It's Going to be O.K.

(but not like we thought)

George
Read it
And you will
Understand
Phil

Pamela Powers Lawson
with Phil Lawson

Spherit
ISBN 978-0615544632

DEDICATED

To You.

September 15, 2011
We've been married 38 years.
We've known each other for 50 years.
It's time to share our poignant journey with America.

ACKNOWLEDGMENTS

Leslie and John: dogs, friendship, projects, fishpond, lifeline. It's *impossible* to thank you enough. Ken and Cozy: you're a *mighty* wind beneath our wings. Kris: relentless advocate, perpetual assignments, eternal gratitude, special friend. Dearest Doug: fulltime editor, part-time teacher, preparing to marry. Still, you found the time to fine tune eight chapters of this tome. So grateful. *(Any boo-boos beyond that point, it wasn't him.)* Precious Jackie: You raised me up from a slump! Great — Scott! Greg: "Momentum is mass *times* velocity — not *plus!*" Thank you clever friend. Dr. Dan: "Full-sight" — love that phrase! — greatly appreciate our relationship. Dr. Joe: five hours of your mentoring went a long ways. Dr. Sherod: Phil smiles every time he remembers what you thought, and later said, about the first time you met him: *"... I looked at him and thought this guy's either nuts or he's a genius. Turns out I think he's a genius."* Dr. Tom: you're prolific at sharing statistics. We used a few. Maestro Michael: You're always there for us. Even as a midnight soundman and graphic designer. Micki: I did it! Ron: I may have lost a brother but I gained one in you. Steven: what you did was exceptional.

Cozy, Leslie, Jackie, (DL), Danny, Cindy, Greg, Sonja, Rachel: grateful beyond words for your feedback/insights/attention to detail when reading the manuscript.

Brief clarification to readers: You may note an age discrepancy in the dedication of Phil's original book, Being Spherical, and this book, It's Going to be O.K., on the topic of when Phil and I first met. We had remembered it as about the age of 7, and he had recorded it as such on the dedication page. Only afterwards, during more comprehensive family interviews for this memoir did we discover we were a few months off in our calculations. It appears we were actually 6. No big deal, just saying ...

"No one is as capable of gratitude as one who has emerged from the kingdom of night." — ELIE WIESEL

Table of Contents

Introduction

(Circa: 2008-2011: from the Great Recession to the historic downgrade of America's credit rating)

I had to do it. Capture a snapshot of America during one of its most unfathomable moments since the Great Depression — at the very same time that the world at large was seized with alarm. I studied that snapshot with a magnifying glass. I searched for my reflection in it. I smelled the picture, tasted it and swallowed it. It swelled my belly, then stained the blood that coursed my veins. And I knew ... then, I knew, that I and you, dear readers, are the ones who have been blessed with the whole burden.

This social memoir, two-and-a-half years in the writing and a lifetime in the making, promises to be a colorful read. But more than that, it is my intention that this book — a collaboration between myself and my husband, Phil — offers up an antidote for society's queasiness; for our uneasiness about what lies ahead. Tall order, I know. But Phil and I have a contribution to make — a message from the front lines of bewilderment. And I'll bet there are others out there like us who do too. If only America can hear us; if only she can see us.

America, we are changed — permanently changed. And now we must walk into it — fully into it, to save ourselves.

Enter the aftermath ...

chapter 1: Stage

There are moments in time, despite our purest heartfelt intentions, when things are not going to be O.K. Not as we believe they should be, or hope they will be.

That realization occurred to me after a family tragedy in 2007, compounded by a book I read a year later about Abraham Lincoln.

"It's going to be O.K.," were the final words of a distant relative, the day she lay dying in a crushed SUV on a two-lane mountain road in Colorado. A spring blizzard was spitting cold at the windows as she consoled her 2-year-old son, who was crying. A damaged 18-wheeler sat cockeyed nearby, having slammed to a stop in the head-on collision.

But things were not O.K.

The young woman, a nurse by profession, was soon dead — her tiny boy, motherless; her husband, widowed; her carefully planned life, derailed.

I recalled her haunting words — passed on by her sister, who was driving that fateful day — when I was immersed in a historic anthology about Abraham Lincoln.

Lincoln was forced to deal with what author Joe Wheeler described as a "*ticking time bomb*" set 85 years before he became president, at the birth of our nation, when American democracy was too delicate and the colonies too divided to disarm it. That centuries-old issue was slavery, and it blew up in Lincoln's time, costing the lives of more than 620,000 countrymen in the American Civil War.

Lincoln could not escape his destiny. And neither can you or I. Something is amiss: a widespread disturbance, cumulative in nature — bequeathed to us by previous generations. Unavoidable, like a semi in your path as your car slides on ice.

— — —

As you will read in this book, I'm all for living in the now; living life purposefully; choosing my actions carefully and thinking positive thoughts *(though that last one took some work)*. I know it's possible to experience quantum leaps in awareness and lifestyles. You will read about it here.

But what happens if our lives are suddenly and permanently changed, despite the power of our intentions?

If our beliefs are challenged, how do we get through a multi-dimensional crisis, such as the one we are experiencing today?

Talented, hard-working Americans are slipping through the cracks. They have lost jobs, homes, health care and financial reserves in one fell swoop — in unprecedented numbers. Many are being forced to navigate their way through parts unknown where the rules of engagement are vague.

Despite proclamations in the media that The Great Recession technically ended in the summer of 2009, citizens from the "right" and the "left" keep whispering *(and shouting)* to each other in coffee shops about a feeling of great unease ... something they can't put their finger on ... that smells like *regression* — a real decline in our quality of life, and most likely that of our children and grandchildren.

Things are not O.K. — *as we have known them*. But there may be another way for things to turn out O.K. And that makes this a scary but exciting time for you and me to be alive.

chapter 2: Leap

I quit my job in the fall of 2008, smack dab in the middle of America's global economic crisis.

Of course, my timing made no sense.

One friend I told was stunned by my announcement. Every sane person she knew was staying put, laying low in a rapidly declining job market.

I couldn't tell her the real reason why I left my nine-year stint as a reporter, in a community I loved, working for a gifted editor who beseeched me to stay.

I couldn't say I quit because of three Bible characters I read about when I was a child — inspiring figures that still had an unavoidable influence on me.

I couldn't explain the "knowing" I had deep in my soul that it was time to write this book no matter the cost. And let me tell you, I was vulnerable. I had no retirement fund and no alternative employment options arranged when I finished it. Considering I was 53 — and no spring chicken — the decision required a significant level of conviction; or madness; or both.

A historic election was pending, the stock market was convulsing and financial institutions were toppling like trees with rotted roots.

For those who asked my reason, I produced a fairly believable one: My entrepreneurial husband needs help with his business (which he did). And I plan to freelance and write a book (which I did).

But the legendary stories of Abraham the patriarch, Moses and Joseph were, in a roundabout way, the real reason for my departure, because of the lessons I learned from them at an impressionable age. *(I suspect I would have admired gallant women, too, as a child, had the elders of my evangelical faith spoken more of them.)*

I lost my religion in my 30s. But I will never forget the excitement and unease that once stirred within me upon hearing the stories of these three men. It was a sense that I too might one day be tested by extreme circumstances in my life.

Here are their ancient instructions as I remember them: 1) You're never too old for miracles. 2) You must first wander 40 years to reach your promise land. 3) If your life is stolen from you, and you're made a slave, pay attention — the fate of your people might rest in your hands.

That brings me to a modern-day tale, one I have lived intimately. It's about losing everything — repeatedly — and keeping your wits. It's about losing them too from time to time and finding them again. It's about being worth less and, in the end, worth more.

— — —

I wasn't the only one that took a leap of faith as 2008 gave up the ghost. America elected its first African-American president (after considering its first female presidential nominee), and for one moment expectation in America transcended our angst. Whether we favored the man's politics or not, his rise to office reminded us of what this country stands for on a good day: equality and infinite possibility. If you work hard enough for something, you'll reap the rewards.

Right then, certain struggles of the past 50 years made sense.

In 1954, the year my husband, Phil, was born — along with Oprah Winfrey, James Cameron and Condoleezza Rice — the Supreme Court had just ruled that segregation in public schools was unconstitutional. Meanwhile, I squealed my way into the world among Steve Jobs, Tim Berners-Lee and Bill Gates in 1955. The year a "colored" woman named Rosa Parks refused to give up her bus seat to a white passenger.

When I entered first grade, the year Barack Obama was born, "freedom riders" had just tested new laws against segregation by riding public transportation systems in the Southern United States, provoking violent reactions.

I moved to the Deep South myself at 19 — a young white woman with my young white husband ready to expound the principles of civil liberty for an evangelical religion that was intent on integrating its black and white churches.

Of course, that's all I have in common with the first black president. And that's an imperceptible link at best. His life journey — which includes degrees from Columbia University and Harvard Law School — and mine vary greatly from there.

I was raised to believe that college was a downer — a hotbed of mind-altering hallucinogens, illicit sex and ungodly scientific theories. And theology outranked politics of any kind, for any reason.

And Phil experienced the same fate, having been raised in the same puritanical faith.

That upbringing sent us packing along the back roads of society as adults. It branded us outsiders, doomed to run alongside the fast track to prosperity without a boarding pass.

While a few of our counterparts grew up to be some of the most powerful, rich and influential people today in media, politics, entertainment and technology, we by comparison have nothing to show for ourselves. We appear to be certifiable losers ...

But I'll share a secret with you: You haven't heard of Phil and me before now because it wasn't time. We had to reach this very moment before you could see us; before you could hear us — when your perceptions of life are beginning to fail you. Now, you will find meaning in our journey.

chapter 3: Lost

I began losing things at the age of 5. That's when my female role model died of multiple sclerosis. But my sense of worth began slipping away a year or so before that, the day I spilled detergent soap in the kitchen sink.

My father was at work. And mother was chained to her bed by a crippling disease that daily wrestled the life from her. I was in the kitchen of our tiny Denver apartment, having hatched a plan to be helpful. I would wash the dirty dishes ... with laundry powder, which at the time made sense.

I dragged a chair to the counter and climbed onto it. I turned the big box over and began to pour, but the powder came out fast — too fast. It filled the sink, then filled me with worry. I tried to clean it up, but there was too much of it.

When my father came home to the mess, I saw on his face a great weariness, and a sense of burden washed over me.

It doesn't take much to sketch a picture of your life at an impressionable age. Just a few experiences here or there, trivial or traumatic — or both intersecting — that transform a feeling, a remark or an image into a perception. A perception that influences a decision, which becomes a pattern, which becomes a journey.

My father's own perceptions of life had long been established by the time I was born. Cleve C. Powers had been a certified evangelical missionary for more than 15 years, having preached the gospel in churches from Washington to Connecticut, addressing a plethora of topics from *"It is High Time to Awake! — Are your eyes open or shut to the signs of the times?"* to *"Educating Ourselves for Peace and Life! — Does higher education free or enslave; protect or destroy?"*

Evangelism, it would seem, was encoded in my family genes. In the early 1920s my father's father, Dennis (Bert) Powers, a Minnesota farmer, was the first to embrace the writings of a deceased protestant evangelist named Charles Taze Russell, who believed he had, during his lifetime, discovered God's blueprint and measuring rod for all humanity.

Russell's book "Divine Plan of the Ages," and his monthly magazine, *Zion's Watchtower and Herald of Christ's Presence,* provided the foundational beliefs of what became known as the International Bible Students Association. Grandpa Bert joined up and was baptized along with his wife, Sarah. They were certain they had found the "truth," and none too soon — for the end of days was at hand.

Grandpa Bert died prematurely of pernicious anemia in 1926, when his five children, including my father, were all under the age of 12. But his religious devotion was evident down to his last breath. As he lay dying in his bed — his wife and youngest daughter curled up beside him — he clutched a *Watchtower* magazine to his chest.

Grandma Sarah's kinship to the Bible Students Association only grew stronger after that, as she raised her children alone in the midst of the Great Depression and moved her family from Minnesota to Oregon in search of a better life.

It was five years after Grandpa Bert's death, in 1931, that the second leader of the Bible Students — a man named Joseph F. Rutherford, a lawyer and imposing figure dubbed "the judge" — changed the name of that religion from the International Bible Students Association to the simpler but commanding title of Jehovah's Witnesses — a title that, eventually, was handed down to me like a medal of honor. Grandma Sarah often listened to a phonograph record on which Rutherford could be heard to say: *"Religion leads men to destruction; [but] Christianity is the way to salvation and life everlasting!*

"Religion is wrong and a snare because it deceives the people. But that does not mean all who follow religion are willingly bad ... Religion is a racket because it has long been used, and is still used, to extract money from the people upon the theory and promise that paying over money to a priest will serve to relieve the party paying from punishment after death and further ensure his salvation! Surely, Almighty God is not a party to granting favors upon on a money consideration ... Christianity means to follow exactly in the footsteps of Christ Jesus by believing and teaching the Bible, the word of God, and which is given for the instruction of all people who love righteousness," Rutherford preached on, introducing two publications he had written that would surely help "*sincere persons*" to

"*choose the right way*" to worship. Rutherford wrapped up the recorded message, more or less, with this forewarning: "*THE TRUTH is placed before the people that they may have the opportunity TO CHOOSE which they desire: Religion with death, or, Christianity with life.*"

Under his reign as president, which was book-ended by World Wars I and II, Judge Rutherford offered up more revelations for salvation for his weary but loyal brethren, prioritizing one activity, for the most part, over and above all others: Preach God's word — everywhere, at anytime — if you want to save your hide and everybody else's. Therefore, Grandma Sarah did not shrink from the task of declaring her beliefs door to door, or shouting *"Religion is a snare and racket!"* on street corners, to ensure her place in the hereafter.

O.K., so you've figured out my family wasn't Catholic. There are no stories here of nuns cracking my knuckles with rulers. My family's faith is on exhibit to illustrate this: A belief of any kind, gifted by our ancestors, can be one heck of a thing to lose.

Back to the story ...

My father — nicknamed "the Swede" for his blond hair, fair complexion and tender baby blues — was Sarah's second eldest son. A shy but colorful boy, he was known to duck below the dashboard of the family's Model A when Sarah went calling on the homes of strangers.

But eventually he came around, like good sons do.

By the time my father and his siblings were grown and married in their early 20s, they were swapping homes and possessions for camp trailers to become traveling "pioneers" and "overseers" — titles that described the most devoted of Jehovah's Witnesses who spent hours each day preaching the gospel. They traded jobs as brick-makers for disciple-making, toting suitcases of literature and portable phonographs playing prerecorded scriptural messages for city folk and farmers along the Oregon coast and into Utah, Arizona and Colorado.

Note to self: No wonder I'm comfortable in small spaces. Note to readers: Yes, yes, I pioneered from camp trailers too when I grew up — that's what good daughters do.

Of course there were casualties along the way. My father's first marriage, which produced a son, ended in divorce when the boy was 5. About the same time, two of his siblings were divorced from their mates ... but the family pressed on. There's was a God-inspired movement — part of a prophetic, soul-shining mission, they believed — that was under way at the perfect time, on the brink of Armageddon: *"It was high time to turn right and go straight before it was too late."*

That level of conviction produced a martyr's courage, which came in handy in the months following the bombing of Pearl Harbor, when my family traveled to Klamath Falls, Oregon, near the California border to attend a Bible conference.

It so happened that the citizens of Klamath Falls had a heightened sense of patriotism in 1942 due to rumors of a possible attack by Japanese forces along the coast. A naval air station had been established nearby to provide combat training for fleet squadrons in the Pacific; locals were volunteering for civil defense positions and the ambulance corps, and newspapers were running ads on what civilians should do in case of air raids. Klamath Falls was also a supply point for a Japanese internment camp a short distance away, which had townsfolk on edge regarding outsiders of any kind.

Then along came the Witnesses — proselytizers who did not salute the flag or serve in the armed forces. An estimated 1,800 convention-goers arrived a week ahead of schedule in the fall of 1942 to build seating benches for their scheduled gathering in Klamath Falls and blitz the town with pamphlets and placards advertising the event.

That enthusiasm exhibited by a horde of unpatriotic strangers led a thousand angry locals to protest the program. As the assembled throng listened raptly to the main address, titled "Peace — Can it Last?", broadcast via telephone lines from Cleveland, Ohio, riots erupted between the townsfolk and Witnesses when the telephone cable to the building was cut. Fistfights and clubbing ensued. Car windows were bashed and automobiles capsized; stink bombs were thrown at startled bible-thumpers, and literature and phonographs were confiscated and tossed onto bonfires, forcing town leaders to call in the state militia to subdue the uprising.

The windshield of my father's car was shattered by a rock. My uncle's car was turned upside down and the oil drained from the engine. That night, he and my aunt slept on the ground in a nearby field — a double-bladed ax beside them — worried that disgruntled townsfolk might also torch their camp trailer.

The message from locals was loud and clear: *Get out of town ... while you still can.*

Attempts to later re-enter Klamath Falls proved futile, but the overall battle for free speech was hardly a waste of time for my father and his comrades.

They were in the midst of a historic campaign by Witnesses all across the country spanning more than 20 years that was setting landmark constitutional precedents and strengthening American civil liberties. During that time, Jehovah's Witnesses won 45 Supreme Court cases involving free speech and civil rights. And there was no shortage of tales about those victories among my family.

(A loud 'Ooh-rah!' seems in order here, don't you think? **OOH-rah!**)

As you might guess, my family and their friends were on a roll. Enduring harassment for their beliefs, and hearing stories about thousands of fellow witnesses who were boycotted, attacked or imprisoned during the war years in America and in Hitler's Germany, only elevated their mission and strengthened their willpower.

Eager to do more, one of my uncles applied and was accepted to foreign missionary school in New York, and my father soon followed in his footsteps. An aunt likewise moved to New York to serve at the international headquarters of the Watchtower Society. She married an exceptional man who, among his many duties at headquarters, once served as legal secretary to the infamous Hayden S. Covington — vice president and chief legal counsel to the Watchtower organization. That same aunt and uncle were in the "inner circle" of friends in those days that rubbed shoulders with the president of the Watchtower Society and other prominent figures who were directing the growing population of worshipers worldwide.

My family was well connected. They had risen through the ranks of a "theocratic" order — of a solitary, special and closed society. One that was impossible to escape, without dire consequences.

You might say it was a simple scheduling delay that derailed my father's goals to be a foreign missionary. His studies were behind him, and all that remained was to receive official word of his foreign assignment. But paperwork of that kind, at the end of World War II, often took months to administer.

By the time the letter arrived from Headquarters assigning my 31-year-old father to Panama, he had met an attractive 20-year-old brunette named Phyllis at a pioneer camp in Iowa. And it was this beauty, unprepared for missionary service, who derailed my father's plans for good.

It was 1946 when my father and mother tied the knot and set their sights on the Midwest, where Headquarters had reassigned them to serve together as pioneers. Their union expanded the breadths and depths of my Christian ancestry to include even more devout grandparents, aunts and uncles on my mother's side, some of whom likewise were missionaries and pioneers.

My family was to Christianity what the Kennedy family was to politics. Family gatherings were often purposeful affairs — a hushed prestige about them marked by passionate and pious farewells: *"If we don't see each other again before Armageddon, we'll see each other on the 'other side!'"* they'd cry as they slapped each other's backs. *"Other side"* meaning that they were pretty darn sure they would escape God's wrath and live to tell of it.

That collective zeal sustained my parents for six years in their ministry work, until my mother discovered she had multiple sclerosis and she and my father were forced to focus on their own dire circumstances.

My parents welcomed me into their arms when my mother was 28 and my father 39, with their perceptions of this sinful world firmly in place — prompting them early on to whisper God's word in my ear for safe measure.

So it was that I began this journey in Seattle, Washington, in 1955 — my DNA encoded with mankind's doom, my mother's life in jeopardy.

By then my mother could not escape the fatigue. Her vision had blurred; small objects fell from her grip; her feet felt "spongy," and her toes dragged along the floor as she hauled her body around the room, grasping the furniture.

I was 2, when my parents traveled to Spears Sanitarium — a large charitable hospital in Denver founded years earlier by a crusader of chiropractic medicine. My mother checked in for a month, followed by frequent visits to physicians thereafter. Still, her health declined.

As I grew 5 more inches, my mother grew more frail: her cheerfulness snuffed out by melancholy; her forehead often pinched in pain; her poise stripped away along with her clothing when my father or grandparents (who came to stay in the final days) hoisted her from her bed into milk baths, or into a wheelchair to travel to Bible meetings, unaware that her nylons were twisted wrong at her ankles. But mostly I remember her knee, the one that rose up through the bedcovers like a mountain, over and over again, from uncontrollable muscle spasms. How I loved to leap on that knee and force it back down, over and over again, as if my mother and I were playing a game.

It was a Wednesday — the day after Valentine's Day, in 1961, when I heard my grandmother scream.

I ran to my mother's room clutching my quivering stuffed tiger and found her lying there, quietly, with brown fluid on her chin that had somehow spilled from her lips. I saw my father standing in the corner, stabbing a finger at a tear. Then, he moved close to her and gently pressed his hand against the mountain rising up through the bedcovers. I watched it fall down and stay perfectly still.

chapter 4: Found

Fortunately, I found a boy the year I lost my mother.

He was an adventurous child, four months older than me — a cowboy who had galloped in from Dallas to Denver on the dust of his parents' fear. His baby sister was dying. And his mother and father, who were barely in their 20s, did what they had to, to save her. They found Spears Sanitarium, a facility that championed alternative medicine and accepted hardship cases. It was the same hospital and doctors that had attracted my own parents from Seattle to Denver in search of a cure for my mother.

Under different circumstances the young cowboy named Phil might not have grown up so fast. But his spirit was defying his age by the time our paths crossed at 6, and his presence in my life was a chance for me to turn a page in my own lonesome story.

Not that I was *that* lonesome. My father and I had a special bond, crafted of necessity over protocol. We knew what mattered and what did not. It had formed long before our train ride to Iowa to watch my grandparents bury my mother at a cemetery near their home, before the two of us moved to a tiny, humble dwelling in Denver to regroup.

It started with half-eaten suckers stuck to a shelf in the buffet, saved for my father but forgotten. It continued when he shared his morning coffee with me; when we hung out together on car lots, shopping the best deals; and when he tucked me in at night in the big bed and then went to sleep nearby on a cot.

It reached controversial proportions when I found my dead mother's makeup, smeared pink rouge on my cheeks and wore red lipstick to a Bible meeting. Dad didn't make a fuss, much to the horror of other mothers in the congregation.

The results of his parenting showed up on my first-grade report card: *"Pamela is a cheerful and willing worker,"* wrote my teacher, Mrs. Franzent.

It didn't matter to either of us that we lived behind Mrs. Heinz's house in a converted shed. That my clothes often fit poorly and I was, on occasion, as wild as the feral kittens I chased and caught in the alley (which could explain my second-grade teacher's report, which in part said: *"Pamela ... sometimes has to be reminded of good sportsmanship."*)

And those things didn't matter either to the young blue-eyed boy who had first laid eyes on me — not at Spears Sanitarium, but at a local Bible meeting — and, by the age of 7, had wooed me into his bed.

(If you must know the dirty details, we fell asleep on the top of his bunk bed while watching "The Twilight Zone." What'd ya think I was going to say?)

Phil's family lineage was far different than mine, its 19th-century roots summed up in a news clipping about his great-grandfather's retirement party at the Kansas City Club — a posh 14-story establishment from basement to roof garden that attracted the most elite members of society. *"Phillip Harry Lawson, general superintendent of Flour Mills of America, Inc., one of the most widely known milling superintendents in the United States, today announced his retirement from the company with the opening of May,"* the announcement read.

The announcement also reminded readers that the Missouri native — whose illustrious career included a decade as superintendent of the Aunt Jemima Mills Co. — was a 32nd-degree Mason.

Upon retirement, Mr. Lawson planned to "*catch up on fishing*" when he moved to the Texas farm he co-owned with his only son, Harry, the notice further read.

That farm was in Hunt County — a few short miles from the county seat that boasted this greeting on its water tower: "Welcome to Greenville: The blackest land, the whitest people."

"Two grandsons, Harry Lawson, 16, and Phillip Lawson, 14, both named for Mr. Lawson, are waiting to join him in the fishing," the announcement concluded.

And that's how the Phil I know (not yet born) came by his full and given name, "Phillip" — the third in a long line of Phillips — who might otherwise have had the Roman numeral "III" after his surname, had his paternal grandmother not bestowed a different middle name on her son, Phil's father, that reduced his pedigree to "junior."

It was an odd middle name as middle names go — a last name, actually, attached to a character of blemished origins. It was, simply: "Wood" — a four-letter word with two meanings, depending on whether you picked the Old English adjective from the dictionary (*insane*) or the modern noun (*xylem: the hard fibrous substance that makes up the greater part of stems, branches, and roots of trees ...*)

Turns out both meanings carried some measure of foreboding for the youngest of the three Phillips, in part and parcel because of the chain of events that had played out long before he was born ...

Bushyhead Wood was 17 years old in 1902 when his father petitioned the Department of Interior in Tahlequah, Oklahoma, for Bushyhead's mother to be added to the rolls of the Cherokee Nation. Bushyhead's father was Cherokee, but his mother was white, making Bushyhead and his eight siblings "half-breeds."

According to family lore, the father of Bushyhead Wood was a tribal chief. His sister was a "wise woman," and another sister trained horses for the tribal nation. But family history was fading fast by the time Bushyhead Wood's children were grown and being assimilated into society in the mid-1930s. It was a volatile time for people of questionable roots — when it wasn't uncommon for a black man to be lynched for no good reason; when Mexicans were hidden out of sight on working farms; when Indians were stashed on reservations with enough white flour and alcohol to kill them.

It's no surprise, under those circumstances, that Bushyhead's youngest daughter — a short but appealing Cherokee with round face and broad nose who loved to dance — listed her race as "white" on the birth certificate of her third child born in 1935, a boy she named after her prominent father-in-law — the general superintendent, Mr. Phillip Harry Lawson. But she traded the middle name "Harry" for "Wood," linking her child permanently to his heathen ancestry.

It was no secret that the White Cherokee's husband, the general superintendent's only son, was a "mother's boy" — and remained so even after the two had met at a dancehall (when he was in college), married, and moved to the family farm. "Mother" was an officious, duty-bound matriarch who influenced her son from afar — from the Kansas City Club, where she and her husband remained boarders. Mother was the daughter of a doctor; reared in a private girl's school, who championed the customs, and cautions, of her elite social circle. And though Mother politely included her son's wife in her societal activities, Mother was none too fond of the White Cherokee.

The marriage failed when the third child, with the middle name of a half-breed, was in the third grade. Not a word was spoken as to *why*. But it has been said that business folk around town closed up shop to attend the court proceedings — throwing their support behind the father and not the mother in that shady union, costing the White Cherokee her chance, despite her protests, to complete the rearing of her offspring.

Her disappearance cast a shadow on her children, despite their above-average existence on a suitable farm, with ample land and water, a herd of cattle, a large barn and a fine house (complete with "colored" housekeeper) that had electricity, which was rare in their town in those days.

Her disappearance was burdensome for Mother's Boy, too — for he found it necessary to beat his children, much more than they felt they deserved, to ensure the farm thrived through their labor. He relied when possible on the support of Mother, who, in addition to her duties as a war volunteer, helped raise the children during summer visits and felt it quite responsible of her to compile the children's weekly list of infractions, which, each Saturday, were duly addressed with a whipping.

Soon enough, Mother's Boy again dated, married briefly, and then quickly divorced, with each of his children reacting to the confusion in their life in his and her own manner. His oldest, a girl, ran away. The middle boy, a scrawny specimen, began to vandalize the town — once destroying the big screen at the local theater, which cost Mother's Boy handsomely. On other occasions he broke into and trashed a local school; and later still wrecked the family Jeep, which landed the scrawny middle boy and a friend, traveling with him, in the hospital.

By the time the third child of the White Cherokee reached his teenage years, he could not escape the stigma attached to his family's name. When he and his older brother walked Main Street, townsfolk bristled, worried that the boys — at least the older boy — would steal from them in broad daylight.

The third child, by comparison, was a handsome son, with thick chest and smooth, rose-colored skin who wore pressed clothes, began piano lessons and had learned his manners. Who remembered with fondness his excursions as a boy to the Kansas City Club, where he played in the corridors on visits to his grandfather, the general superintendent. He was the "good son" — good at boxing and football and embarrassed by his older brother's shenanigans.

But for his head-strong nature, the Good Son might have abided by the demands of Mother's Boy — might have fully applied himself to his schoolwork that, to Mother's Boy, took precedence over his desperate desire to be on the high school football team. Except, like his father, the Good Son was impetuous, and by the age of 14 he had bolted from the family farm in a series of fitful landings before he took up residency at the home of a widow woman, where he worked as her hired hand to finish school.

Even so, the Good Son may well have followed in the general superintendent's footsteps, had he not instead followed a 16-year-old beauty to Dallas, where she had gone, quite boldly, to find work. The Good Son quit the day he was hired at the Robin Hood Flour Mill in Greenville to chase his dreams with the freckle-faced introvert — a romance that had begun, reluctantly on her part, in junior high.

The feisty redhead, of Irish descent, was a straight-A student — a child of great promise who aspired not to be a stewardess, like her best friend, or a teacher, like another girl she knew, but rather "a mother" — purely and wholeheartedly, without a doubt.

All she lacked was a little self-esteem — which often comes with the territory when you've picked cotton as a child; when you're the youngest of six; when you're father is a weekend drunk, and during the week, a sharecropper, who had, off and on, worked the land of Mother's Boy.

But her confidence began to surface soon enough ... two days, in fact, after her arrival in the big city, when she was hired as a billing clerk then advanced, rather quickly, to switchboard operator while studying nights for her high school diploma, something few dropouts did in her day.

Four months into her 16th year, the Feisty Redhead and Good Son married — as if that pairing of Promise and Prestige could produce something perfect. Ten months into her 16th year the Feisty Redhead was pregnant with her first child — an "XY" chromosome that would be born blond, with blue eyes and a Hollywood smile concealing his native past, yet still the owner of short, wide feet gifted by the White Cherokee.

All was right with the world in that moment — the sting of their wedding eclipsed by the fruits of their union; their steely resolve braced against the reality that their own fathers had not attended their nuptials because they had come to despise one another. The Good Son had married beneath his station. And the Feisty Redhead had married the son of a lofty incompetent.

So it was that Phil began this journey in Dallas, Texas, in the winter of 1954, his DNA encoded with pride, prejudice and something to prove. His path reinforced by the men of influence in his life who were, by contrast, headed in opposite directions.

Mother's Boy, by then, had returned to the university to complete his physics degree. He had married an English teacher — an old maid with social skills and ample opinion — and he would soon enough become a college physics professor.

The Good Son, on the other hand, was being sucked into the lucrative and limitless world of sales. He was a contrast of characters, which enticed and perplexed the Feisty Redhead. Before she married him, he once told her he'd "never live to see 21." After they had married, he assured her he would "retire rich in his 20s." She couldn't know that pattern would expand, divide and multiply to intolerable proportions. There was no time for such scrutinizing. She had become a mother and was revitalized by the role. A second child arrived three years after the first, a precocious baby girl — a child that by the age of 2 had fallen deathly ill.

By the time the Feisty Redhead and Good Son had spirited their family from Dallas to Denver in search of a cure for their precious cargo, Phil-the-third had softened the heart of his maternal grandfather. The sharecropper adored his strong-willed grandson and, before he died in a car driven by a drunken driver, had taught the boy this important life lesson: *If you remove the training wheels from your bike too soon, then lose the bolts to replace them, you'd better: a) Learn to live with it, and b) Learn to ride without training wheels.*

As for timing, my family arrived in Denver on the doorstep of the controversial Spears Chiropractic Sanitarium in 1957; Phil's family arrived in 1960. We climbed the same circular pink-stone steps and wandered through the same long hallways of the spacious facility, which boasted two large units, for adults and children, each with hundreds of beds.

We lived four-and-a-half miles apart, in the poor section of Denver, reserved mostly for coloreds and Hispanics. We played in the earth near train yards where smelting plants had once spewed toxic waste and would, years later, be deemed Superfund cleanup sites by the federal government.

But Phil and I might never have connected if it weren't for a pesky Jehovah's Witness who worked as a salesman alongside the Good Son. One afternoon the pair went to lunch with two other salesmen, one a preacher, the other an atheist. And the topic of hellfire surfaced. And the Jehovah's Witness fetched his Bible from his car. And, during the heated conversation that followed, the Good Son was struck by the man's aptitude for scriptural analysis — in particular, his perfectly plausible summary of Jesus' tale of the Rich Man and Lazarus — the *figurative* versus *literal* explanation. In the end, a salesman had sold a salesman, and on that day the Good Son agreed to a free home Bible study. Months later, the Good Son toted his whole family to the Kingdom Hall of Jehovah's Witnesses at 22nd Avenue and Gaylord Street.

That, in a roundabout way, is how I met Phil-the-third. Or rather, he met me, for he's the one that remembers our first encounter: Me, standing next to two more kids — a black boy named Donnie and a pale-skinned girl named Renee — inside the tall brick entryway of the church, built to resemble the watchtower of a medieval castle.

For three years our paths crossed.

During which ... Phil's little sister recovered her health after being hospitalized on and off for two years.

During which Phil earned the nickname "Toughy" from his dad when he stomped on the foot of his father's employee, a sleazeball of a salesman who had grabbed Phil from behind in a sinister headlock — sending the gasping man hopping around the room on one leg.

During which Phil learned a sense of worth from his mom the day she stormed from a doctor's office, her bloody son in tow, as the doctor, armed with a needle, told the crying boy with the sliced-open lip to "*Act like a man!*" And she yelled back at him: *"BUT HE'S JUST A BOY!"*

During which ... Phil, Donnie and I once escaped the city for a hair-raising mountain drive in the backseat of a 1955 Cadillac — a gargantuan yellow model — with Phil's 26-year-old mother, the Feisty Redhead at the wheel on her very first drive in the mountains. The road she chose, perhaps too boldly, was dubbed by locals as "Oh My God Road" — a steep, treacherously narrow gravel passage through historic mining country suited for mountain bikes and four-wheelers that trailed on for nine miles, with washouts and sheer drops to the valley floor; with switchbacks and blind curves (even passing a car on one of them); that offered no chance for her to stop and retrace her tracks. *(A road, I might add, that 45 years later still scares the sh** out of full-grown men.)*

Then, in the fall of 1964, Phil's father took a sales job in West Virginia and moved his family there. And Phil-the-third began his roller-coaster ride to enlightenment — a journey that, inspired by his middle name, would produce, either: a) *insanity,* or, b) *complex tissue that conducts water and nutrients upwards from roots.*

The next thing I knew, that fascinating boy who had stirred something inside me had vanished.

chapter 5: Commiserate

(One day during the writing of this book, after I had persuaded Phil to recall his childhood memories in an exhausting conversation between us, he dozed in the green leather chair in our living room and had a brief dream.

It was of himself as a small, dirty, orphaned boy, about 5 years old, standing on parched ground that resembled a war zone. He lived in a hole in the Earth and from there scavenged for food.

Another individual appeared in the dream — a figure so large the boy could see only the bottom half of his body. The visitor walked toward him, as if sensing the boy had something important to show him — something the boy had found — though the boy himself did not know the object's meaning.

The child then crawled into the depths of his cave to retrieve it. When he returned, he was cradling a round basket covered by a piece of cloth. Standing before the large figure, the boy lifted the cloth and revealed a glowing sphere of energy.)

— — —

A murder revived the connection between Phil and me when we were barely teens. It was the Christmas of 1968, and four years had passed since Phil's father had spirited his family to West Virginia and the light of his love had disappeared from my life.

That winter they had returned to Denver during the holidays to visit friends, and it was then that we reconnected under the darkest of circumstances.

The day after Christmas, the adults were gathered around the dining-room table playing cards, while Phil, uninterested in their game, looked for something to read. Reading was his favorite pastime; it provided him escape from his chaotic life as the son of a traveling salesman. He even read the newspaper, which wasn't typical of other 14-year-old boys he knew. But this time it unnerved him. Scanning the headlines, he stumbled across the story of a brutal murder of a little girl. It happened on Christmas Eve. She lived in Iowa. And her name was Pamela Powers.

Phil froze at the sight of it. My mother had been buried in Iowa. And my name too was Pamela Powers. It didn't sink in that the dead girl was only 10 and I was 13 and almost Phil's age. Or that I still lived somewhere around Denver. Phil was shaken by the experience — despite reassurances from the adults at the dining room table. He knew right then he had to find me. He had hoped to before he read the story. But he was a pimple-faced teenager — an affable introvert who could have easily put off the potentially embarrassing encounter.

But now there was no stopping him from tracking down my family, which had grown to include a high-strung step-mother, and three stepbrothers who made farting sounds by cupping their bare hands under sweaty armpits and fanning their elbows.

When I first heard his voice on the telephone, I couldn't believe my ears — or the words that burst from my mouth: *"I still have a crush on you!!"* I giggled, dashing any chance of camouflaging my feelings.

But seeing each other in person, that winter, proved impossible due to his family's travel plans.

Thus began the letters ... punctuated by school photos and the occasional drawing — a girl wearing bell bottoms, her hair in a flip (from Phil); and from me — when I was feeling particularly righteous — a colored-pencil picture of paradise, featuring a lamb snuggled up to a lion.

Our reunion in 1968 would prove to be the beginnings of an unorthodox experiment, though we couldn't have known it then: of losing and finding; of resisting and attracting; of shape shifting.

Decades later, Phil would co-author a book about it. And develop a patented technology to help people connect the dots of seemingly unpredictable life experiences by integrating information from the left and right hemispheres of the brain — the path to a whole new level of awareness. And a whole new lifestyle, our circle of friends expanding, eventually, to include many PhDs, a few Hollywood types, and even a software engineer who oversees a team charged with validating the performance of payloads for interplanetary spacecraft sent to Mars and Jupiter.

But, I repeat the phrase "decades later." It took us a long time to comprehend that field of attraction we had experienced as teens and maintained as adults. Decades during which we more or less killed ourselves attempting to unravel the mystery. *(I hope that's not because we we're stupid.)*

At the age of 13, however, Phil and I were still learning our boundaries in a sinful world and, for that matter, our worth in the grander scheme of things.

We were, we had been assured, *"good-for-nothing slaves, doing what we ought"* — a message that Watchtower Headquarters had relayed from Jesus. We were incapable, we had been reminded, of *"directing our own steps"* — a message Headquarters had mined from the writings of the prophet Jeremiah.

From our vantage point, there was no such thing as destiny, or karma, or good fortune — admonished as we were to eliminate those words from our daily vocabulary, along with scientific terms that did not serve or preserve Holy Scripture.

And frankly, that reality was comforting. We had direct access to God — or could have — if we simply obeyed him (and remembered to use Jesus' name in our prayers). We had access to the answers to all life's questions — or could have — if we were serious about our Bible lessons. Most of which buried our minds in the *past* — in the failings of the forefathers — for the sole purpose of protecting our everlasting *future*.

But none of those lessons, strangely enough, taught us to tune into now — *Right Now*. As if connecting the past to the present might somehow alter our understanding of the future entirely.

Instead, we were preoccupied. Our families were devoted to the promotion of an exciting new book just released by our organization — a tiny blue hardback no bigger than a woman's wallet — that condensed Bible prophesy into a manageable 22-chapter overview, humbly titled The Truth that Leads to Eternal Life, a marketing feat extraordinaire on the part of Headquarters. It was a time-saving approach to gaining knowledge about an ages-old theme that was catching on like wildfire and would eventually require so many printings, in so many languages, as to earn a mention (years later) in the *Guinness Book of Records*.

Meanwhile, in 1968 ... 1,271 miles away, a man named Ludwig von Bertalanffy, an Austrian-born biologist and a professor at the Canadian University of Alberta, had just published a book too, "*General Systems Theory.*" It contained information that he had stumbled upon 40 years earlier, in 1928, two years after my Grandpa Bert died.

And his book contained a lot of BIG WORDS: "*Compared to the analytical procedure of classical science with resolution into component elements and one-way or linear causality as basic category, the investigation of organized wholes of many variables requires new categories of interaction, transaction, organization, teleology,"* Bertalanffy wrote. "*These considerations lead to the postulate of a new scientific discipline which we call general system theory. Its subject matter is formulation of principles that are valid for 'systems' in general, whatever the nature of the component elements and the relations or 'forces between them ...,"* he continued, adding: "*General system theory, therefore, is a general science of wholeness ..."*

— — —

"To a real nice girl, who is a lot like me." That's how Phil signed the back of the first school photo he sent me after we had found each other, again.

Mine to him, on the other hand, read: "*Don't be disappointed. I'll try to get a better picture if I can.*"

And, when I did send a better picture — a strip of black-and-whites from a 25-cent photo booth — the messages written on the back weren't, exactly, sentimental. Instead, focusing on the benefits of "*DOING JEHOVAH'S WILL*" — written in all capital letters — followed by "*AND YOU WILL SURELY BE BLESSED WITH A GREAT REWARD*" — finished off with, "*THEOCRATIC LOVE, YOUR SISTER PAM*"

At 13, I was a quirky concoction of culpability and chatter. My forehead pinched in a vertical crease of eternal concentration. As if I must manage things on my own, when adults I knew were undependable. And if I couldn't, I'd beg God to hold my hand, promising him my soul in return for his assistance. He and I were a team, and for good reason.

Three years to the month after my mother died, my dad met Loretta Lynn at a Bible convention. It was February 1964. By March, they had "tied the knot," on the cheerless anniversary of Christ's death.

Dad's Loretta Lynn didn't sing for a living (and that wasn't her real name). But she did have this in common with the country music star: Both were married by the tender age of 13 ... to honky-tonk men — Dad's Loretta whacking hers on the head with a frying pan before divorcing him.

That impetuous act solved several worries, instantaneously. *(Not the frying-pan incident, but the sudden wedding on the cheerless anniversary of Christ's death.)* Dad snagged himself a wife — a pretty thing, 21 years younger than him, with chiseled cheekbones and soft brown hair teased high on her head. And I scored a mother. In that order. Loretta Lynn secured herself a man of God; handsome and praiseworthy, with an irresistible sense of humor. And her three boys — the youngest my age, the older two barely and almost a teen — got a role model, presumably.

I was three weeks from turning 10, and my father was 48, when the simple life we shared — cruising town in his red and white Plymouth Fury; staying up late to watch "The Mitch Miller Show"; scaring each other with plastic spiders — had vanished, folded into the struggles of an apprehensive but rigid young mother striving to shelter her unsettled sons, who slapped each other on the back of the head at every opportunity.

What happened next is best described in canine speak: This little bitch was added to a pack of dogs — their routines and relations set — penning me as the disruptor.

— — —

The year my father married Loretta Lynn, Phil's father, the Good Son, moved his family to Charleston, West Virginia — an industrial river town belching the exhaust of chemical plants, glass factories and coal mines, where "the *smell* of money" drew little complaint from local residents.

Too bad the first position the Good Son had been hired for — selling garbage disposals and Electro-Sink-Centers — dissolved shortly before his family's arrival, when the two business partners who owned the company unexpectedly parted ways. Before the family could unpack their yellow Cadillac, they traveled 60 miles downriver to Huntington, on the promise of a similar job. Then, in the weeks and months to follow, another move, across the river to Ohio; then back across the river to West Virginia; then back to Ohio, then, two more times in Ohio ...

Had Phil been an Army brat, there would have been a measure of respectability attached to his mobile lifestyle. Instead, he was the son of a salesman. An attractive good ol' boy who sold Electro-Sink-Centers — space-age stainless steel faucet ensembles with hot and cold water buttons, a temperature regulator, soap storage, infrared sterilizer lamp and — get this — an attached blender *and* an ice-cream freezer, on either side of the spigot.

Folks could experience a little futuristic utopia by just signing on the dotted line and forking over $449 (on sale), which included a five-year guarantee!

It's unclear why the Good Son assumed Huntington, West Virginia, would be fertile territory to sell those space-age sink machines — a city with a declining population, in a state where many did not yet have a television or radio — or, for that matter, electricity or running water.

It's doubtful the Good Son even knew that President Lyndon B. Johnson, that same year, had launched his War on Poverty, targeting, of all places, West Virginia and its neighboring states along the Appalachian Mountains — where roughly one in three people lived on an annual income of $3,000 or less.

Had the Good Son moved in 1964 from Denver to Boulder, where he once ran a business — a city bursting with growth, Hippies, and students attending university — Phil's childhood memories would not have included the four-room school on a dirt road in West Virginia where he had a teacher by the last name of McCoy — a granddaughter of the Kentucky McCoy clan, as in Hatfield-McCoy, the infamous feuding families who killed each other in the late 1800s.

Under those circumstances, had Phil not been a voracious reader — escaping his confines through science-fiction books and Bible literature — he might not have fared so well. But he was, and therefore, he did.

By the age of 11, Phil had landed his first job at the local drugstore, to earn his own spending money. By the age of 12, he had rescued a school bus stuck in the mud, with his father's International farm truck.

The Good Son — gone at all hours of the day, or weeks at a time — left Phil to manage the family's 50-acre farm while he attended junior high school: slopping hogs, chopping wood, milking cows by hand, rescuing a calf caught upside down in a feed trough — even riding to Bible meetings in the rain on the flatbed farm truck, his two sisters occupying the two-seater cab with his mother, who was driving.

Living on that farm necessitated a lifestyle that did not match Phil's era and required chores that his father did as a boy. But the 18 months Phil was there, disrupted by a move to the city, and then back again, did provide the only refuge of Phil's childhood — where he could wander 50 acres unaccounted for; where he could commune with nature. And the memories of that farm would sustain him for years.

By 14, Phil had worked a paper route and sold Rawleigh Products door to door. And, by that age, childhood was just in the way.

To that end, he wrote the high school principal, followed by the school board, and convinced them of his plans to be a minister. He begged them to let him graduate early, devising a way to arrange his school credits so he could.

Phil was 15 when he entered his senior year.

He traded his horse for his first car — a rusty Ford Falcon — and worked nights to pay for auto insurance. It was an unsightly vehicle, which prompted his father, in a moment of pity, to upgrade it, slightly, to a tanker

— an old Jeep Wagoneer. Neither of them resembled the muscle cars the cool guys drove to school.

Phil graduated high school at 16, in 1971; he was inducted, that same year, into the junior national honor society.

— — —

By the time Phil and I laid eyes on each other, seven years had passed since my father married Loretta Lynn. Seven years since the Good Son had spirited his family from Colorado to West Virginia, a family that now lived in Texas, where the Good Son sold light bulbs.

My unlikely family had, by then, found a way to coexist. My friendly father had become distant; my stepmother, moody; her oldest — a handsome teen — had become a Romeo; her youngest, always angry; her smart middle son, the jokester; and I, the peacemaker — kissing my parents on the cheek each night before bed. All of which inspired us, more than ever, to *"keep our eyes on the prize"* in the hereafter.

I was, by 1972, swapping high school lunch breaks to preach the Good News door to door in nearby neighborhoods, joined by a freckle-faced strawberry blond girl who was equally enthusiastic about doing "God's work." On cold days, she and I hopped into my 1961 Comet — with the leaky *(gushing)* radiator and the temperamental *(useless)* heater that, to stay warm, required I bang on something under the hood with a hammer.

Phil and I were both 17 — Phil having driven from Texas to Colorado for a Bible convention, accompanied by a vanload of converts.

I opened my front door that summer to a handsome man-child in gold corduroy bell bottoms and burnt orange shirt — his stature modest, his posture tall. His chest broad, his stomach flat, his thighs built like a football player's. His once-blond flattop was now brown, thick and wavy, and his piercing blue eyes followed my every move, putting in motion a bellyful of butterflies.

Fortunately, I was of modest stature too — the "prettiest girl" he knew, inside and out, by his observations. We were a matched set — a pair of salt and pepper shakers.

We saw each other one more time, after that summer, before we got engaged.

chapter 6: Commence

As I write this chapter in March of 2009, a populist outrage is underway regarding a major American insurance corporation that just doled out $165 million in employee bonuses, after receiving $170 billion in taxpayer bailouts from the Federal Reserve, due to its involvement in the 2008 banking scandals.

It was the largest government intervention (to that point) involving a private company in U.S. history and triggered death threats and demands that the money be returned.

THIS, after the American public has witnessed in recent years the downfall of respected corporations such as Enron, WorldCom, Adelphia and Tyco, where corporate executives used company funds and resources as personal piggy banks and went to jail for it.

FOLLOWED BY well-known brokerage firms paying hundreds of millions (each) in penalties for knowingly recommending the above-mentioned fraudulent stocks to investors! Respected brokerage firms (ever heard of Merrill Lynch?) that, 48 months later, went out of business because of their participation also in the subprime mortgage scandal that followed! A subprime fiasco that rewarded lenders with greater sales commissions for the more risky mortgages they secured, and drew unqualified buyers to the table, lured by the patriotic promise of the American Dream, who couldn't possibly afford to pay for it. SCANDALS, the results of which, cost millions of middle-class American jobs, destroyed retirement funds and toppled the financial infrastructure of Iceland (Google it).

Whew! How did this happen? Who gets the finger? Well, that will require a little history lesson. And I'll get to that soon enough. But it's premature at this stage of the story.

So, the short answer is ***(drum roll, please)****: Our world is a web. Though we are just beginning to grasp the implications of what that means: that everything we do affects the next fellow. You see, our society is still living by a centuries-old metaphor — we're all "parts" in the big "machine" — built on the premise of stability and predictability.*

What a rude awakening it's been to discover that our world is chaotic, that it's interconnected and self-organizing, that emerging "systems sciences" are reshaping e-v-e-r-y aspect of our worldview.

Then again, some of us learned that awhile ago ...

— — —

If words have power, as personal gurus claim, then our path was cemented on our wedding day when we read aloud the words inscribed at the base of a plastic statue of a happy, hugging couple given to us as a gift: *"We're in love, we're together, does anything else really matter?"*

A better sendoff might have been, "Wishing you health and wealth!" But there were no gifts or cards with that message, so far as I can remember.

Phil and I were surrounded by self-sacrificing well-wishers — a sizable crowd of family and friends with carefully crafted perceptions of virtue. And we were the epitome of their dreams — a principled pair armed with God's word, ready to save souls in a preaching mission, with no financial assets to our name.

We married in 1973 in the tiny town of Las Animas — a dusty community 200 miles southeast of Denver where my family had moved three years earlier in mission work.

The historic town had an ominous reputation. Legend was that Spanish explorers once perished at the mouth of a nearby river after a priest abandoned the expedition. The river was dubbed *River of Lost Souls,* and the town of Las Animas the *City of Lost Souls*. Thus it was, at the tender age of 18, that Phil and I set sail to conquer the world from the shores of a doomed village.

We were soldiers of peace, willing to die for our cause, which didn't at the time seem paradoxical. Committed to memory was our invisible suit of armor — from the tip of our heads (encased like walnuts in God's helmet of salvation) to the bottoms of our feet (rooted like trees, in a message of goodwill).

Our job was clear; our incentives, explicit: 1) Never be anxious and say, "What are we to eat?" for your heavenly father knows your needs; and 2) With faith the size of a mustard seed, you can move mountains.

It was a neat and tidy package. And off we went to parts unknown.

— — —

"What would you do if I hit you over the head with this?" The large woman asked me as she scratched at her gnarled black wig and reached for an ax parked next to the wood-burning stove.

The question was a ghastly one, and so was the visual — me struck by the sharp, metal object, in the home of a Bible student. It didn't help that my nerves were throbbing that day. And my stomach hurt — nauseous from a lack of sleep and nutritious food, due to dining on the run on macaroni and cheese, beans and weenies, soft drinks and snack cakes.

And then there were my knees — achy from crawling along the bottoms of merchandise gondolas in grocery stores, with a razor blade pinched between my fingers to remove the gunk tracked in on the shoes of strangers.

Employment options that freed up days for preaching the gospel — a wholly non-paying enterprise — were few in Thomasville, Alabama, in 1974.

Located 62 miles from Selma — known for its "Bloody Sunday" civil rights march nine years earlier — and 49 miles from Monroeville — home to Pulitzer-Prize-winning author Harper Lee, who wrote "To Kill a Mockingbird" — the tiny town of Thomasville had a teeny population. And those limits forced Phil and me to venture out to other towns, more than 100 miles away in some cases, in search of cleaning jobs in order to eat. And that required we sleep in our clothes, often, and set three alarm clocks to rise in time each day for morning worship — too exhausted to wake up to just one.

Between the two of us, Phil and I were a scouring-and-polishing force to be reckoned with, even though our floor scrubber was an ancient model and our tile buffer temperamental. But stripping floors for a living was hardly a career to brag about.

"You're going to ruin your insides," citified ladies would say, pushing carts filled with vegetables past me, shaking their heads at my cheap, wax encrusted cowboy boots, as I, at a shrinking 105 pounds, swung industrial-strength mops through dirty water laced with pure ammonia along aisle after aisle of the grocery store, the fumes of which burned my nostrils and choked me.

Ours was a heartfelt mission, nonetheless, born of circumstance over choice. And I dismissed their warnings because I had to. The End was near, we feared. And the town had appeared on a list of needy locations sent from Bible headquarters in New York — rural communities desperate for volunteer preachers to cover vast amounts of neglected territories. By the time we arrived, at 19 years of age, we had been married 14 months, and had tested our strengths in a less strenuous assignment in East Texas.

It seemed right and necessary that we now offer ourselves for greater works. And a handwritten letter we had received, penned in red ink and punctuated by exclamation points, had solidified our decision to branch out.

"*Greetings Lawsons!*" the church elder's letter began. "*I believe you both will find Thomasville the place where the need is indeed great! ...*"

His was a quiet town. More black than white. But progressive, he argued. Even though, we discovered after our arrival, the local hamburger stand had a separate window for "coloreds" and the doctor's office a separate waiting room.

It was here, in Thomasville, that we would — without formal training — learn the hard way to navigate the mental minefields of splintered souls, compartmentalized beings starved of totality.

Like the woman and her ax.

I can't remember her name now, just her oldest son's — one of several children she dressed in wool coats in the sweltering heat of July for their walks to town. His name was King David.

According to rumors around town, King David had lost his father to prison. And his mother had lost her sanity to hardship — despite her attempts to find it again by going *"away"* for help.

It so happened that Alabama ranked last among U.S. states in mental health funding. And living conditions at the state's mental health facility had been likened, in a news expose, to life in a concentration camp.

It's no wonder King's David's mother wasn't at her best the day our paths crossed and she threatened to slice my head open.

To be fair, we had already met, and she'd had time to cook up an opinion of me. The first encounter came months earlier when I knocked on the door of her home, a three-room shanty, and read her passages from the well-worn Bible stored in my literature bag.

It was then that Phil developed a sudden urge to stay in the car and catch up on his Bible reading, refusing to go inside the hut that housed King David's mother, who often heard strange "voices."

Had Jesus himself not instructed me to care for the poor and downtrodden, I might not have entered her world, either. But I did.

And, on the occasions that our discussions turned to the apocalypse, I felt it necessary to read to her the Apostle John's graphic details about it — of terrifying horsemen bringing news of plagues and death to mankind. And it was then that her disposition would shift. And she would cry out in defiance to me, *"GOD CAN'T DESTROY THE **WICKET**!"*— pronouncing "wicked" in her own specialized dialect — before begging, *"YA HEAR?!"* — as if to wake me, as if to get through to me — *AND GOD* — that too many people who didn't deserve it had already been enslaved by that label.

Unfortunately, my reading of those passages linked me to their judgments. And nothing I said thereafter calmed her.

The day she threatened to drive the rusty blade into my skull, King David's mother had turned up announced, clear across town, on the doorstep of another woman with whom I studied the Bible — a petite creature of strong will and character raising four small children alone, a set of twins among them; who worked nights styling the curly locks of dead people. She was — the long and short of it — the Undertaker's Hairdresser. But despite her many strengths, she could not, on that Tuesday, remove King David's mother from her home. It was the very day that I was to arrive for her weekly Bible lesson.

The large woman with the nappy wig had forced herself through the front door; had helped herself to some clothes, from a gift box, and some food from the refrigerator; and was seated in the living room under framed photos of John F. Kennedy and Martin Luther King when I plopped down across from her on a ragged couch, my study book open on my lap, my worn Bible beside me.

To my right sat Phil. Across from him, in a wooden chair, was the Undertaker's Hairdresser.

"What would you do if I hit you over the head with this?" King David's mother dared me, as she reached for the ax parked next to the wood-burning stove.

Phil looked up from his Bible. And alarm spread across the face of the Undertaker's Hairdresser, as I summoned my wits for a response. It wasn't a profound reaction, in the end, but rather breathless and unassuming — as if bolting from the room would be too disruptive, even disrespectful, of her condition.

"*That wouldn't be a nice thing to do, now, would it?*" I whispered, chancing that hers was a passing mood and not life-threatening. "*We can talk about why you'd want to kill me, later. But first, let's read the next paragraph ...*"

Phil and I had no "How To" books to draw upon while stationed in Thomasville. Just a feeble amount of intuition that we kept whittling to a sharp point, like our lives' depended on it.

And there were plenty of chances to perfect our whittling ...

There was the day we showed up announced at the home of a businessman — the manager of a local store. For weeks he and Phil had exchanged friendly chitchat each time they met at his establishment, prompting Phil to take the bold "next step": *"Mind if I come by your house and expand our Bible discussion?"* Phil had asked him.

"If you can catch me," had been the man's daring reply.

But the night we *"caught"* him, he was not alone. Upon our knocking, a bearded man unfamiliar to us had peeked through the diamond-shaped door window and then disappeared, before the store manager ushered us in with a nervous grin.

As we crossed the threshold, we spied the bearded man crouched behind the door, holding a .45 automatic. Behind the bearded man, lining the south wall of the sparsely decorated room, was an arsenal of weaponry; and across the room, a blond woman in a black turtleneck sweater was leaning pensively against the kitchen doorframe.

Time stood still, as each of us peered into the eyes of the other in search of our intentions. Then, after an absorbing silence, we dropped to the couch and Phil produced a symphony of scriptures about hope, love and peace.

The store manager nodded attentively, the blond woman made coffee, and the bearded man sat cross-legged at the coffee table on the floor in front of us, where he broke down, cleaned and reassembled an assortment of guns. One of which was an HKG3 with a sliding stock and bracket designed to hang on a wall for easy access.

I know this because curiosity got the best of me — despite Phil's daggered glance — and I marveled at the unusual shape of it, which led the bearded man to engage in detailed dialogue about its features. Later he even told us where he was headed. But we steered clear of asking any specifics ... about his travel plans to Iran.

Two hours rolled by before the group determined we were no threat to their private scheme, and they let us go.

— — —

You might say Thomasville established our "baseline" — our threshold of pain and our level of authenticity.

And we weren't alone at Boot Camp. Among the colorful characters happy to dwell in Thomasville were those whose spirits had been snuffed out there. Another self-sacrificing couple, who preceded our arrival, had fled in the middle of the night, leaving no hint of their whereabouts.

Ours was a pressure-cooker existence that was bound, sooner than later, to push one's perceptions past the boiling point.

In our case, three distinct components of our lives were converging: our young love; our close encounters with uneasy souls; and the complexities of our newly integrated congregation, governed by two peculiar black elders. To cope, I squandered great quantities of my adrenaline.

In addition, we had to learn a new dialect, of sorts.

It was customized English that favored individuality over standards. For example: *"Litenater"* meant, "Listen to her," and *"Ibeupinyohead"* translated into, "You must be thinking about me."

Sometimes, letters in words were rearranged or had revised endings: "Ask" was pronounced *"aks"*; "Noah" became *"Norah."*

Other phrases included: *"I swaney,"* for "I swear"; *"tumped over,"* for "turned over." And, when a child had perturbed his "peoples" and was due a whupin', he might hear about it in this way: *"I'm gonna rip yo' arm off and beatchu with the bloody stump!"*

Then there was the matter of our own origins, which sometimes got in the way.

Our door-to-door presentations were often interrupted by the following question: *"Who's your daddy?"* Or, *"You ain't from around here; IS you?"*

It took about two years for folks to trust a stranger in town. Then, the local mechanic's shop might very well loan you tools, free-of-charge, overnight, when your car broke down. But an outsider had to survive on his or her own at least that long to earn that trust, which was a sure-fire way to stay hungry. And a great way to try out any new enterprise you could muster in addition to floor cleaning — like sign painting and plumbing and trash removal. It was reason enough to buy a cart full of outdated, bent and unlabeled canned foods, for a real bargain, from the local grocer. And sufficient motivation to store a dead deer in your bathtub, until a neighbor could help you dress it, after the unfortunate creature had leapt in front of your work truck during a snowstorm.

On top of that, life was comfortless. We lived our second year in Thomasville in a 20-foot travel trailer with a 5-gallon hot-water tank, and closet space the width of a man's logging boot, turned sideways.

And that lifestyle was a vast improvement over the trailer house we rented the first year we arrived. That one had been parked for more than two decades under a stand of yellow poplar before it was relocated next to the Kingdom Hall on Spinks Drive, where we moved into it. Decaying trees had enticed colonies of ants, which were now embedded in the paneled walls of the decomposing trailer — ants that marched like armies across the floors and kitchen countertop, and tramped through our underwear drawer. No amount of spray insecticides deterred them (though *I gagged thoroughly* on the fumes) or the cockroaches that ate the corners of our literature and crawled across our bed at night, causing me to shriek and bolt upright. As did the water, which seeped up through the heating ducts because secondhand plumbing, now old and broken, had been crudely installed inside the ventilation system, which required we add a makeshift gas heater in the kitchen — that we cleverly placed over a see-through hole in the floor, the size of a coffee can, from which, during winter, cold air seeped in from the ground below.

But it was these hurdles, in concert with our insatiable transportation needs, that inspired a juggling act as good as any you'd see in a carnival sideshow — our faces pinched in a freakish grin while flipping bowling pins, straddling a unicycle that was balanced on a rubber ball, suspended on a high wire.

You see ...

As if "eating" weren't enough of a challenge, traveling more than 100 miles for extra work; as if keeping a roof over our heads wasn't enough of a quest, requiring we dig the hole for our own electric pole in order to get local service; as if spreading our brand of gospel through Southern Baptist country, driven by vigorous monthly quotas, wasn't enough of a test. Transportation was the lifeblood of our existence in the Alabama backwoods. And there was no such thing as Yellow Cabs to hail or bus routes to rely on — prompting us to burn through used vehicles, speedily, by traveling some 50,000 miles per year. And that didn't include the wrecks.

Just two weeks after our arrival, while driving four miles south of Thomasville in our Mazda RX-3, the car behind us pulled out to pass near a hill at the same time a speeding northbound car crested the same hill. Yep. Freeze-frame that image in your head, and you'll suspect a collision is imminent — as did Phil, forcing him to yank the Mazda off the road so the passing car could re-enter the southbound lane and avert disaster.

And that spontaneous gesture, at 50 mph, sent the Mazda bucking like a bronco along the uneven edge of Highway 43, snapping a tie-rod, which required a 95-mile tow to the nearest big city and two weeks down time waiting for the parts to be shipped ... which led us to the snappy realization that foreign cars, in those days, in that part of the world, weren't, shall we say, "practical."

We pressed on after Phil's parents drove from Texas to loan us a truck they owned. In the interim, I told the story of our misfortune in a letter to my grandparents in Iowa. And they sent this unexpected reply:

"Burdette would like to send you money to buy a car," my grandmother wrote — Burdette being my dead mother's oldest brother, a single fellow with a learning disability who earned a comfortable wage working at a meat-packing plant. *"He will send you $1,500. He hopes that will buy you a **good** car."* It was, we would learn, his contribution to the "cause," since he was unable to spread the gospel full-time himself.

We were giddy with gratitude and pored over our options with a fine-tooth comb before settling on a dependable Dodge Dart, without the "extras." It was a four-door, 5-year-old workhorse — plastic seats, no air conditioning, no power windows — with 49,000 miles on the odometer that had just rolled onto the lot in Mobile after a trade. But for a few cosmetic flaws — a dent in the front fender and a hubcap missing — it was several hundred dollars cheaper than all others of the same model and year. We were pleased as punch that it was right within our budget — down to the last dollar, you might say, even after Phil, tapping his father's salesman skills, convinced the dealership to fix the fender dent and replace the hubcap for the same low price.

Then, shortly after we'd purchased the car, at a midmorning rendezvous with another carload of preachers at the Gosport country store, a solitary structure in the middle of nowhere much 30 miles southeast of Thomasville, we found out we weren't quite as clever as we thought.

Only after the others had driven off did Phil notice the condition of the back left tire. Squatting down while gripping his Dr. Pepper, he peered at a hole the size of a quarter, worn through to one of the last layers of radial banding.

"This isn't good," Phil muttered, rising to open the trunk. *"I hope the car has a good jack ..."* he said, halting in midsentence as he opened the lid and looked in: *"Well ... **THIS** ISN'T good."*

The condition of the jack hardly mattered when he realized there was no spare tire. Nada! And there was no one we could call for help. Never mind the fact that we didn't have money for a tow, should we need one. Or, for that matter, money to buy another tire, until Phil completed his next cleaning job.

And there was the issue of our monthly quotas. We were way behind on them and needed to compile as many hours as we could to catch up. To that end, Phil pondered aloud our minuscule options:

"*We can attempt to drive home, and if we make it, sit there until we go to work tomorrow ...,*" Phil said, dusting off his hands. "*Or, we can keep going until the tire blows and worry about it then.*"

It was a low-percentage gamble — considering our preaching territory that day consisted of miles of dirt roads covered with pebbles that could easily puncture a damaged tire. Roads that were seldom traveled by others.

But nervous as I was about his strategy, I didn't have a better idea.

So off we went, knocking on doors from the Lower Peach Tree community to a neighborhood called Chance, traveling through densely forested areas, at one point eight miles from the nearest residence. It was in Chance that we met a quiet but sharp-witted lady who had swept her dirt yard clean and hung empty bottles on her fence posts — and who agreed, quite easily, to a home Bible study.

By late afternoon we had discovered a vast area of land, once filled with trees, that had been stripped bare by a local logging company. It was a surreal scene — something you'd see in a science-fiction movie: uncluttered, but strangely beautiful — like no other landscape around. It was a contemplative place, and we stood there for the longest time imagining what the earth would look like after Armageddon, since Headquarters had statistical data to prove it was near.

"My spirit flows here," said Phil, vowing to return when his life got too stressful, which, based on that criterion, would be often.

By the time we arrived home that evening around 7 p.m. it was getting dark, and roughly nine hours had passed since we first noticed the damaged tire. Doubting his initial prediction of doom, Phil opened his car door to investigate, while I gathered up my things on the front seat. As he slammed the door shut we both heard a loud hissing noise. And, walking up to the back left tire, Phil watched in awe as it went flat.

That's the day we learned how to let go of fear and grip purpose.

Sometime after that, driving along Highway 43 in our "practical" Dodge Dart, Phil spotted his wooden utility trailer — in his rearview mirror, in a moment of horror — flipping head over heels behind us, flinging floor equipment out the busted back doors. The trailer had somehow escaped the car hitch ... which led us to the astounding conclusion that being practical, in and of itself, does not make you a genius. And being "gripped with purpose" does not, exactly, mean you're invincible.

Anywhooo, as I was saying *(31 paragraphs ago)*, three distinct components of our lives were converging in Thomasville, and our perception of reality was about to be pushed past boiling ...

— — —

YOUNG LOVE

I stored my precious love letters in a brown paper bag — the kind in which you tote home milk and bread — the ones we sent each other as teens, that nurtured our affections before we wed.

I meant to put them in a better place, safer than a crumpled sack stored in a dank trailer closet. Those writings had revealed enough of our hearts that there was nothing much left to say about that.

Only later, driving the back roads of East Texas during the first year of our marriage, our backseat filled with Bible literature, did we learn the limits of those letters — that which had not been said. Hundreds of hours side by side in a dusty, sun-baked car will do that for you. It will shed light on your reality. It will break you ... in.

"Are you trying to tell me you've kissed someone?" was the question that kick-started the catastrophe that followed.

"Kind of ..." was my reply, as if "kind of" was even possible. How do you "kind of" kiss somebody? But I had brought the question on myself, in one of my familiar moments of guilt, in the interests of brutal honesty, to fortify our relationship.

"Is there something else?" he pressed me. As if he were a mind-reader. As if this were a chance for him to test his instincts — since I had piqued his curiosity — and get to the bottom of things. Get to the bottom of *anything* and *everything,* while he was at it.

Phil had that kind of earnestness about him — an ability to drill down, clear down to the root of matters, to protect his sanity. And I, burden that I was to him, and my parents, and mankind at large, slipped into that chair — the one with the spotlight and magnifying glass above it. I allowed him to peer inside me, willing to suffer the pain of extraction.

As it was, our conversations, on other topics, had begun to rival that of older adults we knew; our discussions were deeper by far than anything to which I was accustomed. Because of that, I was beginning to wake up from a daze that had begun at the age of 10 — shortly after my father walked down the aisle with Loretta Lynn and my feelings and opinions overnight were stamped irrelevant.

Now, suddenly, along the gritty back roads of Texas, I was beginning to express myself. I was learning to match my thoughts to words: sort of. It was a choppy experience — like learning to water ski. And I often wiped out.

"I think I haven't told you everything," I said, glancing out the car window.

*"You '**think**?' "* Phil said, a sarcastic tone masking his distress. *"YOU DON'T KNOW?!"*

If I could have snapped my fingers and disappeared right then, to spare him the dialogue, I would have. Instead, we were trapped in a 1964 Rambler near a town called Big Sandy, having sold his sporty 1973 Plymouth Duster — the one he owned as a single carefree 18-year-old — to reduce our monthly bills.

There was nothing I could do but proceed.

"OK, so I kissed a couple a guys," I coughed, working my fingers like I was counting. *"Over a period of two years ... I think."*

There was that phrase, again: *"I think."*

Then, it happened.

As I began connecting the dots, more faces appeared ... ones I had forgotten, or rather locked away inside the brain cells labeled "hazardous" to my pure and pristine image. And that caused me to update my calculations over the course of a two-day conversation with Phil, disrupted by extended periods of silence. A conversation that was filled with sighs: *"Wait (sigh), about three ..."*

And pregnant pauses: *"Might have been (pause) could have been (pause) four ..."*

And the need to clear my throat: *"Um ... five guys (cough), I guess ..."*

Along with rationalizations: *"But one was just a peck on the cheek — **literally,** a **peck** on **the cheek**!"*

Plus, a shocking side note: *"There **was** one older girl (cough) (pause) (sigh) who touched my ..."*

Thinking I was helping matters, I continued to fill in graphic details of my encounters: one kiss with a boy on a ferris wheel, or was it a roller-coaster? I couldn't quite remember. Twice at the movies — and once while spending the night with a girlfriend, when her brother laid a long, uninspiring kiss on me before I fled the room.

When I glanced at Phil, his face had turned green. And it was too late to recall what had escaped me, so I kept going in an act of lunacy with the biggest news of all — an experience that had lifted my spirits at first, before I terminated it.

"The ferris wheel guy slipped his (cough) class ring on my finger," I whispered, remembering he had done so the summer I turned 15, the year my family escaped Denver for Las Animas and I was sure my inconsequential social life, and any link to my old friends, was dead.

"He was very nice — almost 17," I added. *"But I gave the ring back to him."*

(Though I didn't give it back *right then*, exactly ...)

Phil's eyes were glazed over as he stared straight ahead at the pavement. *"You just now remembered all this?"*

"Kind of ...," I hesitated, petrified to say another word but consumed with the need to clarify: *"It WASN'T important!"*

But it *was* important to Phil. Besides the blow to his ego, it appeared that I had secrets. What else was I not telling him, he wondered?

Phil stopped the car on the side of the road and rested his hands and forehead on the steering wheel. Then, after some time had elapsed, he faced me.

"*What did it feel like ... when you kissed them?*" He asked, his head twitching.

I froze, aware that he was now punishing the both of us.

Ours may have seemed like a petty crisis four years after Woodstock, in an era when "free love" was the mantra of young people. But ours was the strictest of upbringings, with our righteousness being tied to our purity. Chastity, in our faith, in those days, included no hand-holding, no recreational dating *or kissing*.

Phil had stayed the course. He hadn't kissed another girl — though he would have liked to — to save himself for the girl he would marry.

No manner of explaining, on my part, seemed to comfort him. And the more we talked — over the weeks and months that followed along the back roads of Texas — the more we both realized our knowledge of one another was limited. The attraction between us that had transcended time and space had been eclipsed by the inescapable debris of our lives.

Nonetheless, by the time we moved to Thomasville, we had more or less laid our issues to rest. Except on days when we were exhausted and overwhelmed, on days when the outside world made no sense to us.

In those moments, when I felt my worst, I would drag the brown paper bag from the closet and bury myself in the past. It didn't matter if there was laundry to do, or dishes to wash, or dinner to cook. I would curl up on the floor, open those letters and escape to a safe place — a familiar one, in search of the missing pieces of my life. And sometimes ... I forgot to return.

That's how Phil found me one evening after a long and difficult night of work. The dishes were unwashed, the house still dirty.

"*I can't take this anymore,*" he said, suddenly overwhelmed by everything at once. "*If we're going to ever get past this, we have to get rid of the letters.*"

"This" meant so much more than those letters, or, a dirty house. We needed to *get past* our poverty; we needed to *get through* the confounding developments in the congregation. But we were too young and ill-informed to grasp the whole picture. In the meantime, a demon had to be exorcized.

"*You can't be serious!*" I cried. "*What about our memories?*"

"*Those memories weren't real,*" he said, perplexed by it all. "*I can't read them anymore.*"

His solution was staggering.

"*Please ... please no!*" I pleaded. I warned. I begged, bursting into tears. "*I love those letters. I NEED those letters. YOU HAVE NO IDEA WHAT YOU'RE DOING!*"

There it was. The telltale sign that deep down inside I would one day be a writer. It was unimaginable to me to part with such historic documents complete with street addresses and the corny, sappy, ordinary and surprising words we had once penned.

But we had left the safety of our homeland long ago on our journey into the wilderness, and we had planned no exit strategy. Under those circumstances, it was imperative that we keep moving and keep our load light.

That which had once defined us was dragging us down.

I know that now, reflecting back. But that did not ease the acute pain in my heart on the drive to the garbage dump the next day. The dump, in a town I barely knew, that swallowed up my love letters.

— — —

UNEASY SOULS

Some insights can be acquired only by personal interaction, it seems — in real time, face to face. That's what we were learning knocking on the doors of thousands, carrying on dialogue for thousands of hours with people of divergent backgrounds.

It's then you notice the subtleties — that which make a person distinct; that which transcend their assets or job titles, their skills or career — if they even have one. You glimpse their character. But mostly, you see how "beliefs" shape them.

— — —

The Handsome Blond Rancher represented everything I wasn't — though I had always fancied myself a tomboy. A few years older than me, with four kids to her name and a 20-acre parcel of land, she was the head of her household when her truck-driving husband spent weeks on end transporting furniture across America. She mended fences, bailed hay, fed the cattle and chased away the one-eyed, dog-snatching alligator that lived in the pond across the road the day it crawled into her front yard.

I admired her grit. She admired mine. And we became friends.

Phil and I had found her on the outskirts of town while we were hopscotching houses with the insurance man. At the time, insurance agents collected their dues in person. It was, for the most part, the only way they got paid. But some of them were strange birds, we had noticed, when our paths crossed, which they did. It wasn't unusual when we went knocking to find the insurance man at the same house, already inside — sitting with legs crossed at the kitchen table waiting for the occupant to fetch dollar bills from under a mattress. Other times, he'd walk in on us waiting in the living room for the occupant to twist open a sock and pull out a dime for a Watchtower and Awake.

It was on such a day that the Handsome Blond Rancher invited us in. And we passed the insurance man on his way out.

She was an inquisitive sort — full of smart questions. Bible lessons ensued, and she embraced our visits like they were important to her. Over time, she came to the Kingdom Hall on Spinks Drive and once gave her own speech on stage. Eventually, she knocked on the doors of others, clasping her very own green Bible — green being Headquarters' color of choice for Bibles in those days.

She was this close to becoming a believer of our faith when she reached her limits — in particular, her relatives' limits on her husband's side, who lived a few doors down. She was keeping company with "black" folks at that "black" church on Spinks Drive, and her relatives wouldn't hear of it.

One day before we parted ways, she coaxed me into her pickup for feeding rounds. We headed to the barn to load hay, and as she thrust bales into her flatbed, she paused, as if searching for the nerve to say something. We drove across a field. She stopped, then tossed out some bales, but still said nothing. Finally, after her chores were done, she parked the truck and ushered me out. It was a splendid day, warm and sunny, and we walked through the tall golden grass together.

"*I swaney Pam, you have a good right arm for slinging hay. Just develop that muscle more,*" the Handsome Blond Rancher said, squeezing my bicep. Then she cleared her throat.

"*I just wanted to thank you for coming by my house and starting your Bible study with me when you did.*"

As she said the words, her face was a mixture of emotions: Her forehead was creased in a frown, but her mouth hinted at a smile.

"*Because I don't know what might have happened to me if you hadn't ...*"

I looked at her with a puzzled expression.

"You see the insurance man had been coming by for some time ..." she said, looking in my direction to see if I knew what an insurance man was. I did, and I nodded.

"Well, he was a persistent fella ..." she continued, still suppressing a grin. *"And I don't mean about insurance ..."*

The conversation stopped again, and we pointed our faces at the sun.

"He's on the road all time," she said, referring to her husband the truck driver. *"We get along all right, but things aren't perfect. The youngest was starting his first grade ... it was my first time being alone in a long while. Shoot, I was kind of looking forward to the privacy ...,"* she said, filling in odd details.

"I wasn't strongly fixated on him." She looked at me to make sure I was still following along. *"I guess I was just bored."*

She had never been much of a talker — not ever. And I knew this was a big deal for her to share.

"Anyway, I have you to thank for keeping me from messing things up with my family," she concluded. *"He'll never have to know how close I came,"* she said, speaking of her husband, the truck driver. *"But I wanted you to know."*

That was the end of our connection. And I missed the Handsome Blond Rancher for a long time, thereafter ...

Sometimes the outcome was the same in reverse. School Teacher was a dignified woman in her mid-30s when we came to call. The college-educated black woman was a rarity in Thomasville. We relished the time sitting on her brocade couch covered in plastic and analyzing such topics as "Who is God?" "Why are we here?" and "Why do we grow old and die?" from our efficient but tiny blue study book.

But there were strange moments in our discussion when School Teacher was reading aloud, when she would stop suddenly, in midsentence, and pause on a word. Sometimes it was a Hebrew or Greek word found in paragraphs surmising the origins of a Biblical name or place. But other times they were just ordinary words.

When this noble woman had paused too long in silence, we knew it was our cue to say the word aloud, at which point she would repeat it and move on in her reading. About six months passed before she opened up one day and explained her behavior.

She attended modest black schools with only black teachers, she told us. Following high school, she was admitted to a black college. But it lacked the resources, study materials and standards of the white colleges in that era. Despite her hard work, that path had its limits.

"We didn't reach our potential," School Teacher said.

She praised us for our dedication to our work, our punctual arrivals for her Bible lessons and the fact that there was no charge for our services. But mostly she was thankful that a young white couple had been willing to sit on her plastic-covered couch and crack open a book with her. Ours was an exchange that transcended religious doctrine. It was, in those moments, a different kind of divine.

Even so, she had become a respected member of the local black community. And she could not be seen at the "white" church on Spinks Drive.

One day she was too busy to continue her lessons.

— — —

On occasion, though, the now-integrated Kingdom Hall on Spinks Drive attracted folks like flies on honey — no matter their color.

One such bubbly woman showed up unannounced to a Sunday meeting to make my case. She was a brown-skinned creature, but lighter than most, of black and Native American origins — who had been attracted to Jehovah's Witnesses prior to her arrival here while living with her family in New Orleans. It was there that she had found meaning in her life when studying the Bible with the Witnesses. But when she began attending their weekly meetings, her husband got very angry.

He hated *that religion,* he told her more than once, before packing up his family and moving them back home to Dixon Mills, Alabama — a sparsely populated community 12 miles north of Thomasville — to property that his bubbly brown wife had inherited from a relative. And there, he erected a small Jim Walters Home.

At the time, Jim Walters Homes were a popular housing choice for those with modest means. They were shell homes constructed by the manufacturer that landowners finished out themselves, in their own time, whenever they had the money, which often never happened.

And Bubbly Brown was glad to be back, to be living in her very own unfinished Jim Walters Home, surrounded by dense woods where she might *"walk bucks naked and not worry 'bout a thing,'"* she often laughed. *"Not saying I would, but if I wanted to, I surely could ..."*

Despite that perk, her purpose went missing after she moved to Dixon Mills. And she fell ill.

A trip to the family doctor convinced of her of what she must do. *"Get to the bottom of this,"* the doc had told her, knowing full well that what ailed her was not "physical" in nature.

And so she did, by begging her husband, much to his chagrin, to *"find me Kingdom Hall."*

"You won't like it," he threatened her, once he'd found one, 12 miles away on Spinks Drive. *"White peoples go there."*

But Bubbly Brown didn't care. To her, it was exciting news that white people and black people congregated together. And the very day she walked through the double doors on Spinks Drive, her spunk resurfaced, for she had once again found the way to expand herself.

It was my good fortune that she and I connected that day, that she agreed to study with both Phil and me. For we got front-row seats to her persecution, and she got front row seats to our persistence. And we gave each other strength.

As soon as her enthusiasm returned, so did her husband's hatred of her religion. And only on rare occasions did he dare allow us to set foot inside his unfinished Jim Walters Home for our Bible discussions. Mostly, Bubbly Brown met us outside. She'd slip into the backseat of our practical car, along with her two small boys, and we'd drive to a suitable parking spot to begin our lessons.

It was under those circumstances — all of us piled into a sweltering car, or a frigid one, depending on the weather — that I'd often become drowsy. My head would fall backward on the front passenger seat, my eyes closed tight as I slipped into a deep sleep.

"Girl, you always be sneaking a wink," Bubbly Brown would say, tapping me on the back of my head from her backseat vantage point and startling me awake. *"You got anemia or somethin'? You be skinny as a rail ..."*

But I'd just ignore her, as if her spot-on observations lacked know-how. You see, Bubbly Brown "came down" with her two children like you'd catch the flu: *"Let's see, I came down with my BeBe the month of ..."* she'd say, describing one of her pregnancies — a terminology that made my head snap backward against the front passenger seat in a cackling whiplash.

But her obligation to those two boys was not lost on her. She was their one and only spiritual sage. And when the mood struck her, she'd sit her boys down, no matter the lateness of the hour, no matter their drowsiness, and disperse scriptural wisdom to them.

Her youngest, a 3-year-old with a mind of his own, was by her side — as was I — the day she knocked on her very first door in town in the preaching work.

"Good mornin'!" Bubbly Brown beamed, standing on the porch of an old woman who had reluctantly opened her screen door to three strangers. *"We be sharing some Good News with your neighbors today ..."*

Bubbly Brown stopped, looked at me for reassurance, then politely continued: *"Fact is, we be asking your neighbors this question: Does you know that God has a name?"*

It was a different question than we'd rehearsed, and I fidgeted a bit, knowing right then she was winging it ...

"The first time I learned his name, I was so ***amaze'*** *..."* Bubbly Brown kept on, speaking from her heart and transforming my worry into delight.

Things were going very well, I decided, as Bubbly Brown whipped open her Good Book like a seasoned Bible-thumper and began to read the old woman a Scripture. But that blissful moment was dashed by the sound of running water on the ground behind us.

We swung right around to see her tiny boy, his suit pants down, peeing on the lady's sidewalk. Drained of our smugness, we froze, at which point the old woman cleared her throat and said: *"Now don't y'all worries about dat'. The sun will dries it up, and the wind will blows it away."*

The old woman's unassuming nature, devoid of devilment, was a relief that day to Bubbly Brown. Mostly because her own neighbors, some of whom left voodoo dolls stuck with pins on the front steps of her unfinished Jim Walters Home, weren't nearly as forgiving of her or her faith. And neither was her husband, who often made the car unavailable on meeting nights, requiring she hitch a ride with anybody she could find, last minute. Who also made the front door impenetrable upon her return home, which, if it happened to be a frosty night, required she hole up under the house in a crawlspace, wrapped in a piece of burlap.

He was always sorry later, she'd tell us — trapped as he was between his prejudices and his affection for her.

"My husband's like an itty-bitty kitty that climbs so far up a tree, he gets stuck," she'd tell us, as if she could see through him, like she could see through me. *"He don't knows how to get back down, or go higher ... so he just sits there."*

Eventually, Bubbly Brown was baptized. Then, her husband moved the family away, and she found the next Kingdom Hall, in the next city, and worshiped there. But this time, her husband stopped mistreating her. She had pursued her happiness, with immense persistence, and mellowed the meanie.

— — —

By then Phil and I had expanded the breadths and depths of our door-to-door skills to chest-swelling proportions. We had at our disposal a boundless number of sound bites to attract the interest of total strangers on their own doorsteps: a 30-second sound bite, if the householder was especially busy; one minute, if time allowed; and five minutes if the person had no willpower to say, "Shove off." Above all else, we could handle marathon discussions whenever the opportunity presented itself. Like the ones we had with the Church of Christ minister that often lasted into the early hours of a morning and carried on for weeks. Ours was a display of wit — pitting one religion's holiness against the other — and requiring many hours of preparation.

It ground to a halt one night over a trivial debate about the Apostle Paul. In short: *If he were alive today, would he be qualified to be an elder?* As if one of us, over the other, was capable of reaching the purest explanation of sacred writings. As if everything Phil and I did was building up to something significant — not only involving our preaching skills but our behaviors. As if buying four-door sensible cars instead of two-door flashy models — to accommodate a full load of proselytizers — inched us closer to God. As if deadening our desire for material objects or designer homes or lucrative employment options could transform us into the holiest of human beings on this contaminated planet.

In the end, Phil and I argued that the Apostle Paul would have been qualified in his day for eldership — after all, HE WAS THE APOSTLE PAUL. But our opponent firmly disagreed. He assured us that the list of "elder" qualifications in the Bible, as penned by Timothy, was emphatic that elders should technically be *"the husband of one wife."* That singleness, which the "single" Paul advocated aggressively, the big disqualifier for Paul to have ever held the office of elder *(which was an inferior role to "apostle" in the first place — so who cares?)*

Suffice to say, neither of us won the battle spotlighting a 2,000-year-old dead man. Neither of us inspired the other to "switch camps." We both shook our heads and retreated to our selective belief systems and, soon after, ended our weekly rap sessions.

But I will confess: Something about that exchange gnawed at Phil and me for a long time after — even though we didn't dare discuss it with anybody else. Neither of us appeared to be evil or undeserving of God's favor — though both camps seemed quite certain that only one would inherit God's kingdom.

After mind-bending experiences like that, I found it oddly pleasant to frequent the homes of strangers who didn't question a thing I said. Who had no expectations, whatsoever, regarding my intellect, and who preferred simple companionship instead of sparring over finite technicalities about Biblical revelations.

"My backside's sore. Mind if I stand while you read your turn?" said one such woman, as she warmed herself next to the stone hearth in her sparsely decorated shack, which lacked the modern convenience of plumbing.

"I was chopping wood yesterdee, when I had to stop and pee ..." she continued, as I looked up from my study book, my curiosity piqued.

I studied, instead, the image of her: a stubby, sandy-haired lady, presumably of Appalachian origins, with tobacco juice on her chin; the mother of 21 children *(if you count miscarriages, as she did)* who were now mostly grown but for two unkempt teenage boys, who peered at me and sniffed the air like wild dogs.

She was a spent woman — depleted of her stamina and resources, relegated to the role of beggar, for the most part — who shuffled about her world in search of kind-hearted souls willing to give her food: a chicken to boil, some lard, whatever she could muster.

Stationed in the same small room, in the only chair, was her husband — a pencil-thin figure sitting mute and motionless in a string tie and hat — the ghost of a man who once worked as a traveling salesman. I sat nearby, on her crumpled bed, careful to keep my skirt tucked between my legs and the soiled bed sheets, while Phil remained outside in the car catching up on his "Bible reading."

"... I'd barely cleared the door when I ran for the pee pot under the bed," Spent stopped, to spit in a can. *"But dang if somebodee hadn't moved it."*

She grabbed her crotch and scrunched her knees together as if illustrating the previous day's predicament.

"I look around nearly a' panic for something else and ..." she continued, almost breathless. *"The first thing I see is a pan a' water sitting next to the pile a farrrwood ..."* she pointed to the stack beside her. *"And I dropped down to pee in that ... until ... HOT DAMN!"* she froze, her face twisted in horror. *"One a' them boys had just moved it from the farrr!"* she paused to cradle her backside: *"Burnt a complete circle on MY BUTT!"*

My head snapped back and I gasped for air, turning toward the "mister" to share the hilarity. But there was no light left in the old boy's eyes.

"Course, the mister's medicine keeps him drowsy ...," Spent spoke up, on his behalf.

Then getting back to the business at hand, Spent winked at me and whispered: "*I thank ye' right now for bringing me another blue book,*" she said. "*Used the last one you gave me for kindling.*"

CONGREGATONAL COMPLEXITIES

Headquarters, like any organization worth its salt, had its rules. There were duties and titles, tracking systems, reports and quotas. There were incentives and goals that, when adhered to, reflected the level and speed of a person's spiritual advancement. Most of all, there were protocols — certain steps that must be taken when things weren't running smoothly in a congregation.

And those protocols, if not followed exactly, could jeopardize everything we had worked for as card-carrying Pioneers on our God-inspired journey.

— — —

"I'm so scared my thart is humping," I told Phil, clutching my chest, after carrying on too long about the bizarre behavior of an elder of God the first year we arrived in Thomasville.

"How does a thart hump, exactly?" Phil replied, his whole body shaking with laughter.

"HUMP THARTING!" I repeated, trying in vain to pronounce the words correctly. It was beginning to disturb me that I was scrambling my speech more often than most people. Nervous, I reached into the refrigerator for a carton of milk, lifted it to my mouth and took a swig.

"*There are glasses for that sort of thing*," Phil barked.

"*What do I need glasses for? My eyes aren't bad ...*" I snapped at him.

We weren't the only ones distressed about the elder. Whispers were increasing among members of the tiny congregation on Spinks Drive about the giant black man who led the flock — a controlling fellow who expressed himself often with freakish glee; his eyes fixed in a wide stare; his mouth spread in a ghastly grin as a *"he-he-he"* escaped him. Of course, the congregation was made up of less than a dozen members, so, statistically speaking, that didn't count for much. And one of them was the Giant Black Man's wife — a pencil-thin woman with pursed lips who, by a tragic turn of events, had colon cancer.

The only other elder, also in his 40s, was a quiet man by comparison, articulate but sheepish, who wore clothes pressed to perfection and responded to our congregational concerns by pointing heavenward and shaking his head in sympathy before lamenting: *"Jehovah sees; Jehovah sees ..."*

Turns out the Giant Black Man, who expressed himself with freakish glee, and the "Greetings, Lawsons" elder, who had penned the fine-looking letter in red ink wooing Phil and I to Thomasville, were one and the same. And it was "Glee" who would test our endurance in a more profound way than any of the uneasy souls whom we'd encountered in the ministry.

"You'll never believe this," a Portuguese man told Phil not long after we moved there. The Portuguese had arrived in Thomasville from Florida with his family of five a short time before us. He was a passionate man, quick to speak his mind. And he couldn't stop speaking about Glee.

"It's TOO much, man," he said of a recent visit from Glee and Jehovah Sees. They had both arrived unannounced at his home for an "obligatory" shepherding call, in their role as local elders.

*"HE brought up **SEX**,"* the Portuguese gasped, as if it was a bad thing. But it wasn't the topic itself that riled him. It was the *way* Glee had introduced it, *how* he expressed himself, that worried the Portuguese most.

"This is what he tells me," the voice of the Portuguese grows louder: " *'Your kids are growing up! Pretty soon, you and your wife can't run around the house naked anymore!' Then he cups his hands to his chest to mimic my wife's breasts and laughed his stupid 'he-he-he-he-he.'* "

"*We never 'run around the house naked!'* " the Portuguese was almost shouting now. "*I should have thrown him out, but I'm ashamed to say, I just sat there ...*"

Once the Portuguese had told that story, he couldn't stop talking about other strange encounters he'd had with Glee, quoting Glee verbatim: *"I suppose by now you've noticed that **white** women want me. ... He-he-he."*

Glee and his wife, with the pursed lips, were card-carrying "Special Pioneers" — the rarest kind — who received a modest monthly stipend from Headquarters. As pioneers go, there were three varieties, in this order, not counting foreign missionaries: 1) "vacation" pioneer: one who enlists for one month at a time and dedicates 75 hours that month preaching the Good News. 2) Fulltime Pioneer: One who enrolls as a permanent preacher of the Good News; who agrees to knock on doors 100 hours a month (or, 1,200 per year); who has met strict spiritual criteria; who has been approved by a body of elders; who has been confirmed in writing by Headquarters and issued an official "pioneer card." And 3): Special Pioneer: an exemplary servant, granted the privilege by special recommendation only, who spends half-again the number of hours full-time pioneers do and earns a modest monthly stipend from Headquarters, which, in return for that support, has the right to relocate the Special Pioneer on short notice to expand God's work in remote areas.

On average, back in the day, Special Pioneers might spend two to three years in a town before they were reassigned by Headquarters. They lived the simplest of lives and most often occupied small mobile homes they could easily transport when they got "the call" to move on.

But Glee and Pursed Lips had been in Thomasville for nearly six years by the time we arrived, which was highly irregular. What's more, it didn't appear they were going anywhere soon. They had purchased land on the outskirts of town and had filled it with an assortment of cars — from Volkswagens to a flashy Cadillac. They had strewn it with discarded containers of cleaning chemicals, used in their janitorial business. And they had parked three weathered trailer homes on the lot, one of which had burned in a fire and was now a box of charred metal.

As visuals go, something about Glee's personal surroundings did not match his devout image.

Complicating matters more was our place of worship. Glee somehow owned the building on Spinks Drive — which was highly irregular as well. Normally, church buildings were the property of the congregation that gathered there; they were not owned by a solitary member.

Furthermore, this place of worship did not resemble the clean and neat ones that Phil and I had been accustomed to as children growing up. It was an unsightly cinderblock structure. The unfinished, rough-hewn floors had holes in them. Dusty piles of lumber were stored on stage behind the speaker's podium — presumably to one day cover the ugly cinderblock walls. Until then, Glee had partially bathed the walls in a combination of hideous colors — olive green and canary yellow — rummaged from a clearance sale.

Adjacent to the stage was the toilet, with a short plastic shower curtain for a door. The wall between the stage and toilet was made of cardboard boxes tacked flat to a frame made of two-by-fours. Folks waited for a song to relieve themselves — otherwise, the speaker and the audience heard the "tinkling." In the wintertime, the pipes froze, forcing people to "hold it" until they got home. Along the north wall was a wood burning stove; beside it was an old piano with a partially scorched keyboard. And there were holes in the roof — when it rained, folks played musical chairs, scraping them across the wooden floor to avoid the drips and drizzles.

But the literature counter stood out most of all. It was a Playtex Living Bra stand that Glee had found in the alleyway behind a local department store. Bibles and books now filled the bins that once held boxes of girdles and bras — the Platex logo still emblazoned, plain as day, across the front.

Phil had sensed something strange about Glee the first time they traveled around town together in search of janitorial work. When Glee passed black folks on the street, he'd pop his fist out the window and flash the black power sign. That behavior seemed an odd contrast to his anti-activist speeches at Bible meetings. But he did try to explain himself: *"I do it for **them**, you see,"* Glee had told Phil, followed by his freakish "he-he-he."

His leadership skills, as an elder, were even more confounding. He quoted from outdated Bible publications, which was highly frowned upon by Headquarters. And one meeting night, smack dab in the middie of an otherwise solemn presentation, he broke out in song — a hearty version of a Beatles tune — as if to flabbergast those of us in the audience: *"She loves you, yeah, yeah, yeah. She loves you, yeah, yeah, yeah. And you know that can't be ba-ad. Yes, she loves you, and you know you should be gla-ad. Ooh!"* At which point the tiny son of the Portuguese man laughed out loud, triggering cackles from the rest of us.

It's anybody's guess when Glee's irrational tendencies began to overtake him. Surely, before we got there — but when?

Something was eating at him: He wasn't from around these parts and was quick to point that out. He spelled his surname different than other black folks whose name sounded the same, and he pointed that out, too. Not to mention that his wife had attended a prestigious California university, which he liked to remind us; and both he and his wife had attended missionary school in upstate New York, just like my father once did. But Glee and Pursed Lips never received their coveted overseas assignments, and rumor had it the reason was that Glee had pissed off certain higher-ups at Headquarters. That he had challenged haloed members of the inner sanctum. He had noticed, and he told them so, that there were "no black men" on their board.

Sometime after that, Glee was assigned to Thomasville — to the middle of nowhere special — retaining, instead, the title of Special Pioneer that earned him a modest monthly stipend — not enough to escape his predicament, just enough to go mad. Of course, that was only rumor.

And there were other rumors ... passed along by members in nearby congregations that shared territorial borders with Thomasville — rumors of a man, the spitting image of Glee, who had allegedly engaged in certain indiscretions in the backwoods.

By the time we took up living in the dilapidated trailer, owned by Glee and located next to his church on Spinks Drive, Glee's door-to-door habits had become a mockery of Headquarters' procedures. He rarely joined members of the congregation in the work, preferring to go it alone. But when he did partner up, his associates were stunned by the sheer volume of literature he left behind on the doorsteps of residences — even when no one was home — as a quick way to achieve his magazine quotas.

By the time we began to *reluctantly* invite Bible students to the church on Spinks Drive, Glee had become a force of intimidation. He preferred to monopolize all tasks. And even though it was annoying, it was, at the same time, quite theatrical.

In the midst of headlining one such meeting, he discovered he had forgotten a book containing a passage he planned to read aloud. But instead of borrowing one from a church member in the front row, to avoid a disruption, he stepped off the stage, walked to the back of the room to a giant white man newly converted to the faith, and whispered in his ear.

The audience watched in disbelief as the white giant rose slowly, pure of purpose, and the pair headed to the Playtex Living Bra stand. Then the giant pulled a book from the rack and handed it to Glee. And Glee pulled a quarter from his pocket to pay for it. And the giant dutifully filled out a purchase receipt for 25 cents. Then Glee returned to the platform to complete his presentation.

His antics might have deserved a round of applause were there a hidden camera and someone announcing, "Surprise!' It's 'Candid Camera' " But his was not a prank. And we were beginning to feel like imbeciles at Glee's beck and call — who didn't dare cross him.

"I know some stuff on you — and don't you forget it," Glee told the piano player on a Thursday night, when, in a moment of bravery, she had stood up to him.

The piano player was a cheery woman, married to the supervisor of a local paper mill who, when he took to drinking, was known to beat her. She lived in limbo — between leaving him and raising *his* precious children (whose mother had died) until they were safely grown. To hide her fluctuating emotions, she laughed a lot. And she experienced bizarre mishaps.

"I hit another cow!" she said one morning during the preaching work, talking about the collision she'd had the night before. *"He's going to kill me — dead,"* she said of her husband. *"It's the third cow I've hit this year ... and that doesn't include* ***the deer*** *..."* She spoke fast and furious about the dangers of the back roads she traveled to and from meetings — narrow paths often populated by darting or slow-moving animals.

"The last cow I hit didn't dent the car. But this one got back up and kicked my grill!" She hooted. *"I saved the pieces! Tried to glue 'em back on when I got home — but they didn't stick!"* she laughed, again.

Then one Sunday, before the main discourse, as the Cheery Cow-Hitter rose from her seat and headed for the piano to play the introductory song, a fleshy redhead jumped up and beat her to the bench — creating an awkward moment between them, before all onlookers. The redhead was Glee's newly appointed piano player — the wife of the giant white man — though Glee had failed, quite deliberately, to announce the change to the cheery cow-hitter. Humiliated, she laughed louder than usual, then collapsed into her folding chair.

By the time we arrived in Thomasville, Glee's wife was a shadow of the person she once was, from what we could determine. She had been his compass. And now, he was losing his way. He began to miscalculate the people he had attracted to Thomasville — in particular, one young man with something to prove.

"I was very disappointed in the letter you sent (to Headquarters) about me," Glee told Phil one night at a Bible meeting, holding a copy of it in his hand. How he *got the copy* worried Phil — terribly.

Phil had felt compelled to report Glee's conduct to the higher-ups. The tiny congregation on Spinks Drive was unraveling; and worse, it was backsliding. Fear had set in, along with doubt, despair and gossip. Phil couldn't wait any longer, especially after his pleas had fallen on deaf ears. Jehovah Sees had failed to stand up to Glee and also failed to disclose Glee's actions to the Traveling Overseer who had just paid a visit to Thomasville and was not due back for six months — which seemed an eternity. Traveling Overseers were charged with monitoring local elders, but Glee had escaped that checkpoint, too.

And so Phil, like the Lone Ranger, did what he thought was right and responsible: He jotted down his concerns and sent them directly to New York. But he did not expect Headquarters to send the letter right back to Glee and Jehovah Sees as part of a disclosure process — to see if they could first *handle* their own problems *internally* without involving outsiders.

"In that case, I have a letter I've written about YOU, too ...," Glee told Phil, his tone intimidating, having cornered Phil near the olive green cinderblock wall with a shamefaced Jehovah Sees standing beside him. Then Glee leveled his threat: *"If you don't retract the letter you wrote, I will send my letter (to Headquarters) in response to it."*

Glee's letter was filled with an assortment of insinuations about Phil — from talking behind elders' backs to allegations of prejudice and unscrupulous conduct. Phil knew this because Glee had, oddly enough, presented him with a copy.

"Okay, I'll write another letter," Phil replied in a solemn voice, careful to slip the copy of Glee's letter into his pocket.

Glee had finally met his match – though he didn't know it then. But Phil knew it. Somebody was about to go down if he followed through on the rest of his plan. Either way, it was time, he believed, to end Glee's harmful charades.

That night Phil could not sleep, aware that our dreams could be dashed in a heartbeat if Headquarters rejected his strategy – aware that all the hours we had spent preaching along the back roads of East Texas and Alabama could lead to nowhere. That our encounters with King David's Mother, the Handsome Blond Rancher and The Teacher; with Bubbly Brown and the Church of Christ Minister who demoted the Apostle Paul – might all be wasted experiences.

What Phil was about to do was *beyond* risky – and, because of that, I could not sleep either. He might very well be judged a heretic and I his accomplice. We could be excommunicated; we could lose our family and friends.

But there was no turning back now. And Phil did not lose heart regarding what he had to do next. He would contact Headquarters a second time and include Glee's letter, without his knowledge.

This was Phil's argument, in so many words, as he presented it to them: If he, Phil, were truly guilty of the accusations outlined in (Glee's enclosed) letter, then Headquarters should, by obligation, remove Phil at once, without hesitation, from all his duties – including that of card-carrying Pioneer – for he was no longer worthy of those God-inspired tasks.

But, if Phil was not guilty as charged ... then clearly Glee was capable of employing such slanderous accusations as merely a bargaining chip.

Phil had played the cards he was dealt. And he could only hope that someone at Headquarters was gifted at reading between the lines, that they had received the encoded message that "evil was afoot" in Thomasville.

Phil never heard a word back from Headquarters. But a few weeks later Glee cornered Phil again. And this time, when the towering 45-year-old spoke to the short 20-year-old, he seemed troubled.

"Have you heard about the committee meeting set for Wednesday?" Glee tested Phil.

"No?"

"Just be there," Glee snarled, offering no more explanation.

When Phil walked through the doors of the cinderblock building that Wednesday night, he discovered three men — one white and two black — who had traveled many miles to be there.

They were seasoned leaders from other congregations who were now tasked with unscrambling the mystery that was Thomasville. And that meeting was just the beginning. Over the next 18 months, under even more highly irregular circumstances, they returned over and over again to question members of the congregation.

But that first meeting, on a Wednesday night, was the "make it or break it" moment for Phil. It was the night that the committee — after extensive cross-examination — determined he was not a threat to God's flock. But that Glee was.

In the weeks and months to follow, as Glee's world began to crumble, Phil's status rose in the congregation as he received more honorable assignments. And my heart swelled with pride.

We had gone to Thomasville on a mission of peace. But we found ourselves in a skirmish we had not volunteered for — against our own kind. A clash we could not escape, without consequence to our character. A conflict that had presented us with three choices that we knew of: run; die inside, or charge the hill.

But that's not the only thing we discovered in Thomasville. We began to wake up to our assets — and I don't mean money or belongings. I mean people, unconventional as they were. Others who had likewise been captivated by Glee's invitation, in cursive handwriting, to move to a place where *"the need is indeed great!"*

Without them, despite displays of daring on our part, it's doubtful we would have carried on.

"Come onnn, come onnn, *you can do it!"* said the Push Feeder from California offering me, then Phil, another fat sandwich from a picnic basket spread open on his car hood. It was a tasty distraction on a hot day, enveloped as we were by a swarm of mosquitoes being chased by dragonflies.

His hospitable nature was infectious, his stories of trips abroad entertaining; and we lived vicariously through them.

"Come onnn, come onnn *... have another milkshake!"* the Push Feeder had said that very same morning, before we slipped into his station wagon, with his only daughter, prepared to knock on doors. The milkshakes were a happy surprise, the result of his early trip to a local grocery where a freezer had just malfunctioned on aisle five and cartons of ice cream were being sold at a "steal." And the Push Feeder — a divorced retired electrician who played classical piano, fairly well, with his sausage-size fingers — simply *could not* pass up a good deal.

His daughter was our age — with talents that outshined ours, as janitors, in every way. For instance, she made her own clothes, cooked gourmet meals and spoke more than one language. She was single and free to travel the world with her father, having sold the family home in Beverly Hills to do God's work. In fact, the pair had sold virtually everything they owned to prepare for their quest, but for a few specific luxuries. Such as a dining table that expanded to seat 10. Silver candlestick holders, for special occasions. And assorted kitchen items the likes of which I had never before seen.

They had settled into a modest rental home in Thomasville — a third bedroom filled with cases of soda pop for guests only, bought on sale, and the freezer filled with meat, "properly aged" (*which, meant, as bargains go, meat on the verge of turning green)*. And, come winter, they heated only the bathroom, to conserve electricity.

But they had no qualms about spending money on their travels. Of Polish ancestry, they embarked come summer on clandestine trips to countries where the preaching work was banned. Where they met other worshipers in hidden forests, in secret gatherings, to disperse Bibles and songbooks, or to regurgitate lectures they had memorized after attending summer conventions in the United States.

Caring for their spiritual comrades was of utmost importance to the Push Feeder and his daughter. That's why they hosted the occasional party and invited the most self-sacrificing guests. It was when they unfolded their dining table that seated 10 and adorned it with a lace tablecloth, fresh flowers and candles. The evenings also featured servings of fine wine; multi-course meals topped off with exotic desserts scorched with a torch; and finished off with a reel-to-reel Disney film — a perk from his former Hollywood connections.

It was an odd experience to eat a meal fit for a king, in a house with no furniture, in a town with no class. But it was a welcome reprieve from our otherwise wretched existence.

It taught us that here — in the middle of nowhere — we could still make a few useful connections. They would not get us to the moon. But they inched us along in our purpose, nonetheless.

For different reasons entirely, I treasured the black nurse from Minneapolis. She too had moved to Thomasville to "pioneer," and her presence in my life had a calming effect on me. Her appearance — accented by gold-rimmed glasses and a turban — showed me the image of dignity. And she spoke with grammatical precision.

"You must pay attention to the body's warning signals," the nurse fussed over me, worried about my lack of stamina.

Despite her concerns, I could not bring myself to tell her about an alarming experience I'd had at the home of a Bible student. While Phil read from his study book, I felt the strangest sensation come over me — like something had shifted inside me — and I did not "know" myself. My surroundings felt surreal, and my thoughts were unrecognizable. I had lost control. It lasted only a moment, but it frightened me deeply.

In that state, I was grateful for the distraction of another pioneer who arrived from Texas — a plain single woman with wide hips and a missing eyetooth who — for a lot of reasons — had lower self-esteem than I did. I laughed hysterically the day she flushed the toilet in our travel trailer and broke off the valve, the geyser of water drenching her and flooding our bathroom. I felt sorry for her the day she lost her job at the local TG&Y, when she mispriced a shelf full of small appliances, causing unexpected mayhem for the management.

"If I die, you can marry her," I told Phil — who choked. I was certain that the girl with the missing tooth would never upstage me. *(Eventually, she married a man missing all his front teeth.)*

Some of us had moved to Thomasville to find ourselves; others, to give ourselves away. Some were hiding; some dying; others, poised to fly away.

Glee's wife was among those pilgrims ...

We visited her in the hospital just before her death, and that's when we saw the frail side of Glee. *"Now you be careful, and you behave, you hear?"* She told him, as a parent might comfort a child, as if some part of the big man was still a child. And it was the reason for the "he-he-he" that escaped him as he carried his wife's casket during her funeral, with his pants unzipped.

After losing his wife, Glee lost other things, too: his eldership; his Special Pioneer card — even his church, after the traveling overseer, on one of his trips through, engineered a purchase agreement with Glee transferring ownership to the congregation.

But the congregation on Spinks Drive began to thrive. And other worshipers from surrounding areas came to visit, to see it for themselves.

Eventually, the outside walls of the cinderblock building on Spinks Drive were painted a warm brown, and the inside was covered in blond paneling. The rough-hewn floors were covered in carpet, and a lovely chandelier was hung on the finished stage. A cottage-style entry was added, along with fine-looking "his" and "her" bathrooms. An upscale heating system replaced the wood-burning stove, and a bona-fide literature room replaced the bra and girdle rack.

Most important, the building received a new roof and structural braces. And it didn't come too soon. During the memorial of Christ's death that spring, before renovations began, we had a standing-room-only crowd. That was when we heard the strangest groaning sounds coming from the roof and basement. When elders checked on the noise, assuming it was a prankster, nobody was there. The next morning a carpenter from Demopolis inspected the building and discovered it was ready to collapse. The weight of the crowd had strained its limits.

The lyrics of Clarence Carter's song *"Patches"* — about the dying last words of an Alabama man — painted a hauntingly accurate picture of the world we had come to know: *"Life kicked him to the ground. When he tried to get up, life would kick him back down ..."*

But we had witnessed for ourselves a remarkable transformation under the most unlikely of circumstances at the church on Spinks Drive. Had we fled the scene too soon, before the little congregation had recovered its spirit, our lessons there would have been unfinished and imprecise. We would come to depend on those lessons during perilous times ahead.

We had by then exhausted our practical Dodge Dart and found a dandy deal on a used Plymouth Fury with cloth seats and air-conditioning. We had by then sold *(for a handsome profit)* our tiny travel trailer — "tiny" being the obvious reason — and we had lived for one year in a two-bedroom Jim Walters Home next to a pond. We furnished it for a song, thanks to the generosity of a furniture store owner who had once hired us to clean his building.

Near the end of our stay, we bought a charming, lightly used 35-foot trailer — white with red shutters — for our next adventure. No more ants in the walls for us; no cockroaches in our drawers, or dishwater in the heating vents. We'd be in control of our own well-being at our next location, we had decided.

We may have carted off our childhood memories to the dump soon after we arrived in Thomasville, but we had managed to make plenty of new ones in the three years we lived there — some too memorable to forget, others too potent to share, apparently.

"You need to destroy those letters and move on," a new white elder told Phil not long before we left. In this case, the elder was speaking of the three letters exchanged between Phil, Glee and Headquarters — words on paper, as unsettling as the scene of a car crash. A transplant from Seattle, this

elder was unnerved by the drama that had unfolded before his arrival. He was a secure, non-confrontational man who had a stable job, a pretty wife and two darling daughters that wore flower-print dresses with crocheted collars and ribbons in their hair. The family had moved to a good neighborhood in Thomasville, giving our congregation — which had quadrupled in size — a new air of respectability.

So Phil burned his prized letters — the proof of his first "test by fire" — to accommodate that elder's romanticized vision of his world ... and to re-establish Phil's duty to his hierarchy. It was a desperate attempt to conform: As if his experience with Glee had been a fluke — an anomaly — and not, as he feared, a pattern.

— — —

Our three years in Thomasville were the closest we came to brushing up against a moment in American history now known as the civil rights movement.

Had Phil and I lived in Alabama 10 years earlier in 1964, when Martin Luther King marched through the streets of Selma, 62 miles from Thomasville, our time spent there would have overlapped events that sparked national news, like the "Freedom Summer." But we were 9 years old in 1964. And in 1967, when Sheriff's Deputy Cecil Price (and six others) were tried by jury and charged with the murders of three civil rights workers in Mississippi — one of whom hailed from Meridian, 90 miles north of Thomasville — we were only 12.

We arrived late — when there was no national media attention; under the leadership of a cautious religion, that preferred to stay 'off the radar.'

We were nothing but the maintenance crew, for a shift in public consciousness that was already underway.

We had moved to an unknown town; filled with humble, unassuming folks who were scarred by racial inequities, for sure — like the 70-year-old black man, his eyes focused on the ground, who said, *'yes sir, boss man!'* whenever Phil brought him Bible pamphlets. But, like slaves after the Civil War, there was no easy way for folks in Alabama to grow, even if they were now "equal." Integration was mandated. And yet, the whites in the South still found ways to get around it. They closed public swimming pools so blacks could not swim with their children. And they opened private schools.

Southern blacks had not found their voice, yet. In the meantime, they were free to vote for the white person of their choice. When it comes to civil rights, the 1970s aren't talked about much from a historic perspective. And we did our mission work in the South, right then.

Phil and I could only hope that our experiences would somehow, someday, matter.

"Brother Lawson ... we feel that you have seen and learned things that men much older than you have not experienced," The three men on the special committee told Phil one day toward the end of Glee's hearings. *"It would appear that God is training you for something."*

However, that compliment was followed by this forewarning:

"But you have an independent spirit and strong will," the special committee said, reminding Phil that Glee had similar traits. *"Beware that it does not get in the way of your training ..."*

— — —

We left the fall of 1977. Despite our now vested interest in our surroundings. Even though we had learned the local dialect; and townsfolk trusted us. We were 22. We had been married four years. And we had come of age in Thomasville.

It was our cat that showed us the way out. The day she found the door of our work truck open and got stuck under the seat — between the cushion and inner springs — and nothing we tried pried her lose. She yowled and hissed and growled and banged about, like a Tom and Jerry cartoon. Until she broke free, on her own, after one hell of struggle ... because nobody else could do it for her.

As our schoolmates were settling into trades or completing their college degrees to ensure better futures for themselves, we were traveling in the opposite direction.

Ours was not a journey to wealth, in those days. It was about what we could become, without it. And the thought of jeopardizing that God-inspired path was more than we could bear.

In fact, we were chomping at the bit for something more — a change of scenery — and we wrote Headquarters volunteering for greater service. We even offered to move to New York and help with construction of new buildings there, or clean toilets if we had too. But, our timing was off — once again, as evidenced in the following correspondence we received:

Dear Brother and Sister Lawson,

Your letter has been received wherein you inquire as to the temporary construction work at Watchtower Farm. The Society has for the past few years been carrying on quite an extensive construction program in the United States. However, we are now phasing out this program as we have completed all our present planned construction and hence, we are not, at this time, calling in any additional help. The society appreciates your interest in offering your services and we will keep your letter on file with others who have likewise made known their availability ...

We would suggest that you consider working the congregation in Florence, Alabama, or Oxford, Mississippi. Florence recently advised us that they have sixty-eight territories which were not worked in the past year and Oxford reports that they have forty-eight such territories. We believe your assistance would be very useful in either of these congregations. To inquire about local circumstances, you may write the presiding overseers at ...

We pray Jehovah's rich blessing as you reach out for the fullest possible share in his service. We send our warm Christian love, WB&T

As luck would have it (and we didn't believe in luck) the elder in Florence lost our letter of inquiry and by the time he found it and apologized, we were on our way to Oxford — an historic Ivy League college town and home of the late Nobel prize-winning author, William Faulkner.

(If you're wondering if I'll ever get to the dang point of this book, I am begging you to stay with me. You're halfway there! Did I say halfway? Partway ...)

— — —

Meanwhile, 1,323 miles away — during the very three years we lived in Thomasville — a professor at the Massachusetts Institute of Technology, named Edward Lorenz, was gaining notoriety for pioneering something called Chaos Theory, after winning a prestigious award for his studies, the year we were married.

Chaos Theory, examines the behavior of "dynamic systems" — systems that are highly "sensitive" to initial conditions — sensitivity described by Lorenz as the "butterfly effect." In fact, he once posed this very question to the American Association for the Advancement of Science, when speaking on the topic of Predictability: *"Does the flap of a butterfly's wings in Brazil set off a tornado in Texas?"*

chapter 7: Newsflash

It's Sunday April 19, 2009. About four months has passed since I began writing this book. I peer out my cabin window at three panels of color: a thick band of blue, a thin band of green and a deep layer of white — the remains of a winter storm that dropped 36 inches along Colorado's Front Range snuffing out power for two days to 15,000 homes and businesses, including mine.

The power is back on, but the plowman is still missing and my car is buried under a mountain of snow. I am reminded of how fragile our comfortable existence is. And when Phil turns on his computer this morning and scans today's news online, I am reminded of how fragile my fellow Americans are at this time in history. A Maryland man has just killed his wife and three small children before killing himself. There were indications of "financial problems" and "mental health problems," one reporter stated.

This on the heels of gloomy news two weeks ago regarding other people who were losing control: "Forty-seven people dead in the past month in American mass shootings and their aftermaths ..." wrote an associated press reporter who also stated in the same article that "663,000 Americans lost their jobs in March."

I am frustrated for not finishing this manuscript sooner. Not because I have answers, because I have a key to a door that leads to another place ...

chapter 8: Crash

"Dear Pam, I love you very very much. You is a good person you is my friend I like you I love you I hope you feel better."

A touching note from a six-year-old; from a chocolate-colored child I was fond of in our new congregation in Mississippi. But I doubted her hope would stick to me. I was sick — so very, very sick.

So sick that I checked into a hospital the summer of 1978 and watched eight doctors poke and prod me over a list of more than 20 physical complaints — from unbearable fatigue to numbed limbs; from chest pains and jumbled speech to extraordinary mood swings; from light sensitivity and joint pains, to horrific menstruations where my cheeks turned white and my lips blue as I vomited, repeatedly.

The fact that my mother had died of Multiple Sclerosis was of keen interest to the doctors. And they pondered the news that my grandfather had died young of pernicious anemia, and so did all his brothers.

But standard medical tests ruled out more widely known crippling disorders like MS or Lupus or Rheumatoid Arthritis, leaving the doctors scratching their heads.

"Mrs. Lawson, are you experiencing severe stress in your life?" they asked me toward the end of my week-long hospital stay. But I had no frame of reference for that question. Did I have stress? You betcha! But I was doing God's work. Stress came with the territory. So did persecution ... and naysayers. That's what I had been taught since childhood. It was for the greater good.

When that angle didn't work, the doctors asked me if I was experiencing stress in my marriage. But I had no frame of reference for that question, either. How could I explain our eccentric partnership without being criticized for it? Our lives overlapped in every way. We worked together.

We preached together. We lived in cramped quarters together. It was a 24/7 relationship: business and personal *and* stressful. But it was also comforting, fulfilling *and* special.

Did the doctors think I was imagining my pain? Or creating it? I wondered, paranoid by their interrogation.

I didn't know it then, but my beliefs had trumped my well-being in every way. They had dictated my lifestyle. I was protected by them, but also confined by them. And the doctors were confined by their standards. Something about my life didn't jive to them. And that clouded their vision. It gave them permission to stop digging further for answers regarding my condition. In the end, they could do little for me.

In a final attempt to *do something* one doctor recommended a "steroid" prescription to ease my discomfort. But my admitting physician did not approve the advice, due to its side effects. I needed solutions, he decided, not more complications.

I returned home dazed and confused. Months went by and my symptoms worsened. Often, after a deep sleep I felt paralyzed. Upon waking, I would reach consciousness but could not open my eyes; could not turn my head or move my limbs as if my neurological network was malfunctioning.

Stretched out on the living room floor of our trailer one afternoon I slipped into a deep sleep while Phil and a friend, seated nearby, studied together for an upcoming Bible meeting. The friend was a stout sarcastic girl, three years younger than me who shared Phil's passion for research and analysis, which bored me.

That's when I heard a deafening buzz. But I was paralyzed and could not open my eyes to see the bumble bee that had zipped through the doorway riding a breeze and was circling my head, furiously. *It's going to sting me* is all I could think, unable to shoo it away; unable to roll over or dodge it. I was a mummy fastened in place by an invisible weight. All I could do was beg for somebody to save me.

It started as a tiny voice in my head: *"Help! Help me! It's a bee! It's a bee!"* And I repeated the words until they traveled from my brain to my throat, turned to sound and escaped my lips.

As my eyelids began to flutter I could make out the giant faces of Phil and the Stout Sarcastic Girl. Both had dropped to their knees and were hovered over me.

"What's she saying?" One face asked the other face.

"Something about a bee ..."

"What about a bee?"

"There must have been a bee ..."

"Why's she talking so low?"

"I don't know."

"What's the matter with her?"

"I don't know ..."

Suddenly, a hideous laugh escaped me — a hysterical weeping madness that stung the two giant faces.

— — —

We washed out of Alabama on a rainy August morning in 1977, exchanging nervous chatter along the 250-mile route to Mississippi on our CB radios — me, in the Plymouth Fury, Phil, the work truck, pulling our cute trailer home with the red shutters behind him.

The Magnolia State, as it was labeled for its sprawling trees dressed with giant white blooms, was a place of contradictions. It had the largest Bible-binding plant in the nation and more churches per capita than any other state. But it was also the birthplace of the pelvis-swinging Elvis Presley, a teen idol for rebels.

And there were other oddities. Twenty two years before the Civil War, it was a ship captain from Mississippi who took a bold step and freed his slaves, arranging their passage to the West Coast of Africa. Even so, Mississippians fought to maintain slavery in the Civil War suffering the largest percentage of casualties for a single state with 59,000 dead and wounded.

It was also a paradox that the first state-supported college for women in America, charted in 1884, hailed from Mississippi. But a mere 15 years before our arrival, back in 1962, segregationists fought federal authorities amidst bullets and tear gas (killing two people) to overturn the court ordered admission of a 29-year-old black man to the University of Mississippi in Oxford.

But pain gives birth to pure ideas when folks are hard-pressed to overcome their obstacles. That's what we would come to know when we plunged ourselves into this beautiful clammy state brimming with catfish and watermelon; swarming with ticks, mosquitoes and snakes and clothed in fields of cotton.

No sooner had we arrived — having parked our trailer on property owned by a church elder — a tar and asphalt man by trade — when a stranger drove up with terrible news. The church elder had been in a car accident the stranger shouted and could we *'please tell his wife and kids?!'*

Overcome with awkwardness, we scurried down an unpaved driveway to inform a plump pink-faced woman, whom we'd never before met, that her husband had been whisked to the hospital. Quickly, she squeezed herself out the door leaving us in charge of her pink-faced brood.

Thus began our tumultuous life in William Faulkner's home town — a novelist who, it has been said, often "wrote of fiercely intelligent people dwelling behind the facades of good old boys and simpletons." It was a seven-year stay that shattered our lifelong plans and forced us to reinvent ourselves.

That first 12 months passed by in a rugged rush, busy as we were tutoring a bounty of Bible students who were eager to trade their distasteful habits for a bond with God. During that time, Phil gave Sunday discourses nearly every weekend in Oxford, or its surroundings, from Batesville to Columbus.

Had our life been perfect I might not have collapsed.

But we had begun to experience more of the same adrenaline-draining incidents that were familiar to us from our life in Thomasville — oddly unavoidable catastrophes bundled up with the strains of everyday life.

One of them occurring, as it turned out, during a return visit to Thomasville for an official dedication ceremony for the restored church on Spinks Drive — a trip we didn't dare miss despite that season's moody weather.

We were partway there when torrential rains whipped up a flashflood event in the very vicinity we were traveling — a flash flood that turned an entire valley on either side of the road into a lake, a slab of gliding water that engulfed the road itself quite suddenly, sweeping away the car in front of us. Horrified, Phil kept his eyes fixed ahead managing to steer the car in the general direction of where the road once was, making his way finally to dryer ground. Even when we were safe, I couldn't shake the terror that incident had awakened within me. The fright from another storm we had experienced when we still lived in Thomasville. The hurricane style rains we had driven through on an otherwise ordinary day.

We were traveling in two separate cars between Thomasville and Sweetwater. Phil was in the Dodge Dart pulling his equipment trailer and I, the old Chevy pickup on loan from Phil's parents. He was ahead of me by a few cars when without warning howling black rain swooped down and swallowed me. Catching my breath I made out the faint red glow of a taillight in front of me. I locked onto it like a beacon aware that if it veered too far to the left it could be the death of both of us. That section of road had a steep embankment covered in kudzu vines and I would have followed that taillight like a puppy dog into the abyss. By the time I rendezvoused with Phil in the town ahead, my skin was soaked and my clothes drenched. The fierce winds of the storm had forced rain past the rubber seal of the truck's front windshield soaking the inside of the cab.

We could have assumed that Thomasville was cursed, but as I wrote moments ago, oddly unavoidable catastrophes continued to occur in Mississippi.

My grandmother dies — the one that came to stay, during my mother's last days. And during our emotional drive to Wisconsin for the funeral we are caught in a perilous ice storm — a storm that causes two cars to crash on the road in front of us. As we come upon the wreckage we see a woman's bloodied body protruding from the back windshield of her car. There is a dazed boy standing next to her. We stop and give him a blanket.

This experience followed by the death of Phil's grandmother a few weeks later, requiring another unplanned trip out of state, this time to Texas.

These and other stressful events began to take their toll on our bodies. For months Phil battled a difficult case of strep throat. Meanwhile, my body grew weaker and weaker.

And, as previously mentioned, I landed in the hospital in Dallas the summer of 1978 but found no answers to my declining physical condition despite my weeklong stay.

After that, I willed myself onward like a wounded animal in search of a safe place to die.

But that winter, in the midst of my anguish a welcomed turn of events lifted my spirits temporarily when Phil and I were invited to attend a new education program for pioneers instituted by Headquarters.

"Pioneer School" was being introduced around the country and required that participants travel to centralized locations for two weeks to receive customized training and we were assigned to Memphis.

Phil and I were "golden" after attending pioneer school. Only seasoned pioneers were enlisted in the early days of the program, and course instructors had the authority to fast track the applications of attendees who requested admittance to foreign missionary school.

And this was exciting news. We had attended every pitch about missionary school at every summer convention since we were teenagers. Had Phil and I applied right then, we would have been accepted.

But timing was never our strong suit. We could not conscientiously apply to be missionaries when we knew something was terribly wrong with my health. So ... that coveted opportunity slipped away from us.

Afterwards, my inadequacies as a human being overwhelmed me. I felt I was nothing but a burden to Phil. MY health was holding HIM back from exciting opportunities.

— — —

"Do you love me? I'm mean, ***really and truly****?"* I probed Phil one afternoon, seated beside him in our work truck on our way to clean a vacant rental property owned by a fussy client.

My episodes of paranoia were escalating.

"I love your beautiful breasts," Phil teased me.

"But do you love ME?" I pressed him, just for clarification.

"Yesss ... I love YOU," he sighed, the lightness of the moment passing.

"Exactly, ***why*** *do you love me?"* I grilled him some more. *"I mean, what do you love about me — specifically?"* Then, feeling especially pitiful: *"What IS there to love?"*

Before Phil could formulate an answer to the trick questions I had posed I gasped suddenly, doubled over, grabbed at the darkness beneath my seat then screamed: "*WAIT!*"

It was just like that: First, a gasp; then, me doubled over, like a whiplash in reverse, followed by the scream — as if the world had just come to end with me in it.

Phil yanked his foot off the gas pedal in a panic, stomped his foot on the brake, looked around for signs of danger, then hollered out: *"WHAT THE HECK?!"*

I barely found the nerve to say, after a pregnant pause, in a detached voice, the following:

"I thought I left my purse at home. But I found it, whew."

At which point Phil was admittedly confused, then angered:

"Wait a minute ... that's it? You nearly caused me to wreck, AND THAT'S IT?!'"

"Sorrrrrryyyyy ..." I said, like a teenage girl who had just spilled her nail polish. Then I attempted to explain myself: *"I'm shot, do you hear me? My nerves are dead!"* At which point I abruptly changed the subject and asked for the time.

"4:25," Phil deadpanned.

"Oh no!" I gasped, again. *"We're going to be late!!"*

"You worry too much," Phil brushed off my concern.

"But you told the lady you'd meet her at FOUR THIRTY! And the house is at least 10 miles away!"

"We'll be fine ..."

"Why are we always late?!"

*"We're not **always** late. We're late **sometimes — like today,** because **you** were dragging behind, **as usual. Remember?"***

*"As if **you** don't drag! Blame me. You should be glad **I help you at all!"***

"It was your idea to come. I didn't ask you!"

*"Just how would you have finished **all that work** by yourself?"*

*"I'd have gladly managed — **believe me."*** Phil snapped.

"Most women would refuse to help their husband's clean dirty, stinking carpets and mop ugly, filthy floors," I began to cry. *"...with gum and spit and **crap** all over them."*

"Quit saying CRAP!"

"It's not a cuss word — so, what's the big deal!!"

"You're making me crazy." Phil sighed.

*"Why is it **me** that always makes **you** crazy?"* I pressed him to absurdity. *"As smart as you are, you should have waited to find the perfect wife!"*

"That's enough!"

"I'm thirsty." And just like that I had changed the subject, again.

"You want me to stop now?!"

"Yeah! Why not?"

*"I thought you were in such a **BIG hurry**?"*

*"But **YOU** said it **didn't matter** if we were late."*

About then Phil pulled into the parking lot of a convenience store and ordered me out. And I refused to go because my blouse was ragged and my hair was uncombed. And he said, *"These people will never see us again!"* and I said: *"How can you be **absolutely** sure?"*

By the time Phil had returned with two icy Dr. Pepper's, I had rewound the tape in my brain.

*"Could you **please** tell me one good reason why you love me?"*

"Not AGAIN!" Phil shouted. *"Something's WRONG with you."*

"You DON'T know ME!" I deflected — a sense of defiance in my voice like King David's Mother had once been defiant to me.

I was a lost cause. But I wasn't. I wanted somebody to save me. But I didn't.

"I'm scared," I whimpered folding my arms tight to my chest, the fight finally drained out of me.

"I know."

"I'm in a dark tunnel and there's no light at the end," I whispered.

"I know ..." Phil repeated the tone of his voice now gentle. *"We've got to get help. I'm calling that doctor I heard about in Florida."*

Phil was speaking of a tip he'd received from a traveling overseer about an unconventional doctor who had helped his wife when she fell ill.

"But we can't afford it," I sobbed, knowing full well we hadn't paid off the debt from my hospital stay in Dallas, now five months behind us.

"It doesn't matter." Phil spoke softly now firmly rooted in his plan to save me.

— — —

After Phil had made the call to the doctor in Florida a great urgency engulfed us.

"How old is she?" the doctor had asked, after hearing a description of my symptoms.

"23," had been Phil's answer.

"Get her down here right away," the doctor said next. *"I haven't lost a young person, yet."*

"How long will she need to stay?" Phil tested to comprehend the price of that phone call.

"At least two weeks," was the doctor's answer. At which point he offered the name of the historic Ormond Beach Hotel located near his clinic that offered cheap, clean rooms.

"If you can't afford that, you can stay in the manger," the doctor added, having detected a prolonged silence on Phil's end.

"The manger?" Phil repeated.

"The floor of my office," the doctor replied. *"It's a place to 'lay your head' — you know, like Jesus. We get a lot of your kind down here."*

— — —

Had the doctors in Dallas identified the mysteries of my health I would have never ended up in Florida in the first place. In the office of an alternative healer who worried often, and for good reason, that the Florida Medical Association was about to shut him down due to his unconventional methods.

"Dick" was the doctor's name. A witty, balding man — the father of five grown children — who was unafraid to cite the findings of professed "medical heretics." One of which was Robert Mendelsohn, a long-time physician who had determined that Modern Medicine's treatments for disease were seldom effective and were often more dangerous than the diseases they were designed to treat. Mendelsohn had also concluded that the testing approaches of medical laboratories were scandalously inaccurate; that roughly ninety percent of surgeries were a waste of time, money and lives, and that hospitals were a dangerous oasis for sick people.

Dick Doc himself had a cross-pollinated list of credentials that made him appear queer to his more conventional colleagues, who preferred to specialize in a given field.

In short, he was a licensed chiropractor. But he was also a nutritionist and biochemist. And his qualifications, as he explained them, had included eight years as a surgical and obstetrical assistant in a general hospital in Missouri. And, he was once director of research at a biochemical research corporation, where he wrote patents and processed biochemical remedies.

On top of that, he advocated the work of a deceased dentist, Dr. Royal Lee, who had pioneered the value of *"whole, natural unadulterated foods with their vitamins and minerals intact"* — which meant Dick Doc himself required that his patients consume only the most natural foods and supplements ... before stores like Whole Foods Market populated the countryside.

By the time we had crossed paths with Dick Doc, he was learning to tap whatever means necessary to heal people —whether his techniques were popular or unpopular.

It was our good fortune that Dick Doc was a member of our faith and understood what motivated us. That connection allowed us to trust him more than usual — even though, leaders at Watchtower Headquarters had reservations about the doctor's eccentric practices.

"I have reviewed your list of symptoms and they are rather extensive," Dick Doc said on a January day in 1979, not long after our arrival in the Sunshine State.

He paused to look at me, then Phil, who shifted nervously in the next chair.

We had $50 to our name after driving 750 miles from Mississippi to Florida. We had no idea how we would last two weeks — the amount of time the doctor had requested to run the necessary lab work and begin treatments and observe my illness firsthand.

But we had tested our limits in Thomasville the day Phil discovered the hole the size of a quarter in the back left tire of the Dodge Dart. Against all logic we drove nine more hours on that dangerous tire — along dirt roads filled with sharp pebbles arriving home safely before the tire went flat. In the process we learned to lose fear and embrace purpose. We would have to tap that same resolve once again during our stay in Florida, which seemed impossible to pay for.

Just then, Dick Doc got to the point: *"You are suffering from acute polyneuritis,"* after which, he further explained my illness, also known as Guillain-Barré Syndrome that often paralyzes its victims.

(I did not know at the time, that Guillain-Barré Syndrome 'is an uncommon disorder in which your body's immune system attacks your nerves. Weakness and numbness in your extremities are usually the first symptoms. These sensations can quickly spread, eventually paralyzing your whole body. The exact cause is unknown, but it is often preceded by an infectious illness such as a respiratory infection or the stomach flu. In its most severe form, Guillain-Barre syndrome is a medical emergency requiring hospitalization' ... Source and more info: Mayo Clinic)

A great relief washed over me. My health was a mess for sure. But there was a plausible explanation for my pain. And, I would later learn, a plausible explanation for my madness.

In that first week of our stay many other details surfaced about my health, too. I had a hormonal imbalance; I was suffering from emotional and physical exhaustion and from malnutrition — from a poorly crafted diet that was affecting my wellbeing in countless ways.

Dick Doc also identified ways to address the cysts on my ovaries, without surgery, that had been discovered by a previous physician.

"Your body has been deprived of the essential elements to function properly," Dick Doc told me. Then he took the time, despite his busy schedule, to enlighten both Phil and I on the impacts of that statement.

"Anxiety, rage, fatigue, depression, vague fears, acute agitation, tremors, and hallucinations, even feelings of grandeur, are often strong symptoms of nutritional deficiency," he said, adding: *"Though some people may be genuinely schizophrenic,* ***a large majority*** *of the cases of severe mood swings are treatable by lifestyle education and proper nutrition."*

A spark of hope stirred inside me — a flash of possibility beyond death or a limited and restricted life.

"You are obviously under a lot of stress, and stress is a universal problem today, although stress in and of itself is not bad ..." Dick Doc said thumping a book on his desk as if it was jarring a memory. *"A person with normal adrenal function, adequate B complex, optimal mineral and trace element availability; proper protein balance, and reasonably good overall nutrition, can cope with stress. And, if one can cope with stress, stress in itself does not have a harmful effect upon a person's physical or emotional well-being. This then tells you why a person with a prolonged B*

complex deficiency — ***if under continued stress*** *— in many instances, suffers adrenal exhaustion or the "nervous breakdown.""*

As I continued listening I began to tremble uncontrollably, overwhelmed by what I was hearing.

"With adequate glucose for muscle and brain energy, one can fight or survive," Dick Doc continued. *"Without that emergency energy, the person will flee or cry or hide. Emotionally, they usually hide or separate from reality."*

When he had finished, I understood mankind's plight in a whole new light.

Dick Doc's next step was to prescribe an extensive selection of vitamins, herbs and minerals that I would take in "low dosages" at specified times each day to begin rebuilding my body and mind.

The purpose of nutritional supplementation was to help restore biological and physiological harmony, Dick Doc explained. If a person has biological and physiological harmony, that person has health.

The reasons why a person loses that equilibrium in the first place were mind-boggling unto themselves ... Something about our food being grown in depleted soil, compounded by the infiltration of pesticides and other pollutants. Not to mention the food processing and storage practices instituted at the beginning of the 20th century that drained vitality from fresh foods. Followed by the way we humans tend to overcook our food which decreases its value even more. All of which meant that ... much of our food is stripped of its nutrients before it reaches our mouths.

It wasn't hard to comprehend, as Dick Doc furthered explained it to us, why heart disease, cancer, diabetes and depression were a 20th Century phenomenon. Diseases that now fueled billions of dollars annually in research for cures and drug-related treatments, the results of which created drug-related deaths.

What little we could do to protect ourselves, according to Dick Doc, was choose and prepare our foods carefully.

He then handed over a piece of paper that read: *"GENERAL DIETARY SUGGESTIONS,"* which included this specific list:

Fresh raw fruits and vegetables, cooked vegetables, lean meat, eggs, fish and cheese, honey or pure maple syrup for sweetening (raw or Tupelo honey) real cottage cheese, real butter, raw milk, cow or goat if available, brown rice, steel-cut oatmeal. FROM THE HEALTH FOOD STORE: Soy-o pancake mix, sea-salt (non-iodized); Hain cooking oils, (safflower, sunflower or soy); good peanut butter (non-hydrogenated); stone-ground whole wheat bread (un-enriched) and raw nuts."

Reading such a list today might seem less daunting to highly-informed, health-conscience individuals. But 31 years ago — when alternative practitioners were being sued and put out of business and "wellness" magazines were in short supply on newsstands — Phil and I lived on canned foods. We ate from boxed foods designed for instant preparation. And we consumed soft drinks and snack cakes on the go.

Even as a child, the meals prepared by my stepmother reflected the modest weekly food allowance she received based on my father's humble salary. A budget that forced her to park her food cart in the aisles of grocery stores and tabulate her purchases, to the exact penny, before she reached the checkout cashier. Our family dined frequently on boiled pinto beans and cornbread. But our diet did not include a lavish daily selection of fresh fruits and vegetables.

In short order, it was beginning to dawn on me that my recovery would require a complete overhaul of my life. And the thought of it, on top of my exhausted physical state, seemed at first impossible.

More disturbing, however, was the realization that none of the well-dressed doctors who had visited my hospital bedside in Dallas, checking off forms with their fancy pens, had been willing or able to draw me the map out of hell to health.

Yet this quirky healer with a lobby-full of ill and desperate souls was willing to do just that — demystifying the doctor/patient experience by converting it to a two-fold collaboration.

Besides Dick Doc's list of "general dietary suggestions," he also included written guidelines for foods to "avoid." And Phil read this information with great interest:

"Margarine & hydrogenated shortenings (hydrogenated and partially hardened mean the same thing, essentially); all refined carbohydrates such as candy, cake, pie, ice cream, cookies, soda, etc.; high potency vitamins which are mostly fractions, pasteurized milk (use sparingly if at all); most cracker & potato chip products."

Phil stopped and re-read the list again pausing on one phrase that stood out to him. An expression that prompted him to ask a question that would, in the end, alter our future in its entirety.

"What do you mean by 'high potency vitamins that are mostly fractions?'" was Phil's simple inquiry. But he asked it of a man who believed, **'if you were *big enough* to ask a question; you were *big enough* to live with the answer.'**

At that point, Dick Doc grabbed a yellow legal pad and a fine point magic marker and proceeded to draw a circle on it. Then he drew lines that divided the circle into several parts of unequal widths. Then, he began to identify those parts that comprised a whole vitamin.

'This is a vitamin C,' he told us, before scribbling in each of its factors by their initials, such as, "BF" (for bioflavonoid); "AA" (for ascorbic acid) and "TYRO" (for Tyrosinase), along with other factors with the initials of "J", "K", "P" and so on.

Then he said these mind-altering words: *'A vitamin comprises interrelated and interdependent parts. All of these parts make up one complete vitamin.'*

Phil was stunned. And so was I.

Of course there were circumstances, as we understood it, when "components" of a vitamin in isolation were useful. Just one example being Alpha Tocopherol, a component of vitamin E, that works wonders when applied topically for burns.

But that wasn't the heart of the conversation, this was: Whole food vitamins are alive. They consist of nutrients, enzymes, coenzymes, antioxidants, and trace mineral activators **that must work together for synergistic function.**

On the other hand synthetic vitamins, what were described to us as, 'man-made fragments, in chemically pure form, and manufactured in high concentrations,' could have a different affect on the body.

Dick Doc's assessment of those went something like this: 'Vitamins that contain no live enzymes can deplete the body's own mineral reserves. That can happen when a synthetic vitamin, once ingested by a person, draws upon stored elements in their body in order to function as a whole unit, which in the end depletes their body more.'

Even worse, we learned, few vitamin companies actually produced "whole" vitamins. Many instead are mass-produced products, refined without enzymes to last longer on store shelves. That's why Dick Doc selected the vitamins and herbs he prescribed carefully, even creating some product formulas himself.

Wait! Vitamins are not necessarily our friend? They can be the enemy? Yet we don't get enough nutrients in the food we eat? Causing food manufacturers to "fortify" our food with synthetic vitamins?

How frightening and confusing it was to me.

Dick Doc's rants seemed too sensational to swallow. What had we gotten ourselves in to, we wondered?

But it didn't take long to recognize we were there to learn from this rare man.

Something about the vitamin illustration had struck a chord with us. It's value more than a formula scribbled onto a piece of paper. **It was a metaphor for life.**

That thought may have never occurred to us under any other circumstances. But the decline of my health had forced us to, once again, face our limits. It had caused us to step outside our comfort zone for answers.

As we felt more at ease with this man and his unconventional methods we began to notice peculiar but refreshing quirks in his behavior. The thoroughness of his approach and the way he interacted with his patients. How he observed minute details about them — as if they were all clues to their wellbeing: the abnormally extended abdomen on a teenage girl, thick hips on a man or thinning hair at the temples, or, for instance, the man sitting in his lobby bundled head-to-toe in winter clothing when everyone else around him was dressed in shorts.

Dick Doc treated more than a person's complaints. He poured over their lab work like an archeologist on a dig, searching for the subtleties in data that defied the law of "averages." He looked for indicators of a person's *dis*-ease before their symptoms had even manifest. A practice Dick Doc called "pre-clinical" readings.

His approach was due in part to his obsessively observant personality. And in part to the circumstances in life that he'd been dealt.

Many who visited Dick Doc were in dire straights. They had traveled far to be there, even from other countries. Most were on their last nerve having tried conventional medicine to no avail. Drained of all their resources they arrived one-by-one on his doorstep with nothing left to lose.

Those conditions produced a kind of urgent-but-eclectic care. It inspired an oddball sense of camaraderie among his overworked staff, and also among his patients, who often assisted one another in the process of healing.

It was all quit bewildering. And yet, it was also invigorating. The encounter with Dick Doc had expanded our horizons.

That two-week stay in Florida proved to be a precious reprieve for Phil and I — a timeout from our challenging life in Mississippi. It allowed us to stop and reflect on our circumstances; to interrupt our daily habits and envision a different outcome (than death) for me.

It was the beginning of more changes to come, of monumental shifts in our behaviors and actions.

— — —

Dick Doc would have never labeled my condition if he'd had things his way. He would have never told me I had Guillain-Barré Syndrome. Labels were inconclusive, he believed. They prevented some people from pressing past their limits once they had been branded by them. But society-at-large seemed to crave labels, as did I.

I had to have some way to explain myself when we returned to Mississippi.

I felt the need to justify my recovery process. Defend my soon-to-be reclusive, unproductive lifestyle. It would be baffling to my fellow pioneers who had the tendency, though hardly deliberate, to put "selflessness" on a pedestal.

But these had been my orders from Dick Doc:

"Pamela needs to take time off and do ***absolutely nothing,****"* he had instructed Phil, with me seated beside him as if I lacked the willpower on my own to follow through.

*"****No*** *deadlines,* ***no*** *responsibilities, unless* ***you feel like*** *doing them,"* He said looking directly at me, and my body, that was curled up in a fetal position in his office chair.

"It's possible to regain your health but it's a process that takes time. It took time to get in this shape it will take time to heal."

Under Dick Doc's watch I would be taking the slow and deliberate path to health. No shortcuts for me. No prescription drugs to mask my pain or preserve me "as is."

We had learned about prescription drugs too, from Dick Doc. How certain ones, in large quantities, could set off a chain reaction of complications he having treated many people damaged by them. People, who had, as he described it, "reached the end of their drug rope." A journey of maxed out results — of taking one drug, that had side effects, that required another drug, which had side effects, to fix the original side effects ... press the repeat button here.

The slow path Dick Doc prescribed for me involved overcoming complex nutritional deficiencies. For some people that process took many months; for others, much longer, I would find out.

"We will re-work your supplement schedule every few months, for the best possible outcome," Dick Doc had said, concluding our first visit to Florida.

Back home in Mississippi I settled into a life of nonexistence. And Phil kept me company whenever possible — reading an entire set of encyclopedia's in his spare time.

Phil would dress me when I was unable. He'd coax me out of bed when I was unwilling to leave it, pulling me by the hand along sun baked dusty roads.

In the end, it took two years for me to heal and it required three more trips to Florida. But the outcome was unmistakable. My eyes were bright, my hair radiant, my speech clear, my stamina and mobility recovered.

One day during the midst of my resuscitation, I scrounged around the top of a closet in our trailer and pulled out a 35 mm camera. An old, Russian model Phil had acquired in a trade before our first trip to Florida, having swapped cleaning services for it. He had hidden it there when film and processing costs made it impossible to use it. But he had not regretted the trade — having been infatuated with cameras since the age of 11, the day he quite impulsively purchased a Kodak World's Fair Flash Camera with money he had earned to buy a watch.

Now, as I caressed the object, costs no longer mattered. Costs were relative Dick Doc had taught us. You paid one way or the other when you didn't take care of yourself.

Each and every time I picked up that camera, Phil watched my spirits soar. When I photographed the Pudgy Pink-faced Lady's brood plucking corn, when I photographed a barn leaning in the wind with tall grass.

My creativity had returned; creativity that had surfaced when I was a child. And nothing now would stop it, lest I surely die.

My love of art began when I was five, in the house where my mother died, the day I found a wooden paint box in the basement filled with tubes of oil paints left there by a former tenant. Throughout my school years I won ribbons and awards in competitions. But I had buried that gift as an adult believing it to be unnecessary.

That camera resurrected me. And as my strength gathered, as I began to wake up the parts of me that had been disabled, I remembered the depleted souls I had once known in Thomasville. Some of them "fractured" beings, which, like fractured vitamins, could not activate themselves, could not experience "synergistic function" without the necessary elements. And it occurred to us, to Phil and I that people should have the right to be whole too, just like the very best vitamins.

Little did we know it then but a door was opening for us, if ever so slightly, to another place. And it happened after this harrowing chain of events: I nearly died. Our lives came to a full stop. We sought help but conventional routes failed us. Someone unexpected came to the rescue. We were forced to ask tough questions. We were transported outside our comfort zone by the answers. All of which, caused us to shift our perspectives and engage in the process of change.

Whew! Here I am at the end of this chapter, and one last question remains. How did we manage to stay two weeks in Florida, in 1979, with no money to speak of?

Well, it went something like this ...

On the very first day of our arrival we were ushered into a room filled with chiropractic equipment. The room was separated by makeshift dividers. As we lay there, our spines tingling from the vibrating tables beneath us, a stranger struck up a conversation with us from the other side of a partition. He was an architect from Chicago. He had a heart condition and was experiencing severe and frequent anxiety attacks.

We never saw the man's face when he left the room. But we would come to know him well soon after. When it was our turn to leave Dick Doc slipped a piece of paper into Phil's hand. On it was the name of a hotel.

"The architect would like you to be his guest," Dick Doc said. *"With his condition, he's afraid to be alone."*

The architect paid for our own room in a charming beachfront hotel in exchange for our company during his moments of anxiety. He treated us to appetizing meals in quaint seaside restaurants in return for walking with him along sandy beaches so he wouldn't be alone if his heart failed him.

It was a collaboration born of necessity. That turned to friendship. That was filled with grace.

chapter 9: Soar

"Wow! This is a check from Harlequin! As in Harlequin Romance?" the teller blurted out, ignoring customer service protocol in the bank on Ventura Boulevard the spring of 1993.

"Yup!" I said, like a goofy cartoon character, embarrassed by the question yet strangely pleased by it. It was the first time a bank employee had ever been amazed by the origin of my income. The check was for a book cover I had completed, a Harlequin novel named *Forgotten Past.*

We had just moved to the Hollywood Hills, to an eclectic home sandwiched between Sunset and Ventura Boulevards that had an indoor hot tub, crystal chandelier and vaulted glass ceiling. And our life was engulfed in exotic experiences — Phil, now a management consultant traveling abroad frequently, and me, a photo-illustrator doing projects for books and magazines. We were a two-person theater troupe donning multiple hats — equal parts left and right brain, suits and blue jeans.

(If you're wondering as a reader why I just jumped ahead 14 years in the timeline of this book, I will tell you. You needed a break from the poverty and drama. You needed to know that quantum leaps are possible in the most limiting circumstances. And this is but one of them.)

"I can't believe this..." the bank teller persisted, glancing at the dollar amount of the check that had three zeros behind a number, which triggered another foolish grin from me. *"What career path did you follow to land such a great job?"*

Whatever I had done, she was about to steer her own daughter in the same direction if I could just explain myself. Too bad my answer made no sense.

"Well, I ... ah (cough) lost my career to get here ..."

"I don't understand?" the lady blinked at me.

I had yet to craft a logical explanation for my life gone awry; for a journey that began as a self-sacrificing spiritual quest but had, at the moment, become a blissful walk on the wild side.

Instead, I took a breath and hit her with an odd short story. Disjointed and disturbing. Something about 'fresh out of high school entering the ministry' then heading to Texas, Alabama and Mississippi, in that order, wrapping up the story with this uncomfortable revelation: *"That was the first 11 years of my life after high school. Before I* ***lost*** *that calling and was forced to get a* ***"real job."*** *I was* ***heartbroken*** *over that ..."*

After an awkward pause between us, I continued: *"I didn't have a college degree or the money or to earn one, so I worked real hard, real smart, real fast and got* ***here*** *anyway"* — here, meaning the Hollywood Hills.

Secretly, I was proud of the ways Phil and I had learned to skirt convention. But we had no way at the time to explain it.

When I saw the puzzled look on her face, I swiftly added this clarification (so I didn't seem like a smarty pants):

"I can safely say it "cost" a lot to get here. We just couldn't get here the conventional way."

The bank teller stood there in silence a moment peering right through me. Then she looked heavenward and said: *"Well, it looks to me like somebody up there thinks you did it the right way. Will that be all for you today, Mrs. Lawson?"*

— — —

Ours had been an improbable path to success until our late thirties, when we found ourselves swept up in whole new worlds of opportunity by means of unanticipated fields of attraction.

By then Phil had carved out a niche for himself as an "industry guru" (to quote one tradeshow organizer) serving corporate and independent service bureaus; agencies, that produced high end computer graphics for business presentations.

Phil soared like a bird riding the wind — speaking at international conventions and writing magazine articles and technology reviews for trade journals. In those days, Phil produced confidential studies for industry giants like Kodak and Agfa Matrix. And he compiled comparative analysis manuals for corporations on a variety of topics from "facility management" to "sales techniques."

What a leap we had made from our days in Oxford, when Phil swapped cleaning services for an old 35 mm camera. And I retrieved that camera, from the top of a closet, and took photos of pink-faced children plucking corn.

Little more than eight years had passed since our departure from the Magnolia State, but Phil had already been the president of a multi-media firm in Dallas, growing it from a handful of people to nearly 40 in four years, expanding that facility to 8,000 square feet.

And now we were living in the Hollywood Hills. And Phil was an "industry guru."

"*We were successful our first week when applying your professional sales techniques, receiving orders of a 30,000 pounds ($54,000) per year imaging contract and a 4,000 pound ($7,200) custom order,*" wrote the co-owner of a graphics company in the UK about Phil's sales manual. "*We have copied your scripts from the book and sent them out to all 26 bureaus in our UK network. Your vision and techniques are international in scope and apply in the United Kingdom as well as they do in the United States with no modification.*"

It was an anxious time. A decade after the personal computer began making inroads into the corporate world, causing a transformation in business that was upending linear processes by integrating job activities.

It was the early 1990s ... and Tim Berners-Lee, a British Software Engineer, had just released and was testing his model of the World Wide Web as a free service to the public via the Internet (though it would take a couple more years, to officially catch on).

In the decade prior, scientists and academic researchers were virtually the only people sharing computer data through the Internet. But Berners-Lee's creation made it possible for everybody to bridge time and distance and break down cultural barriers. It knitted the world into a **sphere of interconnection.**

Buzzwords like "information overload," "learning revolution" and "productivity paradox" were splashed across business headlines when we lived in the Hollywood Hills. And companies and their employees were plummeting into chaos and uncertainty. Overnight, life-time employment and so-called stable career paths had become obsolete.

Funny thing was the general public was finally getting a taste of our own life experiences — of flying by the seat of our pants without a net.

Phil and I felt a kinship to fighter pilots. Those skilled fellows forced to fly through difficult terrain, even low to the ground, if necessary, with little or no margin for error.

Phil traveled to Europe on his first international business trip the day George W. Bush Senior launched Operation Desert Storm. Over the next 18 months Phil would travel abroad nine more times expanding his worldview during late-night dialogues with foreign businessmen over seven-course meals in ancient stone mansions. He debated war, the future of business and what a person might do if they had millions of dollars, while sipping fine scotch in darkly lit smoking rooms.

"I'm lying here in a hotel room 13 feet below sea level," Phil told me early one morning during a long distance call from Amsterdam.

"Can you see any land?!" I gasped, imagining his hotel was submerged underwater like an aquarium in an amusement park. To be fair, *he had* awakened me from a deep sleep.

"You're kidding, right?!" Phil questioned me, wondering if he should, once again, be worried about my mental health.

"Of course ... I'm ... kidding," I laughed nervously, as it dawned on me what "below sea-level" actually meant in terms of elevation. At which point Phil changed the subject and told me he had fallen off a bus. And I gasped, again.

"I landed on my back, in my good suit," he explained, still shaken by the experience. *"My laptop computer went flying across the sidewalk ..."*

Surprisingly, his suit was not damaged, and neither was his computer, encased in its padded nylon carrier.

"A whole crowd of people gathered around me to see if I was okay ..."

Phil was in the zone — or pretty close to it back then. He devoured some 70 magazines a month and several daily newspapers to stay abreast of his field, fancying himself a minor-league visionary. Helping his clients connect the dots of their companies in synergistic and holistic ways.

Holistic business consulting, what a hoot! For a short fellow with no college degree Phil had him some balls.

But there was more to it than that. There was more than a vitamin analogy motivating him now. Phil had begun to trace the modern efficiency movement back to its roots at the turn of the 20th Century — a movement that had run its course, but still had a profound influence over everybody.

We read about Henry Ford's assembly line and Frederick Taylor's 'principles of scientific management.' Taylor, an efficiency expert, believed the production systems of his day were wasteful. And that applied to the people who operated the machines, too. Taylor analyzed the minute details of the production process and human performance. He counted the number of steps workers took to do a task. He looked at the positioning of the machinery and observed the way people walked, bent down, reached and grasped objects.

And Henry Ford embraced his views.

"Why, when I only want to hire a pair of hands, do I get a whole person?" Henry Ford once said.

By combining his assembly line methods with the principles of scientific management, Ford reduced the time to build a Ford Model T from 14 hours to one and a half. And the cost to buy a new automobile dropped to one third of its original price. Eventually, Ford was producing 48 percent of the automobiles made in America using only 16 percent of the labor pool. And his innovations were quickly and widely imitated.

It was time for "organizational" diagrams to define and assign us our duties.

When factories were small and team-oriented, an owner or foreman could easily watch over the productivity of all workers. But large factories required a second tier of employees to act as supervisors over the line workers. Floor managers watched over the supervisors. Department managers supervised the floor managers. The larger the factory, the more the layers it required. To keep track of the management structure, factory owners drew diagrams in which individual tasks were identified by rectangles. The diagrams revealed at a glance where everyone fit in the production process. The model, with its stacked boxes, became known as the "org chart."

Eventually, the principles of scientific management permeated white collar jobs, too. It was implemented in schools and education systems; in the production of food and medicine — even embraced by Headquarters in New York.

People grew accustomed to being parts in the machine — until it began to horrify them. And artists, philosophers and writers began speaking out. One of them, H.G. Wells, penning these words: *"We must not allow the clock and the calendar to blind us to the fact that each moment of life is a miracle and a mystery."*

By the time Phil and I stumbled upon this realization in the early 1990s, machine-like thinking and behaviors had infiltrated society for many generations.

I can't tell you why, exactly, that Phil and I were so profoundly shocked by this reality. We had been trained that the world was coming to an end, anyway, so who really cared about the operating systems of society at large? God was in charge. And nothing we humans did amounted to much. Until it began to dawn on Phil and me that humans "out there" were actually running things. That it wasn't, for crap sakes, a fallen archangel, doing his dirty work. And yes, I said "Crap!"

One clever man named Henry Ford, at the turn of the last century, implementing the efficiency theories of another clever man, had managed to put a car in everybody's driveway! He had become the "symbol of 20th Century Industrialism!"

Not to mention what other efficient men and women had done over the last 100 years to perpetuate it.

Phil and I hadn't begun to learn what prompted this machine-like thinking in the first place. But the more we researched the topic and pondered the matter in context with our upbringing, and our experiences, Phil was overcome by a great restlessness.

Why spend all his time helping people escape their miseries, by clinging to a vision of the hereafter, when he could help them ease their distress right here, right now?

"Holy man" took on new meaning as he began to offer a presumptuous array of services to help his clients connect the dots of life, to flex and adapt in the business world and learn to see the "whole" picture. Peculiar services, like: *"strategic resource integration;" "management flexibility audits;" "technology integration;"* and *"flexible resource management."*

And every experience he was having seemed relevant.

Sitting in the lobby of a luxury hotel in Santa Barbara in 1992, Phil came face to face with the chairman of Sears Mortgage Corporation, having been introduced to the man by the salesman of a leading quality training group.

The Sears Chairman latched onto Phil's message right away. He liked the idea of "resource integration" and was, in fact, already a champion of the idea. So, he hired Phil, along with the salesman who introduced him, to complete a "resource audit" on the internal activities of his organization.

What a rare opportunity, it was.

To accomplish the task, Phil introduced something quite out of the ordinary during his first executive meeting. He brought in an audience response technology that utilized keypads and allowed participants to respond anonymously to a series of questions Phil had devised.

The senior management team, a boardroom full of MBAs, was aghast at the chairman's decision to hire Phil in the first place. And, when Phil presented his findings, recapping his final report aloud, the room erupted into bickering and then an uproar before the chairman finally shouted: *"That's enough! This is exactly [the reaction] I was hoping for!"*

Phil would later learn that he had been used, more or less, by the Sears Chairman, to flush out internal issues among his staff that would have otherwise been more difficult to expose. In return, Phil expanded his client roster to include another corporate giant who had granted him entry.

Life crackled and popped with activity in those days. We had paid our dues, or so it seemed. And we were poised to reach our objective — hard work produces prosperity.

Our encounters with the "privileged" population only increased when we were invited to live five weeks in London while Phil directed the London, Paris and Brussels operations of a New York-based visual communications company.

We took up residency at the Montrose House in Belgravia near the Turkish Embassy, also occupied by an ambassador that included around-the-clock police patrol.

Within walking distance was the famous Harrods department store, the décor of which resembled an Egyptian museum spanning more than a million square feet with hundreds of departments filled with every kind of gift, and a food hall filled with unimaginable delicacies — whole pigs, shelves of caviar and pates, raw milk cheeses and elaborate confections.

Browsing through a *Tattler* Magazine *(similar to American Vogu*e) in Harrods one afternoon, I discovered a photo of a woman who had recently invited me to her three-story flat for lunch. She was the daughter of a shipping tycoon and the wife of a businessman with whom Phil was engaged in his consulting work. There she was, pictured on a society page along with Joan Collins, the Princess of Wales and Evangeline Blahnik.

And I had just eaten lunch at her house. Surrounded by a group of lady friends that, as far as backgrounds go, came from "old money" or were "married to money" or, "married to someone of prominence," which meant they knew people who "had money."

The idle chat on that day was like nothing I had ever heard before.

A tall striking woman, eight months pregnant, dressed in a short black and white hound's-tooth smock, black leotards and knee-high leather boots, carried on about the apartment building she owned.

"Good God, the building's been there since Queen Mary," she conversed with her friends. *"But I can't get that through to this sad old man who keeps complaining about the condition of his flat."*

I couldn't decide if I should feel sorry for the old geezer, or the pregnant woman in leotards.

Then the 30-something-year-old host, that had appeared in *Tattler Magazine* tattled on her husband who had foiled her chance at a pricey birthday gift from her father.

"Daddy was going to buy me a new car!" she told her lady friends over lunch.

But when "Daddy," the shipping tycoon, shared his secret with her husband, her husband was so excited by the news that he forgot to keep his mouth shut about his own birthday plans.

"Ha! I was going to buy her a car, too!" her husband stupidly replied.

"Well, then, I'LL LET YOU!" was Daddy's delighted response.

As fits of laughter escaped the ladies in the room, I marveled at the nonchalance of her story, as if buying a car to "them" was like picking up the dinner tab at a restaurant — *"Say, I've got this one, don't you worry about it."*

I relaxed into the concept of *"having"* for a moment — of having anything you need or want at your fingertips and barely heard the hostess tell her audience that she (and her thick-headed hubby) were heading to the "country house" for the holidays because Daddy always throws a splendid party there.

At that point there was a knock at the door and upon answering it the hostess discovered a man in uniform.

"Excuse, me madam, but we have reason to believe ..." The Metropolitan police officer said.

Those of us in the room couldn't make out the rest of his words, as he turned his head toward the street and pointed at something a few doors down, which we would later learn was a parked car.

"If you could pull down your shades, Madam, stay inside and stay away from the windows until we can ..." he turned his head in the opposite direction and gestured toward a group of policemen headed his way who were about to investigate a mysterious paper bag stuffed under the car.

"Another bomb scare," the unruffled hostess said as she sucked hard on a cigarette and closed the door behind her.

It was then that it occurred to me, that exhausted, overworked "poor" people tend to respond differently to potential disasters. It ignites "fight or flight" behavior — as if *one more thing* in that person's life is simply too much to bear. They get nervous and talk too fast. I know this from my own experience. They become suddenly apathetic and say insensitive things, like, *"who really cares"* because *caring* takes energy, and they have none to spare.

I struggled to wrap my mind around the world in which these women moved about. Their triumphs and tribulations in no way resembled mine. I felt transparent, uncomplicated and uninteresting.

Fortunately, my artistic talents were gathering some steam and were mildly intriguing to them. I had completed a seven-page spread for the prestigious Palm Springs Life Magazine, in collaboration with Phil. And the creative director of the publication had liked our work enough to feature a brief story about us in the magazine. He had also assigned us the coveted cover for the hardbound summer edition. A special, annual edition placed in the hotel rooms of resorts that featured luxury vacation spots and celebrity profiles.

And it didn't hurt me to namedrop, either. There was that Nicole Kidman movie poster I did for Turner Broadcasting. And living in the Hollywood Hills was a bit glamorous, too. But it hardly compared to the lives of the rich and famous, the likes of which I was beginning to cross paths.

— — —

Living in the Hollywood Hills seemed a fairytale. The peaceful hillside community nestled in the midst of Los Angeles featured quaint bungalows wedged between mansions and the occasional castle. Birds chirped loudly and frequently and resembled the sound track of a Disney animated movie.

We were living the good life.

Our bank was on Ventura Boulevard; a handy coffee shop we frequented, on Sunset Boulevard — not far from where Harold Arlen parked his car in 1938 and wrote "Somewhere Over the Rainbow."

We drove Mulholland Drive almost daily, a street named in ballads and movies. We traveled through Laurel Canyon to the grocery store, a canyon once home to Frank Zappa and Harry Houdini, Jim Morrison, Carol King, Joni Mitchell and Graham Nash. Carol King wrote "Tapestry" while living there; Joni Mitchell, "Ladies of the Canyon," and Nash wrote, "Our House."

We ate lunch at the Canyon Store, the *"store where the creatures meet"* that Jim Morrison sang about in "Love Street."

The Hollywood Hills was a place where freaks and fantastic folks flourished for their differences. And predictable people rarely fit it.

We thrived there. It felt like home.

Our friends were gifted. One, an artist who created movie posters for top grossing films by Stephen Spielberg and George Lucas, classics like, *Star Wars, ET, Indiana Jones and Back to the Future ...*

And I had by then learned the art of networking — of private gatherings at Julie Andrew's home where talented ladies gathered to support each other's endeavors.

Because of that group, Phil and I once dined with a famous movie critic. And we were invited to display our artwork at a celebrity art show, where a screenwriter bought one of my illustrations. It was there that I envisioned a new art series I planned to produce, one featuring aging celebrities who had sustained their passion for life. The first in the series would be Phyllis Diller.

Our lives had shifted so entirely from our days in Thomasville that I couldn't help but tell somebody — a dear friend who had once "pioneered" in the town next to Thomasville, with her young husband, when we still lived there. She was now the mother of three, but her spontaneous nature remained in tact, along with her pleasant southern drawl.

On the night I felt compelled to *share* my experiences with her, she had called me. She had poured herself a glass of wine at the other end of the telephone and had settled into her bed prepared for a long chat. For it had been *too long* since we last connected.

"Guess what? I photographed my first celebrity," is all I said, a slight pitch to my voice.

But it came across as a joke to her that provoked a sarcastic response:

"Oh Babe, Surrre ya' did! And I just won Publisher's Clearing House!"

As I began to defend myself, Oh Babe lost interest and instead launched into a story about a spectacularly foiled party — one, a friend of hers had planned, but could not carry out, because she'd had a meltdown.

"*'Look honey,'* I said to her, *'why don't we do the thing at my house,'"* Oh Babe told me on the phone, pausing to sip her wine. *"I'll throw a ham in the oven, make some homemade rolls; you can bring a large salad, we'll pull a few more things together, I'll tidy up the house — Oh, Pammy, I used to do this kind of thing all the time! No problem, you understand? And she was grateful..."*

But as Oh Babe continued, I sensed something had gone terribly wrong.

"Course, I didn't get home [from knocking on doors] until 1 p.m. and I hadn't fixed lunch for the kids, yet," she rattled on. *"I was looking forward to a relaxing afternoon cooking the ham and cleaning the place up, but I began to remember things,"* Oh Babe said, the tone of her voice strange. *"I remembered ... I had to pick up my oldest at her friend's house at 2:30. I remembered ... I had a hair appointment at 3 p.m., a baby shower at 4 p.m., and I hadn't even bought a gift, yet."*

I pictured Oh Babe as it must have been that day — her staring blankly at a clock, calculating how she might fit 53 things into a three-hour window plus host a party that night.

"How could you have ***possibly*** *forgotten all that ..."* I blurted out, in astonishment.

"SHUT UP," she cut me off, like we were sisters and had earned the right to be rude to one another. *"I used to be a MUL-TI-TASKER — do you hear me?"* she defended herself. *"I just couldn't figure out why things*

weren't coming together this time. 'Cause, you see, I had also ***forgotten*** *... we'd made plans to take the kids BOWLING."*

She was proof-pudding to me, right then and there, of why I didn't lead a so-called *"normal"* life. But I didn't dare tell that to Oh Babe, who was still dishing the blow-by-blows of her catastrophe.

"Soooo ... I canceled my hair appointment, bought the baby gift and then drove around town for over an hour trying to find the house where the baby shower was being held but never did find it, huh! NEVER DID. All the while I'm thinking something isn't working, here ... THEN, I get this bright idea that if I just call all the people coming to the party and tell them to bring their own food it would solve my problem — everything would be fine, you see," Oh Babe paused, taking a breath. *"The party would be at my house, they'd bring their own food; we just wouldn't be there, we'd be bowling. But when I dialed their phone numbers, NOBODY WAS HOME! Oh, Pammy! I figured they must have all gone to the baby shower! Soooo, at 5:15, I called and canceled the WHOLE COTTON PICKIN' THING,"* Oh Babe said abruptly.

"After that, we grabbed a bite to eat, the kids bailed on bowling and we rented a video," she yawned. *"On the way home I stopped by my friend's house to see how she was doing, and she was quite PEEVED at me. Her husband had forgotten to tell her I called and canceled. She didn't find out until last minute. She had to call everybody again, then frantically put together some munchies,"* Oh Babe said chuckling. *"I stayed and helped until she got things* ***mostly*** *under control. It was the least I could do you understand,"* said Oh Babe, before changing the subject. *"Well, enough about me, Pammy! Here you are this big ole' world traveler ..."*

Each phone call from Oh Babe, I was beginning to believe, could have qualified for a skit in a Hollywood sitcom. Like the time she called to tell me she had just sold the furniture out of her house, on a moment's notice, without mentioning her plan to her husband. How he'd come home from work and it was just gone. How it had shocked him senseless. And he'd made a big deal of it, for reasons Oh Babe could not fathom.

Something was upside down in that head of hers, and Oh Babe had yet to come to terms with it. But that had nothing to do with our current phone conversation.

"I'm serious!" I finally cut-in. *"I photographed Phyllis Diller at her fantabulous Brentwood home."* Then, to be sure I got Oh Babe's attention; I kept talking without stopping until I'd told her the rest: *"And, Phil and I had our picture taken with Ed Asner!* ***And****, I saw Chuck Norris at my friend's art show,* ***and****, Priscilla Presley at an antique store,* ***and****, actress*

Rebecca De Mornay at the movie rental place, ***and****, Ella Fitzgerald's son ate dinner at our house,* ***and****, we ate dinner at a friend's house with Michael Jackson's sister, Rebbie,* ***and*** *... Wonder Woman lives in our neighborhood!"*

I imagined Oh Babe's jaw dropping on the other end of the line, and right then, as if on cue she burped the words, *"Well, I'll be dipped in horse shit!"*

At which point I said: *"If you insist."*

And we both burst into laughter.

Eventually, after fits of coughing and heehaws, Oh Babe spoke up again, this time in a voice that was almost hysterical.

"HOW in THE world ***DO YOU DO*** *all that? How pray tell did you get to Phyllis Diller?"*

It was a difficult question to answer. Finally, I muttered something motivational, something about *'taking advantage of every opportunity that comes my way,'* before mentioning I'd read an article in the *Los Angeles Business Journal* about an entrepreneurial woman with the job title of "find-ologist" who did research for the movie and automobile industries. How, for some reason, I'd been motivated to contact her. And this fascinating woman invited me to a networking group that gathered in a home 90 miles away. But I'd gone despite the distance, which led to unusual encounters with other fascinating people, and an invite to an event at Phyllis's house, which led to ...

"I can't believe what I'm hearing!" Oh Babe declared, before her tone turned serious and she added, almost whispering: *"Oh, Pammy ... aren't you worried you're getting a little 'too far out there?'"* as if I might very well slip into the hands of the Devil, forcing me to assure her, before we said our "goodbyes" that night, that I had not yet, to the best of my knowledge, succumbed to his trickery.

We were simply waking up, I explained; waking up to a more expansive view of our world. And what a view it was.

"When I sit here on this couch and stare up at the sky my heart heals," Phil said, rubbing his chest with the palm of his hand one afternoon after Oh Babe's phone call. He was, at the moment, gazing up through the vaulted glass ceiling of our Hollywood Hills home. *"My chest used to ache, physically ache, from all the things we'd been through. Now, slowly but surely, the pain of all those years is melting away..."*

Celestial Winds by David Young and Lisa Franco was playing on the CD player and a cool breeze from the open patio doors was rustling Phil's hair when he shared those feelings with me.

"I know what you mean," I replied, remembering how I often felt inclined to belt out a song in the expanse of our lovely living room for the shear pleasure of it.

And just then, I started to sing, a cappella style, something daring and difficult. A song from Whitney Houston's *Bodyguard* CD, because of its sappy message:

"I hope ... life treats you kind. And I hope YOU have all YOU dreamed of," I crooned to Phil, in a rare and sentimental moment. *"And I wish you JO-OY and happi-neessss ... but ABOVE ALL THIS! I wish you LAHHHVE ..."*

Phil's blue eyes sparkled as I endeavored to reach the high notes, and a smile spread across his face. And it occurred to us that the high notes of life are so beautiful too, when you hit them.

By then, Phil's photo had appeared on the cover of the Century City Chamber of Commerce Newsletter featuring his special presentation, *Taking Responsibility for Your Personal, Professional and Business Destiny.* He had been appointed to the speaking board of that organization, and had arranged a series of upcoming programs designed to explore the radical changes occurring in the business world. The announcement appeared alongside notices for the 14th Annual Golf Tournament at Braemar Country Club and a Nordstrom Fall Fashion show presented by the Women in Business Council.

Phil's message was in keeping with the news clippings, charts and scribbled notes he had taped across an entire wall in his home office — the makings of a book he hoped to one day write.

One person scheduled to attend Phil's speech in Century City was a business writer who had, for a short while, followed Phil's work. In fact, that writer had once mentioned a project of Phil's, in a book he wrote for BusinessWeek. This writer, like Phil, was intrigued and perplexed by the changing business climate. And it seemed to him, there might be an opportunity to coauthor a book about it.

"You're top of the heap, man!" I said, slapping Phil on the back during that period of our lives.

By then, a 30-something MBA executive from a top consulting firm, sent by his CEO, had shown up on our front doorstep unannounced one afternoon after receiving a marketing piece from Phil in the mail. It was a single-page letter, void of gimmickry that featured a series of provocative one-liner questions. The man came by to *check out* the competition.

That same marketing piece aroused the interest of a CPA, the owner of one of the top 25 firms in the city who wanted to pick Phil's brain. Theirs was a stimulating interchange, if nothing else and included stories about children born to rich families that were often ruined by money, and poor people who became rich, but couldn't adjust to having it.

"Poverty is a disease," the CPA had told Phil that day.

Transitioning from poverty to wealth was far more complicated than we had ever imagined. There was a language to it, a set of clues, codes and networking skills that we had little knowledge of.

Even so, we were giddy about the things we had accomplished, thus far. By the fall of 1994 I had completed a dozen book covers for Harlequin. And Phil had by then created a cutting edge online kiosk for a major Southern California home healthcare provider.

The project had been the dream of the chief technology officer at the company. *"Can this be done?"* he'd asked Phil the fall of 1992, handing him a document inscribed with his vision.

"Sure," Phil had said, after reading it, energized by the challenge. The company was already a client of Phil's. But this project was much larger in scope than anything he had previously done for them. It would require a team of experts, some of which were out of state.

Utilizing advanced technologies, the project made it possible for a person with no computer experience to identify health plans they qualified for, enroll in them, in real-time, and print out an ID Card. The kiosk had audio prompts, videos, access to a database of a physician's education and credentials, even photographs of the doctors, as well as an extensive "wellness" library that could be researched and printed out. It also incorporated a geographical information system, otherwise known as a GIS, to assist enrollees in finding all qualified doctors within 10-miles of their home, helping them meet a state law that other HMO's still struggled to comply with. And it did away with the "map and string" technique, hanging on the wall at the company's headquarters, once used by employees to assist enrollees with their selections.

It was created 19 years ago, with features you'd find on the Internet today, done, the year the World Wide Web was barely taking off.

Phil had managed to convince a set of engineers bound by the complexities of GIS systems — systems they believed took months to learn — to create a simplistic locator application easy enough for a homemaker or truck driver to use. (Phil would use this same approach later to create one of the first GIS applications for the Web.)

In the role of strategic designer, I watched Phil painstakingly create and compile a three-inch binder filled with roughly 400 pages of storyboards and schematics over many months to finish the job. But it was quite the accomplishment.

Phil had an uncanny ability to connect the dots in ways that other professionals could hardly imagine. He tapped a vein of creative power pinched off to most by their efficiency experts.

In the end, the kiosk earned that California healthcare provider some kind of award, the details of which I can no longer track down. Meanwhile, Phil had impressed a few administrators who worked there.

"A manager at [the HMO] asked me the other day what university I attended," Phil said, still watching the sky through the vaulted glass ceiling.

"What'd you tell him?" I asked, worried that too much information about our past might disrupt Phil's rise to the top. Explaining our eccentric path to other people, like the local bank teller, was rather difficult, I had discovered.

"I told him the truth in a diplomatic round about way," Phil said, which included telling a brief history of our time spent in Alabama and Mississippi.

"What was his reaction?" I pressed Phil, anxiously.

"Well, he stood their shaking his head for a minute, and then said, 'It's a long, long way ... from Mississippi to the Hollywood Hills.'"

chapter 10: Pure

Michael Jackson died yesterday.

As I scan the online news of his death on June 25, 2009, I am struck by how this artist by the age of 50 had moved millions with his song and dance despite what some described as the tragic elements of his life.

By contrast, Phil and I by the age of 54, have no illustrious achievements at all, despite what some might describe as the tragic elements of our lives.

No wonder I champion old people. I keep imagining that someday, no matter our age, we will muster up a pure thought worth conveying to a large number of people.

But Phil and I do have one thing in common with the King of Pop.

We were raised in the same puritanical religion — a faith that inspired its parishioners to live a special and separate lifestyle, to be "no part of the world." To adhere to the dictates of ancient Biblical commands, as interpreted by those charged with its translation, and avoid the dangers of modern-day scientific and philosophical thought and controversial psychoanalysis.

And so it was, within these confines, with no outside frame of reference, that we blazed our own trail in Oxford at the age of 23 until it burst into flames.

— — —

The knock came in the early hours of a morning.

It was the Pudgy Pink-faced Lady. There'd been an accident ... a fall. Her three-year-old had broken his arm. *"Could you watch the baby,"* she'd asked in a rush, *"She's teething and had a bad night. The others are up and gone to the asphalt plant. Hate to drag her out ..."*

"Sure," had been our reply, both still groggy.

Though, we lived within walking distance of each other, our schedules rarely matched. Her family was up before the chickens; Phil and I, barely to bed by then when we worked nights.

There was one more thing: If complications arise, and she calls us, could Phil hurry to the plant and notify the Asphalt Man because he had no phone?

"Uh-huh."

Too tired to stay awake, Phil and I had crawled into the Pudgy Pink-faced Lady's bed within earshot of the baby in her crib. But the commotion of her mother's instructions had disrupted her and she was stirring, she was whimpering.

Fearing she'd discover her mother was gone, we lifted her up and placed her in the big bed between us and she fell fast asleep. We all did. Until morning sun pierced the darkness and I awoke to the sight of a baby snuggled up against me. Her eyes were open and she was cooing sweetly, staring up at the ceiling, kicking her feet, reaching her hand in the air as if touching something only she could see. I watched her gaze about the room, amazed by it. I saw her smile at nothing and everything — the duck on the dresser, tree shadows dancing on a wall projected through a window. I heard her gasp and laugh as sunlight crawled to a wall picture, then strike the glass and turn it into a fireball.

I felt her breath ...

On the opposite side of her was Phil, facing us, his eyes shut until that last laugh when they popped open. But he hadn't moved. He'd just stared ... at her, at me — our eyes locking. And we knew what we'd given up. The decision we'd made to have no children; to give our time to other people's children. We would never have this experience with our own flesh and blood — our own bundle of joy wiggling and giggling between us.

We stayed perfectly still, soaking up every scent and sound until she looked directly at one of us, then the other. And she knew we didn't belong to her. Then came the wailing ... and we paced the floor together.

— — —

And so it was the children — so many of them, who taught us to seek the whole picture. Like Dick Doc once did with vitamins.

I don't know why we were so drawn to the task: to understand the children. To help them. When you step up, there are consequences. You step across lines. You scare people. But we did it anyway. We did it anyway. To quench the thirst in all of us, I guess — them and us: To be heard, clearly. To be loved, dearly. To be known. To be grown — fully grown; not forced to grow up too quickly. But if one must grow up quickly, and sometimes we must ... Oh, but to know those budding parts of ourselves, those muffled parts of ourselves when they emerge ...

"I want you to write something down for me." Phil coaxed the shy but promising girl sitting in the car behind us as we drove from door to door. *"I want you to dream a minute. I want you to tell me what you would like to be if you had no obligations."*

The request took the girl by surprise and she frowned at the very idea. She was good at frowning, it helped her concentrate. When she would frown, she'd tilt her head, and bite her large bottom lip with her buck teeth.

"Well ... I'll have to think about that," she had said. And later she put her thoughts to paper ...

Our duties became clear as soon we arrived in Oxford. When we met the children without fathers; the one's whose mother's were overburdened raising multiple offspring on their own while working all hours of the day or night ... and the others, who had parents but those parents faced their own personal struggles.

And while it seemed useful and important to shower those children with sagely scriptures to live by, it seemed equally important to take an interest in them personally. And when we did, they began to respond, each and everyone, in their own unique and difficult ways. Sometimes their needs were simple ones:

"To: Phil & Pam From: The Sick One," read the little boy's note. *"I am glad you two drop by my house yeserday. I was really proud to see you all. I went to the doctor after and he said the cold was working on my heart, so I guess I got heart trouble. So I guess you were right about staying in bed so then prouble I can go to school an play, so the best thing is to do is stay in bed and stay in the house. Phil & Pam I would love for you two to go to the library and get me books but if you don't have the time don't you and Pam go out in that cold weather. Don't spend your time all on me, use your time wisely and preace the good news. If your car don't work don't try to get there stay in bed* sleep *Pam & Phil. When I read the note you left for me I could have cried this shows that you love me and not only me you love other people too ..."*

Other times, they were more complex:

"I don't know what I am doing or if its even me," Phil read, unfolding the note from a child that was handed to him — her feeling safe enough to confide in him something she had experienced awhile ago. *"But I am completely tired of this I am sick to my stomach over the though. I once*

said that I though white men were nicer, and kinder than black. That they really cared for people and they wouldn't hurt the people they cared for. I though very highly of them at one time, but now I don't know. I never though I would dought myself in that cuse it was what I believed in for such a long time every since I was a little girl. Well I am a little girl now but then I was even littler about 7 or 8. But in order to come out of this dream world I'd have to go throu real life experiences that are always hurtful. And when something like this happens it really shakes me up. You'll probly wondering what by now..."

The note was hard to read. And yet it wasn't our first awareness that some thing or someone was disturbing some of the children. We'd seen it in Thomasville, when we returned for the dedication of the [church] after our arrival in Oxford.

The tiny girl had been hard to watch, sitting perfectly still beside Glee, her back stiff as a board, afraid to look in any direction but straight ahead. On the other side of Glee sat a younger woman, his new wife and mother of the child. But when that marriage ended suddenly and Glee went to prison around the same time, we remembered the disturbing nature of the man — the peculiar patterns in his actions and behavior that preceded his incarceration. We couldn't help but wonder why he'd been arrested.

And so our curiosity grew as the children opened up to us. What if they could get past the limitations imposed upon them by the adults around them? Imagine what they could do ...

"I would like to become a model," the letter read from Shy-but-Promising began. *"I think some model are very pretty even beautiful. They are so neat and petite. Everything they wear fit them so good. They can fix their hair so unusual and it looks great. But of course they have to mix business and sex.*

"I would like to be a gymnastic artist. I think that that is a beautiful art. The way you can get your body into a very flexible position. It's wonderful. But I am about to late up in my years to do that."

"I would like to be a artists. A natural artist painting real pictures about nature, wildlife family, the sky, the sunrise all kind of wonderful thing that Jehovah made ... " Shy-but-Promising kept adding to her "dream" list, until she finally wrapped it up with:

"I would like to have a friend, a friend I could trust, depend on Help when they need help. Help figure things out together. A friend I can cry with, laugh with, talk to, sing with, tell my deepest thoughts to, get angry with and still be a friend. Some one I can get embarrassed in front of and not be ashamed. What I would give for a true friend."

As so it was that we began to "see" them ... not the image they projected, but what was underneath it ...

"What's a matter, gal?" I asked the Stout Sarcastic Girl; noticing the clumps of mud on the back of her coat, which, I would learn, got there when the old truck she was driving stalled on the drive to town forcing her to pull off and stop; then pull off the distributor cap and dry it out, like her daddy had taught her.

"I think I need a husband, that's all."

"I know you're kidding." I teased. *"Is that going to make your rashes go away?"*

"If I had someone to love me, anyone that would take me, I would feel better ..."

"Where's the rational girl who told us that 'until she found the right man, she would wait as long as she had to because she's seen too many people live in regret?' You had specific plans for your life, remember?"

"I changed my mind. I need out of the house. The Renault only works half the time, I'm tired of driving sixteen miles to town, I'm tired of not knowing what kind of part-time job to get, and I'm tired of Scotty peeing on the carpet ..."

"Whoa ... how you feeling these days?

"What?"

"How's your health ..."

The Stout Sarcastic Girl, who often wore the same plain cotton blouse, with the tiny peach flowers on it; who wore the same unattractive double-knit skirt and comfortable rubber shoes, was losing her cocky edge.

Her weight was rising, the dark circles under her eyes, deepening; the crusty layers of skin caked to her eye lids each morning when she awoke from sleep, too difficult to scrape away. Not to mention the mysterious rashes on her arms and that burning sensation in the roof of her mouth. But it had become her badge of honor; that moment when she was five and fell off the swing. That blow to the head that left a bruise on the left side of her brain. The fact that she began to mature too quickly after that and the family doctor prescribed a popular barbiturate to temper her emotions and slow down her metabolism. By the time she was 15, the drug had taken its toll on her body. She would come home from school in a state of complete exhaustion and go directly to bed. And now, at 19, her body was malfunctioning even more.

"I don't know what that means?" She said, blinking rapidly. *"I've always had health problems. That has never stopped me; it's just life, that's all."*

"Well it's stopping you. And that's a shame. We haven't always seen eye to eye, you and I, but I know a sincere, good-hearted person when I see one ... a selfless person ... a bright person ... who knows how to change her own flat tires."

As I said, we began to "see" them ...

"Well, that all depends. Is it a bad leak?" Phil probed in an easy voice, a telephone to his ear.

'Nah, not really it's been like that for a few weeks,' Shy-but-Promising had said, Phil relaying the message to me when he'd hung up. *'It works better than our old Mercury. It don't drive at all. It was too hard to get someone out here in the woods to fix it so we just parked it and mamma bought another car. That ain't nothing. When we got sick of that ol' piano we pushed it out the back door and over the hill after mamma went to work one night.'*

Phil's face had registered surprise as he pictured the scene; her and her siblings finding an easy way to make space in their crowded living room. But Shy-but-Promising had somehow earned the right to make those decisions, having cooked and cleaned and looked after things for her mamma, since she was little. *"You pushed a piano over the hill in your backyard?"*

'It wasn't any good, some of the keys were broken and it sounded poorly.'

We began to "see" them ...

" ... this evening my mother told me that she could see that I was trying to slip out of the [church] and that Satan had me in his hand! That isn't true," another kid wrote in a letter to me. *"I'm trying so hard to get myself back together and not let me get into a spiritual death! I want so bad to come out of this shell or my own little imaginary world of that everything is okay with me! Why did she have to say that? ... I tried to call you, Pam at least five times but the lines was always busy! I just want to cry and tell you what she had said! Why doesn't ma take time out to be with us and to truly say she loves us. She is a good provider but she doesn't have time to be a real mother. The kind that you can sit down and say: ma, I have a problem. And she says: let's sit down and talk about it. If only she could do that in a loving way. I only wish that more people in the congregation would take more time to show more love to all the teenagers. If the others feel anything like I do. Just for someone to just come up and give you a hug. Or hold your hand just to let you know that they care. They don't even have to say a word. That would mean a lot to me. I truly need someone now ..."*

And, again ...

"It was a very bad day. I got real nervous in bed this morning and I felt as if something was eating all my body up on the inside, all I wanted to do is scream! Why I got out of bed I don't know. I got up and [name omitted] was visiting ... talking real loud and I just couldn't take it, I had asked them to be quiet but they wouldn't, so I just began to cry and scream, why did I do that! I couldn't help it. I can't stand all that noise. Then after I got myself together I went on to the school and they told me that I could't come back because I had moved. That upset me too ..."

And, again ...

"I've made some changes in my life for the good, one that of children," began a teenager's letter, which she had written to us, *"Because of what happened years ago, I hated children up until a few years ago. Believe it or not, I was actually jealous of their happiness. I thought in my mind, 'I wasn't happy when I was your age!' So whenever I was around children, I would try to make them unhappy. That would make me happy. Silly, -----so silly. For the better part of my life I have been running, changing every avenue of my life so that no one would ever suspect anything that happened years ago.*

"Remember when I told you those things about what I did with [name omitted]? It wasn't because I wanted too. I was trying to build that outward image up, and I wanted so much to prove to myself that I wasn't [word omitted] when I was a child, that it was all just a bad dream and that doing things like what I was doing with [name omitted] only helped me to prove to myself that I was a so called normal person with a perfectly normal background and no regrets whatsoever. I thought for sure that I was leaving my childhood behind. If I could only start out new, no one would ever know, it would be just my horrible secret. But it hasn't worked out as I had planned. As I grow older, the more curious I was to learn more about how to change so that no one would ever know. So I became just the opposite of what a [word omitted] child is supposed to be like: **1.** *Shy,* **2.** *Withdrawn,* **3.** *Hate children,* **4.** *Afraid of men. Instead I was outwardly:* **1.** *Not shy at all,* **2.** *Outgoing,* **3.** *Love children,* **4.** *Not afraid of anything.*

"That's the image that I have worked on and if you asked someone if that was what they see me as, I am sure they would say yes. I have worked hard for that phoney image. I can't go through the rest of my life living a lie. One thing that the image hasn't wasted its true colors on is children. I do love them because around them you can be yourself so to

speak no airs, no phoney conversations. So I have learned to be sensitive toward them and not so harsh.

"I have almost killed myself at certain times. I have stayed up night after night, afraid to go to sleep, afraid of the nightmares and reoccurances. But I wouldn't let anyone into my world because of fear of being hurt. Little did I know I was hurting myself. You know how you are always asking me what I am running from? Well, to the best of my knowledge, I am running from reality. For the reason that I have been hurt so bad by this wicked old system that I would rather run than face the truth. But that's all I have been doing for so long, covering the past with a phoney image. Pam, help me to never start paving myself underground again. I must go. Its 1:15 a.m. [signed, name omitted.]"

But there were consequences to our "seeing" the children and caring for them.

"Friday night when I got home I really caught it," began the letter to us from the Stout Sarcastic Girl. *"It started out with me spending too much time with you guys and avoiding my folks. Then it went to the point that I never do anything around the house. I just sat there and waited till they had said all they wanted. When they had finished I started asking questions. Like why did they show such a hostile attitude toward you guys? ... I said that all my life I have wanted a big brother, and now that I have one you want me to forget him ... Then I was told that since I had been sick and spending time with you guys that our family has fallen apart. I said that I disagreed and ask them to think back before I was pioneering and still in school. Did we do anything as a family? Did we have a family study? Did we have family recreation? Did we do anything at all as a family? They had to say no ... I said the reason why I was around you guys was for the encouragement I received and for the up-building association. I was told that I should be encouraging them. I said I knew that and I tried to, then I asked who was to encourage me? Daddy said that he got me a car. I told him that was an act of love as a father, not a source of mental and emotional encouragement. ...*

"I want to run away from the whole mess ... Despite being totally wiped out to the point of aching and trembling, I was able to go to sleep. Then sometime early in the morning, I heard someone in my room. It was Mamma. She woke me up to tell me that she just figured out that she resented me for having friends that love me so much and for having a big room and being able to wear nice clothes. She said she was sorry and that she guessed the resentment started when I started pioneering. She told me she was going to try and work on it but didn't know what to do. I told her

that at the moment she should try and calm down and get some rest and think and pray about it when her mind and emotions were more settled. I wanted so bad to run down and be comforted by you two, but I knew that all that would do was fuel the fire ..."

And the consequences didn't always involve just the parents, but the children too:

"You see I got into a big jealous rage. I thought you were more concerned about the other kids than me," wrote one kid, who liked to call Phil "dad." *"You were always spending time with them and I thought and felt I was being rejected and it hurt me so bad and I just completely stopped caring. But now I know that wasn't right and I just hope you can forgive me for being so childish. Now I am trying so hard to put my jealousness behind. I got to realize that I can't always keep you to myself forever. I hope you understand what I am saying. I was going to tell you this at the hall but I was always so slow about getting around to it. I knew it would be better if we were to talk it over, but there hardly ever time. Just remember I'll always love my Dad and Pam too!"*

Or, this instance:

" ... There I was laying asleep then all of a sudden awful thoughts started to pass through my mind. I began to feel that I'm just being used by Phil and Pam. They didn't really want me to go to the assembly with them; the only reason that they wanted me was because I knew [name omitted]. That's just the start. I began to feel that they must like [another name omitted] better than me because they were taking her even though she wasn't needed. Then I began thinking that I was no longer special. I felt like just one of the crowd, nothing important. I really must work on being jealous of other people that Phil and Pam get close too. They don't belong to me. No one does. I have no one person to love me more than anyone else ..."

But, despite the obstacles there was much progress.

"The other day I found a thank-you card that you guys sent to me in February of 1979. In it you said, "The gift you gave us came in very handy at a very needed time. We put it to good use. Thanks lots!!"

"Well, the truth of the matter is, you gave me a gift, also at a very needed time and it has and always will come in handy," The Stout Sarcastic Girl wrote: *"The gift is yourselves, time and love. I pray that I can put to good use all that I have learned from you guys, because it is part of the gift that most likely will benefit me most.*

A Stout Sarcastic Girl, who over time, lost 60 pounds and changed her attitude. A Stout Sarcastic Girl who sought medical help from Dick Doc and had over time transformed herself into a Thin Gracious Girl. A Thin Gracious Girl who, improved her skill sets, found a part-time job and looked quite lovely in her nice new clothes.

"You guys are excellent teachers let's hope that I'm a good student. Keep up the good work. Thanks so much for everything, [signed, Thin Gracious Girl.]"

Progress came about in many different ways. Especially when the youth learned to "see" us, too — when they caught a glimpse of our own personal obstacles; in particular, while I was recovering my health, as evidenced in this letter written to Phil by a teen, about me:

"Today was a most unusual day. It was a day when I felt my heart was breaking. This was the forth time in my life when I have felt this way. I felt like this when my father died. It hurt me for a long time. I think he new he was going to die, because that night when he went out, he patted me on the head and told me to be a good girl and take good care of the family. He never told me that before. They said it was a car wreck, with him and a few other guys, but I think there was more to it than that. I don't know exactly why I didn't know that much about him. We never talked or played I might have been to little. I do know that through the week he was a dearly sweet man, he didn't hurt anyone or harm me. He was so kind and that's the way I want to remember him. But I can't cause I saw what went on through the weekend. Friday was the day his check and his bottle and mamma went through hell until Monday then we would live half normal lives. I liked it when we lived Monday through Friday morning lives.

"The second heartbreaking thing in my life was when [name omitted] got [disease omitted] ... The third heartbreaking thing that happened to me was when I thought you were going to get to go to foreign country to be missionaries. I hated that. I even hate to think about it. I did not want to care for anyone again because the pain of loosing you was to great. But I can't stop caring ... The forth most heartbreaking thing involved a lady a very beautiful lady, a lady that I look up to more than anyone else next to my mother. Her outward appearance is as a little girl so sweet and gentle never hurting anyone. In the inside she has so much love bubbling forth. She's such a comical character dancing around and prancing around the house like a little busy bee. But I can't understand some one with so much joy and enthusiasm can be so sick. I've seen her suffer today. It was so horrible to see someone suffer, so full of life to have to go through that ..."

And thus, she would join us on the walks, some days, she and other children, as I recovered ... as Phil coaxed me in my recovery — when I was still learning to gauge my strength and limits; when I'd do too much and then pay a severe price for it.

"Get up ... come on lets go for a walk. I need you Pammy. I need you to go on this walk with me. It will be good for you. You need your exercise. Come on ... no, don't sit back down ... (sigh) that's it, what do you mean get somebody else? ... Come on, we'll walk down by the old abandon house and watch for deer. You get your jacket ... oh; I'll get your jacket. Do you want the blue one? Oh, you want my jacket, instead? Are we having an identity crisis? I was kidding! ... Please don't lay back down, Pammy, I need you to go with me, I'm lonely without you. The sun is going down. I'll get your shoes ... that's it ... hold my hand ...

— — —

It was our cars that taught me and Phil the limits of our fellow humans — those assorted machines we relied on that rolled to a stop when we pushed them past empty. Maybe because the adults we knew acted like machines when life spun out of control. They plowed ahead with steely resolve and gauged their worth by high performance.

But we no longer did. And that confused some.

Slim was one of those. A shiny black model; an elder of God tanked with zeal. A West Coast Christian-turned-Mississippian, having moved there of his own free will on his own personal mission; a divorcee, who caused women for miles around to swoon (secretly); a classically trained musician who had to his own admission relinquished his debauched life to do the Lord's bidding, the sacrifice of which no others could possibly comprehend more than he.

And it was he who felt it necessary to correct our course, Phil's and mine, and get us back on track.

If I could've hid the day Slim knocked on my door I surely would have. But I lived in the cute but tiny trailer with the red shutters. And my footsteps could be heard by visitors standing on my tiny porch.

Slim had ducked when he passed through the metal front door before straitening back up again — all six foot of him, the epitome of what he believed about himself, that he could see above and beyond everyone else. Phil wasn't home. It was just the two of us nose to nose; Slim seated across from me in my tiny living room, his Bible splayed on his lap. Tasked he believed to remind me of my duties.

Lifting the good book to his chin, he cranked up his voice like a car radio and read: *"This good news of the kingdom will be preached in all the inhabited earth for a ..."*

The trouble was that scripture, of all scriptures, was the first one I'd learned as a child. I knew it like I did my middle name. It was the very one that had inspired me after high school to embark on a mission to spread the word in three different states. And here Slim was, gilding my guilt with a "do-good" scripture when I was down and out, in the midst of my slow path to recovery, as prescribed by Dick Doc.

And then — as if to overemphasis his point, having observed my lack of attendance at certain Bible meetings he launched into a story about another woman who had been such an inspiration to him when she was sick:

'I knew a sister [out West] who was so sick she was dying,' Slim began. *'Yessir, I was there the day her blood count dropped so low from her bleeding ulcers and I thought it'd be the last time I'd see her ... she was slipping away. Slipping away ... hooked up to all these I-V's, oxygen running to her nose; one of her arms all taped up where they had poked her too many times drawing blood,'* he said, emphasizing her dire condition; doctors having been refused the chance to administer blood since it was against her (and our) religious beliefs to take it.

Just then a visitor arrived and pulled out a plastic bag from her purse filled with capsules of cayenne pepper. She poured a glass of water and slipped a few of the capsules to the dying woman who could barely lift her head.

'Bleeding to death, see, but what did she have to lose?' he said, shaking his head and smiling, *'Cayenne pepper! And she started getting better. The doctors were surprised. They began giving her the capsules every few hours, and unbelievable as it may seem, the bleeding quite. It was really the first time I started understanding that in some situations there are alternatives like herbs and vitamins that can help with health issues, and all,'* he said, attempting to find common ground between us about my vitamin regimens. Then, he got to the main point of his story, by comparing my progress to hers; I, of course, not holed up in a hospital bed with I-Vs stuck in my arms. *'She got back to the meetings as fast as she could,'* he said, knowing well that I had skipped my share of them. *'We even set up a cot in the back of the hall for her. That faithful sister was back before she could walk. She was a real encouragement to the congregation ...'*

But to be fair, I must set the stage for Slim's behavior.

As organizations go; ours was at the end of a phenomenal growth spurt. An energizing eight-year stretch that began two years after my father married Loretta Lynn and lasted through our arrival in Thomasville — a burst so extraordinary that worldwide membership doubled, driven by the anticipation that Christ's coming was absolutely eminent as insinuated by Headquarters.

It fueled an explosion of enthusiasm on the part of the brethren that resulted in a "quick-build" movement. The construction of new churches — in a mere 33 hours — by hundreds of volunteers converging on small towns and cities for action-filled weekends — Phil and I having experienced one of them.

Meanwhile, explicit instructions were being implemented from the top down; new judicial procedures designed to enforce strict moral codes as the organization transitioned into a 'rule by committee' format, an approach that, in the hands of those zealous but inexperienced, reined havoc.

Zealous like Slim. And Manic Man, who told stories of Christians he knew in Hollywood who sacrificed their careers for the cause. And Guitar Man and his side-kick, a pock-faced drummer, both of whom spoke disdainfully, though frequently, of their promiscuous, drug-inspired pasts, before they'd gotten the 'heavenly call' — Guitar Man's wife being an able singer; The Drummer's wife, the antsy daughter of a doctor all among the enthusiastic converts in Oxford. They were in the company of long-standing locals like Asphalt Man and Stocker — Asphalt Man, with his passel of kids from a first wife, before marrying the Pudgy Pink-faced Lady, half his age, when she was still a teenager, producing a new crop of kids — and Stocker possessed of unremarkable drive and opinion — all of which made for a kaleidoscopic collection of leading characters. Not to mention the subordinates in training.

And it was these adults that revealed to us the power and weakness of perception. Strapped to an assembly line of rules and procedures, their momentum in life powered by their own perceptions, they could not "see" us.

As we observed this phenomenon we began to connect a few dots about perception, behavior and other specifics, having learned the value of it from Dick Doc.

Vignettes, like these, for instance ... of Manic Man ...

As soon as a calf dropped Manic Man would scoop it up and place it in a warm corner. He'd talk to it, cuddle it — keep it in close proximity every single day to bond with it. But that bull ... that independent bull ... *'Zat bull makes me sooo angry,'* Manic Man said gritting his teeth. *'He run from me, but right to dead end fence. I so bad beat this bull with a wooden plank there was blood in bladder water for two days!'*

'They liseened thrue the windows,' Manic Man explained, his hand curling into a fist, about the police that pestered his tiny European village when he was young. *'They didn't like? They punch you out.'*

"I'll catch zis thief," Manic Man said running a trip wire from the basement of the hall to the contribution box, then rigging a sensor to the chair where he sat in the audience.

And there was his wife and daughter:

Such a sweet face wrapped in a scarf, Manic Man's wife — quiet wife, busy wife, cleaning her cabinets every three weeks, potty training her baby girl, who was now a teenager — a very, very good teenager — at an unbelievable three months of age. That Sweet Face, good at creating things, building things, growing things, like Manic Man. Dancing, even, the night he swung her round on the floor, his mood ecstatic. But for her headaches ... those headaches that chased her to the hospital. Once, 'a blood clot on the brain,' she said a doctor told her. But she controlled that pain like she did everything else, and to hear her tell it, the blood clot went away.

Then there was the day Manic Man pulled Phil and I aside and told us to our faces: *'Joo are zee best friends I have. I just can't trust joo.'*

The next time we saw his daughter was at the book study group. She walked in and glanced our direction with a look in her eye that seemed to say: 'I have to do this; I can't talk to you anymore' and then seated herself in her chair, sitting upright, stiff as a board, staring straight ahead.

"I could hardly wait to write you this letter because I'm so indebted to you for taking the time and along with my parents making me into what I am," she wrote to us from out of town, soon after, gushing, almost too much, in the letter. *"Thank you so much for teaching me to be humble, to keep pride in the proper place, for teaching me to be me, being down to earth, to have a pleasant personality but not one that is fake or painted on like a smile. I wish you were here so I could give you two a giant hug to show and tell you just how much I appreciate what you have done. Even Biblical knowledge and principals you have taught me with regards to organizational points are so handy, I am youngest but I think I compared to some know as much here. Thank you, thank you so much. I wish everyone had a brother and sister like you ..."*

And there was Asphalt Man who appeared to operate from an out-of-sight, out-of-mind viewpoint. Oh how some of us had cringed when we got word of the advice he'd given Sweater. Sweater — such a big fellow to sweat like that on stage. Sweater, in over his head again, financially. Such a testament to a life improved, he was — changing from a knife-wielding character that drove around town with questionable men in low slung cars to preaching from the pulpit. But he hadn't nailed his money woes, yet — buying this; borrowing that. Takes time to figure those things out. In the meantime he was on the verge of bankruptcy. *'That's not sound of mind,'*

The Asphalt Man had admonished him, being the judge he was; reminding Sweater that being 'sound of mind' is directly related to godliness. *'Why don't you leave the [church] and go bankrupt; and then come back in when you've straightened things out.'*

And there was that other painful incident ...

"Have you seen Dingo?" I had asked Phil nervously, that morning. But his answer had been "no."

"Not even when you read the paper at the picnic table? ... I'm worried ... It's not like her. She's always here, leaning right against the door ..." I said swinging the front door open again to make sure she hadn't arrived. *"Go ask [The Asphalt Man] if something's happened to her, please!"*

"If you insist, but you may not like the answer..." had been Phil's reply.

Dingo, meaning "wild dog" had been the name assigned to her by The Asphalt Man's family; by the Pudgy Pink-faced Lady and her brood. The healthy-looking two-toned black and tan creature, its legs accented by feathers of fur, resembling a Gordon Setter but smaller, had turned up like a stray at their house with a plastic bag tied to its neck. Skittish at first, it had taken a little time to lure her with food before she joined her new pack family and assumed her duties: to keep strangers off their land; to protect their kids and play with them on demand.

One last part of the initiation was surviving "the curve" — the sharp curve on the main road near their driveway — near our tiny trailer with the red shutters parked near their driveway — where more than one dog had lost its life to fast passing cars. One pup of theirs lasted a few months before we heard the horrible yelping and The Asphalt Man got his gun. Another was a female that had learned her duties well — a thin lanky canine with a wispy black coat and white chest, that was prized by the family; that snarled and barked ferociously at me and anyone else who got near their property or their kids. She had lasted a year before one of the Pink-faced Lady's brood knocked on my door in a panic to tell me she'd been struck by a car; that she had run off down the road and "daddy" had followed her, carrying his gun. And I, like a mad woman had sprinted down the road after them, imagining her injury was fixable, that I would repair her; that I would pay for it myself if need be, thinking mostly: *"Why doesn't anybody fight for anybody around here! Why do they give up so quickly? Why must they get their gun?"*

"She broke her back," The Asphalt Man had said that day, his voice gently but resolved, as I walked up to her resting in tall grass, sniffing the air, in no obvious pain.

"She's a good dog hate to put her down," he said some more. *"She can't move her legs. I pinched her toe, she didn't feel a thing ... better go back now."* At which point I hugged the neck of the dog that had often growled at me and made it partway down the road before I heard the shot ring out.

"Dingo's dead," Phil said, slumping down in his chair, jerking me back to the present.

"Whaaa ... t?!" I said; the word escaping my lips in a gasp. *"Was she injured? Was she sick?"*

"The kids were running around when I asked," Phil explained. *"He couldn't talk too loud. Mumbled something low about Dingo not being around much; didn't ever bark, didn't keep people away, wasn't much good with the kids — not like the other dog was ...*

Dingo hadn't done her duties. So the Asphalt Man loaded her in his truck took her to the back field and shot her.

"It was this morning. He doesn't want the kids to know."

And that's when it struck me. That last conversation we'd had. No, it wasn't a conversation. It was a hint. A remark tossed in the air like the butt of a cigarette as he walked past my trailer after a Bible meeting. As he walked home, his suit pants ragged on the back side from dragging the ground, as usual; a passing scene I'd grown accustomed to — him walking by, often accompanied by his children strolling behind him, in a single row, like little ducklings, all smiles, all of them. But he was alone that evening — just him. Just strolling by, not stopping; just glancing in my direction, then down at *his* dog lounging on *my* porch, as he passed by saying something like: *'You want her? She's always here at your place, anyway? She eats and leaves.'*

His comment was so unexpected I had no idea what to say. The tone of his voice, strange: Was it a joke? Was it an offer? Was it a judgment? I knew what I felt, *"Yes! Of course I'll take her! She's a wonderful dog! We've bonded!"* But I hadn't said the words aloud. Imagining I would give him a little time, make sure he was sure; make sure his wife and kids were sure. Not knowing my time had run out, right then, as he walked by me.

As I dashed past Phil seeking air, as I hit the door, ran down the steps and crashed into a tree I could not stop thinking ... if only, if only, if only I had been more clear, if only I had asked one more question, or maybe two ... pinned him down right then — right then and said, *"What exactly do you mean? AND, AND, what* ***exactly*** *is your timeframe?"* Said, *"Well, here's my initial reaction: Yes! I will! Just let me check with Phil!"* Or, *"Can I ask you to clarify your statement? Please!"* If only I'd said, *"I am happy to! Right now! Take her!* Followed by, only after I'd said, *"right now,"* followed by, *'Will your family be okay with this?'* to be polite. Had I just said, *"Absolutely, certainly, and thank you very much! You are a great man for giving her to me!"* ... Oh God, Oh God ... I must always, always, always ask *'What do you mean? What exactly do you mean?'*

— — —

In the midst of our time spent with the children and our time spent studying the perceptions of the adults, we spent time transitioning from janitors to photographers — expanding our photography business that started out working from the kitchen table of our tiny trailer before we rented one room, then two, from a law firm; and finally, rented a seven-room space for our photo studio above Sneeds Hardware on the town square.

"We'll put a darkroom in and not have to walk to Mr. Davis' darkroom anymore," Phil had said of that wonderful office space. We had by then landed a project to restore the pictures of 18 board members at Oxford City Hospital. And a local bank was doing a special mailing on our behalf offering free portraits to its preferred customers as part of a holiday promotional.

Along with our traditional photography services, we were experimenting with a stylized photo-illustration process that involved shooting local scenes in black and white and then painting them with photo oils. In order to test it, Phil hit the streets with framed versions of the artwork, going from store to store to get feedback from business owners, and when possible, selling a few. His methods got the attention of two local banks that purchased originals to hang in the offices of the president and vice president: one bank commissioning a night shot, lights on, of the courthouse; the other, commissioning a print of an historic, abandoned train station.

And when the chamber of commerce approached us to create a brochure that would highlight the extraordinary attributes of Oxford and Ole Miss, we did that too. Reveling in the feedback we got despite a few kinks during the printing of 25,000 copies of it. Such as this letter:

"Dear Mr. and Mrs. Lawson, Recently, while attending a meeting, it was my pleasure to see a copy of the extraordinary brochure you produced for use by the chamber in their community promotional efforts. I shared a copy with my co-workers, and we all agree that this is the finest example of published material being used by any of the thirty-three counties within our service district. The artwork is outstanding, and when combined with the unusual format and the manner in which the

information is presented, it makes this a truly unique product for community image enhancement, tourism development and promotional activities. We hope other communities will avail themselves of your unusual techniques and talents. Sincerely, Ralph D. Ford, Tennessee Valley Authority."

Phil and I knowing full well we couldn't have accomplished so much without the aid of a local bank, Phil writing this *telling* letter of appreciation (something you'd probably never read about "banks" today):

"Dear Mr. Black, Pam and I wanted to write a letter to you to express our deepest appreciation and gratitude for the understanding and support that First National Bank has given us the past two years. James Woodington has been very understanding and supportive as our loan officer. For that we are eternally grateful. James told us of how we were discussed at your bank board meeting. We know we have gotten nearly four months behind on two loans with you and that you had every right to legally foreclose on the items involved, which included our camera that we make a living with. James said you decided to wave the back payments and let us start fresh, even, and just make our payments regular from this day forward. No matter how bad our financial condition was, James was always encouraging, telling us not to be excessively worried about our bills and that he was confident when things got better we would take care of them. He said that he knew we were honorable people, us and the Mormons. His attitude was a great aid in maintaining personal dignity, in that he never treated us condescendingly. You have a great asset in James Woodington.

"Mr. Black ... We are acutely aware that you did not have to go as far as you have in supporting us. It is comforting to know that First National Bank is far more than just a lending institution, but rather it is 'human.' Sincerely, Phil Lawson"

James Woodington, the loan officer who stepped up when our old Chevy was breaking down and helped us buy a nearly new Oldsmobile. *"Go get yourself another car. You can't run a business properly in that thing. It's just a money pit now,"* he'd said, even though we had no collateral to back it up and no money for a down payment.

That old Chevy ... the one we'd bought two years earlier, in West Virginia, in a rush, in a pinch, when our overloaded Rambler broke down on the highway, while pulling a U-Haul behind it, filled with the belongings of four pioneers we were transporting from Oxford to New York to attend missionary school — Phil stopping, periodically, along the way, to throw up on the side of the road, because he was sick.

— — —

And just a little more about perceptions ...

It was a peculiar sight to see Guitar Man and his wife at our-bi-annual convention in Memphis sitting at the back of the hundreds seated in the audience. They, who most always sat near the front row, proud of their status as special pioneers; feeling obliged to speak of their promiscuous, drug-induced pasts to inspire others; happy to tout the number of converts they'd accrued, recounting them on their fingers. And now they were hiding in the back.

"Satan got a good man down." Had been his wife's explanation when we discovered Guitar Man had been stripped of his eldership and his special pioneer card. And we couldn't help marvel, Phil and I, at how often Satan was the scapegoat for our own inadequacies — for our lack of self-awareness about our own strengths and weaknesses; for our inability to see them, acknowledge and address them. Thank God for Satan ...

"Dear Phil and Pam,

Well this letter is long overdue. First let me acknowledge your appointment as an elder," the Pock-faced Drummer wrote; two years after we'd delivered him and the three other pioneers to New York to attend missionary school. *"I know you have been waiting a long time. [Name omitted] keeps us filled in on the goings on in Oxford all the new arrivals. How are things with you two? Pam how's your health? ... Missionary life is a lot tighter than pioneering. The schedule is fairly grueling, even more so than New York. Our home is so noisy that you would not believe it. 24 hour a day pollution of the mind. We really miss the country. How I wish we would have walked more in the woods now ..."*

Phil's eldership indeed had been long-overdue, at the age of 26; he having lived up to the qualifications a long time before he was appointed as one. He, being denied it by the local body of elders, even though the circuit overseer, two circuit overseers, had recommended it: *'By his age, I was in circuit work,'* one of them had scolded the body of elders; he himself having grown up in the faith. *'If I would have been treated the way you are treating Brother Lawson, it well may have stumbled me,'* he said quoting a scripture in Matthew about the scary consequences of mistreating God's flock, something about having a millstone tied around the perpetrator's neck and throwing him into the sea.

But who could blame the body of elders. Phil had become a thorn in their side long before his appointment. As is evidenced by this journal entry:

Journal entry: Tuesday, I came home and I could see cars parked at the hall (next door.) I found out a judicial committee meeting was going on. [Elder name omitted] came over and said they wanted to talk to me and it was obvious they were upset. As soon as I sat down I was jumped on hard, because Pam knew the situation. Pam knew the situation because [female name omitted] called our house in tears and said something terrible had happened and could Pam and I come over to [name omitted's] house and pick her up. I got chewed out by everyone but good. One thing led to another and I got chewed out for several things in just a matter of minutes. I could not understand why I was in so much trouble. I felt the committee meeting was called on "me" and not [the person in trouble]. I was upset when I found that the committee was formed and they had already talked to [female name omitted] without her mother present, which had me upset, because I felt it could have been handled better ... because when we took [female name omitted] home to her mother, I had watched a mother hear that her daughter had been [word omitted] by [male name omitted] that very afternoon. I saw it nearly break her heart, and then later that night she finds out that the elders decided to talk to her daughter without her present and without her even knowing it. I had told [elder name omitted] earlier when I reported the situation that the mother and daughter needed extra love and that the [elders] might want to wait till at least the next day to have the conversation after [the mother] and [female name omitted] could get some rest and talk with each other. [Elder name omitted] disregarded my suggestion. They called a meeting that very night when [the mother] was working ... The committee wanted me to tell them all I knew, but when I asked them why they talked to [female name omitted] who is only fifteen, alone without her mother present, they said that was privileged information and they couldn't tell me. This just added to our strained relationship ... Pam and I were all very close with the family. That is why [female name omitted] had called us on Tuesday ... When it was all over, they told [male name omitted's] wife to go home and forget about it and fix him a good breakfast in the morning ...

(Side note about [female name omitted]: Pam and I have started noticing that some typically good kids keep ending up in very dangerous situations. The situation with [male name omitted] was definitely his fault. But this isn't the first time [female name omitted] has had a problem. If she is not careful, she is going to receive no mercy from the body of elders here. Bad conduct is bad conduct. There has to be something triggering it. Perhaps if we can find it, we can stop this and she/they will stay out of trouble.) (End of entry.)

In response, we set out to improve matters.

Journal entry: Pam and I have started compiling a whole notebook on subject of "Depression," using every article we have had printed in Watchtower and Awake. We have close to 30 articles in the notebook already (still looking), and have cross-referenced material on such subjects as: loneliness, depression, alcoholism, marriage problems, incest, toxic waste and effects on body, mental illness, single parents coping, teenager and parent problems, violent behavior, stress, how to speak consolingly, how to show love, forgiveness and making amends, how to get help for ailments, how others can help, etc. etc. Hopefully we'll learn the proper ways to handle, as well as have on hand to discuss with people to help them cope better during desperate times.

We've tried to keep the kids exposed to a variety of learning experiences. Got the book *How it Feels when a Parent Dies* by Jill Krementz and passed it around. *One Child* by Torey Hayden, insightful! Stories of struggles and triumphs are good for these kids. Pull occasional stories from Readers Digest. [Shy-but-Promising] loved reading the book *The Education of Little Tree.* Went and bought her own book. (End of entry).

But the very act of exposing the children to information and options — and those parents who were likewise interested; of teaching them how to discover such things on their own, appeared as if it riled those in authority even more. It was all so confusing ...

Journal entry: Pam and I having been talking and are concerned about why so many feel the need to spill their guts to us. Think maybe we have done something to cause this. They feel safe, but why? Also why do we allow them to spill guts? Nobody would consider going to a shrink. Should we encourage them to talk out feelings? What did everybody do before we moved here? Was nobody abused before we moved here? Of course not. Most people live life in a coma. Move forward slowly, but never really accomplish what they could have. We think we remind them of choices, a life worth fighting for. But then they are unable to achieve it because they have too much excess emotional baggage. Which is fine if they are going to stay in their coma, but if they want to go places and accomplish things with a clean conscience, it seems to bog them down. They are defeated inside and nothing they do and no amount of good they accomplish is enough. They feel like they are living a lie and that if people only knew what they really were or what they had really done, nobody would respect them or like them. The only thing we have discovered that works to break that mindset is to encourage them to ... Throw off every emotional weight possible. Understand as many of the reasons why it happened, stop the fear, the panics, and then put it behind them peacefully. So far so good, but it is a roller coaster ride ...

— — —

And speaking of my own perceptions, these were but a few I had attached myself to:

"A (good) name is better than good oil, and the day of death than the day of one's being born," I read, slipping into the scripture like a favorite Sunday-go-to-meeting dress.

"As apples of gold in silver carvings is a word spoken at the right time for it," I read, storing the scripture in my heart.

"Love never fails. But whether there are [gifts of] prophesying, they will be done away with; whether there are tongues, they will cease; whether there is knowledge, it will be done away with. For we have partial knowledge and we prophesy partially; but when that which is complete arrives, that which is partial will be done away with ... Now, however, there remain faith, hope, love, these three; but the greatest of these is love," I read, caressing the Bible against my chest and closing my eyes.

And this verse that inspired me to expand my perception of my surroundings:

"For mere oppression may make a wise one act crazy ..." I read, letting the scripture steep like tea in my belly.

Me, adding this prayer to my list of "IOUs":

"Pleaseeee God," I prayed. *"Phil has taken such good care of me during my illness ... pleaseeeee let me live long enough to make it up to him."*

For seven years we traipsed through the hearts and minds of people in Mississippi. And I'd be lying to you if I didn't mention it was, on many occasions, a terrifying experiment. That Phil and I pined over scriptures for direction; that we prayed incessantly. That we even took courage in the sentimental poems of greeting cards and the quotable quotes of accomplished humans seeking answers in them.

"Give sincere compliments freely, more people have died from broken hearts than swelled heads," Read the "Thought for the Day" on the breakfast menu of the local Holliday Inn we frequented for meals.

And when that didn't satisfy us ... we turned up at Headquarters seeking answers. There, in New York, on a sight-seeing tour having planned the trip with a local family to expose them to the world, to expand their horizons; them, on a tour of the impressive block of buildings in

Manhattan comprising the organization's Headquarters. But things didn't go as expected as is evident in this journal entry:

"Then it was time to deal with the other meeting [in New York] that we had asked [name omitted] to arrange with a mature brother just to get feedback. But that went bad. The brother decided at the last minute, that maybe the topic was bigger than he was able to lend a listening ear, so he told [name omitted] the name of another brother that we were supposed to ask for ... we waited in lobby for a while. Then two brothers finally came out and led us to a conference room. We weren't expecting two brothers. We sat at a long table staring at each other. We were a little surprised when they introduced themselves as being from the Service Department, which handles all [judicial] committee matters and complaints and problems all over the United States. It was a little more formal meeting than we had expected. They asked what the problem was, and I said there wasn't a particular problem, but that we just needed guidance. We didn't know if everybody all over the United States was having to deal with the kinds of issues we were running into, and we were just looking for feedback because we were getting tired and need direction and support. But something happened and we are not sure what, because after they listened for awhile they proceeded to read a few scriptures about trials and suffering and the role of the elders in dealing with certain matters. Then they mentioned something about the importance of not 'pushing ahead' or something. They shook our hands and that was it. Over in about fifteen or twenty minutes. Pam and I were not sure what their ultimate message had been. We hadn't received any specific feedback regarding the subject of abuse, or any feedback regarding the cases we had mentioned. It was avoided. The heavy load we were dealing with was still with us. We got the impression from these two brothers that we weren't supposed to worry about it. But you tell that to [kids back home] and all the people who keep asking us for help. You couldn't just turn them away, ignore them, could you? It was strange. It was like they were simply being polite and doing their duty but they hadn't heard a word we said. These men didn't know us from Adam, and for all we knew they probably got a lot of crack pots in there all the time with this problem or that so I guess the fact that they even came out and spoke to us was something. But it wasn't enough. We didn't know what to do from there. We were as lost as we were before we came and more confused for sure. Oh well, we'll figure something out."

But we didn't know what, exactly ...

"Dear Mom," the letter from Phil began. *"It's amazing how in some respects we never grow up. In 10 years of ministry work I have seen and*

dealt with a little bit of everything. Pam and I just counted up the other night that in the past year alone we have dealt with some 26 individuals who have been victims of incest, or sodomy or rape, suicide and murder. We have done extensive marriage counseling and many other things that at this moment I cannot even remember. We have cried with these people. Their pain is our pain. At the same time, we have learned to deal with their situations and not let them get us excessively downhearted. Here, we are adults, these people trust us for help with their problems. Indeed they trust us with their lives. Yet when Pop called Saturday night I was instantly a little boy ... He said you were back in the hospital and it did not look good ..."

Even after Phil's mother pulled through her ordeal, we weren't sure how to proceed ...

"I asked Phil if you guys could do something with me on Saturday. Nothing for sure was planned, then Thursday evening [you, Pam] called and said that [you were] working and that did me in," wrote a young adult we had spent considerable time with. *"There's been so much trapped inside of me for so long that one more thing broke the seams. I'm sorry that you are the ones catching it all. All I could think of doing for the past few weeks was to spend some time with you and talk and hear that I'm still special and that you do care. (I hope after this it's still true) I just need to hear that as well as to just talk. This letter does not make everything all right but it does help some. The shape I'm in, I guess a letter is better, since I can't hardly talk without crying. I could sure use one of Phil's prayers right now, but that would be impossible considering it's after 1:00 a.m. ... "*

At some point our brains began to overflow with the memories, the experiences ... all individual yet all interconnected:

That special day at Wall Doxey State Park, when under rare circumstances, we saw two snakes mating; how we'd been ecstatic to tell The Asphalt Man (among others) and he'd seemed slightly perturbed. Like that kind of experience was reserved for locals, or, those who had certainly lived a lot longer than we had ...

That time Phil and I were asked by a couple to more or less mediate their serious marriage problems. But they were taking Bible lessons from [Slim]; him, studying a book on Revelation with them, as if that outranked all other matters. *'Hope [Slim] doesn't find out,'* I had anxiously told Phil. *'Now to figure out what to do about [that elder's wife] who has confided to us a dark secret'* ... ay-aye-aye.

All those memories, those experiences ... connecting up inside our heads:

Even the evening we photographed Charlie Daniels at the Peabody Hotel in Memphis standing next to a large portrait that an artist had painted of him.

And that day we saw the injured horse. That horse, with the dangling front leg, broken at the knee, *'it'd just snapped,'* the woman's husband had said. Gangrene setting in; him, not having the stomach to put it down — because he was so fond of it, and no money to fix it. Then us returning a week later for her Bible lesson to see the four-legged horse was now three-and-a-half legged: *"What happened to your husband's horse?"* We had asked the wife and she had said *"The pig ate it."* The pig ate it right off the horse. But the horse sort of seemed okay???!!!

And that year or so we'd studied with that student at Ole Miss, that student teacher, on the verge of his PhD in wave motion theory, on the verge, on the verge, on the verge ... for how long now? ... appearing to be strung along by his professors; they, inspired by what they had suffered for their credentials, what he must now suffer for his credentials, as a part of some kind of pious, time-gobbling ritual, which did not seem so different from our own experiences. That walking cup of coffee and a cigarette that emerged from his bedroom, during our visits, shroud in a brown robe resembling a monk and we'd engaged in endless philosophical rationalizations on everything from heaven to damnation.

Along with that interview of ours on stage at the convention. How the Circuit Overseer had asked us about the couple we'd called on for two years; the couple who had just gotten baptized to everyone's delight. Because we'd been 'consistent and never given up hope' the Circuit Overseer had pointed out. The couple having just graduated Ole Miss, and were preparing to move to Louisiana.

And oh, that *other* couple ... the one's getting a divorce. What was it that I'd said? What had I asked him, precisely, sitting in their living room that day (with Phil) during their Bible lesson? What was it ... was it this? *'Well, if you had a choice, would you choose your wife or your career?'* Meant to be a simple illustration. After all, they were college students. And I had simply asked the man: *'If you had a choice, would you choose your wife or your career?'* Not expecting ... not expecting him to hesitate. Me, not prepared for his answer, his choice. Nor, was his wife. And although she later thanked me for exposing his intentions, I did not feel so good.

All those people; all those memories and experiences forming into ... what?

"It takes a great amount of courage and help from God to even attempt to write this letter to you," the adolescent wrote. *"The only way I know how to start is to start from the beginning up to now. When I was just a little girl, 5 or so, I had this cousin, 6 or 7 years older than me. He took me out to my grandfather's pasture and we began to play and wrestle ..."*

And so it was that I snapped one summer evening, at a Bible meeting, cornering Slim in the back of the hall.

"Can't you SEE that although your talk was very nice tonight, it only skimmed the surface of the needs of the people in your audience?" I said, having grown too weary of his superficial presentations that wrapped up everyone's woes in the same neat little bow.

"These people are suffering in ways you may not imagine ..." I preceded cautiously, but obsessively, *"... and yet you are encouraging them to push harder and harder to do only one thing ... go out and preach! But there is so much more to it than that ... we are losing the children to morality and apathy ..."* at which point I began outlining some of the sordid details, also referencing the Bible student that was gutted by a guy with a knife in front of his family, and another guy who was shot five times by his mistress ...

"There's a lot of pain here and it needs addressing," I pressed on, abandoning all my fear, for at least a minute: *"People need patience and direction to rise above these obstacles. Kindness and compassion — there isn't enough time for it. They haven't a clue how to manage their own families ..."* I said quickly, speaking of no one in particular and everyone in general. *"They need to learn how to apply the full range of ..."* I babbled on about scriptural principals. *"I mean, just this week alone we have dealt with three cases of ..."*

Suddenly, as if running from the devil himself, Slim wheeled around without saying one word to me, walked briskly past a group of children giggling among themselves, and stormed out the door. He marched swiftly towards his car, which had already accumulated several riders going his way home and stuffed his long figure into the small front seat of his compact station wagon.

Like a fool I scurried after him muttering something like *'You can't run from it! And it's rude that you left me!'*

As I began to gather my wits, I looked around noticing that a few people had stopped to stare. Phil, among them, on his way out the door; confusion at first registering on his face, then seeing Slim's vehicle scratch the gravel on take off — recognition. Recognition that I had actually followed through, despite him voicing his objections; I'd followed through on my plan to wake

Slim up, to engage him, to get his assistance, to get a little help with the children AND ... the adults.

— — —

It was then Phil and I could feel it ... growing ... a foreign substance under the mantle, irritating the skin, something solid forming in soft tissue: a pearl.

— — —

Out of the blue, Phil motioned me to walk slowly toward the door, his brow pinched in fear. I watched him unwind the lock and raise his hands in the air like a criminal.

Positioned behind him I could see policemen ducked behind parked cars, guns and rifles aimed directly at us. The street in front of the bank had been blocked off and red lights mounted to patrol cars were flashing silently.

Police would discover, after our shakedown that Sunday afternoon, that the high pitch of our carpet-cleaning machine had triggered the bank's silent alarm system and we were released in good standing.

We were sure glad we were selling off the remnants of our cleaning business in our transition to photography, we decided right then.

But the incident was troubling. Was it a signal from the great beyond — a portent of things to come? Something we could not imagine?

chapter 11: Soiled

We turned onto Central Expressway in our Olds Cutlass, an oversized U-haul trailer swaying behind us. Dolly and her pup shifted restlessly in the back seat, panting and smudging the windows. Sheba the cat growled fitfully from her cave under the driver's seat.

The Dallas skyscrapers rising in our view seemed humongous, the busy interstate, complicated. We were about to embark on a technological odyssey the likes of which we had no frame of reference. But we didn't belong here. Faulkner's Oxford was our home — had been for seven difficult but precious years.

We had sold our prized darkroom equipment to pay for the move. All we had left of that life were boxes of books, personal letters, kitchen utensils, my art table, our cameras and a few odd pieces of furniture. Like the antique chair, covered in black and white Houndstooth that once graced the lobby of our seven-room photo studio on the town square. It was the same office space once occupied by William Faulkner's niece when she and her husband started their publishing company, Yoknapatawpha Press, named for a fictional county in Faulkner's novels.

"I hope you realize you're leaving behind something special," a businesswoman told us as we prepared to leave Mississippi that fall in 1984. She had a swanky interior design studio on the square and had once used our photo services. *"You'll never have another place like this — it suits you."*

Our business was taking off when she said those haunting words. We had photographed the families of local lawyers, bankers and physicians. We had completed an innovative tourist brochure, a hand drawn art piece for the chamber of commerce that was so well-received that framed limited editions of it had been presented in ceremonies to the Mayor, the Governor, and businessmen from Japan (and later, we would learn, Miss

America). Framed originals of our photo-illustrations of local landscapes and businessmen hung in local banks, City Hall and the University of Mississippi.

We had made the switch from impoverished janitors to industrious entrepreneurs. We had become part of the community. Only to be forced to leave it.

I clicked open the glove box and removed a small white box and cradled it in my lap. It wasn't the first time I'd opened it along the 540-mile route from Mississippi to Texas. It had brought me comfort every time I thought about what we had left behind — the spiritual calling that had been ours since our wedding day 11 years past.

The contents of the box were of great significance in validating our worth, but to an outside observer might have appeared trite, or worse — offensive.

The box was used, as if someone had decided on the gift last minute and scrounged up an old jewelry box from a drawer. A scrap of notepaper was taped to the lid with the handwritten words *"We will miss you"* in ballpoint pen. But there was no trinket inside it. Instead, I found another smaller box and another note, which read: *"Here is something to remember us by."* Inside that was a third box, with this teaser taped to the top of it: *"Remember all the times when we said we're like no one else ... well ..."*

When I opened that final box, I discovered an Oreo cookie. I smiled at the inside joke — black on the outside, white on the inside — given to us by a shrewd black teenager, at a time, in a place, when that meant she was experiencing personal growth rare to her contemporaries, most often available to whites. This teen had blossomed, along with her siblings, when Phil and I helped them peel back the layers of their mysterious anxieties like an onion to discover their worth. There was no stopping them afterwards as they pursued life's many opportunities. But the personal cost to us for assisting them and others like them with that transformation, we were about to discover, was grave ...

— — —

"Have you got your plane ticket?" I asked Phil, nervously.

"Yes." Was his response, his voice showing no sign of emotion.

We had just arrived in Dallas — had only been there a few weeks. Phil hired to work as an animation camera operator at a multi-media firm; his knowledge of photography providing the basis for his hire — that, and the fact that the owner was a member of our religion and liked to give ex pioneers a break.

It was still hard to comprehend why we were here in the big city of Dallas. It must be a necessary reprieve, we had decided. We would learn things that would benefit us before we once again resumed our work in the ministry. Just until we found a work-around concerning the negative report the elders in Oxford had sent to Headquarters.

I watched Phil pick up his Bible and a notebook and stuff them into his suitcase. Returning to Oxford had been his idea. The hire had happened quickly, and we had packed our bags and moved to Texas before we'd gotten the chance to defend our character to the elders in Oxford in formal proceedings. They had already publicly humiliated us and had no further interest in our case. But Phil wanted his named cleared so he could resume his eldership at a congregation in Dallas. And he believed it possible to do so, with some reservations. Things had not gone well in Oxford during our final days there. What assurance did we have that they would now?

"Say Hi to everyone for me ..."

— — —

Phil sat in a room surrounded by familiar faces. And as the proceedings got well underway, Phil couldn't help but notice that one among them spoke very little; that some spoke more than others and one spoke the most — the off-key tone of their accusations pounding and relentless:

'Brother Lawson, you have shown great disrespect to us by talking to Headquarters about these matters without our knowledge ...'

'What issues were so important to you,' grilled another '... that you had to tell them without first telling us?'

'How could you possibly NOT have known you would be speaking to the Service Committee? You know it is standard policy that Headquarters reports these matters back to the Traveling Overseer. What do you mean you hadn't intended for it to be a matter to report? Then, what were you thinking? Our new Traveling Overseer was confused about why he had not been contacted ... you have shown great disrespect for organizational procedure here ...'

'And what about sister [name omitted's] daughter? That was a serious offense but you set yourself up as judge of it ...'

'Victims? Abuse? I see. Who exactly are all these other victims, Brother Lawson? ... And you think you are doing the right thing by not revealing that information? ...'

On and on went the inquiry; including them asking Phil why he had allowed me, his wife, to address such matters as sex when approached by other adult women in the congregation; why I had taken it upon myself to crack open the Bible or a magazine to answer their questions.

'And that doesn't matter to you? The gravity of this behavior? Do you think that is HER place? Don't you feel that these women should have spoken with elders instead?'

'But would you let your wife do this again?'

'Do you really think that they should view your wife as an 'older woman' [in terms of the Bible's reference to wisdom] since she is so young? Does that even matter that she once studied the Bible with them?'

'Your wife has an independent spirit, Brother Lawson. As you know, ***Eve*** *had an independent spirit ...'*

'Excuse me, Brothers, but we need to move on ... Brother Lawson we feel you have been lying and have abused the platform ...'

'Well, lying primarily by the words of Brother [name omitted]. He says you promised him your car in repayment of a debt.'

'Yes, we know the debt has been paid as you claim ... what? Far over the amount due, if you say so, but ... what? ... No he does not have a complaint at this time. He ... no ... yes ... he seems satisfied with the arrangement, but did you not tell him that you would in fact *give* him your car if you could not repay him?'

'Well, I agree it doesn't seem logical that you would give away your only means of transportation ... okay, of far more value than three hundred dollars you owed, yes, yes ... but did you not offer it just the same? ... Oh, I see, you don't recall saying it at all because it isn't something you would logically do ... Are you saying Brother [name omitted] is a liar? ... So now, if you even mentioned it, it must have been in jest, as a joke ... Brothers?'

'It seems as though you squander your money ... you have two dogs and a cat, for one thing, and you eat out often for another ... Oh, so, living in an 8x35 foot trailer justifies that you do not squander? ... It does not ... Oh, working 12-to-16-hour days justifies that you are not squandering ... Oh, you eat out often because your wife is busy ... you can't expect her to cook all the time and work long hours, not realistic, I see ...'

'So, what you're telling us is ... you actually thought of selling your trailer home to pay off some of your debt and you were actually going to borrow Pam's parent's travel trailer to live in? ... Well ... Tell me, Brother Lawson, if you are really working that hard to stay here in Oxford, and you even considered moving into a smaller trailer than the one you have I ask you, is that sound of mind? Is that balanced? Do you feel you are presiding over your household in a fine manner? ... Um, Brothers?'

'Phil Lawson, we feel you have abused the platform by talking too much about ...'

'Overemphasizing ...'

'Thank you Brother [name omitted], by *overemphasizing* "love" always...'

'And what are these greeting cards with poems on them that you keep passing out; are you trying manipulate people's thoughts and emotions?'

'Would you care to explain, then? ...'

'And you think a few greeting cards will fix everything? You think talking about love will fix everything?'

'And you have *time* for all of this?'

'Brothers, let's not forget the main issue, Sister [name omitted's] daughter ...'

'Yes, of course. We believe you and your wife have set yourselves up as a judicial committee by going to her home and discussing this matter, privately ... No. This was a case of fornication ... It had to be dealt with ...'

'We do not know for sure if she wasn't a willing participant ...'

'Six years old is not the point ... in the back seat of a stopped car in the door-to-door ... doesn't matter, yes ... oh, and ... that he was 15 and has since moved away. *You* might call that a form of [alleged] rape ... but there are other things to consider. It had to be handled to keep the congregation clean ... Brothers?'

'That's exactly right ... you failed to report the matter to us, and [name omitted's] situation too, regarding her sons. The uh ... the problem they're having with self abuse [masturbation].'

'What do you mean you had not intended to keep this from us? What would you call it ... oh ... 'so many other things going on in your life' that you got sidetracked *for a few weeks* ... and now you openly confess your error and ask God's forgiveness. You're sorry that Sister [name omitted] needed our aid with this problem involving her sons ... and you delayed it? That's a nice confession, Brother Lawson, but how can you expect us to believe you — considering everything else ... Well, everything else we have been discussing ...'

'Phil Lawson, do you discourage pioneering?'

'Oh, so because you pioneered for ten years that's supposed to prove that you cannot veer off the path? Deviate? We're only as good as our conduct and actions today, Brother Lawson. We cannot trust ourselves ... we are imperfect ... like the Bible says ... I'll show you ... oh, you already know that scripture, then you know that you can deviate, is that correct?'

'Do you discourage people from pioneering then?'

'That is not what Sister [name omitted] says ...'

'No, that's right, she says that you told her to 'take it easy' ... those can be devious words ... none of us can 'take it easy' in these perilous times. We must keep up our guard, be on the watch, stay busy in the preaching work ... Than what did you mean by 'take it easy'?'

'Of course she has a new baby ... yes. When you said 'take it easy' that was nearly a year ago ... I see ...'

'Excuse me, Brother Lawson, but do you think that just because you studied with her that you have the right to ...'

'*Did you* discourage her from pioneering?'

'Once again, you have no recollection of that type of conversation. Doesn't that seem a little unusual, Brother Lawson ... doesn't it seem odd that these other people are saying ... Yes, she [name omitted] had a serious operation ... life threatening, yes, just before her pregnancy, yes ... what does that have to do with the issue ...'

'Oh, now you are a health expert and you can caution her on how to take care of ...'

'So you're saying you were simply trying to get her to take time for herself and her children? ... But about her pioneering ...'

'Wait, are you trying to tie her daughter's (illegitimate) pregnancy to not spending enough time with her? Yes, we know she's only fourteen ... well ... well some people Brother Lawson, have to answer for their own conduct ... wait, because Sister [name omitted] was pioneering fulltime, you are saying that if she would have spent more personal time with her daughter ... Brothers?'

'Brother Lawson, do you have any apostate material in your home? Yes. No, I am not kidding. I mean do you have any apostate (reading) materials? That's right. Are you sure? Then, about the ...'

'And you would continue to allow your wife to answer questions or even listen to discussions about sexual matters with other sisters, then?'

'You still feel that she is not stepping out of bounds? Dealing with things that only elders are qualified to do ... you're sure ...'

'Just verifying, Brother Lawson ... Brothers?'

'We feel that you are not qualified to be an elder, Brother Lawson.'

'Why? Because ... that's right ... and you are not 'sound-in-mind.' And ... yes, sound-in-mind. You do not 'preside over your household in a fine manner' ... with regards to ... yes, we have ... we have told you ... and there is more. You are not 'free from accusation.' Accusation, that's correct ... well, we have provided you with plenty of proof.'

'You are not loyal, either, Brother Lawson.'

'You took it upon yourself to handle ... it doesn't matter, you did not confide in us ... You have lied and been deceitful ... what do you mean? I ***have*** *given you proof! Not any longer.* ***I will not allow you to drag MY heavenly father's name through the dirt any longer!'***

'We must protect the congregation from wickedness, from you and your wife.'

'It's a shame. You have a strong knowledge of the Bible and its applications — better than just about anybody I know — you could have made a very good Traveling Overseer. We had hoped that you would have seen the error of your ways, but the evidence at hand shows you are not even qualified to be a shepherd of the flock ...'

'We have strong suspicions and clear indications that you should be *put out* of the congregation of God, but ...'

'Oh, yes ... that's right, we have just begun to show you evidence. But for now, at least, you are no longer an elder.'

'We will keep digging until we find more, you can be *assured* of that ...'

'We'll get back with you, Phil ... any other comments, Brothers?'

— — —

(Yikes. That didn't go well.)

— — —

Nearly comatose, I stared at the image of two cockroaches mating — at a strip of freshly processed Ektachrome film stretched across a light box, scanning for scratches and dust spots with a magnifying loupe. An invoice sat nearby with the name of an insecticide company typed across it. Beside it, sat a stack of plastic slide mounts; tacked above me, a sign that read "Quality Control." My hands were dressed in white cotton gloves; my chair boxed in by four sterile walls and I frequently dabbed at salty tears stinging my eyes with my little pinky.

"Checking for vital signs here," Said a voice behind me, as I felt a tap on my shoulder, *"You're the oldest-acting young person I've ever met. I think we need to hook you up to life support."*

It was the mid-1980s. I was 29. And I'd just been hired at the same Dallas firm where Phil now worked.

"I used to know some kids like that," I thought, but didn't say it. Me, having switched places with the children we had once strived to liven up — old faces on a young person's body robbed of confidence who rarely laughed, their trust teetering on the brink ...

I was in the ICU of spirituality, my innocence vanquished. Standing in for it was oppressive guilt.

"It's my entire fault," I told Phil when he'd returned home from the Oxford interrogation. All the beauty that was Oxford, the savage, incomparable beauty of it, had been painted ugly. *"Maybe I AM EVE."* I said attempting to overlay my outspokenness with her independence, even though our stories didn't match. *"If only I'd kept my mouth shut ... I always wanted to be like Deborah, the prophetess, or Queen Esther ..."*

"It doesn't matter," Phil said, facing me. *"It was a witch hunt."*

"But we've been stripped of our good name! Our future, serving this organization with the talents we've been given. We've lost everything that matters to us because of slanderous hearsay and false accusations! Because we were simply overzealous?! A little too energetic, maybe?! And we overemphasized love?!" I was shaken to the point of distraction, but still able to quote scripture like a sage: *"The apostle Paul said, 'if I loved you the more abundantly, am I to be loved the less? I did not burden you down, nevertheless, you say I was crafty and I caught you by trickery ...' These elders can insinuate – SIMPLY INSINUATE –that we are wicked and it stands? It clears? The Bible adheres to the premise of innocent until proven guilty! So do the courts! Criminals are given better protection than we were. What would you call THIS? Excuse me,"* I grabbed Phil's shoulder and shook it, *"What would you call THIS?!"*

He was listless.

"*What you're telling me is ...*" I paused, gathering nerve to finish the sentence, "*... we were not worth fighting for.*"

My head fell forward, as if I were praying. And my chest began to ache with a pain I could not describe as that reality penetrated me, as silence enveloped me.

Until I began to speak in short outbursts clinging to my reason, otherwise I would have collapsed: *"But how?"*

"Majority rules," Phil said in his sternest voice.

"*But why?*"

"To keep the peace."

Silence lingered again, as we both processed what he said. Until I whispered:

"What peace?"

— — —

Slowly, my sense of humor returned. I found it in the comic strips I collected from the Sunday newspaper and, in time, in the company of new friends and co-workers.

"It's true, Hobbes, ignorance IS bliss!" said Calvin, in one such *Calvin and Hobbs* strip, **"Once you know things, you start seeing problems everywhere ... and once you see problems, you feel like you ought to try and fix them ... and fixing problems always seems to require personal change ... and change means doing things that aren't fun. I say phooey to that! But if you're willfully stupid, you don't know any better, so you can keep doing whatever you like! The secret to happiness is short-term, stupid self-interest!"**

"We're heading for that cliff!" Hobbs hollered. **"I don't want to know about it."** Calvin replied ...

Despite our initial resistance, it couldn't have been a more perfect time for us to be in Dallas. To land the jobs we did, as far as preparing for our future — the future that has arrived — that is now.

It was 1984, and that very year the Macintosh personal computer was released along with the IBM PC/AT, making personal computers powerful and easy to use. Those PCs offered functions in a useable format that affected the production services of many companies; simplifying tasks that made possible, virtually overnight, for one person to do the work of several people.

We were in the midst of what Phil would year's later dub the "Invisible Revolution." And it was unstoppable.

"Every advance in human history, every technological advance had always broken complex problems into smaller and smaller parts, requiring highly specialized workers that did one thing well," Phil now often says, explaining that transformational period in the mid-1980s. *"But all of a sudden, a 21-year-old girl with a high school education from a small Midwestern town who can type fast, who is a fast learner, who is not set in her ways, who is open to new experiences, can sit in front of one single computer and do the work of what, at that moment at least, had once required four highly trained professionals — who each took years to learn each of their professions — typesetting, graphics, lithographers, animators ... What just happened??"*

What just happened, indeed!

Phil and I had been holed up for more than a decade in the slow-moving, disadvantaged Southern United States. We'd stifled our exuberance, in our final days in Oxford and over analyzed every thing we said and did — as if training ourselves to be lawyers to dodge the bullets of our adversaries. Until they shot us down, like a dog that hadn't done its duties. Only thing is, we hadn't exactly died.

After that, wounded but breathing, we found ourselves navigating a starship — going from zero to warp speed in four seconds ... er ... four years.

Not one to sit idly by, Phil quickly worked his way from the production department to a position of leadership at the Multi-media Firm — leaping from animation camera operator to salesman, sales manager to general manager, vice president and then president, growing the company in 48 months from a handful of people to nearly 40 employees, expanding the facility to 8,000 square feet.

The building was in a constant state of remodel, which was maddening. Rooms that once housed specialists were overtaken by rows of computers, Phil establishing the company as a beta test center for new technology applications. He knew it was over for the typesetters and camera operators that had spent years learning their high-paying crafts when a Texas Instruments client asked Phil for a "computer generated slide." It didn't matter that the text and graphics were inferior to the high quality slides the firm was known to produce. That client wanted slides made from a computer — period. And they wanted to pay less for them. Even though the technology necessary to create those computer slides back then cost upwards of $100,000, including maintenance fees, to accomplish what folks can do today with a few hundred dollars of software on their home computer.

Backing up a minute, let me explain: In his initial job, Phil sat in a darkened room, huddled over a large animation camera creating elaborately designed slides with multiple exposures for high-end corporate presentations. This was back in the day when those kinds of shows could involve a bank of 20 to 40 slide projectors, creating a 'moving film' experience for viewers, costing thousands or tens of thousands of dollars to produce. That's because our clients, who came to include EDS, American Airlines, Texas Instruments and a number of high profile advertising agencies — were often pitching their company or products to secure their own lucrative contracts and dazzle trumped expense.

But Phil couldn't get ahead working in the dark. So he made the move for sales. Being forced to start from scratch with no client base, dialing for dollars from the yellow pages — the sales manager laying claim to the profits from all preexisting customers. That didn't stop Phil, though. Within a few short months he was matching the sales of the house. Then, after investigating what the industry standard was for monthly sales — believing it to be unimaginative — Phil set out to quadruple that number, and he more than succeeded. Not long after, Phil earned the position of sales manager and the guy who once had the job, departed the premises.

Increasing sales, however, meant overworking the production department. So Phil standardized and streamlined the production processes and techniques, so other employees could at any moment step in and help complete projects if the primary point person was unavailable — even implementing timestamps and daily check offs so he knew instantly how far along each project was. Finally, toward the end of his leadership at the Multi-media Firm, Phil hired a former Xerox executive and then opened a satellite office in the prestigious Crystal Palace preparing to attract a new level of corporate clientele.

The 1.5 million square foot, $85 million Crystal Palace — a handsome glass and iron structure fashioned after the famous historic 19th Century European Exhibition by the same name — had just been built by a noted Dallas developer to serve the needs of information technology companies and offered a permanent trade show environment for information technology vendors. Opening a tiny satellite office there was a ballsy move on Phil's part.

All in all, slides our company produced for clients would eventually turn up in presentations given at the White House and before the King of Sweden. Businessmen from Australia would tour our facilities, having heard about our momentum, to fashion their own company after ours. We were all a buzz, causing graphics students' and artists' fresh out of respected universities to request internships at our firm.

In response to our continued growth, Phil designed a new automated Ciné film processing machine that could handle the workload of three shifts of people. And I migrated from the quality control department to the computer room finally becoming creative director over those three shifts, able to multitask in profound ways (that I can no longer imagine.)

I feel like I'm just ticking off a list of things from Phil's resume here, and a few of mine, which sounds self-serving. (But you do remember the first part of this journey — eh?)

Truth is the whole experience was outlandish. Some 75 employees coming and going throughout that four-year period trying to hang on, stay aboard, and keep up with the growth — many unable to, for various and as sundry reasons, including being fired.

One might wonder how that was even possible. Who in their right mind would have given Phil such an extraordinary opportunity?

And my answer would be: someone who presumably sensed — despite his fitful insecurities — that his industry was changing out from under him. Someone who knew despite his business degree — despite searching the thick business manual resting on his desk — that he didn't have all the answers. So why not give this live wire, willing to blaze a new trail, a little slack?

The owner who loved to play golf had only recently, prior to our arrival, ventured out on his own after a successful partnership at another company in the same industry had run its course. A few others from that company had even joined him in his endeavor, all of them armed with the experiences and history of an industry that had flourished during financially lucrative times.

But they weren't prepared for the oil crash of the mid-1980s. No one was. The crash sent Texas into *"a prolonged economic downturn that caused multiple business failures, high unemployment, and regional real estate crashes,"* to quote one report about it.

As that relates to our multi-media firm, 11 of our competitors went out of business. But we flourished.

The thing is, Phil and I had spent years surviving "prolonged economic downturn(s)" in other locales, and had developed a kind of sixth sense about how to spot them and navigate the pitfalls.

Mind you, it required that the employees (us included) endure those killer weekends, when it was necessary to work 36 hours straight during rush jobs, unwilling to risk turning them down lest we lose the client. But we more or less managed.

In the end, Phil had assembled an extraordinary ragtag team of employees that hardly fit the norm. One's he'd cherry picked for the gifts they possessed, whether they had been trained in that field or not.

There was the delivery boy, hired by The Golfer, that became the firm's unofficial technology expert under Phil's guidance, when Phil tapped into his self-taught skills for computer hardware and networks. A brilliant young man barely out of his teens, who possessed an annoying sense of humor that often rankled his coworkers to a state of desperation (— them often pleading Phil to fire him —) but who inspired from me unexpected admiration.

Other employees included a university educated artist with a keen eye for style. There was the clean-cut former police officer; the tattooed singer, and the 30-something-year-old executive from China who couldn't speak English. New to America, and finding it difficult to secure work, Phil had given him a chance by hiring him for the only position available — collating slides. Still, he was grateful, rising from his chair and standing at attention each time Phil, who was his "boss," walked through his work space.

The notes and letters had long since trickled in from Mississippi by then, about the controversy surrounding our departure:

"You can't even imagine how much I miss you ... I am learning so many things from watching the people here, day by day people are being torn apart ..." " ... The night you left, I cried that night and the next morning. The hug was a lifesaver. Have I been a good girl? Yeah over all ... One more thing before I say good-bye, thanks for trying to help. Believe it or not I really appreciate it." "Send some of the friends a post card or a telegram or something, they keep asking and I have run out of things to say ..." *"I'm very disappointed at all the negative talks and stuff that have been spread around about you in Oxford. You two and I didn't get to spend a lot of time together when you were here, but I know you better than that, I know that stuff isn't true ..."* "... The scripture at Proverbs 18:24 says, "There exists a friend sticking closer than a brother," this scripture really brings both of you to mind for the scriptural encouragement you gave me along with your sincere concern will always be remembered ..." ***"That special part on the meeting about you all, well, I could see right through it. They were blowing things all out of proportion, taking matters out of context. I'm sorry. Please never stop taking an interest in helping people ..."***

I didn't know what to say. If we were a bad influence, as had been the claim by those "in authority," then responding to the letters would be stringing those friends along. They were better off to forget about us and get on with their lives, we decided. If we weren't guilty as noted, rekindling the relationships, and enduring any discussions about what had happened to us, or what we were doing about it, was too painful.

"Make them go away." was my uncharacteristic reaction, when speaking to Phil about those letters. Though Phil did respond to a few:

"Pam found a little $2.50 gift for [name omitted] to thank her for her phone call," Phil wrote in one note to a friend. *"It was a dish of strawberries that would have matched her kitchen. But then Pam decided it would cause more harm than good ... she got depressed and put it back on the shelf. It hit me so hard that I broke down ..."*

In the beginning, Sundays were the worst. We could bury ourselves in work during the week, but not Sundays when we attended our Bible meetings and went door to door. On those days we had time to think. Or sleep, which Phil grew accustomed to late in the afternoons, too depressed to function — even considering with some intensity the idea of disappearing — of just walking out the door and not coming back — but he couldn't find the heart to leave me.

"We're a team," was his final decision. *"What could I solve myself that we can't solve together?"*

What he did do was buy me an extraordinary Lladró figurine, a women 28 inches tall — with a paint palette resting in her hand; her hair swept back as if blowing in the wind — to honor my inner creativity. And make up in some small way, as he conveyed it in a sentimental letter to me, for all that we'd given up in our Oxford days, including our high school class rings that we sold for gold when we needed fast cash.

But our relationship appeared to have faired better than many others in Dallas who'd had plenty of resources and opportunities. And that was quite curious to us. Couple's we'd known when we first lived in Texas before we ever moved to Thomasville — most all divorced; two couples actually swapping partners.

'Went to a party recently,' The Golfer told us not long after our arrival in Dallas. *'Out of thirteen couples married near or around the same time we were, my wife and I were the only ones left married to the original spouse. We've known these people since college...'*

As I said ... how curious.

Another fascination of ours was the number of exotic automobiles on the roads we traveled.

"What have you got so far?" Phil asked me one afternoon after he had quite deliberately decided to keep track of them driving along the North Dallas Tollway. Tired of complaints in the media about how hard people had it in Dallas, due to the oil crisis, Phil had decided to send a letter to the editor of "D" Magazine and include our list. *"A city that's literally hosting a "Finer Things of Life Convention" doesn't have a clue what hard times look like,"* he'd mutter under his breath.

"50 Cadillacs, 29 Mercedes, 12 BMW's, 18 Volvos, eight Lincoln Continentals ..." I said glancing at the growing list of expensive cars I was jotting down on a piece of paper. *"... four Porsches, two Jaguars, and eight 'other' luxury cars — a Corvette, Saab, Lotus, Audi ..."*

"There goes another Lincoln ..." Phil blurted out.

"Look, look! At that red convertible Porsche! ... Ahhhh, you missed it ..."

"What?"

"The license plate said, 'Greed.'"

I'd almost forgotten the way I'd behaved when we bought our own luxury car after our arrival here. It was an Oldsmobile 98, about five years old — the size of a small boat, immaculate inside and out, custom through-and-through and dirt cheap because it was a gas guzzler, making it the most cost effective choice at the time. But I had bolted from the salesman's office in the midst of buying it, in a full blown panic attack, perceiving him to be a manipulate thief; and fearful that I would set a bad example by driving such a luxurious vehicle.

Probably because I was so used to arguing with my Dad about such matters in the cryptic vocabulary we used between us to protect ourselves from worldly pursuits.

"But God chose the foolish things of the world to shame the wise; God chose the weak things of the world to shame the strong," Dad would quote scripture at me, him being too paranoid to replace his worn out living room furniture.

"The sons of this system of things are wiser in a practical way toward their own generation than the sons of the light are." I shot back, throwing in an extra verse for good measure: *"If an iron tool has become blunt and someone has not whetted its edge, then he will exert his own vital energies. So the using of wisdom to success means advantage!"* By that point in our conversations, I was always getting on his nerves.

At any rate, it was time to get me some culture. To get us some culture. And we did, frequenting museums, art galleries, art shows and concerts. Going to art house movies followed by coffee and dessert at a quaint little place where the owner sang opera to his customers. We took dance lessons and drawing classes and visited the very best book stores, where I once picked up an unusual choice from the bargain bin that dumbfounded Phil — a biography of Henry Ford.

We joined a gym and played racquetball. We took a joy ride in a glider along the countryside above Dallas. We bought a sophisticated stereo system and a digital piano with synthesizer. Three-and-a-half years into my job at the Multi-media Firm I quit — Phil's salary ample for our needs — to further explore my creativity. I began taking piano and voice lessons and I even took sculpting classes. Managing to create a bust of Phil that so pleased my professional tutor — a man who created life-sized statues for the wealthy who lived in Highland Park — that he insisted I have it bronzed.

"Another 500 hundred heads and you'll be a professional," he also told me, reminding me of just how much work it takes to become any expert at anything.

Improving our living quarters was among our pursuits, upgrading from a small duplex in an older section of town to a substantial home in North

Dallas with a teardrop pool. It was located near a grocery store that had a waterfall in the entryway and a pianist who entertained shoppers seated at a Baby Grand.

Moving there involved a brainy plan that benefited both the owner of the home, whom we knew, and ourselves. The family had moved away, the real estate market was dead and there were issues over insurance if it sat empty and happened to be vandalized. We maintained the inside and outside of the home and she maintained the payments, leaving us to cover the utilities, all of which allowed us to quickly get ahead financially. In less than a year the house had sold and we'd found a handsome bank-owned, two-story condominium with a sunken living room, and marble baths at a ridiculously reduced rate, but we were careful to first sign a lease/purchase agreement before buying it. We'd also found a nearly new Volvo, bought for a song under unique circumstances, and Phil was on his third, or was it fourth, company car — also a Volvo.

Phil even reconnected with his grandfather, "Professor Vaughn Lawson," as his physics students used to address him before his retirement. And the professor had found good reason to be proud of him.

"My grandson's producing that show ..." He once told a bank officer in his hometown, a hundred miles west of Dallas, pointing to an advertisement in the lobby of his savings and loan that read *"Together, We Can Make It Happen."* The ad featured an upcoming event in which all branches in the southern region of that bank, including over a thousand employees, would be introduced to the new CEO of the struggling enterprise along with his plan to reorganize. *"My wife was just telling her friends at bridge the other day what a mighty fine boy he's turned out to be ..."* the professor said, as he later recapped it for us; then pushing his admiration to absurdity, he added: *"Look him up when you're in Dallas! His name's Phil Lawson. Tell him his grandfather sent you!"*

To immortalize that period in our lives (that had included buying white furnishings and barrister bookcases with leaded glass) I bought a postcard that featured this poem, titled: *The Yuppies Prayer*: *"Now I lay me down to sleep. I pray my Cuisinart to keep. I pray my stocks are on the rise, and that my analyst is wise. That all the wine I sip is white, and that my hot tub's watertight. That racquetball won't get too tough, that all my sushi's fresh enough. I pray my cordless phone still works, that my career won't loose its perks. My microwave won't radiate, my condo won't depreciate. I pray my health club doesn't close, and that my money market grows. If I go broke before I wake, I pray my Volvo they won't take."*

I bought the card because I didn't think we'd stay. Not permanently. Not hopefully. In all honesty, we believed the injustices we'd experienced would some how remedy themselves. That we'd get our old lives back. Only this time, we had some culture and were better people for it.

We worried that if we settled in — completely in, we'd get trapped in the assembly line of life. We'd lose our chance to do something profound. We wondered why others believed they were content there. Why reaching milestones in life had to be lived in slow motion? Why people believed they should be?

I felt we were onto something in Oxford.

I felt it after a catfish dinner one evening out with Phil and a male friend of ours, a short time before our departure. We'd walked to a nearby river in the fading light of dusk and a feeling of clarity came over me. We'd had some extraordinary breakthroughs in Oxford, and I couldn't help but think it was leading somewhere ... to something important. Just then I began to twirl and twirl along that road like a little girl, my arms reaching heavenward.

I presumed that feeling was related to our mission work. But four years later, nothing much had changed with Phil's status in Dallas. He had not regained his eldership.

The conclusions of the henchmen in Oxford, that cast doubt on our character, followed us in a letter they sent with our files to Dallas causing our new body of leaders to observe us cautiously and let time pass. Too much time ...

One day Phil's vision for the company skidded past The Golfer's. I heard his keys hit the table near the door of our condo too early one afternoon and it alarmed me.

"Just got fired," Phil said matter-of-factly, *"Well, more like: 'I'd like your resignation' to be exact."*

The pressure had been extraordinary, recently — Phil pressing on against the odds, learning as he went, dragging everyone with him. He'd even thrown up for two days after a stressful open house at the firm celebrating its most recent expansion.

Phil had been no match in sales, marketing or vision — The Golfer had told him upon his dismissal; later giving him a company car and several months' severance pay in compensation. But Phil was taking the company big when he wanted it to stay small.

"But I thought you were beneficial to ..."

"I'm not now. Neither is [name omitted] nor [name omitted]. They're gone too, he cleaned house, no advocates ... We're back to square one."

— — —

"I especially enjoyed that discourse you gave two Sundays ago," an acquaintance told Phil when she heard we were moving. *"What was the title, again?"*

"Acquiring a Heart of Wisdom," Phil had answered her, a hint of exasperation in his voice.

"Yesss, that's it. They'd have made you an elder here soon I bet! Take care of yourselves."

As we packed our belongings for California — the only stimulating place we could imagine — I poked through the box of comic strips I'd been collecting and pulled out one of them:

"The saga continues next 2000 miles." — Ziggy

chapter 12: Recoil

"Noooo honey, not that piece. The piece underneath, don't you see it there dearrr? Yessss, right there!" the swollen old woman said shoving her finger at the glass counter in the Furr's cafeteria.

"I've told my kids if I ever get that old just shoot me!" a man whispered standing behind her and in front of us in the serving line.

I paused to soak up his comment then resumed my conversation with Phil leaning closer to his ear so he could hear me above the restaurant chatter*: "It's just that all this is familiar to me now ..."*

"All this" being the life we had chosen in a retirement park in Yucaipa, California, at the robust age of 33. Why we had moved there in the first place, two doors down from a relative, in an affordable doublewide, occupied by gray-haired hunched people, reflected our state of mind.

For four action-packed years we had reveled in deadlines and breakthroughs at the Multi-media Firm. And I'd watched Phil's swift and stellar rise through the ranks of that company.

It was unthinkable that the talents he had acquired might be useless. But everybody else seemed to operate by an obligatory code, mechanistic in nature, which had nothing to do with best possible outcomes in the bigger scheme of things.

The more creative he became the less he fit in. And we had never much fit in to begin with.

For a moment afterwards Phil was "hot." Within hours of his firing, as word hit the streets, he was offered a new job with a competitor in Dallas. But Phil couldn't stomach recreating what he had already done, despite the possibility of a stable income.

We knew Phil's chances to capitalize on what he knew of that industry were brief, and his accomplishments easily forgotten. But it was necessary that he recover his dignity and establish his worth another way.

A quaint mountain village named Oak Glen, childhood home to actress Susan Anton, lined with apple ranches, gift shops and specialty restaurants, seven miles from Yucaipa, tugged at our hearts when we first arrived in California. But we had relied too many years on "practical" decision-making and could not justify our frivolous plan to move into a cottage we'd found for lease in the village.

Instead we bought a 21-year-old doublewide in an old folk's park with the Angelus Oaks mountain range visible from a back bedroom window. "God's waiting room" is what locals called that park and others like it in Yucaipa.

Recoiling from life, that's what that was. It appeared we lacked the tools to function well. We didn't "get it." Nothing made sense. The only thing we could do was establish what we *did* know; then figure out *who* we really were, deep down inside, and rebuild ourselves from there.

Taking what appeared to be a major step backward, Phil returned to working for himself, this time as a management consultant at a time in the late-1980s when most all independent management consultants were viewed as unemployed people marking time looking for a job.

And I, after being fired from a landscaping company where I'd worked nine months as a bookkeeper in a slummy section of San Bernardino, decided to make a go of it as an artist — specifically, a photo-artist, because that was the only form of personal expression I knew.

(Technically, I got fired, then rehired — the owner claiming he'd made a mistake — then, I quit!)

Just recalling that scary period makes me want to bite my nails to the quick — both of us working to establish our footing in scarcely lucrative fields; Phil, a business advisor whose earnings depended on his ability to sniff out cutting edge information; me, an artist whose earnings depended on my ability to convey a story through visuals.

But it was a guaranteed way to find out what we were made of ...

"Question: What's pink, white and red all over?"

"Answer: A baby sucking razor blades."

Okay, gross, stupid joke. But it came to me lying in bed one night as I stared at the walls — at the squiggles in the ash paneling. It came to me that when you're helpless and unaware you can cut yourself, you can bleed.

So we set out to change that.

Phil soaking up knowledge and patterns in the business world like a super absorbent shammy — perplexing the mailman who delivered close to 70 magazines a month to our doorstep. And me; exploring countless clever ways to present my artwork.

Any money we made went right back into improving ourselves, Phil spending significant sums each time he traveled out of town to speak at conventions, and me, on expanding my technique and compiling expensive portfolios. Even when we had no money to speak of we plowed ahead, once traveling five hours to Las Vegas by car with only the quarters we'd saved in a plastic bag so Phil could fulfill a speaking assignment at an international tradeshow he'd committed to months earlier.

Our vulnerabilities made us as sensitive and reactive to our environment as the creatures that roamed the Angelus Oaks forest. We lived and behaved in real-time shocked that others did not have to; barely able to stop and rest even after Phil collapsed in excruciating pain one night, naked and shaking on the bathroom floor, requiring an ambulance ride to the hospital.

This time it was not a kidney stone — he'd had five of those already. This time the cause of his pain was unidentifiable, appearing similar too but not exactly like acute appendicitis, due to its location. A worried doctor ordered immediate exploratory surgery and I called in family and friends to sit with me in the waiting room, the doctor having prepared us for worst case scenarios. It was then that Phil broke down and wept. Not because he was afraid to die; because his life felt unfinished. Felt as if he had something to do but hadn't identified it yet, let alone achieved it.

Upon opening Phil's abdomen the doctor and his team found it awash with poisons that had, after all, spilled from a ruptured appendix and after an extensive cleansing of his innards they sewed him back up and he recovered.

Early on, in the midst of recoiling from life we met some friends who were recoiling from their own painful religious experiences, too; a gifted movie poster artist and his wife who was pursuing her interests in psychology — in the works of David Keirsey, Marilyn Bates and Isabel Briggs Myers, along with her interest in Gestaltism. Not that we didn't already have friends, but we clicked with this pair like no others.

We were starved for intellectual conversation and we found it with The Artist and Her Gestalt. We began to explore once unimaginable topics together over dinner or during phone conversations or faxes — burning through reams of fax paper as Her Gestalt and Phil, in particular, exchanged passages from books they were reading.

In time, Phil and I began to see ourselves in context with our fellow humans — all of them, not just our tight knit religious order. We explored our natural skills and temperaments in ways that had never before occurred to us — Phil was a rare kind of introvert, a monastic/crusader type. And me? I had the personality of a journalist. Furthermore, we weren't a good match in the eyes of those experts — my type better hitched to a banker or accountant, and Phil, better matched to an 'in charge' woman — a field marshal or administrator who could 'marshal him towards his distant objectives or insert tradition into his life.'

And that was an odd discovery. We sensed through our own experiences that there was more to it than that, but how could be we possibly explain it? That we'd found, or at least sensed a kind of work-around approach to life's complexities, the details of which were still formulating in our heads.

Meanwhile, we enjoyed what we were discovering in the works of so-called experts.

"Welcome to the ever growing club of new upstarts in the prime of life," wrote Her Gestalt in a greeting card to us in those days. *"Who would have ever thought. I still chuckle when I think of Mr. INFP. No wonder you always had heart,"* she said, addressing Phil's intuitive/feeling personality traits that had been informally identified, along with mine, and hers, and The Artist's. *"No wonder we were all massacred! No wonder we all sing of life & love!"*

Somewhere about then, I began to curse for the first time in my life. Angrily, like a surly old sailor. As the scales fell from my eyes; as I began to process my world with an expanded awareness and realized despite what I knew, it wasn't nearly enough, I couldn't help but swear: "*What in fucking hell??*"

Back then, you see, I didn't know about neuroscience. I didn't understand what was going on inside my head. That the very act of expanding my awareness was taking my mind off autopilot. It was allowing for new combinations of thought, which differed from my childhood enculturation. It was changing the structure of my brain. I was moving away from rigidity and expanding my flexibility. I was linking the differentiated parts of me and integrating my behaviors.

Okay, what I just said is the sensible 'sounds good' version of what Phil and I were experiencing. Now, I'll get to the 'it doesn't feel good' version of what was going on. Something else we didn't know back then, something we felt but couldn't prove ...

Something Phil would read two decades later in a *Fast Company* magazine article titled: *Why Change Is So Hard: Self-Control is Exhaustible*. It highlighted a research project that exposed two test groups of students to two bowls of food. One bowl had freshly baked chocolate chip cookies in it, the other, radishes. Each group was asked to eat only that which was assigned to them, and then afterwards they were given a logic puzzle to solve, which was actually unsolvable, though the participants didn't know it.

Turns out the students who ate the chocolate chip cookies spent 19 minutes attempting to solve the puzzle before they gave up. But the students who had forced themselves to eat the radishes, and who had used additional restraint by not sneaking a cookie when the researchers left the room, gave up on the logic puzzle after only eight minutes.

Why? *"The answer may surprise you,"* the author of that article wrote. *"They ran out of self-control."*

The author then further stated:

"Psychologists have discovered that self-control is an exhaustible resource. And I don't mean self-control only in the sense of turning down cookies or alcohol, I mean a broader sense of self-supervision — any time you're paying close attention to your actions, like when you're having a tough conversation or trying to stay focused on a paper you're writing ...

"And here's why this matters for change," the *Fast Company* article continued: *"In almost all change situations, you're substituting new, unfamiliar behaviors for old, comfortable ones, and that burns self-control. Let's say I present a new morning routine to you that specifies how you'll shower and brush your teeth. You'll understand it and you might even agree with my process. But to pull it off, you'll have to supervise yourself very carefully. Every fiber of your being will want to go back to the old way of doing things. Inevitably, you'll slip ... This brings us back to the point I promised I'd make: That what looks like laziness is often exhaustion. Change wears people out — even well-intentioned people will simply run out of fuel."*

Of course, Phil and I didn't know about neuroscience back then, like I said. And we didn't have that *Fast Company* article to explain WHY THE HELL change was wearing us out.

(And DON'T make me get into to the scientific reasons for cursing ... like it being an instinctive response to something painful and unexpected, or in some cases, a result of damage to parts of the brain, producing a sort of automatic speech, which often consists of conversational placeholders and can include swear words! Grrrrr...)

I'm not saying we couldn't find our way. We did.

Phil was eventually hired to complete costly confidential studies for large corporations like Kodak and Fujifilm. He was hired to do consulting projects for corporations like Towers Perrin and Sears Mortgage. He spoke at countless conventions across the country and wrote 50 published columns and magazine articles for trade journals. He stayed at the Doral

Hotel on Park Avenue in New York City while securing a project spanning several months that required he direct the activities in the London, Brussels, Madrid and Paris offices of a visual communications company, to name but a few of the things Phil accomplished.

Having by then indoctrinated himself in the practices of his peers, driven to uphold profits and deadlines, there was little evidence of Phil's past life, but for the comment of one businessman who attended one of Phil's keynote addresses at the Del Coronado Hotel in San Diego: *"Great presentation, real motivational — you'd make a great preacher!"* that man had said, which made me smile when I heard it.

But our past was still there and it came calling ...

"I've called to tell you some good news," a familiar voice from Oxford spoke into the telephone.

"You're getting married." had been my casual response, which surprised Shy-but-Promising. But she was in her mid-20s by then and it wasn't a hard guess on my part.

"Bet you'll never guess WHO in a million years!"

"If I don't know him, you're right..."

"Oh, YOU know him!" she had said in a hyper voice that unsettled me. *"Think of someone totally off the wall, someone you would never imagine me with ... go on, I dare you..."*

I could only think of one person that fit that painful, appalling description and I knew it couldn't be Slim but I threw his name out there to get a laugh, to 'creep her out' a little. Only it didn't ...

"You guessed it!!" she gasped, especially proud of the answer. *"Are you surprised?"*

And just like that, like a creek spilling over a ledge, came my tears.

"Uh ... surprised ... yes ..." I spoke in spurts, covering my hand over the receiver so she wouldn't hear my sniffling. *"He's ... something like ... 27 years older ... than you ... isn't he?"*

Phil was by then standing beside me, eager at first to speak to the young lady who had long ago called him "dad." But as he began to piece together details of the conversation, watching me speak, then cover the receiver and snivel, he refused to take the phone when I thrust it at him, instead backing slowly away from it.

"Yeah, but it doesn't matter to me," Shy-but-Promising kept talking, oblivious to the drama playing out on the other end. *"He's got some gray hairs, but he stills hold his age good. And he's changed. Are you okay?"*

I couldn't honestly answer her. So I came back with a question in a hurry: *"HOW'S your mamma taking it?"*

"All right, ***now,"*** was her reply. *"But it took her awhile. Mama 'n him are about the same age you know. The single sisters 'round here are real disappointed, too,"* she said referring to the ladies around Slim's age in hers and adjacent congregations who'd had their sights set on him for years. *"He was one of the few available bachelors, especially with his credentials — pioneer, elder, you know,"* she paused to laugh softly. *"I think they're real shocked that he picked ME ... Even the circuit overseer and his wife was. They think we might qualify for circuit work like them since I'm pioneering now. We're so excited! I wouldn't have imagined it, but you have to understand* ***he's changed!"***

As she explained how Slim's interest in her came about rather sudden-like, my mind drifted back to the man who, along with his supporters had choreographed our termination. And the irony was obscene.

We, who had taken her to our hearts and tended to her emotional bruises; who had coaxed her out of her shell and encouraged her to speak her mind; we, who had coached her through the launch of her own teenage business and flamed her aspirations to pioneer. Now, of all the women Slim knew, Shy-but-Promising was the one he prized most.

"Oh, Pam, I am extremely happy. And that's all I know you have ever wanted for me — to be happy."

After that call, her words *"You have to understand, he's changed,"* hammered at Phil's temples to the point of distraction.

He may have changed but our situation hadn't, despite our years of "good behavior."

We had never been allowed to see the letter Slim and his cohorts had sent to Headquarters about us. The elders weren't required to reveal its contents. And neither was Headquarters, based on some privacy rule. Under those circumstances there was no way to defend ourselves. Or, have the issues surrounding that letter exhumed and reexamined. But whatever that letter said, its contents had a lethal affect on our advancement in the organization. This came to light when we inquired about moving to New York and serving at Headquarters, after the letter had been written. A kind gentleman living there checked on the status of our file there and sadly informed us, *'It will never happen. You will never be invited to work here.'*

Headquarters had turned our fate over to the locals. And they had leveled their judgments the day Phil returned to Oxford from Dallas to be sentenced and humiliated by them.

To reference an old television series, we'd been "branded."

The elder's conclusions that cast doubt on our character followed us like a shadow after that ... dutifully transferred from Dallas to Yucaipa, along with our personal records, when we moved again, making *"he's changed"* an especially bitter pill to swallow.

At some point we began to doubt our own motives and our own gifts ... but for a few curious reminders of who we were.

"Is this you Pam-a-la, you ol' dear sweet thang? And how is my dear ol' Phil-lup!?" This time the call from Oxford wasn't Shy-but-Promising. It was a woman we'd studied the Bible with, a dynamic specimen cut from special cloth.

"I have started my own business, Pamela. I went all out, you hear me!" she said, sounding quite pleased. *"I even have business cards that say, 'Stunningly sensational and luring fashions for the strictly full-figured woman. Stirred tapered and enhanced luxuriously to bring out the natural elegance and beauty for confidence in mind.'"*

"You fit all that on one business card?!" I gasped then laughed.

"I did and it looks all right," she defended. *"Did I tell you that one of my sisters lives in California and designs clothes for a living? That's right. She used to send me nice things all the time. Now I am doing my own — it's HIGH FASHION. They bring the material and I get $20.00 to design the dress. These women be looking scary around the house,"* she said about her friends, who had become clients. *"I be shamed to take some of these ladies where I go. They got to take care of they selves ain't no men want you hanging on their arm like some ol' hank, its a reflection of them, you hear me? So I sew these clothes that are lovely and luxuriant and they slip it on and these outfits actually speak, darling, they speak: 'Hello there how are you?' these garments talk when you walk. They be so appreciative. I told my husband that he is one of the privileged few."*

That's not the real reason High Fashion had called me, though. Nor the first thing she talked about. She had called with tragic news — a person we knew in common had been killed in a head-on collision — the cause a *"stupid thang"* — a car traveling the wrong way in her lane as she topped a hill. The crash killed everyone in both cars and High Fashion had rushed to see them.

"I knew all those people from around about; they had them in there laying on the floor all scretched out. Girl, I'm jest sick ..." she said describing the morbid scene before focusing again on the friend we knew in common. *"She was so rare, she come from a tight family all grew up in orphanages, they had weathered all these problems together, such a senseless wastes..."*

The ache of my past life in Oxford came back in a rush as she dished the blow-by-blows to me. And it was a relief when she changed the subject to boast about her business cards and how she'd reminded her husband he was 'among the privileged few' to have her.

"What'd he say?" I asked her grateful the mood had lightened.

"Honey he's like a dawg that's been tied up for forty years. I'm due a break, you hear me. I told that man I ain't no queen bee sittin up hea, he has nuclear warheads for sperm ..."

At which point High Fashion shared a few details about each one of her seven children from the oldest who was 17; about her only girl, who was growing up "pretty" and looked like her daddy's side of the family, to her latest baby that we'd never met. And his name took me by surprise.

"I had gotten to the point I didn't want to hold no babies — nobody else's babies, I didn't even want to look at them. I was through with babies. My baby was five years old, you hear me, then my ol' [husband] had to go and get that other baby made for me, and this is the worst child I ever had, ol' Phil-lup, I was going to call him PamPhilia, hay! But I didn't. That Phil-lup is a mess, you remember that wrestler on TV, Tojo Yamamojo?"

"Ah, not exactly ..."

"My Phil-lup look jest like him, jest as round with his big ol' fat head and he's just as greedy as a pig, he is the life of the party, he is bringing his mother shame, bringing her gray hair down, do you hear me, hay! But he's smarrrt, wooo's he smart. His ol' granddad would be proud. You tell that ol' Phil that he would be proud a how smart he is..."

What an honor. High Fashion had named her last child after Phil. But that wasn't all she told us during that phone call. She kept a photo of Phil and me under her mattress to remember us. One of several mattresses she had stacked high for a bed in her bedroom, the image of which had reminded us when we still lived there of the story of the Princess and the Pea.

"I shore do miss you two dear peoples. And I miss my studies. You were a ray of sunshine that shined sooo brightly in Oxford."

I might have disregarded her comment altogether — that we were once a ray of sunshine in anybody's life — but for the comment The Golfer made, too. Phil crossed paths with him at a business convention, well into our stay in Yucaipa.

The Golfer strolled right up to Phil without greeting him and said: *'We're doing everything you said we should,'* and then walked off. It was his way of acknowledging Phil's vision — which was very decent of him — of acknowledging the timely changes Phil had been implementing at the Multi-media Firm before he'd been fired.

The comment, though brief, provided great relief. Phil had read the pulse of that industry pretty well.

And there was one last validation. It proved certain sensitivities we had developed in Oxford still burned bright within us ...

"Do you always think to call the hospital when you don't find people home at night?" a man on the other end of the phone asked Phil on a typical Monday night.

We'd been waiting for his call — waiting for hours for him to call with his daughter's flight number. There was something wrong with her and he was desperate for help, planning to send her our way for a change of scenery. But we had worked with too many other troubled teens and knew the signs of a life unraveling.

"Not normally," had been Phil's answer. *"You must admit though, you lead a pretty stable life — all the years I've known you raising those kids of yours..."*

"Kind of radical for you isn't it?" The man had joked, which was his nature; before he broke down and cried.

But it wasn't just that, that the man led a predictable life. That a deviation in his schedule would cause an outsider to presume the worst. It'd been our discovery a few days prior that his pretty 16-year-old daughter had wanted to die — a friendly sweet girl that got straight "As" and was an honor student. Until something happened six months ago ... And now she had attempted suicide. And it wasn't the first time. Or the second ...

"She's alive but she's lost her will," the man's voice broke, again. *"Will she try it again next week, I don't know. She fights with the other kids, daily. We can't let her out of our sight; we're going to have to pull her from school for the remainder of the semester. They want to put her in an institution ... it might be the best thing. The resident doctor said she has very troubled ideas about her religion ... and her God."*

The sexual encounter had occurred six months ago, that's what we'd found out. The abuser was in his 40s. He was the step-father of her best friend, a man of trust, who held privileges in her congregation. When the incident came to light, he lost most of those privileges. But the 16-year-old girl, oddly enough, had been reprimanded too. And after that, as the body of elders rallied around the 40-year-old to restore his wounded spirit, they ignored the shattered girl. And, as she died inside, so too did her family.

It was then we knew for sure we weren't the "culprits" in Oxford. We knew we were onto something; that we'd been taken out because of it. We had learned to connect a few dots. And that made us a threat. We asked questions that others didn't seem to know how to ... or, didn't want asked. (Topics that would be addressed in an NBC Dateline expose on our religion about a dozen years later, that program focusing on alleged sexual abuses and cover ups by those in authority.)

Over the next several months — as we traveled out of state to visit the shattered child in the institution, after Phil wrote a lengthy poem for her that fessed up to the inadequacies of certain leaders — a poem she confessed she found comfort in daily — we knew this wasn't our fight. We possessed none of the bureaucratic credentials to lead the way in the struggles of survivors of abuse.

But *where* did we fit in? We had yet to figure that out.

A petite, well-mannered blonde had seen us through most all of our changes in Yucaipa. We had hired her to manage Phil's files soon after our arrival there; first for a few hours a week, then a few days a week; working from a desk on our leaky porch until we remodeled the space into something quite respectable. And that petite blonde began to cheer us on, reporting our progress to her husband at night over dinner.

"[My husband] and I were just discussing last night that even a year ago we would have never believed you and Phil would have come this far..." the petite blonde told me one afternoon. As she rifled through a pile of papers Phil had placed on her desk, she proceeded to boost my spirits by talking to my back as I, facing away from her, opened a letter from St. Martin's Press.

I'd already created one book cover for the New York publishing house, one about the New York Mets, and my contact there had told me she'd be sending along the storyboards for another cover right away, but they had never arrived and I was getting nervous.

"Dear Pamela," the letter began, *"Enclosed is a poor color Xerox of the above named cover. As you can see, we had to change your design around just a bit ..."*

My pulse began to race as I read on, barely able to hear what the petite blonde was saying behind me:

"Although you left enough bleed left and right, you did not allow for bleed top and bottom, something I did not catch in the rough stages ..." the letter from my contact at St. Martin's Press continued, and so did the petite blonde: *"When I started working here, you only had one, four-drawer filing cabinet in your closet, and when Phil told me that we would have all his files organized, welllll huh! ... Now you have six, four drawer filing cabinets and look at you two! And look at you and your artwork! When I started working here, typing on your dining room table, Phil showed me*

all the pictures on the wall that you had done and he said, 'My wife did this one, and my wife did that one ...'"

"... After three chromalins we could do nothing with the background color but produce several different shades of brown," I kept reading the letter. *"The back cover remained a shade of brown-orange and unfortunately we're not pleased with the results. As I'm sure you have guessed, this is one of the reasons why I have not been in touch regarding the Dodgers book ..."*

"... Your pictures were so warm, they told a story," the petite blonde kept talking. *"I was just telling [my husband] that the other night; I think you've really got something here. I don't know ... I mean Phil's company has come so far since my first day, it's really taken off! But it's you, Pam; it's you that I have this feeling about — are you listening to me?"*

I nodded, distractedly.

"I'm sorry to say this because you are more pleasant to deal with than many of my suppliers," the letter went on. *"But with such a small department and you being so far away I can't handle the extra faxes, phone calls and transmissions ..."*

"It's you that I am surprised at and I have this feeling ..." the petite blonde went on. *"[My husband] asked what I meant and I really can't explain it ... It's just that I think your work is really going to take off. Turner Broadcasting loved your work. St. Martin's Press thought your portfolio was great. It's just neat to think, you know, that I knew you when!"*

"I always like to try new people, but unfortunately this situation is just not going to work. Thank you, [contact name omitted], St. Martin's Press."

I folded the letter back up and slipped it into its envelop. I thanked the petite blonde for her generous compliment. Then keeping my back to her I soaked up my tears in a Kleenex.

Despite such setbacks, three-plus years into our stay in Yucaipa, I developed a new kind of boldness pitching a plan for us to move our home offices to a trendy historic building in Redlands, nine miles west, and Phil agreed.

Like Phil's business, the photo-illustration work was catching on, too, with a prestigious magazine spread and cover, poster art, and graphic design work already behind us.

And it was there, at the Redlands office, over the next year, that Phil secured contacts and projects that would have otherwise been impossible without that respectable workplace.

We had finally regained our confidence and were ready to take on even more opportunities.

When it was time to renew the annual lease at the trendy office we bowed out, sensing we were approaching a moment, sooner than later, when we must pick up roots again and move to Los Angeles some 70 miles away. We already traveled there frequently on business. Why not prepare to sell the doublewide and move there? So we squeezed ourselves back into the attached home office and put the place up for sale.

It all made sense but the thought of it was suddenly scary.

"Can't we stay put for a little while longer?" I moaned to Phil in the restaurant line. *"We're always taking the next big step before it's sure."*

"Because we have no choice," was Phil's reply, which irritated me.

It seemed we did have a choice — somehow, someway. I just couldn't explain the sense both he and I had that it was time to move on. I felt it necessary to over-analyze each and every detail for and against the idea, to punish the both of us.

"If I were to plot the wave lengths of your life — if there was such a thing — yours would look like this..." I said, thrusting my left index finger into the air near his eyebrows, then down to his chest, then up to his forehead, then down to his waist. *"And every once in a while, you arc and I never know where that will lead..."* I added, jerking my finger toward his right shoulder.

"That's not kind," Phil said cupping his hand to his heart like it hurt. *"Give me an example of harm I've done?"*

My jaw dropped as if I knew plenty. *"Just the other day when you were going to buy that expensive suit ..."* I said, struggling on a moment's notice to think of an example of his risk-taking.

"I didn't buy it!"

"But you were going to!" I said, suspiciously. *"You most surely would have, had I not objected!"*

"But you're the one who showed it to me!" Phil reminded me, amazed by my illustration.

"Because it was beautiful and the manager would have reduced the price," I defended.

*"Give me a **worthwhile** example of my erratic behavior."* Phil said, now irritated by my charade.

"Don't have one right off the top of my head ... wait ... okay, okay, then, the motorcycle!" I blurted out, glad that I could finally make my point.

"The motorcycle ..." Phil gasped in disbelief, *"... WAS OVER EIGHT YEARS AGO!"*

"But we didn't have the money; it put us in a real bind and YET you spent three hundred and ninety five dollars on it!"

"Three hundred," Phil challenged, *"And I turned around and sold it for $695!"*

"$650," I shot back, certain that I remembered a lower figure. *"You exaggerate the positive!"*

"You exaggerate the negative!"

"YOU blow things so far out of ..."

"YOU could fit your hope ..."

"...proportion that your reality no longer fits on this planet!"

"...on a postage stamp!"

Having selected our food and seated ourselves in the cafeteria, I shoved a forkful of mashed potatoes in my mouth as an old man shuffled by me pulling his oxygen tank strapped to a wheel cart.

"It's just that all of this is familiar to me now ..." I repeated one last time, feeling the energy drain right out of those words — losing my desire to remain in God's waiting room.

chapter 13: Arrive

"Pamela, this is Henny Backus," I heard the woman say on my message machine. *"The photo you like best I like least. If you use it, I'll kill you."*

Earlier that day I had dropped by Henny's home with proof sheets of our recent photo shoot. She had studied the selections and had called my Hollywood Hills home with her choices, but I was out.

Hers was the second shoot in a photo series I began compiling in 1993 entitled, "Young at Heart" featuring talented, people of age who *(vive ut vivas!)* lived life to its fullest. Henny, at 82, was stylish and witty. And she was willing to crank her arms overhead in a half-a-mile of laps daily, in her private Bellaire pool.

Henny's late husband, Jim Backus, *(RIP)* had been the voice of the comic Oscar-winning character, Mr. Magoo and had played the role of millionaire Thurston Howell III in the television series Gilligan's Island. But Henny was no slacker. In her youth, she was a Broadway showgirl, a Vogue Model and the first "Torch Lady" in the Columbia Pictures logo. She was also an author and sculptor. One of her statues, once unveiled on the Jack Parr show — to the delight of the audience — was of a single nude comprised of both Henny and Jim's body parts: her tits; his ass. It was such a hit that small bronze casts were made and fans bought replicas.

"There are two more out in the back yard," Henny continued in her voice message, elaborating on the pros and cons of one of them, which included a shadow on her face and bird crap on a nearby statue. But the photo taken inside by the bar was *"just marvelous,"* she gushed. The pose was *"so natural;" "a real charmer." "It looks as if I have just lifted my hand and waved to somebody!"* she said, before offering this curt critique:

"I look the heaviest in the one you like. You haven't got any goddamn taste that's your problem! Let me hear from you. I will have my phone off at quarter to seven, in an hour."(click)

No sooner had Henny hung up, when two minutes later she called back and left another message; then another; and another — each with specific details as they occurred to her, such as: *"I have just had a jury and they agree with me 100 percent ... The one you picked looks like I have one large boob..."* followed in the third message by: *"Of course I'm going to sign the model release, but I want your word that you'll use one of those two pictures..."* and finally, in her last message 54 minutes later: *"Why don't you give me a ring and pop by one day next week and have a glass of wine with me and we can talk about the pictures ... Give me a ring on Monday around lunchtime if you can. If not, Tuesday; or, Monday between 4 and 6. I'm turning the damn phone off now. Have a lovely weekend, dear."*

— — —

We *loved* Hollywood. It was the first time that we felt at home in our environment — like we could stretch and grow and hustle without being scrutinized. We were in the company of other Bizarros like us. And we sparked like fireworks when our stars crossed.

Hollywood was the antidote to a past life of simplicity and guilt — of control and certainty. As a cure it offered complexity; vulnerability and insecurity. That's because our arrival there was out of order in life. But, we had belatedly discovered, life was never meant to be lived orderly.

And that's how it came to be. In the midst of our travels in those days, as our business opportunities expanded, along with our encounters with exceptional and privileged people; as we challenged the limits of our own knowledge during fireside chats with a rare handful of friends (— one of which had journeyed to a far away land to research the oldest complete version of the Hebrew Bible, the *Codex Leningrad*) it came to be that I found the nerve to test my mushrooming intellect by pecking out a lengthy letter to the editor of the *Los Angeles Times,* which they printed, about the death of Kurt Cobain: *("Hear me out, all you Nirvana fans who are buried in confusion and grief and hear me out all you talented people who don't think you can go on because your own passion and trueness are in jeopardy. The biggest creative buzz of your life comes from saving yourself and filling up with gas for the next run...")* A letter that some time later wound up being partially recited in a piece that ran in *Rolling Stone Magazine*, under the heading "Stupid Fan Letters Written to Newspapers," though the author of that article did write: *"she deserves an "A" for effort"* beside my name.

And that's how it came to be that I found my nerve to speak to local community groups, too (— you heard that right, me once being interviewed on a local television station, though I wished I would have better applied my lipstick —) about the value of we Californian's keeping our perspective, as the state's economy was nose-diving in the mid-1990s, as those expensive homes dotting hillsides and valleys dropped in value so rapidly and drastically that people owed much more than they had paid for them — me, creating business cards that had this adolescent slogan on them: "Chins Up! California." Me, feeling the urge to commission an artist to create logo graphics for a T-Shirt I intended to sell that reflected California's angst — its residents having survived riots and mudslides and fires and economic woes and *multiple* earthquakes within a relatively short period ... as if it couldn't get any worse but, if it happened to, get worse, that there was a workaround — that it was perhaps possible, if we had an entirely different outlook on things, to get to a better place another way. Something about adapting to our evolving circumstances as they called for it. About leaping to a new understanding of things when it appeared we must.

— — —

Phil stood before a whiteboard in an executive boardroom at Headquarters. He'd finally made it there. Not to live and work, but at least to offer his assistance for free, as usual, as an outside business consultant.

Ever since Yucaipa, he'd been sending the occasional correspondence to officials he knew there. Offering whatever consulting services might be useful to them from "the outside." And they had responded on occasion to his findings: *"We have read with interest what you have said about the special conference you attended in Beverly Hills, California. It is certainly interesting to see how economists and others are taking a 'global view' of matters. We appreciate having the quotations you have included in your letter, and we thank you for your willingness to supply more information ..."*

By the time we'd moved to Los Angeles the correspondence had expanded to phone calls between him and them. He even produced a white paper that was articulate enough in addressing a few growing concerns that it was passed around Headquarters, he was told.

It contained information that more or less challenged ineffective and outdated procedures that was now costly on so many levels.

Phil remembered the orphans and widows in Oxford impacted by them. He remembered the zealous converts who had too easily adopted and readily enforced them. Phil had seen the bodies floating by ... seasoned and gifted advocates who were being snuffed out by the peculiar judgments of the less aware — actions that appeared to be lowering the baseline of our organization. An organization, among many, that had emerged from the bowels of America in the late 1900s — a node on the sphere of America.

An organization that had, despite its vow of detachment from her politics, had contributed to America's fight for civil liberties. An organization that had produced the likes of Phil and me: Those of us that were emerging from its bowels, as a reflection of its condition, a node on its sphere.

Phil had seen similar things occur in the business world, too.

Something about it wasn't so personal anymore. It wasn't against us, specifically, it was something else, Phil was beginning to discover, something else ...

As we stepped back, the scent of our own grief still present; as we unfocused our eyes and dared to glimpse a bigger picture, we couldn't help but marvel back then that the activities at Headquarters appeared to mirror the business world at large; corporations like IBM, Kodak and Pansophic Systems and vast numbers of others that had begun to flounder amidst tumultuous change. Some to which Phil had personally consulted — Phil, sensing patterns foreshadowing disruption others could not or did not see.

Driven by an antiquated mindset and perceptions of how the world functioned, most of them appeared to be in the same boat. Some sold film, software and computers, while Headquarters (along with other religions) had boxed up and packaged our intrinsic connection to the great beyond like one might sell bottled water, or canned air, complete with absolute instructions on how to worship.

Procedures — enforced on the assembly line of life: our businesses, our social services, our religions, netting a certain kind of result; benefiting those attracted to it, at least for a while. But we'd seen the children, plugged into that unit. And employees, plugged into their units. We'd watched them shut down, completely, or wake up, rather swiftly, due to what might be perceived as a minor change in conditions.

It was all so unsettling, that an institution such as ours, that had once fulfilled and sustained the hopes and aspirations of my extended family among throngs of others, could run its course — like a mini-series. That it was enough. And now we could grow past it, should grow past it ...

But we'd been grateful for that "packaging" up to that point — both Phil and I; having been robbed, along with our ancestors, of our own sense of direction long before any of us had been born — our lives and world reduced to exact measurements; we humans moved along in precise increments — because it had once been deemed necessary, apparently, to define our existence as humans in that way.

Still, we couldn't forget what we'd observed in Thomasville and Oxford — the imperceptible yet distinctive differences in each person's story — in each child, in each adult, their solutions diverse, not standard. It had all mattered, those tiny pieces of a bigger puzzle. (Did I mention the Thin Gracious Girl did attract — after attentively upgrading her views and image — a suitable man to marry?)

We were learning to identify their individual needs, connect their own critical data, like one might link the colors on a Rubik's Cube, no, not a Rubik's Cube ... something else ... something else ...

We couldn't forget the 75 employees we'd crossed paths with while working at the Multi-media Firm, either. How some of them had surpassed the labels assigned to them. How uncharacteristic combinations of staff could spark inspiration or friction. It was like cracking a combination lock ... no, that wasn't it. What was it?

And what was it we had tapped in ourselves — that consciousness, that innate sensibility, that transformed us from humble servants in Oxford to navigators of a starship in Dallas?

But as Phil stood there, in the executive board room at Headquarters, engaged in dialogue about connecting information to streamline outdated techniques, one man seated among them was visibly shaken, seemingly terrified of the consequences of it; uncharacteristically worried that God himself might be offended.

And Phil became acutely aware of the pain of change — of the physical discomfort of growth — that it shouldn't be, but somehow was difficult — how the fear of it can be systemic, how people can be trapped by it. And that sensation, that vibration, did not feel good.

We had come so far, Phil and I. But as our awareness increased — as the push and pull of our connections — those invisible tensegral forces that comprised our existence — as our fields of attraction expanded and retracted in response to our internal and external stimuli — we arrived at a different place.

chapter 14: Depart

"Did you see the bloody towels in my trunk? I didn't murder anyone, please don't call the police ..." Phil looked puzzled, telephone to his ear, as he whispered the caller's question to me. At which point I shrugged my shoulders and shook my head no.

Fifteen minutes earlier that January day in 1995 the tall, fair-skinned woman had parked her blue Jaguar outside our front door and scanned our personal belongings like a vulture during a New Year's Day moving sale. She purchased a wooden bench from our foyer, once used as a prop during a Harlequin book cover photo session. Phil had helped her load the bench into the trunk of her Jaguar, but he hadn't noticed the bloody towels.

"There was a drive-by," the woman added, now obligated to explain her bizarre phone call. *"A friend of my son's was shot and I forgot they were in there. It's not what it seems ..."*

Nothing was that day. As the parade of strangers, responding to garage sale signs stuck to light poles along Mulholland Drive and Laurel Canyon carted off our possessions.

There was the middle-aged man who scrutinized Phil's handwritten notes taped to his home office wall — the beginnings of a book — and proclaimed to all within earshot that a *"philosopher lives here."*

There was the woman, once an actress, who bought my cherished coffee table. Even though she was homeless and living in a van into which she stuffed it. I wanted to laugh but was too distracted — clinging as I was to an emotional cliff, my fingers wedged in the crumbling rock.

I hadn't asked to live in the Hollywood Hills alongside eccentric beautiful people in a house with a vaulted glass ceiling. I couldn't have fathomed such a life back when I slipped on a borrowed wedding dress at 18, exchanged vows with a bookish boy, and sped out of town in his pea-green Plymouth Duster. But once we had arrived in Hollywood, neither of us could bear to leave it.

A famous quote from President Calvin Coolidge that I had fastened to refrigerators and bulletin boards over the years was a reminder of how we had arrived there: *"Nothing in the world can take the place of persistence. Talent will not; nothing is more common than unsuccessful men with talent. Genius will not; unrewarded genius is almost a proverb. Education will not; the world is full of educated derelicts. Persistence and determination are omnipotent."*

It seemed inconceivable that the Northridge quake that rocked Los Angeles 12 months earlier could unearth so many lives for so many months thereafter, including ours. After all, we'd only lost a fanciful piece of pottery, a gift from a Scottish businessman that tumbled from our fireplace mantel as the city went black at 4:30 a.m. that January morning, writhing into piles of twisted metal and concrete that resembled a war zone. But Northridge would prove to be the costliest earthquake in U.S. history.

And here's what made matters even worse. California was in the midst of a recession.

Less than a month before the Northridge earthquake, the *New York Times* highlighted California's plight in an article titled, *"Humbled by Mean Recession, California Fights for Its Jobs."* According to the article, the state was paying a price after an economic boom that had led to overcapacity, which in turn produced a haughty outlook that opportunity and abundance would never end.

The trickle-down effect to Phil and me was inevitable. We had no fallback position. Even so, we were desperate to stay in LA; determined to keep our friendships and business relationships.

For 11 months we held on for dear life draining what was left of our resources and creativity. But no amount of hard work or fervent prayers — *and I mean heartfelt deal-makers* — could prevent the inevitable New Year's Day moving sale when our furnishings were swapped for emergency cash to move back to Dallas near family and start life over again at 40.

That combination of circumstances, a recession and natural disaster, triggered a life of chaos and uncertainty, the likes of which we had never before experienced. Of temporary jobs and temporary lodging — the first seven weeks in Dallas, a relative's bedroom; the next three months, a loft in a revitalized warehouse district filled with nightclubs, tattooed artists dressed in leathers and chains, corporate dropouts and mysterious characters with peculiar pasts.

In LA a kind lady named Consuela cleaned my house and did my laundry. In Dallas I did my own laundry at the Bar a' Soap — a tavern with a backroom painted in black and decorated with busty female caricatures that housed washers and dryers.

We were free to flounder in this unconventional place but there was no time to recover here, for we found ourselves once again in the crosshairs of nature.

One afternoon, five months into our stay Phil and I were roused to our feet from the confines of our second story loft by the sounds of breaking glass. A menacing storm was bludgeoning our building and a neighbor lady had already pounded on our door seeking refuge from the violent lightning bolts she was certain had targeted her rooftop. We three had downed a beer by the time we stood and peered through the industrial windows of our loft at the noise below.

"Don't worry. This is nothing," we had told the neighbor lady beforehand, a little too cocky for our own good. *"We've seen cars washed away right in front of us during flashfloods in Alabama! And we once drove through a tornado!"*

Glancing down, we saw a man waist deep in water struggling to reach a light pole. Giant wooden crates floated down Commerce Street like plastic toys having busted through the metal doors of nearby warehouses on the back of a brown raging river that now engulfed the neighbor lady's parked car up to its dashboard.

(Feeling stupid was, by now, a familiar sensation to us.)

The Super cell thunderstorm, we would later learn, started in Fort Worth as softball-sized hail and turned into a deluge by the time it hit Dallas and produced flash floods. It damaged hundreds of homes, businesses and vehicles and cost the lives of 16 people, two of which drowned within walking distance of our Deep Ellum loft. Damages soared to a billion dollars and the hailstorm proved to be the most destructive of its kind in U.S. history.

Once again the neighborhood we lived in looked like a war zone. And it took weeks for locals to remove the debris and thickened mud that had destroyed the studios of local artists and entrepreneurs. It also damaged ground floor apartments in our building, one of which should have been ours had we signed the lease papers quicker. But another unfortunate couple had instead.

Soon after, Phil landed a job in Denver — an executive position with a publicly traded Internet company that was rehiring after a corporate recapitalization. By the end of June we had departed Texas for Colorado.

(Ironically, Phil had been in discussions with executives at the Denver firm before our departure from LA. But for some horrific reason the hiring process took far longer than expected.)

I'd be remiss to say I wasn't by now a little paranoid: *"Holy Toledo! Someone is out to get us!"* Experience a bankruptcy and two major moves within a six-month period and you'll likely be shocked senseless. Add two national disasters in the course of 18 months and your nerves will be toast. Find out in the midst of it all that your precious dog has cancer and you'll be tempted to rip your heart from your ribcage.

The truth is we fared better than many of the people who lost homes, businesses, office buildings or loved ones during that recession, earthquake and flashflood.

But we had lost our confidence (again) for sure. After exhausting every fiber of our being attempting to salvage what was precious to us. Only to discover it was irretrievable.

A small reprieve from our uncertainty was the tiny penthouse apartment Phil snagged under rare circumstances in Denver before my arrival. The west-facing view of the city skyline with a backdrop of the Rocky Mountains was breathtaking.

By the time we watched July 4th fireworks the summer of 1995 from our new balcony on the 13th floor our spirits had lifted. If only temporarily.

At times, I felt like a magnet for catastrophe. But on other occasions, when I was alert, it seemed as though we were being exposed to a confounding level of angst in order to comprehend it — in order to examine it and disarm it.

A case in point was Phil's new job as Executive Vice President of a publicly traded Internet company. A longtime business associate was responsible for the hire, which should have ensured Phil a little stability under the circumstances. Another advantage was the knowledge Phil brought to the position. Just the year before, while living in Los Angeles, he had completed that cutting edge, online enrollment project for the large Southern California HMO (that I wrote about in chapter 9.)

At Phil's new post, he dived into designing a related application for an ATM Visa locator, one of the first consumer-oriented practical GIS applications for the Web. He even returned to California on a business trip and met with the company that had built the original HMO technology to fine tune his specs. Too bad the new CEO of the Denver Company, hired three months after Phil's arrival there, a big bullish fellow who had married corporate royalty and had his own rolodex of colleagues, did not grasp Phil's value. He replaced Phil with a friend of his, after Phil had been with the company only six months. Fifteen days after Phil's departure the company closed on the Visa project using Phil's design. Unfortunately for stockholders at the firm, the company never fully implemented Phil's vision for the technology, though VISA used the product for years to come, and a company called MapQuest released its own similar product to great financial success.

It was time to become full-fledged losers. And here's the handy thing about that. You at least know where you stand in the bigger scheme of things. Those who come in contact with you feel empowered to impose their perceptions. It's the loser's curse. You've earned it. And here's how it goes: Despite your past accomplishments you are now perceived an idiot. You are the accumulation of your failures. Everything you have ever done is suspect. You have nothing new to offer. If that awareness frustrates you, take a hike. If you reveal your emotions in a sudden angry outburst, it only reinforces their perceptions. If you become a loner, you are dangerous. If you try to fit in, but are no longer inspired by ordinary rhetoric, you're a disruptor.

Actually, losers come in all shapes and sizes. Some have lost their way and must find it again. Others have yet to comprehend or define their gift to the world. In the meantime, it's hard to fit back into the mechanisms of society that once worked for you. You've sprung free — if you can call it that. But that freedom comes with a price. You must rediscover your place in the world. However long that may take.

The idea sounds brave. But the reality is, under those circumstances, your self-worth continually arrives and departs like an ocean tide.

Months ticked by after Phil lost his job with the Internet Company. He followed job leads and calls from headhunters who were impressed by his resume but nothing transpired. He considered pursuing a new career in the healing arts but it was too tall an order under the circumstances.

Meanwhile, to keep the wolves at bay, we scrounged up freelance photography work from marketing firms and public relations agencies and managed to land an exciting project for the lieutenant governor of Colorado who was championing a new school-to-work program for high school students.

But freelancing in a new town was not a stable plan.

Eventually, we drove our Audi A6 to a dealership and turned in the keys to avoid some kind of embarrassing repossession experience. We had managed to keep it off the Chapter 13 bankruptcy that we filed after leaving LA — a settlement that mandated we continue to pay *hefty* monthly payments to certain creditors. Now we had to let the car go too.

Finally, we caved in a moment of self-doubt. Life as we knew it was over. We should accept whatever jobs we could find in order to eat, we decided. Phil checked out a truck driving position at a recruitment center but couldn't stomach filling out the paperwork. And I took a job with a tire wholesaler. It was dial-for-dollars work, calling tire and repair shops along the highways and back roads of America who serviced the agricultural, construction and mining industries. The company T-shirt featured the caricatures of three girls in bathing suits poked inside giant rubber inner tubes which, for some reason rankled me.

I sat across from a woman in her 30s who was gifted at 'tire' talk. But her body was ravaged by diabetes and she spoke daily, during coffee breaks, to her sister in prison.

Soon enough I was making 85 calls a day pitching tire products, then 100, then 130 calls, until I snagged a $3,000-plus contract for the company within my first month there — an exceptional feat I was told for a new salesperson.

Then one autumn morning in 1996, as suddenly as the violent financial tumble had begun, it ended. And I quit the job with the tire wholesaler after working there little over a month.

Phil had found "the perfect job" to quote a colleague of his. He would become the chief operating officer of a Denver agency with three dozen employees that served international clientele. The position required Phil to utilize all the skills he had accumulated over time. It was maximum satisfaction.

Months into Phil's term there, the owner of the company hired me too after I produced a freelance design project that launched a new national ad campaign for the business, along with other collateral materials I had also done for him. He wanted to "clone" me, he said, so pleased he was with my accomplishments.

chapter 15: Interlude

After our plunge into the depths of ruin we found ourselves in the midst of a breath-taking challenge working for a company in an industry undergoing tumultuous change.

The owner, a flighty fellow who claimed to have been abducted by aliens, found Phil's resume on the bottom of a stack of job seekers that had applied to run his agency the fall of 1996 after the last manager announced his departure.

But Phil was more than manager material, The Alien discovered. Phil was qualified to be a gladiator in a spectator sport.

Captivated by the job, Phil stepped into the ring (— he had no other choice, if you recall the previous chapter —) and he gave quite the performance.

The Agency had offered a good product for many years. But sales were in serious decline by the time Phil came on board. It was part of a lucrative industry — once comprised of many mom and pop-style enterprises that supplied visual content to design firms and advertising departments. But that industry by then had caught the eye of large corporations seeking to expand their product lines. And they began buying up the smaller businesses that served their objectives leaving the rest to die slowly.

The Alien had only recently transported his staff from cramped, dilapidated quarters to a sprawling historic building in a trendy section of the city featuring brick walls, upscale furnishings and an eye-catching fountain in the lobby. And it was the perfect backdrop to attract more international clients and better qualified employees as Phil, in the role of Chief Operating Officer, kicked operations into high gear.

Early on Phil knew what he was up against. In its current condition, there wasn't much to set this agency apart from other similar-sized companies that were beginning to struggle. He knew the drill — had learned it in Dallas at the Multi-media Firm in the mid-1980s when it too faced unavoidable change. Once your world shifts out from under you the "old rules" become obsolete over night.

But at this stage of our journey, Phil and I were just beginning to grasp that our personal responses to rapid change differed considerably from others who had been grounded all their lives by standards and expectations of predictability. They rarely knew how to react instantly and instead moved in slow motion imagining they had time to study what was going on. Or, hold on until things 'return to normal.'

We knew otherwise. In Dallas we had watched long-standing competitors bite the dust during that recessionary period while our company grew and flourished due to Phil's unconventional methods. And those memories would come in handy here. But, during the Dallas experiment Phil was intuitively responding to change while dragging the staff and company along. This time he would endeavor to *collaborate* with his employees and, in theory, navigate rapid change along *with* them.

Phil had been using words like "flexibility" and "adaptability" since the early 1990s when he wrote magazine articles about changes in technology and business management. But that was intellectualizing the subject. Talking the talk and walking the walk were two different things.

"I have now gone beyond my dissection of the past management and gone to the future and I see future management as organic, not mechanical," Phil wrote in his journal the winter of 1996, three months after he joined the Denver agency. *"The illustration that conveys this is the human body and how it is made up of vastly different parts, but they work together. The analogy of the body instantly prevents the idea of power bases and the warring between departments that will not even talk to one another."*

He wrote the entry after an intense company meeting on a Saturday where he allowed staff to speak about a painful experience they'd had with The Alien during a catalog production project, completed before Phil's arrival.

"We spent more than an hour in a group session allowing them to all vent their frustrations," Phil's journal continued.

But during that meeting Phil also learned that introducing new concepts about life and business can be challenging.

"Unfortunately I could see in their faces that they were struggling big time with the analogy of the body," he wrote. *"This is going to be much, much harder than I expected, or more accurately I should say than I*

hoped it would be ... I do not have their overall confidence at this time, they are too damaged to believe that anyone can protect them during the next catalogue production."

"At the same time I see this as the ultimate opportunity for me to prove the validity of Versatile Reality ..." Phil further wrote, speaking of a term he had loosely coined to describe his new business model.

"... Instead of being some consultant somewhere, I will be the person running a company that is living proof of how this concept works in real life."

"Perhaps I should start a regular evening class for the employees and explain about this entire concept and use this as a proving ground ..." he concluded.

Five weeks later he hosted his first after-hours company class:

"For those new to our meeting I will regress for just a moment and explain the underlying philosophy that [this agency] will be built upon: Enabled Organic Entity," he told his employees, using more terms that were unfamiliar to them.

He then re explained his idea of an organic organization.

"In the mechanized model, people are simply inferior machines that do what they are told and don't ask questions. In the organic model, the people are members of an organism, much like the human body, where each organ/member is distinctly unique, provides different value and proactively keeps the organism /company healthy ..."

Phil's enthusiasm for this new business model was infectious. And so was his eagerness to adapt to the changing industry that The Agency served.

He began speaking about those changes any chance he got at international conferences, workshops and retreats; and writing about them in trade journals.

"Making noise" was his way of drawing attention to The Agency. Once he had that attention, he began to build anticipation for new technology products he planned to launch. It was a risky strategy, but the company's chances for long-term survival were slim, he believed, without drastic steps on his part.

His strategy involved CD and internet solutions for suppliers that would provide them independence from the larger corporate entities who had their own agendas. Phil hired technologists to build the products and then ran creative ads to introduce them.

There was nothing else like it in the marketplace. And it alarmed the CEO of a large competitive agency in New York who met Phil at a conference; a man who later began to make curious calls to The Alien.

Over time Phil hired talented new staff, some of which moved in from other states and the management team grew to be an impressive group that earned praise from investors during venture capital evaluations.

The Agency added satellite operations on the East and West Coast; added more quality suppliers and substantially increased its international distribution from 36 to 50 countries. And there was even talk of a merger with another respected mid-size agency.

Phil's approach was distinctly different than a plan The Alien had considered. He had been advised by someone unfamiliar with the industry to reduce staff to a skeleton crew, turn the company into a "cash cow," and ride out the remainder of its days.

But Phil wanted no part of it. He knew the international clients would have bailed under such an arrangement, which would have effectively ensured the company's failure.

"I will not under any circumstances run this company into the ground," Phil told The Alien on more than one occasion. *"I will build it to be something significant. I will buy it myself or partner with someone ..."*

To that end Phil crafted a legal letter of intent to buy The Agency.

I joined The Agency a few months after Phil. As I said, The Alien was impressed with my creative skills and so were certain company affiliates.

"I love what you're doing there — your creative ideas will go a long way in helping the [Agency] achieve premiere status," wrote one content supplier about my work. *"The idea of story sequences and portfolios in the new catalog ... the profiles: great idea."* he said, adding: *"Curiously, are you going to be involved in the design of the next catalog?"*

Indeed I was. And, as I began compiling the material for the catalogue, it was obvious this role was bringing out the best in me. I could utilize all the skills I'd accumulated over time plus learn new ones while collaborating with some exceptionally creative people. My job was amazing beyond words.

As far as The Alien's role, he disappeared soon after Phil's arrival — gone for weeks or months at a time on travels abroad, relying on faxes and phone calls to stay connected. Which meant Phil was also tasked with managing the office building he owned too when he was away, which required Phil oversee renovations for a new restaurant on the bottom floor of his building that had no relation to his duties at The Agency.

Despite the increased workload, life was thrilling in those days. It was full of possibility. We traveled internationally and earned company perks. But it was also tenuous.

"We are running against time," Phil told the senior staff one morning, holding up a miniature replica of a Tucker automobile. *"We are swatting at giants. Being "the best" will not by itself save us ..."*

The Tucker automobile was an eerie illustration for Phil to use.

The car was named after a man who in 1948 oversaw the design of an innovative car with safety features that was years ahead of its time. Preston Tucker had created a genuine crowd-pleaser. But, as the story goes, he made some powerful enemies who tried to obliterate his business, claiming him to be a fraud.

"When the day comes that anyone can bend our country's laws and lawmakers to serve selfish, competitive ends, that day democratic government dies," Tucker once wrote in an open letter to the Automobile Industry that appeared in a variety of newspapers.

By the time Phil reflected on Tucker's story with his staff, time was indeed running out for The Agency. Working capital was running perilously low while Phil pursued serious discussions with upwards of eight investment groups while wrestling with The Alien over painful contract delays regarding Phil's letter of intent to buy the company.

"He goes off to see the penguins in Antarctica instead of signing vital documents costing me three vital months," Phil wrote in his journal about The Alien. *"I am pressed beyond imagination ..."*

Then a suitor stepped forward — one that had been poking around for some time. It was the competitor from New York. And it happened ... but not like we had hoped. The head honcho of that organization began final negotiations to purchase The Agency from The Alien and merge the two companies. But they excluded Phil from the deal.

In the final days before our departure, Phil's journal entries were difficult to read. Such as this one when he was out of town on business:

"Then Pam sends a fax, she backed the Rover into one of the poles at the office, she is so tired and she was so upset. Then Pam calls back and says that I have to get to the office NOW that the shit has really hit the fan ..."

The manufactured smokescreens to cloud the employee's vision of us had begun; the rumors that conjured up blame for our pending demise ...

"[An employee] asked to talk to me and came up to my office and said she had heard that [The Alien] was going to fire me and I told her that was probably true," Phil wrote in his journal nine days later. *"She was shocked. She asked when, and I said probably in the next two hours or so.*

She was amazed at how calm I was. We talked for a while and she said that she found all of this to be very intriguing and she would like to watch it from the outside."

Immediately below that paragraph was this entry: "[The Alien] was very late for the meeting as usual. He wanted to talk about payables and I told him that we had something far more important to talk about. I told him that the employees are asking if I'm going to be fired and so I was asking him. He said "no"; that he had never said that ..."

Phil's entry went on at some length highlighting more intense dialogue between them: *"[The Alien] said I had proved to be very disloyal ..."*

At 11:30 p.m. that night the phone rang at our penthouse apartment. It was the security company in charge of our office building. Someone had triggered the alarm a dispatcher told us. When Phil drove over to investigate he discovered The Alien on premises along with a locksmith who was changing the locks on the doors.

He didn't have the courage to tell Phil to his face that he was fired, after all.

That night Phil handed over the keys to the company SUV then retrieved one last item from a shelf in his office. It was his Waltz blue miniature Tucker Torpedo.

— — —

I was fired too by association. And the blow to my psyche was enormous. It was as if I had lost a child at birth. I began to stutter and my photographic memory went on hiatus.

That's because I was only a few weeks away from completing my precious 372-page catalog — the bread and butter of the company — the one that was producing smiles of approval from any who laid eyes on the proof copy.

It was a project that would have established a new level of credibility for my career. It would have highlighted skills that earned others in the industry a substantial paycheck. Not to mention the rapport I had painstakingly developed with so many sources and suppliers.

Furthermore, staff in my department had found creative ways to shave off gargantuan sums of money in production costs, which was a marked improvement over the last catalog project.

"That baby was 98 percent yours," a colleague told me over the phone one day after my departure. He had been a creative teammate during the catalog design and he knew how I hard I had labored over it.

"You know that and I know that, but who else ever will?" I replied, heartbroken.

In a frosty sendoff, The Alien omitted my name from the design credits as if he could make me disappear. And he did.

I had no strength left to clear my name of the unfounded gossip and no desire to beat the pavement in search of a similar job on the East or West coast while my reputation was hot.

My spirit was crushed. It happened the day after Phil was fired. When I called The Alien and asked permission to pick up personal items from my office.

He had no complaints with me, he had told me over the phone. But when I arrived to retrieve my belongings he met me in the hallway with a woman professing to be a judge, who then rifled through my wallet before confiscating my things. I was too dazed and confused to challenge their shameful behavior towards me. (Soon after, rumors circulated that a private detective had rummaged through our belongings at the company cabin.)

That same morning, police patrolled the building as word spread of many more firings at The Agency. But the display of paranoia on the part of The Alien was strangely misaligned with the quality of people who now worked there.

Immediately after, Phil and I were forced to hire a high-powered attorney to fight for our final paychecks, vacation pay and unemployment benefits, as well as defer outlandish allegations left on our doorstep in a thick document that threatened a lawsuit. The issues were all quickly settled in our favor. But attorney fees gobbled up our final wages.

When The Alien lost that battle, he set his sights on the technologist Phil had hired to build the company's internet product, refusing to pay his bill, then filing suit against him claiming he had failed to deliver on outcomes.

— — —

A lesser man might have tucked tail and run; might have lacked the strength to face a million-dollar lawsuit. But The Technologist valued his reputation, especially on behalf of his family, and braced himself for the lengthy process of a courtroom trial.

Ironically, while still employed at The Agency, I read a book about the real-life story of a horse whisperer; a man who pioneered a way to communicate with animals that challenged centuries-old practices of domination — of pitting man against horse and breaking the animal. While reading the book I was struck by an unfortunate personal experience the horse whisperer had with a businessman — an eccentric millionaire who offered him the dream of a lifetime: build a first class Thoroughbred breeding and training facility and be its managing partner.

Once built, the horse whisperer and his family enjoyed many successes at the ranch over the course of about four years before the eccentric millionaire announced shocking plans to dismantle the operation. Turns out, he suffered from bi-polar disorder and had a nasty habit of building things, only to tear them down again — a condition his psychiatrist labeled "sand-castle syndrome." In the process, he set out to destroy the horse whisperer too by instigating harrowing events — false legal charges, a false arrest, and a scheme to have a thug attack him — before the matter was eventually resolved in the courts in the horse whisperers' favor.

Reading his experience was unnaturally disturbing to me. Was it some kind of a sign? The thought crossed my mind. But it was easier for me to will myself forward with blind optimism, because the opposite outcome was unthinkable.

Still, it happened.

— — —

For 10 days after our departure from the "perfect job" the spring of 1998, we blockaded ourselves in our apartment. We stockpiled it with junk food and pummeled our brains with 27 movie rentals.

We didn't know it then, but this period of our life was nearly over — what I now call the Interlude — defined in the dictionary as "a short intervening episode between the acts of a play."

But we had one experience to go ...

The digital asset management software Phil had developed for The Agency was an impressive technology to some of his associates. Designed for content libraries, production labs, artists and photographers, it enabled them to manage visual content on the World Wide Web years before similar online services existed. Users could scan images, add keywords, and select an attractive background from a choice of preexisting templates to create their own business web site. (Sound familiar? Like something you'd find online today? Well, that was back in 1998!)

Immediately after Phil's departure, he began receiving calls about how he might rebuild it on a different technology platform for mainstream use — especially considering The Agency that fired him had discontinued the product.

"I have never had people pursue me and my work so aggressively," Phil wrote in his journal during that timeframe.

But in all honesty, he would have rather been doing something else.

His real passion was to sequester himself in a room and finish the book project he had begun back in Hollywood — an exploration of the chaotic changes occurring in the business world. He was driven to identify the skills that people needed to respond to the speed, obstacles and conditions of constant change.

"I desperately need time to ***stop and think,****"* he'd say, over and over again. *"I* ***must*** *get my book written and get out there and speak about ..."*

But he had limited financial resources to follow that dream — just a modest savings account we had squirreled away — enough money for a nice down payment on a comfortable home. Trouble was we needed an income again. And, at 43, with limited employment options in Denver, we had no idea what the next opportunity would be. And that frightened us.

So, Phil rented a quaint office in an historic section of town and began to rebuild the technology for mainstream use, working relentlessly with gifted programmers and a business partner from Boston.

Within months they were displaying their product at international trade conventions.

And it was featured in trade magazines.

And people ogled it, for there was nothing like it.

And they got clients including Fujifilm.

And they explored additional and varied applications.

And investors asked for business plans.

In fact, Phil's financial advisor was so impressed with the Fujifilm project that he was certain Phil and his partner would soon be millionaires and he told them so having run the preliminary numbers based on factors related to their client base and additional applications and markets that were available to them.

Then the U.S. Federal Reserve began increasing interest rates.

And the economy began to slow.

And the middle-manager at Fujifilm, who had embraced Phil's technology product, got promoted to a different division.

And our working capital dried up, having drained all our savings.

... Our dot-com bubble burst six months before that phenomenon occurred internationally. By then we had developed quite the knack for being ahead of the curve.

chapter 16: Scream

It's the morning of September 28, 2009. Phil rises from his computer and heads to the kitchen to make coffee mumbling something as he passes me about the power of perception. A snippet of a New York Times article he just read online about a widely studied psychological phenomenon.

"If a waiter tells diners at a restaurant that the wine he served them is an expensive, estate-bottled variety, chances are they'll like it — even if it's a bargain bin cabernet," Phil related as he scooped spoonfuls of Russian Roulette coffee out of a bag. "They'll linger over dinner longer, and enjoy the food more. But!" he said, holding his finger in the air like an exclamation point: "... if you tell them it's a low-end wine from North Dakota, they won't like it as well, won't like their food as much, and they'll finish their meal faster."

Then he zeroed in on the punch line.

"The difference involves the perception not the reality," he said, referencing the article. "Mindset drives the experience."

— — —

I rose from my bed and slipped through the sliding glass door to the balcony. It was cracked open as usual inviting air into the stagnant living quarters of our tiny penthouse apartment. There was no worry of intruders — not 13 stories high. It was 3 a.m. and the houses on the streets below were draped in shadows.

Grasping the railing I coiled my body, dropped my head, and let out a blood curdling scream, followed by an almighty list of expletives. My distress had turned to fury, my numbness to pain. I needed somebody *out there* to hear me, to end my anguish.

"GET ME THE HELL OVER WITH!" I cried, as if my life had turned out to be *somebody's* bad experiment.

But the unblinking sky did not reply, did not flicker a star in my direction.

Here it was 1998, and twenty five years had passed since Phil and I said our 'I-do's' and embarked on what we believed to be a purpose-filled life. Yet, what did we have to show for it I wondered as I gripped the handrail?

We had become complex adaptive creatures able to navigate change and uncertainty like no one else we knew — perfecting our inner game, without consciously following step-by-step rules. But we were incapable of securing a stable lifestyle as defined by so-called experts.

We were misfits.

In that role, however — leaping from one experience to the next — we had discovered something astonishing about our fellow humans: mindset determines their experiences. And people are mighty protective of their mindset, even if it becomes harmful to them.

But what if our perceptions of life were nothing more than stepping stones to a more expansive existence, Phil and I pondered. If people could grasp that, change wouldn't be so scary.

We hadn't fine-tuned the idea, but we were exploring it. Since we had been compelled to abandon ours, over and over again, by a force we couldn't define or escape.

We weren't the only ones to have our perceptions challenged. Everybody does sooner or later. But few seemed to embrace their new vantage points like we did. Most, who were stretched past their limits, snapped back like a rubber band to the familiarity that once was.

And snapping back is understandable. You often lose more than your perceptions when you let them go.

One day, I was especially distressed over losing so many friends. Some lost when we left our tight-knit religion. Others; vanished when the winds of change lifted us like feathers from our settled places and blew us towards the horizon.

I couldn't even find "Oh Babe." One of the few friends I had kept hold of since Thomasville. I'd called her number but it was disconnected. I'd searched the internet but found no new address in her name. I'd searched obituaries.

"I met with my shrink yesterday," Oh Babe had said in one of our last phone calls. *"But I wanted to talk to you, too."*

"I'm flattered. Please send me $100 an hour," had been my snide response.

*"My real shrink doesn't get **that much**,"* she had reminded me, in her comforting southern drawl.

"Fine, $75 will do ..."

"Shut up and listen to me ..." she'd growled, as usual, like a sister, before her tone turned serious. *"We were at a friend's house the other night when this public service announcement came on TV ... it showed a father choking his son ... and my son chirps up: 'Look mommy, that's what daddy does to us!'"* Oh Babe had told me. *"I could have died, Pammy — just died, right then and there.'"*

And now Oh Babe had disappeared into thin air. And my heart had disappeared with her, me being worried sick about her safety. But, her disappearance stirred up another worry in me too ... I realized there was no one left but Phil to vouch for me. To validate anything I'd ever done.

Sitting cross-legged in a park that afternoon, I stretched my arms heavenward toward God like a child reaching for its father. But the elementary image of him I once knew was gone.

A feeling of emptiness enveloped me and I felt eternally lost.

But over time, as I revisited that emptiness, I began to feel connected to something else — to what I can only describe as an invisible "umbilical cord" linked to a vast universal consciousness.

Deciphering the sights and sounds of it, however, seemed a daunting task. *"Great, as if I need another baffling challenge!"* I would grumble bitterly to myself on those occasions.

Goodbye, Descartes was an apt title for a book that Phil read during the interlude period of our lives. Written by a Senior Researcher at Stanford, it addressed our personal predicament in scientific terms. The book tackled the centuries-old concept of rationale thought, argued so famously by Rene Descartes — the belief that we have an abstract rational mind, separate from our bodies, one that is ruled by the laws of logic. To discharge that notion, author Keith Devlin referenced advances in artificial intelligence and natural language programs that do not begin to approximate actual human abilities.

"It is time, to come to terms with the fact that logic simply can't capture the real processes of human thought," the author conveyed on the book's dust jacket. *"We must begin to appreciate that our minds are intimately intertwined with the world around us, and that our feelings and perceptions play crucial roles in the marvelously complex dance of the human condition."*

In his book on Descartes, Devlin cites research from the book *Mind Over Machine* written by two brothers Hubert and Stuart Dreyfus, armed with Ph.D.s in philosophy and mathematics. They presented a five-stage model of human performance that Phil and I, in a loose way, had learned on our own while navigating the abrupt changes in our lifestyles.

For their comparison of computer systems to human performance, the Dreyfus brothers studied the skill-acquisition process of pilots, chess players, car drivers and adult learners of a second language.

The five-stage model included the following, which I will paraphrase here: **Stage 1: Novice:** The beginner simply follows the rules in an unquestioning, context-free fashion. **Stage 2: Advanced beginner:** The advanced beginner modifies some of the rules according to context. **Stage 3: Competence:** competent performer still follows rules, but does so in a fairly fluid fashion — at least when things proceed normally. Instead of stepping from one rule to another, makes a conscious decision of the next step at each stage; has a much more holistic understanding of the rules. **Stage 4: Proficiency:** For much of the time the proficient performer does not select and follow rules. They've had sufficient experience to recognize situations as very similar to ones they've already encountered many times before, and to react accordingly by what has become, in effect, a trained reflex. **Stage 5: Expert:** Terms such as rule following, decision, mechanical, and knowing facts do not really apply to the expert performer; rather, one speaks in terms of skill, know-how, intuition, instinct, and expertise.

Then in his book, Devlin summarizes his take on the Dreyfuses' above-mentioned experiment.

"Notice that the Dreyfuses are making a very strong claim with regard to expert performance," Devlin writes. *"They do not claim that the expert is someone who has learned to follow the rules in a highly efficient and rapid fashion. Rather, they assert that the expert* ***is not following rules at all,*** *not even subconsciously. Rules, they say, are there to help us learn how to perform a task. When we become expert at performing that task, we no longer need rules."*

Even so, Devlin's students were disturbed by that information, he said, quoting: *"On a number of occasions I have explained the Dreyfuses' theory of expertise to classes of college students, and I have always met with considerable opposition. Fresh on the heels of many years of fact-and rule-based high school education, most college students seem to find the idea of rule-free expertise completely counterintuitive. "Experts simply know the rules better and are much better at following those rules," they assert. They seem shocked that a mathematician such as myself could even entertain the suggestion that human beings are equipped to acquire skills that eliminate the beginners need to follow rules."*

I was giddy as Phil read to me from professor Devlin's book. *"Here, here!"* I cried, exuberant that the skills Phil and I had acquired navigating relentless change seemed explainable in scientific terms.

Phil and I were becoming self-motivated characters in a land of rule-following machines. We looked the same as our fellowman, but we did not click with them. We had lost our rivets and appeared broken.

"Everything that we do is done in, and influenced by, a context," professor Devlin further explained in his book, which Phil in turn read to me. *"Moreover, the context of any action — including conversation — potentially includes everything that happened to us in our lives up to that moment. But context is only part of the story ... "* he added, elaborating on what he described as compatible communicative skills developed by means of the same environment or culture.

"Exactly!" I thought. No wonder we weren't connecting particularly well with anyone anymore. Our experiences were a compilation of several environments, of several cultures. We had vastly different frames of reference, which altered our conversations, our behaviors and our actions.

One could argue that highly educated folks likewise experience different cultures and have diverse frames of reference. But "educated," is the operative word, and those models come with shiny hubcaps, an extended warranty and owner's manual.

We didn't have those luxuries. And that often had a blinding affect on people. They couldn't see us. Or hear us. And if they tried, they rarely understood us.

"Pioneer" had been our title during our religious missions and that title fit us once again as we explored how to see our world anew.

But pioneers have few counterparts let alone advocates. And they frequently come face-to-face with danger.

(Oh, Phil insists I mention Watson here. IBM's computer named Watson that during the writing of this book beat humans at a game of jeopardy. Does that discredit what I just wrote as far as humans performing differently than machines? Hardly, Phil says: "Watson can't feel. It has no personal history or any way to experience its existence in context. Watson memorizes content and application problems but is unable to become flexible and adaptable to humanistic and changing realities." Good job, though, eh IBM!)

— — —

The night before our 25th wedding anniversary, four months after we had been fired from The Agency, Phil's mother called — that fiery redhead who had taught her son by example how to persevere. She was compelled to share a quote by a man named Moshi from a book that she was reading and Phil and I were both on the line:

"When heaven is about to confer a great office upon a man it first exercises his mind with suffering, and sinews and bones with toil; it exposes him to poverty and confounds all his undertakings, then it is seen if he is ready."

"Who's 'Moshi?'" I challenged, deliberately ignoring the inspirational message to question the authenticity of the author. But Phil's mother knew nothing about him.

Deep down, however, the message stirred something dormant inside me. I wanted to leap for joy. Our life would make sense one day, I thought to myself. Our path was worthy. But we had struggled too long. We had not yet accomplished our purpose. In fact, I *screamed* at Phil frequently about our confounding circumstances. I couldn't seem to help myself.

"That's what people who never 'make it' say about their lives to make themselves feel good," Phil told me after his mother's call dismissing Moshi's words.

And I adopted his skepticism ... though some part of me was deeply saddened by it. Phil had become a Doubting Thomas, and I, an inconsolable bitch.

chapter 17: Violence

Phil eyes popped open and he gasped the morning of April 20, 1999, awakened from a deep sleep by a profound dream.

He was inside the shack of an old black woman ... in the South ... some place like Louisiana. He sensed she was a Shaman, or perhaps a spirit guide. He was exhausted when he arrived, with no knowledge of how he had gotten there, and he lay down on a bed and went to sleep. Until the old woman stroked his hand and told him very clearly that it was time to *"WAKE UP!"*

And he did wake up. Right then, at 4:30 a.m.

It wasn't the first vivid dream he'd been having lately. *(Or, was it a vision?)* But the uncertainty of our lives had caused us to seek answers in unconventional ways. A year had passed since our brutal departure from the perfect job. And we had yet to find tranquility. So Phil increased his meditation practices and carefully recorded his dreams. Those dreams had run the gamut in recent months from flying an air force jet accompanied by an overweight female instructor who walked with a limp; to Phil and me buying takeout food from a restaurant that was filled with people who had once worked for him.

Then there was this dream: *"Wake Up!"* the old woman had plainly said. Phil lay there for half an hour pondering its meaning, too tired to rise, until he finally did and headed to the living room of our penthouse apartment to meditate on the futon. Still, he had no inspirations about the dream.

Eventually, his mind drifted to other matters; to a rendezvous he'd had five days earlier on a trip to Los Angeles — an intimate interview he'd conducted with our old friend The Artist.

The two were working on a project together. It was an interactive CD that would feature his movie posters, along with rare sketches, an exclusive peak inside his personal studio plus details of his painting process.

But as usual with Phil and The Artist, the conversation had wandered off the subject of art as they examined the importance of being true to one's self. That's the key to real success — and doing "good" for others, they had decided. Being true to one's self would enable a person to accomplish more real good than any other course of action.

The Artist had found his path and stuck to it early on in life. But Phil's journey had appeared much more convoluted to outside observers — like a cripple wandering a dim lit road, mistaken for a drunk. Even now, as Phil worked diligently to take his latest technology venture to market for his financial well-being, he couldn't help but speak of a conflict in his soul: the craving, the necessity, to write his book. No matter the cost.

"Have you ever, in your classes or seminars talked much about the underlying core foundation principles of your life? And why people need, themselves, to adopt solid principles?" Phil remembered asking The Artist during that conversation.

"Whenever I talk, I'm asked to talk about my art — because that's what they see; that's what's out front," The Artist had said that day. *"But the power of the art comes out of the personality of the human being. Inevitably, you 'can't paint what you ain't.' So, you want a good painting? You've got to be a good person. You want the ability to be encouraging? You have to be that person. You can't hide it. You might paint your soul. That's why there's so many dark paintings out there. 'Cause the souls that paint them are dark. So, I can't help but talk about it,"* The Artist said, speaking softly.

"In general, if I'm able to squeeze the words out, which is very difficult for me, people like it. And I'm not surprised. I utterly believe, at least in this way, that I'm an optimist, that I know that all souls, all people, need to be loved. They need the big three things. They need to get love, give love, and feel like they're lovable. That's what they need. So if you speak in a way that gives that to them, then they're going to listen to you. I think the badness basically comes out of the misdirection that they can get it through other ways ... they wish their boss loved them, and they don't know how to go home and tell their wives. So they get mad and they overreact and they say the wrong thing, and nobody understands. So, of course everybody gets in contentious arguments, because nobody seems to be reading the heart of the other guy. And all the other guy really is saying is, 'please understand me, please love me, please care about me.' And they don't know how to go about it."

As The Artist continued his musings, Phil couldn't help but feel that the interview that day had significance. But he had no idea what it might be.

"I mean even the sickest of people, that's all they really want," The Artist went on. *"It's what people need, trade you a kiss for a loaf of bread, you know. A kiss will go a lot further. It just does. People haven't come to accept that. And, you know, the President gets up there and it's, 'two chickens in every pot, and a car in every garage,' instead of the constitution, how does it go? The inalienable rights? The right to pursue happiness, blah, blah, blah. They knew it. Why are we missing it? They knew it. It's a wonderful piece of literature. It's all there; every artist every author writes about. It's every painting that's worth its salt is ever about. It's what every song, every dance is all about. What, love? You know, nine out of ten songs is about love. Everybody's saying it, but nobody's living it. What's the deal? 'Cause when they say, 'You want this check? Kowtow to me!' And love goes out the window. You gotta' find that self integrity. To pay the price I guess. I pay it every day, not just when the work arises."*

As the conversation continued The Artist reflected on his work.

"It's been my dilemma all my life. How do you get through to people?" He said. *"And at least I've learned in my older, middle-age here, that it's not the point, it's not how many. You just do the best you can. I do it in every fiber of my being, the best I can."*

Then, he reflected on communities.

"People want to be needed and so generally they join a part of a community," he added, again illustrating his point. *"What is that except them wanting to be loved and acceptable?"*

"Unfortunately, they give up a lot of what they're looking for as soon as they join. Without freedom you can't love. You know, 'If you love it let it go; if it loves you it'll come back.' Even God got that. 'Let's see, if we make them all that is loving, we've got to give them all (that is) freedom or they're not loving us, they're just robots.' So, yeah, what you wind up with is the freedom to not love, when you give them the freedom to love."

A few hours after Phil awoke from his dream on April 20, 1999, two teenagers stormed Columbine High School.

As local news anchors began reporting on the gruesome details of the massacre that occurred shortly before noon, in a suburb 14 miles from our Denver neighborhood, we were caught up in the grief of an entire city.

In fact, our financial business advisor had two daughters who attended Columbine. They were not hurt in the shootings but his family was reeling with pain along with the rest of that community. And that made it even more personal for us.

There was a disturbance in the force and total strangers could feel it.

Two days later, news continued about the catastrophe. By then a nation-in-mourning sought to identify reasons for the killer's behavior. Citizens in Colorado and elsewhere contemplated ways they might help heal the hearts of those whose families had been destroyed. And Phil could not shake the dream he'd had about the old woman. "Wake up!" she had told him.

Finally, something came to him.

He picked up the phone and called The Artist.

"Do you want to paint a poster for the children of Columbine, for the children of the world to give them hope?" Phil asked him.

"Yes!" was his instant reply.

But both knew he'd have to act quickly for it to be useful. Fortunately, The Artist was already scheduled to be in Denver the following week for a Star Wars convention to promote his latest movie poster. The timing couldn't be better. He could create a painting for the students and community; have posters made and be in town to meet with them. Any poster sales would benefit a survivor's fund.

"I know a few people and will make some calls," Phil said before hanging up.

One contact Phil called was a business investor he met before he was fired from The Agency. He claimed to be a mover-and-shaker in Denver and after Phil had convened for two hours with the man and his son in his office, sparks flew and momentum spread throughout their network of business acquaintances.

Things happened swiftly after that. The Artist settled on an image for his painting and the theme, "Love Endures," and within a week he had finished the piece and shipped it to us.

Phil sat in front of the massive painting once it arrived, contemplating its message. It featured an angel carved in stone, with weather streaks on its face that resembled tears. The sky behind it was dark and ominous; but it had a bulbous center, whiter in appearance, from which a rainbow appeared.

"You'd swear she's going to start talking to you at any moment," Phil said that night, mesmerized by the large work of art.

Afterwards, respected businesses stepped up to cover costs of color separations for the poster and printing and related expenses.

Soon enough the group of us began contemplating ways that the painting and theme could serve a grander purpose. An opportunity to launch a healing organization related to art that would also serve future survivors of violence. The Artist's painting could travel to other schools and communities as the need arose to inspire much needed dialogue — to help people heal. But also engage those who were troubled in life; who were contemplating violent acts.

"It could serve as a catalyst for change," Phil explained, noting that The Artist's notoriety and his morality made the idea seem quit feasible.

The Artist was one of Hollywood's most renowned talents. He had completed artwork for roughly 150 movies, including many of the best known films ever produced. And he was a favorite of film directors Steven Spielberg and George Lucas.

But he walked his path with humility for someone of that stature. That's because he had a few battle scars of his own. He was dyslexic as a child. He was held back a year in school. And in college he was not granted his masters degree when he failed to write his thesis properly. He could have easily drawn it, but that alternative was unacceptable. Then there were the greedy businessmen and jealous associates he had been forced to deal with in the art world.

If anyone could reach frightened children or the disenfranchised he had a shot at it more than most, Phil rationalized. And, as the foundation found its wings, the works of other artist's would also be featured, allowing for different viewpoints.

Phil selected a name for the foundation, "Art for the Heart," and secured the URL. The Mover-and-Shaker tapped his legal contacts to begin the paperwork for a full-fledged non-profit and he secured pledges to the fund. In addition, our financial business advisor suggested a model for distributing the funds raised. It was an organization he knew of in Washington D.C. that helped the families of fallen policeman and firefighters. It was a "quiet" approach, without media attention, and it reflected the sentiments of all involved with Art for the Heart.

But we weren't the only ones with a plan.

"People from all around the country are being drawn together for one common purpose," said a Denver composer Phil met during that time. He too believed it was about the healing and recovery of a community and nation.

That composer produced a CD of songs for the victims, and in collaboration with Art for the Heart, used The Artist's poster image as the album cover. And there were many other groups fueled by their own angst that raised money for Columbine families, or strategized school programs that they believed might prevent disasters like it from occurring again.

Two weeks to the day after the Columbine massacre The Artist and other representatives of the Art for the Heart foundation met privately with a couple hundred Columbine students at a local restaurant. Students had just returned to school that week. And the chance to meet the Star Wars movie poster artist provided an uplifting experience for them. The Artist handed out free posters and signed them. And many of the students signed one of The Artist's posters in return, as a gift to him, making the exchange an especially cherished one for all involved.

A week later the Rocky Mountain News ran a story about the collaboration between Phil and The Artist. But certain board members of the foundation that represented different business sectors began to verbalize their anxiety over the design of the painting, that depicted an angel, as well as a scripture The Artist had insisted on adding at the bottom of the poster that read in part, *'neither death nor life ... can separate us from God's love.'*

The Mover-and-Shaker was bowled over by the petty conflict that ensued, especially, under the circumstances. In response, he considered burning the posters as a public statement to freedom of expression. So much for healing the disenfranchised, he thought.

Opinion had trumped good intentions.

Meanwhile, discussions in the media explored the need for increased security measures at schools. And people offered up their judgments for why two teens might kill 12 of their peers; kill a teacher, and injure 21 others — reasons that included possible mistreatment by their peers.

During this time a businessman Phil knew who lived out of state had a conversation with his 11-year-old son about the school shootings. *'I understand why those kids would do that!'* the boy had told his father, which shocked him. In fact, a board member with Art for the Heart remembered being severely mistreated as a teen and retaliated one summer by beating up his foes. Those stories and others seemed to underline the merit of the non-profit.

Despite the hard work of many people involved, however, efforts to light a hearty fire under the foundation fizzled. And that bewildered us all.

But then, bewilderment had become quite familiar to Phil and me — as if we were mining the breadths and depths of that emotion for a reason.

By all outward appearances we were success-disabled. But, people with disabilities would argue that they often develop remarkable gifts that others do not have.

In our case, our lack of victories caused us to challenge every idea we had and every situation we experienced. It forced us to confront our motivations and evaluate our resources — as if every ounce of our being must be carefully rationed to stay alive.

"I was very excited about this yesterday and things really look good," Phil wrote in his journal about the foundation during that time. *"Today I think it is a great idea but I am already tired. We were running on empty before this and this will take the fumes of gas we have to survive on and use them up. We must be crazy to do this ..."*

In another entry, Phil was even more distressed.

"I believe we have both come to the very strong conclusion that paying attention to dreams is not good for us. I listened to the shaman woman who told me to "wake up." As a result I started Art for the Heart and it isn't working and just made our situation much worse. Dreams are not giving us any direction; meditation is not giving me any. I simply feel that we just simply must not belong here. That there is something very wrong and it is way, way beyond us to do anything about ..."

But we weren't as far off as it seemed from our purpose. And the theme of the dream was not useless.

It was indeed time for us to "wake up" to our disturbed fellow humans and to our own role as part of the human race. Something was amiss — a widespread disturbance. And it was about to get much worse.

The kids at Columbine were the canaries in the mine ...

— — —

As the air escaped Phil's internet bubble the fall of 1999 he was forced to appear in court as a witness for The Prosecution in charges against The Technologist, whom had been sued by The Alien for a million dollars the year before.

On the second day of the trial, after grilling other members of Phil's former staff, Phil took the stand prepared for the "four hours" of questioning The Prosecution had scheduled for him. They had made it clear during pretrial depositions that it was their intention to put Phil on trial even though he wasn't named in the suit.

But, as he detailed the strategy he had implemented at The Agency, a thunderstorm swooped into downtown Denver and began battering the hell out of it. A violent downpour marked by ferocious lightning strikes that forced me to the balcony of my penthouse apartment — with its envious view of the city skyline — to observe the disruption.

It was a sight I won't soon forget. There before my eyes bolts of electricity appeared to be lashing the rooftop of the courthouse at the very moment that Phil was in the building.

Only later would I discover that the brutal storm I had witnessed had discombobulated The Prosecution. As the attorney began his interrogation of Phil, lightning bolts slapped the building and rattled the windows so hard that his inquiry was inaudible. Each time he tried to speak, thunder split his questions in two. Stopping abruptly amidst the racket, he requested a sidebar with the judge.

As The Prosecution left the bench he glanced over his shoulder in Phil's direction and muttered, *"I have no further questions."*

On the third day of the trial, after final arguments, the judge apologized to the jury for wasting its time and dismissed the suit as having no merit.

— — —

Two weeks prior to the hearing we'd been given 30-days notice to vacate our penthouse apartment. We'd lived there four years. But the building had been sold suddenly and management informed us it was being turned into condos. Certain apartments would be offered for sale at reduced rates to tenants, they added. But our unit — and select others with "views" — were not available because the developer had special plans for them.

About now you readers are probably thinking, 'It's time these knuckleheads go to the mountaintop and figure out some shit!'

And that's exactly what we did. We moved to a mountain cabin. Above the front door hung a weathered wooden sign, left there by a former dweller who had named the place. "Walhalla," it read; the name of Odin's mythological hall of immortality for heroes slain in battle. *(Usually known as Valhalla, they'd chosen the Old Norse spelling of it.)*

It was beginning to dawn on us, as we settled into our new surroundings, that few people venture to their outer limits without a road map. And for good reason: You can die there.

chapter 18: Submerge

It's the end of September, 2009. Phil climbs the hallway stairs headed for the kitchen to make coffee (as usual) recounting something as he passes me about an Internet story he just read regarding the surprising way that metaphors shape our world.

"Psychologists have started to take an intense interest in metaphors," Phil said paraphrasing the article. "Cognitive scientists are discovering that metaphors are more than literary phrases, they are keys to the structure of our thoughts — they are how we think."

— — —

It was time to plunge to our depths.

This leg of our journey they don't prepare you for in school. It surpasses dreams and degrees and the promises of those pursuits. It's the clarion call.

The signal was at first faint in 1979 when I fell ill and we met Dick Doc and he scribbled the sum parts of a vitamin on a sheet of paper and showed us our first "whole."

But it became an unmistakable summon in 1993 when Phil felt compelled to plaster his office wall in our Hollywood Hills home with notes, newspaper clippings and pages ripped from magazines to connect the dots of the rapidly changing business world.

That grew louder a year later, when Phil spoke at a chamber of commerce event in Los Angeles and grabbed the attention of a business writer he knew seated in the audience — an award-winning journalist who had for years written about the ways in which rapidly advancing technology was "stitching human beings and the world together into a vast electronic quilt."

It was a call to action that inspired the two men to band together in creative collaboration; to drum up a message fit for publication. They crafted the first draft of their book that same year. But their message was missing something so they decided to do further research.

When earthquakes, and major moves and new jobs and middle-school soccer practice distracted one or both of them they still couldn't shake their attraction to the book-writing project. They wrestled often with the urge to put their lives on hold and finish it. And they experimented with ways to better illustrate their message with various visual models, one of which was a sphere, a shape they'd settled on, the year before, for its multifaceted features.

Then, five months before we moved to Walhalla in 1999, Phil was reading an issue of *Inc. Magazine* and came across a commentary written by the editor that further fueled their desire to halt their busy schedules and dedicate their lives fulltime to the book.

The Inc. editor described his habit of asking CEOs he interviewed to draw diagrams of their organizations. And over the years the Inc. editor began to witness a provocative change in their artwork. In the early 80s, the CEO's diagrams featured the classic pyramid that had been in existence since the turn of the century featuring key managerial positions represented by boxes at the top and workers at the bottom.

But, by the middle of that same decade, the CEOs' drawings were changing. *"There were gyroscopic concentric wheels; complex molecular forms that turned in on themselves, helix-like; [and] elaborate solar systems. Most striking was the originality of the drawings — no two were alike,"* the Inc. editor wrote. In fact, one CEO suggested the name of the diagrams be changed to "disorganization charts."

Phil told his writing partner about the editorial and he was equally disturbed by it. It seemed to both of them that business leaders were on the verge of figuring out what Phil and RLL knew — that society was seeking a new metaphor to live by and work from — a new visual model to express themselves.

"How do you say, in French ... Holy Sheet?" was RLL's email reply after reading it himself. *"They feel it. They sense it. They awkwardly try to define it ... visually! And yet, they all depict it in different, useless forms. Its organizational Alzheimer's at the highest. There is no communal vision. No central, guiding form. No pyramid, no Stonehenge. No way for execs or anyone else to comprehend ... GEOMENTALLY. So, at the end, he asks the Inc. readers to create their own org charts and put them in an envelope! Management time capsules? The editor adroitly describes the outlines of the lurking, evolving geometric creature, and then can't see it himself.*

*"He's tacked a big, f**kin' sign on our door! God help us if we miss the chance to pass on the message."*

RLL had a way with words. And that made the collaboration between him and Phil especially sweet. They each brought unique talents to the table if they could just see their goal through. If only.

"So the madness continues for me," Phil wrote in his journal the same day RLL responded to the Inc. editorial. *"I have [the makings of a] book that is so timely that it kills me to even think about it and [RLL] sees the same thing and yet I don't have one iota of energy to devote to it. I have worked and worked and worked and worked, I don't think you can work harder. We don't do anything but work and try and stay alive..."*

— — —

Five months later we received a gift.

Though, I hardly saw it that way at the time. We were forced to evacuate our penthouse apartment on short notice. And that's when we found Walhalla — the charming rustic cabin with metal kitchen cabinets built in 1929 in what was then a colony of writers and artists.

We discovered it in the want ads under "mountain rentals" and had beaten out several other people interested in leasing the home that was situated on four acres and included a small detached office. Probably because of the mini-biography I included with our credit application, complete with photos of our past residences and a few of our accomplishments, to offset the bankruptcy on our credit report. It was my desperate but creative way to defend our character.

Turns out the cabin owner was a Mark Twain scholar who taught information and communication sciences at an out-of-state university and had once written his college dissertation at Walhalla. He was struck by Phil's passion to write his book in solitude there and granted us that wish despite our financial instability.

It was one of many lessons we were beginning to learn about life rearranging itself in peculiar ways when you press on with good intentions.

But we would also learn this: the difference between good intentions and final outcomes requires unwavering devotion.

Especially if your odds of success appear abysmal as was the case with Phil who graduated high school at 16, had no college degrees — thus, no academic titles — and yet was trying to write a thought-provoking book about what he believed was an emerging worldview.

"If only we had gone to college," I often lamented to Phil, saddened by what we might have become under different circumstances. But he always disagreed with me.

"In my case, it would have destroyed my credibility," Phil would argue, defending the value of his uncharacteristic path. *"I couldn't be somebody's protégé to learn what I know. I needed to think my own creative thoughts."*

Occasionally, he'd concede that attending college had its merits.

"I don't disagree that critical skills and training are vital. It's the best course for most. But for certain "creative's" it's not. It actually stifles. It harms you if you have a radical idea ..."

Then he'd remind me of the times he'd "been in board rooms of multinational companies with a team of MBAs" who had "paid him" to "hear his views" about the changing business world.

Or, he'd tout the speeches he'd given in the early 1990s *(as if I'd forgotten them)* about the accelerated rate of change in the Information Age — how information, by conservative estimates *(back then),* was doubling every five years. *(Now its every 18 months!)*

"Colleges need a new approach to match the times," he'd say, further stating his case. *"They are rarely at the bleeding edge of a revolution. They can't put together curriculums fast enough to stay abreast of the changes ... They require students to "pick a major" — and then screw you if you want to change that — and the higher you go in education the more you specialize — the more you are trained to filter out the noise — and that can limit your views."*

There was no end to Phil's rationalizations.

"My work is the exact opposite. It involves pulling everything together to look at the whole. I never stop learning; I'm never done. I read tons of books and magazines in all kinds of fields. I'm constantly connecting new information; I'm continuously connecting the dots."

I knew he was right. And the thought of it was exhausting. We could never rest on our laurels. We were always improving our game ... even when our college friends didn't think they had to. No wonder it was so important for Phil to write his book. It was his only chance to establish a little credibility.

To submit himself, at this point in his life, to the training of a standard university with classes designed to help students "fit" a typical profession would have disrupted his clarion call. Worse, it would have extinguished his exuberance. His favorite ceramic coffee mug, after all, was inscribed with this quote by Einstein: *"I was supposed to choose a practical profession but this was simply unbearable to me."*

But that didn't change the fact that he had no easy way to make a living as he aged, nor did I.

"Yeah, yeah, yeah, I've heard all your reasons before," I'd reply, wounded by the conversation. *"I still think that if you could've attended a GREAT university ... could have been around OTHER GREAT MINDS ... you would have at least LEARNED THE ROPES. You might have gotten SOME BREAKS!"*

"I'd have killed for a ***great mentor,****"* he'd say, sidestepping my observation.

Phil craved the company of rare beings. But he now craved them in concert. He desired interchanges with scientists *and* psychologists; with philosophers, technologists *and* business specialists. But that was impossible to do in an education system that resembled Henry Ford's assembly line.

Instead, Phil faced the harshest kind of future. If the book's message had merit, he would have to overcome unavoidable prejudices by so-called experts who felt it their duty to discredit his vision.

That's why his collaboration with RLL was important to his journey. RLL had earned college degrees and had been raised with privilege. He had established a comfortable lifestyle with his family in an upscale suburb of Los Angeles. He was a soccer dad and offered a different perspective. He knew the lingo of the secular world.

And that gave me considerable peace of mind. Finally, Phil had someone other than me with which to brainstorm — since I was about dead from being his wing(wo)man.

— — —

"Well, Phil, You extreme extremist you ..." RLL wrote late one night in an email exchange a few months after we'd moved to Walhalla.

There was an air of practicality in his response to Phil's mind-walk about the importance of humanity adopting a "spherical" mindset.

Mind-walks were a phrase Phil borrowed from a favorite movie by the same name, and they were often long-winded interchanges that examined a string of thought.

"Your manifesto on the essential need for Sphericity was best summed up with "Will Sphericity become the vehicle to help get this mindset across to the world?" I don't know. I hope so. But whether it is Sphericity or some other vehicle that accomplishes the goal, it must be done," RLL wrote.

"I agree deeply and completely. Humanity must come to recognize, internalize and live the message we are trying to convey in Sphericity or the species is doomed. The only hope of a sustainable future for people is a deep recognition of what we are trying to say. But will the language, models and publication methods of Sphericity accomplish that task? Who knows?

"Many other people are trying in many different ways to convey the same basic message of the interconnected and interdependent nature of life. Holistic philosophy and thinking is as ancient as the campfire. Rachel Carson is an excellent analogy. She did not just point out the unseen long-term dangers of chemicals [in her book Silent Spring], she rekindled the deep feelings of interconnectedness that we all have inside. She showed by example the interdependence of nature and, therefore, humans as well. Your manifesto could well have been written in 1965 at the height of protest against the established order, the ruling class and the rape of the planet in the name of profit and materialism," RLL continued.

"When I said I don't think people need Sphericity, I meant they don't necessarily need our approach. Because it may not be the right one. It may not strike the chord. We may not be the right voices. Or the right metaphor. Or have the necessary funding. Of course, I believe with you that in the long-term (maybe shorter, rather than longer) the message of Sphericity is "'absolutely essential for the continued existence of mankind on this earth.'"

"Part of me thinks humankind is already too far gone. But another part of me, mostly the father part, insists that the turnaround in mindset and action is entirely possible."

The word "Sphericity," which means the state of being spherical, or having the form of a sphere, was so much a part of Phil and RLL's vocabulary during that period that they used it in the title of their second book draft completed around February of 2000. It was called, *Introduction to Sphericity,* though it was far too clinical a term for the average reader even with its elaborate subtitle that read, *Death of the Box: How the World Goes Round in the 21st Century.*

By then, I had tracked down a noted political cartoonist who lived in New York that was willing to illustrate the book (for less than his usual fees) after I explained the book's message, which impressed him, during a rather lengthy phone call between us.

"It is overwhelming when I sit and think about the ground we are trying to cover in an extremely simple 150 page book that is full of pictures ..." Phil wrote in mid-January of 2000 shortly before the second

manuscript was finished. *"Everyone has been looking for the seven steps to a better life. That is mechanized Newtonian thinking. It "works" — if it does — only in an environment where we believe that everything can be controlled and organized. But the world can't be controlled or organized. It is chaotic in nature and will self-organize in non mechanical ways. But there is no one explaining that in a manner that the average person can understand it and take some comfort in it. We are trying to do that for the world."*

A short time later, Phil followed those observations up with these, which revealed his inner turmoil: *"I think the book is an important work. But the challenge will be if it is* ***close*** *but not on target. Even if it is, it may well die yet, as I certainly don't have the means to spend any more time on it. I am so out of money I don't have a clue how we will exist, we don't have a dime to pay the rent for March. I haven't thought about any of this and can't until next Wednesday..."*

Concurrent to their book writing Phil and RLL also pursued avenues to introduce their concepts to the business world. They wrote comprehensive business plans and aroused interest from the Mover-and-Shaker Phil had met during his days at The Agency, the same guy who was later involved with the Art for the Heart Foundation after Columbine.

Then, in late February, Phil and RLL headed to Atlanta, Georgia, where they revealed the contents of their masterpiece during a *Presentations Expo 2000* event. They were among several scheduled keynote speakers that week that included MIT's Nicolas Negroponte, Desmond Tutu and political commentator Ben Stein.

Nearly 400 people came to hear Phil and RLL speak. And many were jazzed afterwards about the message the two had conveyed during their multi-media presentation — people that ranged in age from their 20s to their 60s who went out of their way to offer feedback to Phil and RLL — visitors from Spain, Thailand and Canada — even people from Italy who wanted to translate the book, when it was finished, into their own languages and distribute it in their own countries.

The next step was to get feedback on the working manuscript. Before the conference, Phil and RLL had already begun sending it to a few select readers — close business acquaintances that they hoped would provide perspective before they completed the final edits.

By the end of March, however, Phil's expectations hit another low with this entry in his journal: *"I still can't believe I have not heard a word from anyone I sent the book to, not a word. It is (or was) my only hope. It was the unfinished thing that kept me going ... Now, not only is it done, but I get no response to it."*

As Phil and RLL waited for comments they began to revisit the material themselves and were not happy with what they read.

"Where's the INSPIRATION?!!" Phil pondered aloud, at which point RLL concluded that the script was indeed *"underwhelming."*

Their fears were realized when reactions trickled in from manuscript readers. There was "quality information" and "good storytelling," they were told, but there were no "aha!" moments.

That's primarily because Phil and RLL had worked too hard to blend the features of a prosaic business book with a 21st century philosophy-for-living book, making compromises that were now haunting them.

"The reaction of the [live] audience in Atlanta seemed much more enthusiastic than anyone who has read the book," RLL lamented to Phil. *"Clearly, a lot of what worked in the presentation was our enthusiasm and clear personal explanations. It may be that we are not translating that. Is it even possible to do such a thing?"*

A harsh realization was beginning to dawn upon them, despite the time, energy and money already expended. They would have to let the project go or face more grueling rewrites.

(Sound of fingernails on chalkboard here.)

In the midst of that disappointment Phil and his old friend The Artist had a strange falling out over a CD project that they and a third partner had completed — a difference of view over marketing issues that tragically — during a series of uncharacteristic email exchanges between them — destroyed an 11-year friendship.

In fact, the third partner retreated too. And I, at some point in the hours and days that followed, decided my presence in Phil's life must be toxic. For I had edited the documents he sent to those two partners but had failed to mask the angst that plagued Phil in those days. That necessity of Phil's to defend his honor and his worth at all costs. As if that image was the only asset he had left.

On that note, it seemed prudent for me to leave him, to let him travel his own uninhibited path to enlightenment. And when I threatened to do just that, he did not blame me.

The sky was a dazzling blue the morning after Phil emailed his last bit of correspondence about the fallout to his third partner in late May. And to hear him tell it, he felt "incredibly good" all things considered when we left the cabin around noon for a trip to town. His fingers thumped the steering wheel as we meandered up the dirt driveway to the gate and he exited the Jeep in a carefree mood to open it.

Then disaster struck.

We will never know if the Jeep popped into gear that day, or if Phil, an otherwise careful driver, failed for some unknown reason to push the gear shift firmly into park. All that remains of that memory is the piercing cry that escaped my lips as the Jeep plowed through the locked gate with Phil nowhere in sight. Enslaved by my seatbelt on the passenger's side, I was helpless to stop it, until I gathered my thoughts and clawed to release the seat buckle. By then the Jeep was on course to crash through the neighbor's gate on the opposite side of the road when I dove for the brake at the same instant that Phil thrust his right foot through the open driver's door and stamped the pedal, which jerked the Jeep to a stop. Then, just as suddenly, Phil staggered backwards and collapsed on the ground.

Rushing to his side, I found him pale and faint, and it took me several minutes to piece together what had happened.

How, when the Jeep charged the gate where Phil was standing, he had swiveled around to stop it but was knocked under it by the open door. How, as the Jeep moved forward, the back left tire rolled across his left foot, crushing it. How, in a final rush of adrenaline, he had stood up on his mangled foot and rammed the other foot at the brake pedal preventing his beloved four-wheel-drive, and perhaps himself, from destroying anything else.

— — —

As much as Phil was driven to write a book, so was I.

I began recording vignettes of our personal journey in the early 1990s sitting at the dining table of our doublewide in the old folk's mobile home park in Yucaipa; and later, in the tiny flat in London, in Belgravia Square, during our five-week stay there.

I remained obsessed with it during our final days in Hollywood, after the Northridge earthquake shook loose our hold on that lifestyle.

By early 1996, I had completed my first 423-page manuscript in the penthouse apartment in Denver — having secured the editing services of a grad student at the University of Denver who was completing his Ph.D. in English Literature and Creative Writing. *"Your work reminds me of Eudora Welty's,"* he once told me, for I wrote in long rambling sentences back then.

I even snagged interest from book publishers after mailing out my very first query letter, one of which requested to see my manuscript.

But I sensed the story was incomplete. Had it gone to print too soon I feared its ultimate purpose would be lost, along with my efforts. Thus, I never sent the manuscript to that publisher.

By 1999 I had started over, hoping the ultimate meaning of our story would reveal itself if I wrote a new manuscript. But a warning from a rather intuitive medical doctor, with whom Phil conversed one day, after our arrival at Walhalla, caused me pause. During their phone conversation that spanned many topics Phil explained his book-writing project to her. Then, he mentioned mine — which involved reliving the difficulties of our past to properly portray our journey.

"How's her health?" the doctor asked Phil with genuine concern in her voice. When he conveyed her message to me I sensed I should heed it. I was too fragile and unprepared at that moment in my life to follow through. It wasn't the right time and I wasn't ready.

A few weeks later, when Phil was reading the local newspaper he noticed a job posting for a reporter. *"You should apply,"* he told me, at which point I balked and reminded him I had no journalism degree. *"It doesn't matter, you should apply anyway."*

I stared at that posting for many days before I found the courage to pass along my unqualified resume to the editor.

But it was another one of those moments ... when the rules of life seemed to rearrange themselves in a merciful way. That hardcore newsman contacted me. Then he hired me over his other job candidates after I successfully completed a trial assignment for him.

It was up to me, however, to decipher the meaning of that collaboration. To respect it and build upon it, to soak up the experience as if my future depended on it.

In fact, it was up to me to make sense of my life in general — to reconcile my torments and crystallize my contribution to society.

And that is exactly what occurred when we submerged ourselves at Walhalla. Well, eventually.

"Hey Pamela, Take 'em by storm, girl!" wrote a writer friend from Los Angeles in an email soon after I landed the job at the newspaper.

"When Phil told us you were working as a reporter I said 'hot damn!'" she wrote. *"I thought of Hemingway running all over the world doing that sort of thing and thought 'yeah, I could have done that and I wouldn't have been half bad, either.' I really enjoy poking my nose all over the world scene, seeing what's out there and then having something to say about it in one form or another. Isn't that what Hemingway and other great journalists did? Remember them all encouraging one another*

especially during WWII to get out there and get involved? They had a very distinct point of view of what was going on around them. So when I heard you were doing that my first thought was 'yes, she's found her home.' I think you will be wonderful. It is you. Art is OK. Photography is OK. But ... we are verbal, girl, and we have a lot to say and I think that's what it takes. You lure people in with wonderful storytelling ability and then take them on a wild ride," she concluded, having read my original 423-page manuscript. *"Use it, use it, use it!"*

So I did.

As Phil and RLL wrote their story of how *"scientific discovery, mid-millennium philosophies and the Industrial Age combined to condition us to a view of the world as a collection of separate and distinct parts ..."* I wrote about a scandal at a local church involving an elder and a teenage girl that cost him some jail time.

As Phil and RLL explained how *"mechanistic and reductionist thinking produces a sense of isolation and separateness that prevents us from seeing the complex interrelationships in our lives, organizations and societies ..."* I wrote a two-part series about Bridging the Digital Divide between rural communities and the world-at-large with high-speed internet access.

As Phil and RLL wrote about the "qualities and characteristics necessary for mankind to survive and thrive in the 21st Century," I landed a story about midget football.

"Gosh! How many midgets are there?" I asked the mother of one player over the telephone. I was stunned by the fact that there were enough midgets in the mountain community where I lived to form a football team. I hadn't seen one, not one, in the local grocery store.

"About 23?" was the mother's curious reply.

"I had no idea!" I gushed. Then, careful to be politically correct I added, *"They are technically called "LITTLE PEOPLE" aren't they?"*

The woman seemed confused by my comment, then defensive.

*"Well my son **IS** only **10**. I guess you'd call that **little**!"*

It took me months to live down that incident with my fellow reporters who were far more informed about the names of children's sports leagues than I was.

But I wasn't the only one suffering humiliations.

"I've decided on a career change. I'm going to go to work for the CIA as an undercover agent," Phil told me one afternoon after he was forced for financial reasons to deliver mail as a part time postal worker.

"My ability to create a believable cover is so good I can't waste this talent," he continued, his voice filled with sarcasm.

By then, Phil's past life in technology — of creating practical applications years ahead of his competitors — was but a memory. And that realization was quite painful to him.

"Yesterday, when I was heading out to deliver a new mail route an assistant manager handed me her cell phone to use in case of problems," Phil explained. *"'Have you ever used a cell phone before?'" she asked me, before carefully instructing me how to 'turn it on' and 'turn it off!!'"*

It was nearing the end of 2000. More than a year had past since we'd moved to Walhalla. Nearly six months since Phil's run-in with the Jeep, which had required major foot surgery and 10 weeks in a leg cast.

And now Phil was working as a substitute rural carrier for the U.S. Post Office that functioned by a business model established in the Industrial Age, which proved to be blatantly ironic based on the message he and RLL were championing in their book. That it was time for us to let go of outdated modalities that harm us and see the world anew.

The words of Henry Ford now haunted Phil. *"Why, when I only want to hire a pair of hands, do I get a whole person?"*

Phil himself had become a "part" in the machine. Filing and delivering up to 10,000 pieces of mail daily during busy periods, while learning 23 different rural routes; monitored, at specific times of the year, by "counters" who timed the actions of employees with a stop watch, some of whom had the inhuman job title of 204B.

Phil's days were long, the work strenuous and repetitive, often prompting him afterwards to soak his arms at 20 minute intervals in hot, and then icy water, to reduce the swelling. He was now blue collar. Exhausted and wary that he would get trapped in that role.

Still, he pressed on. Stealing every moment possible to work on the book — rising at 4 a.m. to pour over the material a few precious moments before heading to the post office each morning. And, and upon his return home, willing himself to his detached office — a small log bunkhouse located a short walk from our cabin where creamy yellow light glowed from the antique window panes late into the night.

At times, the difference between our lifestyle and RLL's would overwhelm Phil.

"[RLL's] leaving for a week in Hawaii with his family," Phil would grumble. *"Last year it was France to watch the eclipse of the sun."*

But Phil couldn't seem to change his own financial circumstances despite every attempt to do so. And he certainly tried, sending out countless resumes — handsomely crafted documents that frequently earned him praise.

"In my 9 years of recruiting I have not seen a resume like this," wrote one corporate recruiter, before noting: *"It's really a lot more interesting than just words on paper. In looking through this, I have to ask, what would make you interested in joining a company in a fulltime capacity at this point in your career?"*

And that was the crux of it. Phil's accomplishments were vast and varied making him over qualified for many of the postings he applied for which made no sense to head hunters. The white collar machine was designed to produce success stories, so why wasn't he already a monumental success?

To picture it, Phil's life resembled that optical illusion people used to fax or email to their friends. Perhaps you remember it? It was a black and white sketch of a woman. *'What do you see,'* people would ask, *'A pretty young lady or an ugly old hag?'* The answer of course depended on the way you looked at the drawing.

Even so Phil talked his way into interviews. But in the end there were no takers.

"I believe the [CEO] felt it would be too much of a risk to take at this time and we have some other candidates who more closely fit the background and experience we desire for this position," wrote the above mentioned recruiter, before adding: *"I would like to know how your Sphericity concept takes off. Stay in touch and I will do the same."*

Ah well, no matter.

Had Phil found a way to reenter the corporate scene, as all-consuming as that was, it's fairly certain he would have never finished the third and final phase of book rewrites.

The post office worked his body like a slave but it freed his mind for pondering his latest discoveries about Sphericity as he stuffed envelopes into mailboxes along the Rocky Mountain Front Range.

And there was plenty of research to consider.

*"Holy sh**! I really don't know what to say!"* Phil emailed RLL after he discovered a comprehensive paper online written by systems experts that was suspiciously similar to their book topic. *"You must read every word of this document. If someone did not know for a fact that we had our philosophy and the characteristics of the sphere and Sphericity all defined, and they read this, they would assume that we read it and stole it to come up with our book. It is very, very, very eerie."*

Phil was particularly stunned by the age of the document.

"This paper was so close it is unbelievable, yet the timing was wrong," Phil continued. *"Published originally in 1978, they were on an almost exact path we are on with tensegrity in organizations and social structures. In point number 3 they are even explaining tensegrity of nodes as we have designed it for [our Spherical Modeling Tool]. But as they go on they get a bit lost as they try to apply all of this to explain existing hierarchical structures instead of seeing the need for a spherical structure, but then again they did not have the Web as a guide."*

Phil rambled on and on about his findings before sending them to RLL.

"I just got your barrage of e-mails highlighting the UIA papers ..." RLL replied, rather shocked by the news. *"Don't have to look too hard to see that, except for the use of the sphere as a model, these people were onto the same thing we are more than 20 years ago. I'm dying to know if work has progressed from there."*

"Clearly, we will have to absorb the information and investigate to make sure that we acknowledge earlier work. Even though we came up with our concepts independently, that's not how it might appear to the authors of the UIA papers on the Web ..."

It was as if Phil and RLL were among a select few experiencing a new and emerging awareness that could change mankind's understanding of everything.

Had they not stumbled upon a simple ingenious visual to explain their message, it's possible their endeavor would have died. But they did. It was called The Sphere. And no systems experts were using that model.

The Sphere originally surfaced when Phil was still working at The Agency in 1998. It happened during a visit from RLL, who had traveled from California to Denver on business.

Phil was standing before a flip chart in his Santa Fe-style office in downtown Lodo, illustrating the activities of his international agents, when he began to draw a diagram that was circular in nature and filled with interconnected lines that represented the links between his agents by means of the Internet.

'That's a Sphere!' RLL exclaimed; both he and Phil recognizing it was an important revelation for their work.

Later that same visit, Phil began to expand upon his spherical drawings by attempting to illustrate the interconnected parts of a human being. It mimicked a powerful shape he'd seen long ago when Dick Doc drew the sum parts of a vitamin on a sheet of paper and showed us our first whole.

Something about the shape defied linear thought. Phil saw it and RLL saw it. And they began to consider ways in which it might have relevance to their book project that was on hiatus at the time.

"I encourage you to continue to work on the idea of a graphic of some sort that repeats throughout the book," RLL told Phil a few days later. *"I'm not sure just what it should look like, but it undoubtedly should be 3D and should demonstrate both the dis-integration and the re-integration theme as it pops up in management structures, computer networks (the Net) and life models."*

Phil's doodles on napkins after that were often spherical in nature with nodes and lines between nodes as if he were tapping into the cosmic remains of Buckminster Fuller, an American architect and inventor who had popularized the geodesic dome, even though Phil had not heard of Fuller when he began those drawings.

On a lazy afternoon that September of 1998, the shape became more precise. Phil had scanned the newspaper as usual and then began reading a book called *The Four Fold Way* about an indigenous medicine wheel and the circle of life. Then, he sat down at his computer and began to create two sphere graphics based on two ideas that had been bouncing around in his head for more than a week. One, designed to offer insights into a person's health, and a second, that would identify what he called "business equilibrium."

This time the drawings resembled a medicine wheel but included many nodes of information.

Unconstrained by the divisions and rules in the fields of medicine and psychology, Phil sketched in all the aspects he could think of that might contribute to or diminish a person's health — from nutrition and diet to physical complaints; from environmental influences and exposure to chemicals, to one's emotional history and genetic predispositions. At first pass, he identified 16 distinct elements that a person could rate on a numerical scale. These data points were then displayed on the sphere graphic to show an instant snapshot of their wellbeing. Then, at the outer edge of the circle, he penciled in three different sectors: intervention, intuition and investigation.

The business sphere was even more comprehensive at first pass and included 32 nodes of information divided into six sectors: prospects, customers, associates, management, investors and environment.

Afterwards Phil was on cloud nine.

He had devised a technique that, if developed properly, could provide a holistic snapshot of a person or a company instantly. It was like nothing he'd ever seen before.

"This is truly a momentous occasion," Phil declared, dubbing it the Philos Sphere. *"While the chart is very crude in comparison to what it will become, it is the essence of what the final spherical charting will [be]."*

"You are in quite deep," wrote The Artist back in 1998, after Phil had emailed him a sample copy of his designs. *"Good for you. You've got something here. You're going to be great on the talk shows."*

— — —

Discovering The Sphere, however, was only one of several critical breakthroughs that would be necessary for Phil and RLL to complete their book. They must define its worth in the bigger scheme of things. And time marched on ...

"It's Tuesday night. The cabin is dark except for the light of the laptop," began an email sent from RLL to Phil on May, 29, 2001. In the subject line RLL had written: *"The Journey to Sphericity and other stuff"* and it was sent late at 10:45 p.m.

"I'm picturing a young Phil Lawson choosing to suppress his doubts and sublimate his instincts to a group that promises answers to his biggest questions. Then, decades later, having discovered the lie, there he is thinking his way to freedom like someone climbing out of a deep cave with only their reason to guide them.

"It is the hero's journey. Prometheus bringing fire to mankind. Sir Gawain and the Green Knight. Whatshisname slaying the dragon of Thou Shalt," RLL continued, as if he were giving Phil a pep talk.

"You have great courage. Most of your peers in the cult did not escape and their souls will most likely not survive. That you have survived to pull back the veil that covers the sphere is neither accident nor destiny. In spherical terms it is simply an intention toward roundness — the courage and power of thought to see the true shape of things.

"Curiously, just today, it occurred to me that my spirituality has always been based on one thought. Not a question. And not an answer — I long ago stopped believing in answers. In songs and poems, in half-written books and screenplays, in late-night conversations I have always looked for the simplicity that is always there, but is always smothered by complexity (and partmentalism).

"I guess that makes me somewhat Aristotelian in that I have always envisioned and sensed that separateness is a delusion and that there is a

thread that weaves through all experience and all life. I have always been seduced by the idea that life is one simple, elegant and beautiful idea," RLL's email went on at length.

"I may have mentioned that my visualization exercise (very much like prayer or meditation) when I was a teenager, and sometimes still today, was to mind travel into the smallest smaller then go smaller still and imagine even smaller. Or, I would imagine the largest large and travel into increasingly bigger realities. In either case, I knew I was on a journey into the infinite. And I knew at some point, that the two journeys were the same, as if I was traveling two directions on the same circle. I found and still find this to be a highly satisfying conceptualization that merges reality and spirit for me. At the very least, it always helped me calm my mind so I could sleep.

"During a long and swift hike today, I got to thinking about spheres within spheres. Quite some time ago, I may have mentioned that the image of endless spheres of influence extending to the infinitely small and infinitely large feels like that same mental meditation that I have been using for about 40 years. Today, I found that all I had to do was imagine one connection in my life and quickly all the nodes and interconnections formed, I was in that sphere, which instantly revealed its connection to uncountable other spheres and in a flash I was seeing spheres within spheres within spheres. There I was, laying in my bed in my old room in my family home thinking about the smallest small and the largest large again.

"I am less inclined to use the sphere to answer questions. I seem to use it more often to ask questions. Of course, that is how I make my living. For me personally, the sphere is emerging as a way of seeing inside and outside myself at the same time. The sphere reveals the simple, simple beauty and unity that I have always wanted to be there. It is the one-line poem that includes all poems. It is the one painting that includes every color and thereby reveals that the blank canvas was not blank at all.

"As you know I have been a fan of Joseph Campbell's work for a long time. In the audio tape of his conversation with Bill Moyers, when he says that we humans have lost our mythologies and thereby lost our guides for how to live human lives, he sounds horribly sad. All the air leaves his lungs as he says it.

"We might be nuts to think that we can reveal a living mythology that will communicate universally with simple, poetic elegance, but it is damn well worth the try.

"To be perfectly honest, I never felt that the business book would change anything. Cynically, saw it as a chance to be iconoclastic and cool, to inject reason into absurdity, and to make money. [But] Sphericity is proving to be quite a different story."

As I said, time marched on. Each day seemed a replica of the last.

"We met with [name omitted] for 2 1/2 hours," Phil wrote in his journal, on another occasion when RLL came for a brainstorming session. *"The short story here is that she feels this is the multi-billion dollar idea and that major consulting firms will soon have a practice or discipline of Sphericity just like they have IT, Strategy and Change Management today. She was very excited and supportive and knows a partner at Deloitte that she was going to call over the weekend to see if she can set up a meeting with and try and take us into Deloitte. To say that both [RLL] and I were overwhelmed when we got home is no understatement. I have heard some of these same comments before but this is the first time he heard them and they are unsolicited comments that this is going to be huge ... Then Saturday morning we had a conference call with [name omitted]. The company he now works for has received major funding from Accenture and a partner from Accenture sits on the board of his company. He also sees this, Sphericity, as a major, major deal that can have incredible value. We then had a late lunch meeting with [name omitted] and before we went I told [RLL] that if she on her own says this is the billion dollar idea I will scream. I am so overwhelmed with people telling us this is the big one and yet I am starving to death and still facing homelessness each day ..."*

Life seemed to move in excruciatingly slow motion. And one thing dominated our lives: The Sphere.

"I think about The Sphere, write about the Sphere, bore my friends with The Sphere. I noodle on The Sphere more and more, especially in my dreams and waking dreamstates, even as my journalistic work fades away with the slowing economy," RLL wrote to Phil late on a Tuesday in August of 2001, responding to an email from Phil that had "Mindwalk Mania" in the subject line.

"I spend absurd amounts of time crafting and creating ideas and images when I should, according to duty, be doing other things to support my family.

"I send my ideas on to you. You send ideas to me. We synthesize, massage and question. We spawn new concepts and new insights like green-thumb philosophers, but in the process both of us have ceased to be the primary breadwinners in our homes.

"Is this good?"

A soft rain pelted the tin roof above Phil's head as he finished reading RLL's email. He rested his hands on his chin and stared into space for several minutes before writing his reply.

"As I said, Sphericity has taken over my life [too]. Your comment that the same thing is happening to you did not surprise me. You act different. It's as if it has taken possession of you in spite of your attempts to keep your life in balance.

"Good? Pam and I have spent a great deal of time asking that question and there are only two viable conclusions. One is that we — you, me, and Pam (for supporting me) — are totally crazy, that we are suffering from delusions of grandeur and will pay a horrible price for our egotism or insanity.

"The second conclusion that can be drawn from this is that there is something going on here that is bigger than you and me. That we are in some way harmonically connected to universal fields and that we are in effect "channeling" this stuff. That there is a purpose, though we may not yet be aware of what that actually is ...

"Sometime ago, I really don't know exactly when, but sometime during the past year, I have started to become painfully aware ... that I no longer have any control over my life. No matter what I do, now matter what I try, I wake up everyday and it is Groundhog Day again. The only thing I can do is think and work on Sphericity, to attempt any other activity will absolutely not work. Not only will it not work, it keeps me from working on Sphericity and that keeps me in this situation all that much longer.

"Yes, I believe this is what it takes, at least for us with Sphericity. Good or bad has no bearing. We went on this journey, whether we volunteered for this or were drafted is of no consequence. We are the ones that have been allowed to see the re-emergence of the Sphere. We are far into the wilderness, far beyond where any person has gone before. Our maps of how we got here are of no value to get us back to where we came from, we cannot go back to that place anymore, we are different. The Sphere is the only way out of this place. Without it, I fear we may be more lost than we imagine.

"I am inclined to take this very seriously. There is only one thing scares me worse than the reality of our horrible and deteriorating financial condition and that is that the "quantum harmonics" that we are experiencing with the universe will cease.

"We must finish the book as we see it and we must do so very soon. Not that the universe is time sensitive but our financial situations are

extremely time sensitive and I see only two ways for both of us to address our finances. One is stop this nonsense, throw it all away and try to go back into the world, get jobs and live (that is assuming that the universe will allow us to do this which is very questionable to me, understand that I am serious about this comment). Or two, finish the book so the universal fields of attraction can go to work at finding ways we may be able to eat doing this or even something else. Right now we have nothing on paper to really attract anyone.

"OK, this next comment is unrelated, or is it? For some reason, I don't know why, but for several weeks I have been thinking that you need to be out here for a few days. I don't know why, I have no agenda ... the main thing I want to do is to take you up to the top of Mt. Evans. I don't know if you have ever been there before but it is the most sacred place I know."

And so RLL came. The very week terrorists flew two planes into the World Trade Center and another into the Pentagon. And his stay grew longer when all air travel was suspended.

"Wednesday I [delivered mail] and then yesterday we were supposed to work on the book but we both knew we couldn't," Phil wrote in his journal the week of 9/11, both he and RLL shocked by the attacks they had witnessed together on television. *"We went to the top of Mt Evans for a couple of hours. It was a cleansing and really helped."*

As RLL waited out the travel delays he responded to emails from friends who were checking on his whereabouts.

"Here we have a textbook example of the shrinking globe and what it truly means to our future," RLL wrote to a friend in Canada. *"That this horror causes not only America but the whole world to tremble is, perhaps, a very positive development in the condition of humanity.*

"In spherical terms, what we are experiencing is the strong tensegral connection between our personal spheres. You immediately feel the effects of the attack through those of us you know as friends. We immediately feel your caring and concern. In some small way, the shape of our individual lives are changed by the interaction of our spheres."

"Canada is behind you!" his friend emailed him back. *"We have 17 grounded planes in Winnipeg and thousands of people across other Canadian cities. The response has been overwhelming with people lined up to donate blood, opening their homes to stranded passengers and volunteering to help. Local governments and medical response people are mobilizing to assist. We will be there for you. Our hearts ache and reach out to you ..."*

In the days that followed, Phil continued to record brief observations of a country and a world that was as he put it, *"fundamentally and irrevocably changed."*

"As I sit here thinking about the illusion of stability I find it very interesting that in addition to everything else the WTC attack showed us, it revealed to us in real time before the entire world that the buildings that we believe to be our monuments to our lives, that will be here for generations to come, the ultimate representations of what stable means, crumbled to dust in about 40 minutes as we watched," Phil journaled.

A month after 9/11, my father died. He had slipped into a coma in a Texas hospital by the time I arrived to say my goodbyes. As I sat beside him, my fingers resting under his palm, he squeezed my hand. Was it a spasm? Did he know I was there? Was it the same grip that reassured me as a child? Either way, I felt comforted by it.

'Your father had surgery, it didn't go well and you'd better come quickly,' had been the duty call from Loretta Lynn.

We hadn't spoken much in seven years. It had been that long since I lost my religion and gave up my family's traditions. And from my father's perspective there was little left between us to talk about. During the rare times we did connect, our conversations would start out cordial but digress when he felt the need to interrogate me: *"Pam, are you at least reading your Bible? Do you still get the Watchtower in the mail?"* At which point I would balk, and in an angrier voice than necessary, defend my choices and my character.

But during our last phone call together, a few short weeks before his death, something felt different. He had listened with interest as I carried on about my personal life as a journalist living in a mountain cabin. And that gave me peace in the days following his death. When the link between my step-mother and I was severed — she having no desire to stay in touch with a heretic. An attitude that stung even worse when it cost me my relationship with my loveable blonde-haired, blue-eyed, baby brother — a child produced from her union with my father who was now in his 20s and remained her loyal advocate.

Had I not written a story about a man with Usher's Syndrome, during the early days of my career as a reporter, I might have been overtaken by loss after my father's death. But his story set a new benchmark for human endurance.

The man had lost both his hearing and his sight to the disease in his mid-40s. Before then, he was a gregarious dentist married to the love of his life and the pair had raised four children. When our paths crossed he was

86. His wife, who had been his "eyes and ears," had recently died, and he had been forced to move in with his son. And yet, he had not lost heart. In fact, he played the piano for me during our interview — a classical piece performed from memory, though he could no longer hear the music.

These and other encounters I was experiencing as a writer served more than my job. They were my reality check.

Each breaking news story; each community event or highway accident that I covered interrupted my own whining — which had become quite repetitive as I frequently, and earnestly, recounted to Phil all of my failings. And each of my achievements that had gone unrewarded. Like the prestigious catalogue project I had produced for The Agency which, I was told, had become a "best seller." I had spent nearly a year of my life on that catalogue and it was heartwarming news. But it was also bittersweet since The Alien had in a moment of cruelty removed my name from the production credits before the catalogue went to print.

My painful memories were ripe for the picking. And pick at them I did. Until the day I stopped talking. And for what seemed like months barely spoke at all around the house during a self-imposed time-out. My mind was booby trapped with emotional triggers that seemed impossible to disarm.

Meditations barely soothed me. So I kept experimenting. Caressing beautiful stones during my contemplations to tap their energy, including a magnificent slice of a petrified "palm tree," Phil had bought for me. It had been found in a Colorado River (Colorado doesn't have palm trees) which was quite extraordinary and meant it was millions of years old. Pressing that slab against my heart, connecting me to an ancient past, made my anguish seem irrelevant.

At Walhalla I began to look inward in ways I had never done before — and outward. I became especially sensitive to my surroundings. The dozen or so baby mice I found trapped in a sink, which I scooped up one at a time and released safely in a field. The magpie hanging upside down 30 feet in the air, its leg caught in fishing wire it had used to build a nest — the sight of which, neither Phil nor I could bear. So he climbed the tall skinny pine, despite the risks, and rescued the bird.

Everything around us had relevance — even the snake that had shed its skin before our eyes the week before our arrival at Walhalla when we were visiting an historic Indian site. As I began to explore animal totems, I learned that in certain cultures seeing that phenomenon symbolized rebirth and transformation.

And perhaps that summed up our lives, for we were in the midst of a great transformation.

"Something's coming," Phil would say — as if his whole body was bracing itself for yet another inspired thought. *"There's something here. I can feel it. It's like a bubble,"* he'd continue as if tapping into a greater consciousness. *"I have so much information in my head — so much more than I can express..."*

But he kept at it until he did find a way to express it.

One of the early driving forces for writing his book was to make sense of why the business world and life in general no longer worked the way people had been taught it should.

Understanding both the "how" and "why" caused Phil to follow a trail of information back to the Renaissance — a cultural movement generally seen as a period of intellectual transformation that profoundly influenced literature, philosophy, art, politics, science and religion.

"Why, in a relatively short period of time, in a very small geographic area, was there an explosion of knowledge that changed the world?" Phil wondered.

RLL was well versed in the liberal arts and was quite informed about the Renaissance, which was helpful to Phil. Even so, during further research, they found little that addressed *why* it came to be.

"Everything I read tells me ***what*** *happened,"* Phil would say, exasperated. *"Galileo did this; Copernicus did that; Descartes said this; Michelangelo created that; Newton wrote this; Sir Walter Raleigh thought that ... but my question is* ***why*** *did it happen?"*

As he examined the history of the Renaissance, that spanned about 300 years from the 14th through the 17th centuries, he began to see what he believed to be an obvious tie to that period and the one mankind was living in now.

"There comes a point when our experience contradicts our training — what we've been taught of how the world works," Phil would say, attempting to verbalize what he was sensing. *"And we face the conundrum of 'do we accept what we were told and deny what we see and experience,' or, do we reject it, leave it behind and embrace what we now see and experience that is proving to be true?"*

Phil wondered if there was a word or phrase to define what he was thinking and searched a variety of cultures to find one.

"Hmmm, "prescient" comes close, but it's not perfect."

Until the day he came upon the word "consilience" coined by a 19th century Philosopher named William Whewell in 1840. Consilience derives from the Latin consilere, meaning to leap or jump together. Whewell used the word to describe the interlocking of explanations of cause and effect between academic disciplines.

Phil latched on to the word believing its meaning could be expanded upon.

"When Whewell coined the word he was trying to understand and explain why scientists at similar times could have similar discoveries and not be connected to one another," Phil would elaborate. *"But I am expanding his use of consilience to include all human activities — those moments in time when a "jumping together" of people, ideas and events occur and alter an entire civilization."*

Attempting to explain why the Renaissance occurred and how it mirrored society today was a grandiose undertaking for Phil.

"The only reason I have these thoughts is because of my experiences," Phil would say. *"You don't have these thoughts when you are 'in the system' and it's working for you. [RLL] didn't have these thoughts. But my world view, everything I had been taught prior to this, how man came to be, what we are supposed to do and believe, why we are here, I found to be limiting at best and wrong at most. I understand how Galileo felt, how Copernicus felt, and this is key ... every one of those people from Copernicus through to (Isaac) Newton were very, very staunch faithful supporters of the Church. None of them were seeking to overthrow the Church. Martin Luther was questioning it, but he's not on my list. All they did was look up and say, 'Oh sh**! I keep watching the stars and I don't think the earth is the center of the universe. Holy f**k, what does that mean? The Church says everything revolves around the earth and man ...'"*

Phil paused and remembered the January day in 1995 when we left the Hollywood Hills. His two sisters had arrived from Texas to help us pack up the remainder of our belongings. Phil had grown a beard and his hair was longer than usual and one of them was very worried about his spiritual well-being.

"We're eating at the Outtake Café on Ventura Boulevard," Phil recalled with detail. *"And she is basically pleading with me, 'Why can't you just submit to the Governing Body [at Headquarters in New York]. And I said, 'Because they are wrong. They don't have it all figured out.' I either had to deny my intelligence and my experiences, deny what I had seen and learned and just believe that these people are God's chosen ones even though my senses told me otherwise. Or, I had to step into the unknown. Lose my history, my friends and my family — everything we had worked for. Because of that, I was able to understand what Copernicus and*

*Galileo and Descartes went through. They were not trying to disprove the Church or discredit the Pope. It's just that the body of knowledge ... by simply opening their eyes is all they did, when they opened their eyes and looked up they said 'Sh**! The earth is not the center of the universe!'"*

*"Do you think they actually said 'Sh**?'"* I butted in, but Phil ignored me.

*"Once you find one thing wrong, then its 'oh, that's not right either.' The mathematicians figured out the science of probability and chance. If enough people cross the road in front of enough horses and carriages, people will get run over. It's not God doing it. Holy sh**!"* Phil said again, obviously distressed by the implications of what he was saying.

"Even Benjamin Franklyn played a role later on by learning the science behind lightning strikes — and oh, it's not God punishing you!

"Collectively these people, none of them leading the way, none of them trying to take out the Church, or take on the order of the world, had these recognitions. Then they realized 'Oh my God, I can't talk about this because I will die!' It was after all during the Inquisition. Many refused to have their works published until death because of it.

"That's how I was prepared to see something almost no one else could see," Phil said, managing as usual to work his own story into it. *"...Because my experiences mirrored so closely those of Descartes and Galileo. I understand how they were thinking and how they made the leaps they made. That's why I like the word consilience. Whewell was looking only in science. I say it applies to everything. When humanity's experience exceeds the limitations of their worldview — their mindset — that's a great word, their mind-is-set — we are now forced to make a decision. Do we revert back, as my sister wants me to do, or, do we leap into the unknown, into the incredible possibilities?"*

So there it was. During the Renaissance a collective group of people began to see their world differently — began to challenge their belief systems, some of which, had been in place for thousands of years. And they needed a way to explain it.

So, someone stepped forward.

"The whole visible world is as if it were a machine in which there was nothing at all to consider except the figures and motions of its parts," wrote French Philosopher and mathematician René Descartes in the mid-16th century. Descartes was a revolutionary character, now deemed the father of modern philosophy.

He penned his view on the heels of discoveries by Galileo and Sir Francis Bacon.

Galileo, an astronomer and physicist believed the universe was written in the language of mathematics, and Bacon's system of logic implied the mysteries of the universe could be examined, studied and solved using rational, scientific methods.

Some 50 years after Descartes, mathematician Gottfried Leibniz proposed that even human thinking could be reduced to a mathematical method. If the right formula could be arrived at, he said, any human problem could be settled through mathematical calculations.

Then as the Renaissance neared the end of its run along comes the embodiment of all the great mechanistic thinkers. Influenced by Copernicus, Galileo, Da Vinci, Bacon, Descartes, Leibniz and others, Sir Issac Newton in 1687 published *Principia*, often called the greatest science book ever written. He crystallized and solidified the notion that a universal mechanism exists, and that its universal laws apply even to the origins and nature of mankind.

Out of many generations of questioning and probing, a different picture of reality emerged — one that replaced superstition and arbitrary church control — without a war or revolution — one, that vividly depicted our bodies, our thoughts, the physical universe and all of space and time as a masterful machine at work. And in such a reality, understanding any aspect of our existence required only that we investigate the underlying mechanisms.

The machine as metaphor had been born. And society embraced it without a doubt.

As those thoughts took form on the pages of Phil and RLL's book, I couldn't help but marvel at the creative process. And at their gumption to keep digging (— much deeper than I have touched upon here —) to discover the basis of society's belief systems — the one's that have defined our behaviors for the last several hundred years.

Beliefs that gathered steam and enthusiasm during the 18th Century Enlightenment movement — when philosophers and social engineers of that era dissected the mechanisms of government and economics like laboratory specimens in an attempt to redesign and control society.

By the 19th Century, we were using mechanical models for agriculture and manufacturing, and factories were rapidly overshadowing farms and guilds as the major employers in Western nations. We even engineered our institutions to conform to the factory model. Then, we applied those same production methods with equal enthusiasm in our schools, hospitals, banks, political systems and other social institutions. We built Newton's picture of the physical universe and Descartes' vision of the metaphysical realm into all of our assumptions and attitudes about health, education, career and politics.

During the final two decades of the 19th century, we applied genetic, statistical, historical and experimental methods toward understanding one of the most fundamental mysteries of life: human consciousness, so that even our brain became a machine.

At the beginning of the 20th Century prominent American psychologist John B. Watson introduced the theory of "behaviorism," that was quickly accepted by many, proposing that all human and animal behavior results from an organism's response to external stimuli rather than internal mental processes.

The ideas put forth by Watson and others created the notion that the human mind is a *tabula rasa* (blank slate) on which can be sketched whatever designs we desire. Watson boasted: *"Give me a dozen healthy infants, well-formed, and my own specified world to bring them up in and I'll guarantee to take any one at random and train him to become any type of specialist I might select — doctor, lawyer, artist, merchant, chief, and yes, even beggar-man and thief, regardless of his talents, penchants, tendencies, abilities, vocations, and race of his ancestors."*

Finally, by the mid-20th Century, we humans were horrified by what we had become, how we had become parts in a machine. The artists, philosophers and writers among us were particular appalled —*"We must not allow the clock and the calendar to blind us to the fact that each moment of life is a miracle and mystery,"* wrote novelist H.G. Wells — they feared mankind was losing its collective soul to the machine. And it nearly did.

But there was a shift in awareness already happening among a select number of scientists. On-the-ball folks who were making their views heard.

Among them, was Ludwig von Bertalanffy, an Austrian-born biologist, and professor at the Canadian University of Alberta, who was exploring "the general science of wholeness."

Remember him? I wrote a teaser about him earlier in this book. You see, two years after my grandpa Bert died Bertalanffy stumbled across information that he would eventually write about 40 years later in 1968 in a book called *General Systems Theory*. And that book contained a lot of big words in it. Like this:

"Compared to the analytical procedure of classical science with resolution into component elements and one-way or linear causality as basic category, the investigation of organized wholes of many variables requires new categories of interaction, transaction, organization,

teleology," Bertalanffy wrote. *"These considerations lead to the postulate of a new scientific discipline which we call general system theory. Its subject matter is formulation of principles that are valid for "systems" in general, whatever the nature of the component elements and the relations or "forces" between them."*

And he was not alone in his pursuit. From the 1950s to the late 1990s others including mathematician Edward Lorenz, inventor Buckminster Fuller, scientist Murray Gell-Mann, scientist Peter Senge and organizational development expert Margaret Wheatley stepped forward with their studies and observations, too.

Lorenz, a professor at the Massachusetts Institute of Technology, began challenging linear statistical models in his field in the 1950s, which led to his pioneering *Chaos Theory,* a field of study that examines the behavior of dynamic systems. In fact, he earned prestigious honors and awards for his contributions. (He coined the term Butterfly Effect, remember?)

"Bucky" Fuller, a designer and futurist who popularized the geodesic dome especially intrigued Phil, now that Phil was finally reading the man's books and memoir.

"I find society is just groping around with parts, never understanding wholes and continually being surprised by them," Fuller once said.

Then there was Gell-Mann, a Nobel Prize recipient and co-founder of the Santa Fe Institute, who wrote in one of his published papers that it is *"essential"* for humanity to *"take a crude look at the whole picture, taking into account, as much as possible, the strong interactions among the various parts."*

Senge contributed his own view on humanity's need to change its mindset in his national bestseller written in 1990 titled, *The Fifth Discipline: The art and practice of the learning organization.* His book presented organizations as dynamic systems, in a state of continuous adaptation and improvement. Senge, a director at MIT's Sloan's School of Management, wrote this:

"I have come to believe that there is an opening today for a new movement of meaning and change. Our traditional ways of managing and governing are breaking down."

But Senge knew well that our "traditions" are deeply imbedded in our vocabulary and thinking ...

"It is extremely awkward in normal verbal language to describe circular feedback processes," Senge wrote in his book. "So, by and large, we give up and just say, in effect, "A caused B, which caused C." But this convenient shorthand suggests to the subconscious mind that "A ***did***

cause B." Subconsciously, we tend to forget that "B also caused A." If all we have is linear language, then we think in linear ways, and we perceive the world linearly — that is, as a chain of events. It is impossible for us to grasp the scope of the consequences, but we know they are sweeping," Senge continued.

"However, if we begin to master a systemic language, all this starts to change. The subconscious is subtly retrained to structure data in circles instead of straight lines. We find that we "see" feedback processes and systems archetypes everywhere. A new framework for thinking becomes imbedded. A switch is thrown, much like what happens in mastering a foreign language. We begin to dream in the new language, or to think spontaneously in its terms and constructs. When this happens with systems thinking, we become, as one manager puts it, "looped for life."

"As organizational theorist Charles Kiefer puts it, "When this switch is thrown subconsciously, you become a systems thinker ever thereafter. Reality is automatically seen systemically as well as linearly (there still are lots of problems for which a linear perspective is perfectly adequate). Alternatives that are impossible to see linearly are surfaced by the subconscious as proposed solutions. Solutions that were outside of our 'feasible set' become part of our feasible set. 'Systemic' becomes a way of thinking (almost a way of being) and not just a problem solving methodology.""

Even Wheatley pointed out the fallacies of our compartmentalized world in her book, Leadership and the New Science, when she wrote: *"We have broken the world into parts and fragments for so long now that we are ill-prepared to see that a different order is moving the whole ... one of our greatest challenges, after so many centuries of separation and fragmentation, is to discover new ways of thinking and sensing that allow us to comprehend the whole."*

But only Fuller and Wheatley's quotes would end up in Phil's and RLL's book. They did not want to make it too "technical" a read, but rather an engaging one.

"Murray Gell-Mann speaks the language of physicists. He discovered quarks! He stopped speaking English along time ago," Phil would say, in an attempt to be clever.

"We are not scientists. We have no credentials. We make no claims to be creating a new science, nor are we attempting to explain what scientists have discovered in technical terms," Phil would defend. "The driving force in everything I am doing is based on two things, really. The South; where we had to deal with people with little education who had

complex problems and needed to figure out how to get through them. And the corporate world — I experienced the exact same thing there, business people who were overwhelmed with the radical changes occurring; the end of lifetime employment, of new technologies altering everything overnight and globalization...

"Our book is about practical applications of systems science without using big words. We say there is a villain — The Box — we put everything into boxes based on our mechanistic thinking — versus The Sphere. And this is how The Sphere works — it has an underlying systems science basis — but you won't find systems scientists defining its common characteristics. We extrapolated those from our own life experiences — the "fly-by-the-seat-of-your-pants" way to understand the inter-workings of "systems" for the common man. That life is made up of interconnected nodes, fields of attraction, and fields of nascency. All we're doing is providing a way to understand that — to not get in a tizzy about it — it's not about "what's wrong with you" — it's not about fixing "broke parts."

"How do we reach stressed out busy people with this news? That our understanding of our world is expiring without notice? That there's a shift happening? That the sphere of our existence is interconnected and self-organizing? That we must "see" whole to "be" whole?

"Oh, and by the way, we don't have 300 years like our ancestors did to switch to a new "mental model" of life! We have less than 30. It's time to 'shift or die.'"

Phil knew time was short. That people must be told. But forward thinking scientists were themselves trapped in the boxes of their institutions. They were bound by outdated methods to substantiate their views and they were obligated to protect their names, tenure, reputations and esteemed jobs to continue their work and preserve it.

But Phil was not. And perhaps the Universe knew it, I would sometimes think to myself.

Here's this yahoo who has nothing left to lose. If only he and RLL can piece together enough essential clues to break through to the masses. To break through with this message: that humanity is once again in the midst of a great consilience — a leaping together of people, ideas and events that is completely altering our worldview, but at warp speed this time, thanks to the Internet and constantly advancing technologies. If only they can get this message across: That it's time to wrap our minds around a sphere. That a sphere as metaphor, as a new visual model to live by, can help us see past our outdated mindset that is linear and mechanistic and dangerous — a mindset that restricts our flexibility, adaptability and responsiveness at a time when we need it most. The Sphere introduces us to what makes us whole. And once we experience that, a whole new picture of our world emerges.

"I feel more and more that the next thing we need after the book is the institute," Phil wrote in his journal late one night. It wasn't the first time he'd explored the idea and now he was revisiting it. *"[RLL and I] talked on Sunday for 2 and a half hour's about it and he said that as I started to say this he was thinking the exact same thing. I told him this is so big, so important and that changing a person's mindset will not happen in an hour presentation or a one-day seminar and that people need to get away and have time to hear, think, mediate, ask questions etc. But you know what I have been suspecting is holding everything up? Us. Phil and [RLL]. I think we have tried to force Sphericity to be a business or something and until we are willing to let it be what it wants to be and we are ready to stand up before the world and say with a straight face that this is vitally important, it is not going to happen ... It is 11:00 p.m. I have to be up in a little while and I have to do the dishes first. Goodnight."*

Along with The Sphere came a new vocabulary for Phil and RLL and new ways to explain the human experience:

"As it is with music, color and form, the field energies of our spheres sometimes combine in advantageous ways," RLL began to massage the words into place.

"In The Sphere, as field energies overlap and interact they blend, much like tones in a musical composition or mixtures of color on an artist's canvas. When two or more fields interact propitiously, we experience harmony. In spherical terms, we refer to this phenomenon as field harmonics ..."

Sixty-five chapter's rich with information took shape filled with characteristics of The Sphere. Phil and RLL explained how we can shape-shift by means of The Sphere. How, like nature, all the nodes and interconnections of our spheres can rearrange themselves in response to internal and external stimuli. How, through an invisible web of tension, information can be transferred, exchanged and shared throughout our spheres.

"Out of field interactions emerge the qualities and characteristics of our lives, our world and the Universe," they explained.

They even introduced readers to what they called the "universal sphere."

"When we envision with clarity the field energies of every sphere interacting with the field energies of every other, we see that all spheres

influence all spheres, even across spans of time and distance. When we look at or think about the all-inclusive sphere of interconnection and interdependence, we are looking at, or thinking about, the universal sphere.

"The universal sphere is not hypothetical or abstract. As with all aspects of The Sphere, the universal sphere is a representation of something real, something everyone knows exists. We might call it by some other name, or think of it in some other way, but the universal sphere is as real as we are. The universal sphere represents all that is knowable and all that is unknowable."

On and on they wrote, keeping the chapters short, two to four pages in length, and adding nearly 90 illustrations.

Finally, *Being Spherical: Reshaping Our Lives and World for the 21st Century* was published the spring of 2004, nearly five years after we'd moved to Walhalla.

But it was a handsome work of genius upon its completion. A book signing party at Walhalla followed, attended by friends and business acquaintances that had offered feedback and cheered the writers on.

"Being Spherical is a modern philosophical treatise that is attractively bound and illustrated ..." wrote one book reviewer with a PhD, a brief summary of which went something like this: "It espouses the need for complete social integration as the next step in the evolution of our civilization, a step that may ultimately be essential to the very survival of the human race. The authors, in a thorough 65 short-chapter presentation, seek to convince the reader of the necessity of replacing the current worldview ... The book has great merit. It targets, gives practical tools to, and is best understood by the thoughtful individual ... who is concerned with our world, its long-term direction and our long-term survival ..."

The book even succeeded in accomplishing what scientist Peter Senge and organizational theorist Charles Kiefer said occurs when people actually "get" the science of systems.

"What Phil and [RLL] have given us is not merely a new lexicon of terms to describe our business and personal environments but a radically different way to comprehend and interact with them," wrote a college educator who read the book. "Since being introduced to Being Spherical, I find myself building mental spheres for both my personal and professional environments. The process is strikingly effective."

Phil and RLL toasted their success at the historic Fort restaurant in the Colorado Rockies, a place often frequented by celebrities and dignitaries.

They had stayed the course despite the price paid and it was time for a shot of whiskey spiked with gunpowder.

— — —

It happened over those five years that we shook off the heat and chills of our past like a bad fever.

And the storm of my anger dissolved like a cloud, along with my perceptions of life.

I understood the dog-eared characters that frequented mystic fairs and visited fortune-tellers — those that had tried to "fit in," in everyway possible to no avail and were now searching for solidarity among men in ponytails wearing talismans and women dressed in velvet reading auras.

We found ourselves transported to a mysterious but comforting subordinate reality — the intermediary spaces of the universal sphere, the intermediary spaces of us, the IS of US, that had its own powerful properties.

Our awareness of it materialized slowly at first ... a few months after our arrival at Walhalla when Ben our 11-year-old Welsh Corgi suffered kidney failure. It was the same pup who waited patiently at the front door of our double-wide, in Yucaipa, on the exact days the Petite Blond arrived for work. (Oh, how he loved that woman!) It was the same dog I had nursed back to life after a bout with cancer at the age of six when we left Dallas in a rush for Denver.

Ben was so attached to Walhalla, nestled as it was in a forest, that when we toured the cabin before moving there he had refused to get in the Jeep to leave, instead standing firm by the front door as if to say, 'I'm already home.'

It killed me that 'home' would be a short stay for him — that 18 weeks after our arrival his body would wear out. I could not bear to part with Ben, especially not then. And for many days Phil flushed his kidneys with an IV solution to ease his discomfort. Until a cold January day when a stranger arrived at Walhalla, a nurse, there to verify our health stats for a life insurance policy.

It had snowed that morning and the roads were icy. And Phil had agreed to meet her at the nearest post office, his four-wheeler being a safer option than her car for the last two-mile leg of the drive to our cabin.

She was a warm person, easy to laugh and fascinated by Phil's ramblings about the book he was writing.

Ben had been totally silent during her visit, hidden out of sight in the middle bedroom, resting on his favorite sheepskin rug, until it neared time for her departure. Then he suddenly barked once.

"You have a dog?" the nurse replied, being a dog lover herself.

"Yes, but he's very sick," I had answered her, the sound of my voice strained.

"Can I see him?" She had pressed me.

"No!" had been my unfriendly reply.

Then the phone rang — a call Phil needed to take — and I was charged with driving the nurse back to her car.

On the way there in the center of odd chatter between us the nurse blurted out, *"You need to tell him, it's okay to go."*

I swallowed hard, kept my eyes on the road and ignored her suggestion, steering the conversation in several different directions.

But I knew what she meant. I had seen the resolve in Ben's eyes a few days earlier, during one of his last visits outdoors, as he took in the sights and the smells, then turned to look back over his shoulder directly at me. Still, I couldn't turn loose of him, fighting to hang on to the link between us like a drowning woman. I could not — would not — lose one more thing.

Parked in front of the post office, cold air swept into the cab of the Jeep through the passenger door as the nurse transferred her equipment to the front seat of her car. And it was then, in the midst of her clamoring that a small dog with scruffy hair leapt from her car to the ground, then, onto the seat beside me.

As our eyes locked, the creature lifted its front right paw and began to wave it at me, as if it were in a hurry, as if it had something to say.

"Oh my!" the nurse cried out, reaching for the little fellow. *"This is quite unusual behavior for him!"*

We smiled said our goodbyes and I headed home, unable to shake the sensation that something inexplicable had just happened — a message, sent to me through a total stranger and her dog.

When I arrived home I slipped into the middle bedroom preparing to give Ben his daily medication. I scooped my little boy up to my chest — that handsome fellow with the short white legs and magnificent red coat — and I closed my eyes.

"Its okay if you need to ...," I thought the words, but could not speak them.

When I opened my eyes Ben gasped, then gagged and died in my arms.

An indescribable pain seized my heart in the weeks that followed — the culmination of everything I'd ever lost. I was in trouble; I couldn't imagine getting attached to anything else.

Before Ben died, I had considered getting a puppy. I had been strangely attracted to a medium-sized curly breed I'd once seen while walking Ben through Denver's Cheesman Park. I had tracked down a breeder, after we moved to Walhalla, imagining a puppy might energize Ben. Phil and I had even visited the breeder's home and cuddled a chocolate brown boy that had a gold ribbon around his neck. But our veterinarian was weary of the plan, worried it would stress Ben more than it would benefit him, at that late stage of his illness.

It was three months after Ben's death, on the eve of spring in the Rockies that a friendly voice turned up on my answering machine.

"Where'd you go?" said a woman in her late 40s. *"I still have that curly brown boy! If you're interested, give me a call."*

I got the message on my birthday, and I admit it excited me. In three months time I'd decided the heartache of losing a pet paled in comparison to life without one. But it was critical that I connect with the right pet. Scanning the papers and visiting the pound had not produced such a match. But I remembered that curly brown boy with fondness. He was special, I decided right then and there.

When Phil and I showed up for a second look, the puppy at 16 weeks had grown into a gangly specimen, its hair nappy, its face resembling a gorilla's. But it didn't matter. He was 'the one' — though I didn't know how I would possibly pay for a purebred Portuguese Water Dog in our financial state.

Affordable, practical, realistic — that pup didn't fit any of those criteria. Still, we managed. First, a down payment that sufficed, followed by a variety of trade outs on my end that settled the bill.

That's because it wasn't just about the dog, which I grew to love deeply. It was something else, which manifest slowly over time. It was about the woman who owned the dog — a business professional that bonded immediately with Phil and the message in his book; a woman who came to champion his cause. A woman who later sent paying clients his way; who later introduced him to other important contacts that likewise hired him for projects and became advocates of The Sphere.

We were tuning in to the IS of US — a realm that defied the steps and routines of life and the carefully crafted conclusions about it. It was a space that transcended clicks, secret societies and the boxed-in kingdoms of sophisticates. It was an interconnected place — where head and heart cautiously co-mingled and birthed new behaviors.

The clues appeared to be everywhere. Even the energy healer I visited on occasion embodied them, a woman who offered a lower price to me, without asking, if she "felt" I was strapped for cash.

And so did the Parkinson's Man, embody them.

As a young pilot, he once flew anti-submarine warfare aircraft for the Navy, before becoming a systems engineer and computer scientist in the space business, all of which came to a grinding halt due to an "unfortunate convergence of bad politics and the limits of modern medicine," as he would explain it. By the time we'd met him, introduced by a friend, his central nervous system had failed him and he was no longer employable. He'd undergone a risky surgery and received a brain implant, a pace-maker like device to minimize the body tremors from advanced Parkinson's disease. Now strapped with the rules of disability, he could not engage in paying projects, lest he jeopardize his disability income and the needs of his family.

Seated before Phil, in a small dimly lit room sandwiched between an electric keyboard and a computer station, the Parkinson's Man listened intently to Phil's speech about The Sphere, the principles behind it and his technology goals. Transforming The Sphere from a paper idea into an actual technology had turned into quite the undertaking. Phil had designed the software specifications, but no technology companies he solicited knew how to build the display for the visual model.

But Parkinson's Man believed there was a way he could help. It would just take a little time on his part.

Before we left that evening, he shared an intimate experience with us. He turned off the pace-maker in his brain, with a handheld programmer, and showed us the severity of his condition. Over a 10-minute period his body began to shake uncontrollably and his speech became undecipherable. When he turned it back on, he regained his composure and drove home.

Sharing that intensely private moment with Parkinson's Man gave us the chills. And when he did later custom design the visual display without charge, the chills returned. With his design in hand, Phil was finally able to hire a firm to build his online sphere technology. A man off-grid with a brain implant had saved our ass.

Phil and I were swimming in the chemistry of life — unrestrained by the mechanisms that man had built to contain it.

But clueing in to it, into the obviousness of it, on a regular basis, at least, required skills. Fortunately, I had the perfect job to hone a few of them.

"Tell me you ARE NOT still verifying quotes!" one of my editors would often grill me.

*"What? Um ... well, only the **important** ones ..."* I would admit to him, without clarifying that all my stories were important. And it wasn't just key quotes I verified; I often verified key details in a story, too. Sometimes even reading the whole story to a person I had interviewed.

My editor had been taught that was a "no-no," that people could use it to their advantage, could change their statements if it suited them and that was bad journalism. But it didn't happen that way for me. Perhaps it was how I explained myself when I phoned people back. Perhaps, I had listened carefully enough during the initial interview. Whatever the reasons, it was rare that anyone challenged the material I read back to them. *"That **is** what I said ..."* was most often their response.

I couldn't easily tell that editor I verified the quotes for *me*. Well, *them* and *me*. It was my way of "tuning in." I considered myself intuitive by nature, but my instincts were hit and miss at best, which frustrated me. That's because I'd forced myself to "conform" for too long.

But connecting with other people on a consistent basis — sensing and feeling and translating thousands of their stories helped me refine my own internal guidance system. The more accurately I reflected them the truer my own instincts became.

That didn't mean my stories were flawless, or perfectly written. It merely meant my intention to stay true to the message came through. And when I covered stories that involved three different sides, and all three later contacted me and thanked me for correctly portraying their views, I knew my technique was working.

In the midst of my "tuning in" efforts though, I was shaken by an experience involving one of them.

'Was that YOU that wrote THAT EDITORIAL?' A woman grilled me after a firefighter meeting. The fire agency had been embroiled in heated controversy for an extended period and those involved wanted heads on a platter. I had been covering the unfolding events in my usual way and people had grown accustomed to my storytelling. The matter had reached a climax when the head of my department promised to write an editorial piece in the paper to inform voters of the newspaper's view of the controversy, right before board elections. But that person had dropped the ball — one of many, struggling with his own personal problems. Thus, I felt

compelled to step up at the last minute and keep his promise, for too many reasons to explain here. But writing an official editorial, taking a stand on the emotionally charged subject was a highly inadvisable step on my part, considering I was the sole reporter covering the crisis. As you might imagine, it blew up in my face.

'Well, did you?!' The wife of a board member glared at me. 'Your writing is always fair, but that piece was awfully biased.'

After mustering a pitifully evasive reply that went something like this, *"oh, um, the editorial department produced it," (which I was a member of)* I left the scene disturbed by what had happened. Why would this woman, who didn't personally know me, ask if I'd written that editorial? One that took a stand, no holds barred? Especially considering I never wrote the editorials.

I'm guessing she sensed *me* in the words, my authentic tone that was present whether I was channeling the thoughts of others or scrambling to assemble my own. And it occurred to me that we, stripped of our motives and enculturation, are not empty shells. There is something there ... that *is us* — our constant, even when the outer world is spinning. The key is to stay in tune with it. And listen for that authentic sound in others.

It was all part of the awareness I was gaining on the job, though it had little to do with my job criteria. Nowhere had I read in the journals of journalism that, 1.) People, in general, have built-in honesty meters, but 2.) Motive trumps honesty, 3.) Perception trumps motive, 4.) Enculturation shapes perception, and 5.) Metaphor powers enculturation, however ... 6.) When our honesty shines through we can often, underneath it all, still reflect it in others.

My life — Phil's and mine — had taught us that we were more than our enculturation. And we can change our metaphors.

Which is why Phil made his spheres, all kinds of them by then, having filed a patent the year before the book was finished for the spherical modeling tool.

The Sphere was designed to be a mirror. When people used it they saw a reflection of their own perceptions. It was a simple mental exercise that allowed them to see the views of their life in context — linked together, in a circle, on a single page. It freed them from the step-by-step thinking that had been imposed on them for the last few hundred years — that prevented them from seeing the whole picture. That had reduced us all to parts in the machine and restricted our dynamic human potential — even made us fearful of it.

And it did more than that, as Phil would later find out working with PhDs who had studied neuroscience. The simple design of The Sphere, that displayed words and a visual together, allowed the left and right brain to co-mingle, bypassing the fight or flight trigger in the brain. It also helped people overcome the limits of working memory that prevents most of us from juggling more than about seven things in our brain at once. Those features and others made it possible for sphere users to have much calmer and briefer conversations regarding sensitive, complex or controversial topics. It wasn't a sexy looking system, but as Phil continued to get clients and fine tune its features, even meeting with specialists who guided him through writing better online questions, The Sphere became remarkably purposeful.

That's not to diss machines. I've bonded with my fair share over the years (Love our Jeep!) But we humans are not machines and never have been. We are organic and biological. And in biology resilience comes from diversity. In fact, specialization decreases diversity and sets the stage for catastrophe.

Remember the Dust Bowl of the 1930s? Drought conditions coupled with decades of poor agricultural practices — of extensive farming in the same locations, without crop rotation and erosion prevention — led to severe dust storms. It made millions of acres of farmland useless and forced hundreds of thousands of people out of their homes.

"And then the dispossessed were drawn west — from Kansas, Oklahoma, Texas, New Mexico; from Nevada and Arkansas, families, tribes, dusted out, tractored out," John Steinbeck wrote in his 1939 novel The Grapes of Wrath. *"Car-loads, caravans, homeless and hungry; twenty thousand and fifty thousand and a hundred thousand and two hundred thousand. They streamed over the mountains, hungry and restless — restless as ants, scurrying to find work to do — to lift, to push, to pull, to pick, to cut — anything, any burden to bear, for food. The kids are hungry. We got no place to live. Like ants scurrying for work, for food, and most of all for land."*

The realization that we humans might have done the same thing to ourselves — to our schools, our institutions, our religions, our politics — that those farmers had done to the southern plains was overwhelming to Phil and me during the writing of *Being Spherical.* We humans had specialized and compartmentalized our world to such a staggering extent, that we'd depleted our own value and our own strength. The results of which caused us to make unwholesome decisions and take unwholesome actions.

After that, The Sphere became our safe haven, our neutral zone — a space to reflect and recover. Dogma was missing and that was refreshing. We could connect the dots of life without shame or penalty. The Sphere renewed and strengthened us.

— — —

Its doubtful Adam Smith saw the machine age coming, let alone its demise that is occurring right now.

Smith was the 18th Century Scottish Philosopher who introduced the idea of rational self-interest and competition. Smith laid the groundwork for free trade and capitalism. He pioneered the logic of greed. He reasoned that the most efficient methods of production maximized profits and ultimately benefited all.

His magnum opus, The Wealth of Nations, would become one of the most influential works on economics ever published. This, about 100 years after Descartes had determined the world was a giant machine. And fifty years after mathematician Gottfried Leibniz proposed that human thinking could be reduced to a mathematical equation.

How could Smith have known that over time, as his work coalesced with that of Descartes' and Leibniz — as those theories were experienced *concurrently,* culminating in the efficient Industrial Revolution, that something dastardly would happen: That we humans, who had become parts in the big machine, could no longer feel any responsibility for our indulgences. Or, grasp the harm we were doing to ourselves.

Mechanized free enterprise — what an oxymoron, eh? Once free enterprise had been boxed in and locked down, its limits, and ours, were set.

As you might imagine under those circumstances pioneering a hybrid business model as Phil was doing — that featured The Sphere in multiple, profitable applications, plus a 'do-good for the world' component — was hard for investors to wrap their minds around. How does one position a new metaphor for society in the marketplace? And what "box" does The Sphere fit into? Know what I mean? (Sound of sad violin playing here.)

"Everyone wants three things in a book, to be richer, thinner or prettier," Both Phil and RLL often moaned during the writing of their book, and during their early experiments with the spherical modeling tool.

"People won't hear us until things get bad," Phil would add, though he didn't know *when* that would be, precisely. Or, that RLL would no longer be in the picture when that time arrived.

— — —

The split began with three little letters: "IRS." More specifically the tax returns Phil and I hadn't ... exactly ... um ... filed with the IRS ... *for awhile.*

To be clear, our predicament was tremendously troublesome. But there was little we could do. We were trapped, as is often the case when you step off the assembly line of life. The costs are impossible to calculate. The endless hours spent working away at your mission, without relaxation or financial compensation, while holding down fulltime jobs. The dread that accompanies those unexpected expenses; the worry, on bad days, that your efforts will never reach fruition. The bills and paperwork you stuff away, unable to face them.

We lost an IRS refund one year when we were too overwhelmed with other responsibilities to file our returns. And we jeopardized another sizeable refund before realizing last minute we could salvage it. But other years we owed money and had none to spare. We could only hope we'd find a way to pay when we crossed over. Crossed over to the rewards of our hard work, not, you know, the "other side" as in the place one fellow went to (that I did a story on) who off'd himself when he couldn't pay his taxes.

Phil hadn't bothered to mention the issue to RLL until the book was done. No reason to worry him, Phil decided. We had all committed to the journey. Following through to the end was the right thing to do. But RLL had tapped into his surplus to complete the project. Endangering his family's status and wellbeing was inconceivable to him.

We, however, had taken four rookie missionaries to New York Headquarters when they were called to duty during our Oxford days, because nobody else was available. It didn't matter that we had no money to speak of. Or, that our car died on the way and we had to borrow somebody else's car to deliver those rookies to their destination. Or, that we had to go in debt for a replacement car, upon our return home. It was the right thing to do.

Phil and I had developed an embarrassing level of stick-to-itiveness. We didn't know how to quit. Didn't know you could or should quit until you 'got there.' That fortitude would prove to be critical to The Sphere's survival in the years to come but it jeopardized every facet of our own wellbeing.

On the matter of the IRS, we presumed we'd find a way to rectify it in due time. But what proof could we logically offer to RLL?

The news was difficult for him to hear. *'That's criminal,'* was RLL's reaction, as Phil remembers it, which stung Phil's dignity beyond measure. Other matters too had begun to gnaw at them about the company they were trying to form. They had different views and approaches to the workload and compensations.

'I need some silent time,' Phil decided one evening exhausted from many months of dialoguing between them. Phil could not sign the document that would have cemented their long term business marriage. He knew he must now go it alone. The partnership had been an extraordinary one. But it had reached its limits.

A visual kept reoccurring in my head in those days about how dangerous our journey had become. One from a story I'd written about a mountain climbing team who helped a blind man ascend Mt. Everest. During their journey they past the frozen dead body of another climber, reminding them of the risks involved. Once they'd made it to the top they could not linger there due to changing weather patterns. And they still had to make it back down to safety. On the way up they'd been forced to cross a deep crevice navigating a narrow, spliced ladder — a rickety contraption they dubbed the "Jesus" ladder. On the way back down they faced the same crossing. Could they possibly make it a second time?

The Jesus ladder ... We had to cross one or two of those, too.

Phil had made it to his destination. He had thought deep thoughts that few steal the chance too. He had read dozens and dozens of books for research purposes; had let his hair grow long like a mountain man, and had recorded 4,000 pages of his experience in his personal journal. But we could not linger in that space. We had to re enter society. And our passage remained perilous.

During the writing of *Being Spherical,* Phil spoke publicly about The Sphere to any business groups, women's organizations and school administrators that would listen. (He even once mentioned The Sphere to Futurist Alvin Toffler, when he was seated across from him during a special business luncheon; and he once slipped a sphere chart to Al Gore, having waited in a long line of people to hand it to him, when the former Vice President was in Denver on a book signing tour.) This on top of the few paying clients he managed during that time to continue to validate The Sphere technology. But a year after the book was finished, it was necessary to take a leap of faith and let go of his anchor pay check at the post office to champion The Sphere fulltime.

— — —

Four months after we moved to the rustic cabin in 1999, Phil's father and the Feisty Redhead arrived from Texas, there to experience the freedoms of retirement. First, a short stay with us; then, to a cabin they bought on a mountain draped in shadows. Until they returned to Texas abruptly, were gone a few months, came back, stayed a few months, sold the cabin and then moved away.

But we had learned by then to take nothing and no one for granted.

"At this very critical moment in my life, when I had to get this book out, they came," Phil wrote about their stay in his journal. *"They offered us credit cards to finance my writing. I know to some that is a stupid thing but in our world it was incredible. It was the only way we could survive. When they couldn't stay they left their car ... without them we simply would not have made it,"* he kept writing. *"As the oldest child I had always carried the burden of the family... They were not there for me when I was young ... [But] Pam reminded me today how many, many times I used to say 'I just need time to think. I have to have time to stop and think to hear what is inside of me and get it out.' Well, I got it."*

Of course, credit cards alone didn't save us; there were those monthly payments to contend with, the late fees and exorbitant interest rates. Though admittedly those little pieces of plastic felt as life-saving, at times, as the mask, snorkel and fins we once wore on a sea diving expedition.

Truth is it was the only way the old system worked. We couldn't get loans or grants for our kind of adventure.

And, it was the only way *our* system worked — the routines and patterns of which had become us, at an early age, by our reaction to our environment. The mental model of need and plead; of working and working and waiting and waiting for a promise land that was not of this world, that could not exist in this world, as it had been told to us, repeatedly.

We were cursed. And if not literally cursed, branded, and if not absolutely branded, presumed to be heretics, when we struggled to free ourselves from our confines, and whether we actually believed that lunacy or not, it dusted us with doubt. It painted us martyrs, positioning us to die one way or the other.

And we might have died, had we not discovered the IS of US. But we had seen the signs — intermittent as they were that signaled to us something different was 'out there,' something possibly but not actually contradictory to everything we'd ever known. Experiences that we might have once explained another way ...

The Post Office accidentally overpays Phil then oddly enough sends a letter from its corporate office establishing a pay schedule for him to return the money in installments, which unbeknownst to that institution, happened when we were in desperate need of cash for Jeep repairs.

What was that? And why didn't it happen more often?

And what was this? A stranger angrily chews me out in a grocery line one day when I accidentally cut in front of him, reducing me to tears. And, *that same week,* Phil gets chewed out by a resident while he was delivering their mail.

Why, when I was dreadfully depressed over my finances did I get a story tip to interview a homeless woman named "Pam"? And why, when I was desperately tired of those relentless news deadlines one day did I respond to a blind job posting online — only to discover that the corporation that had spiked my interest and had, in fact, responded to my cleverly written resume, had the word "sphere" in its company name?

WHAT WAS THAT? Ahhhh ... Ohhhh ... Those reflective elements of our existence on this planet — those interrelated, interconnected, attracting, repelling and mystifying elements that we are just beginning to understand.

— — —

After eight years at Walhalla it was time to go. I knew it when a splendid sensation swept over me the day I learned the cottage next door to Walhalla had unexpectedly been vacated around the same time as our annual lease was due. And it was more affordable, giving us wiggle room to begin our financial recovery.

When I first introduced the idea to Phil, he wouldn't consider it. The home was outdated and less romantic than Walhalla and was in need of much repair. It was a step down in his mind and we had always imagined that when we left the cabin we would step up in the world again.

But my intuitions had remarkably improved by then. I had removed many of the emotional filters that had once jerked me around. Before then, I couldn't much decipher the difference in my so-called "gut" feelings. *"Please, please you have to believe me, we should do this,"* I would beseech Phil as if I knew exactly how to handle certain situations, only to discover later I was wrong. Other times, I was intense, almost mean, almost obsessed that I was right. *"I don't care what you say! I know this; I absolutely know this!"* At which point an odd peacefulness would envelop me, as if I were suffering a cause.

But that was not, I would come to realize, what genuine intuition feels like. When I experienced it I felt light, playful and loveable. There was no resistance or intensity. It was as pleasant as walking through an open gate to a flower garden.

"Just wait and see," I smiled at Phil, once I'd learned that the owner's of the cottage were planning to remodel it.

Much to our delight, when the renovations were complete, it had a measure of character and our furniture and belongings blended perfectly. And it was more functional than the rustic cabin we left behind. For one thing, we no longer had to traipse 100 yards through five-foot snow drifts come wintertime to reach our cars parked near the main road on snow days.

We named the cottage Camp Dodge after the practical Dodge Dart we once owned in Thomasville.

As far as transitions go, we couldn't have predicted this one — moving right next door to the cabin we'd lived in for eight years. But the new landlord knew us and did not resort to typical credit checks before leasing us the property. And that was fortunate. We were by then so far outside 'the system' it would have been virtually impossible to qualify for such a comfortable place under any other circumstances. And moving into lesser quarters would have demolished what remained of our confidence at this late stage of our grueling journey.

We were surfacing, it seemed — preparing to expand Phil's work in new and exciting ways.

It was at Camp Dodge that we got the call notifying us that the patent for the Spherical Modeling Tool had been approved by the U.S. Patent Office. We had waited five years and it was glorious news.

And it was at Camp Dodge that we got the call from a former teen we had spent time with in Oxford. One of the girls we'd taken to New York City along with her family 25 years ago. Who had once penned this poem to us titled "Me":

I feel as if I'm in a world alone, with no one here to sing me a song.
I once thought I heard thousands of footsteps,
just rushing for me to meet, and to them I would greet.
But soon to my regret — I found out one day
that loneliness was all I'd get.
Then along came they, who had at first, very little to say.
Then they said "My goodness, this is a lonely child,
if we don't help she might go wild!"
Well, the light of the world is shining on me,
my motto is L-O-V-E.
This child no longer sits in a dark and lonely hole,
viewing all, just like a mole,
but is being surrounded by TLC, that's tender, loving, care, to me.
And my friends, that brought me out of that hole & world,
may not be Richard Dawson, but is Phil and Pam Lawson.

As it turned out, "Me" now lived in New York City and was a Wall Street analyst.

(Oh, and if I might back up a second, Oh Babe resurfaced when we lived in Walhalla, which was a great relief to me. After leaving her husband, she retreated in silence to a relative's home (with her children in tow) to heal and recover. She later resumed work in the medical field where she once earned upwards of $75,000 for her unique self-taught skills before training to work and travel for a major insurance firm that served communities affected by natural disasters.)

— — —

Our understanding of our past, and our present — of all the people we had crossed paths with came full circle at Walhalla.

We remembered the intricacies that comprised their personalities, their sparks of color. How their light grew dim or brighter based on their own qualities — on how they'd been handled; on the luminosity that surrounded them and the black holes that pulled at them. How the light of some shined beyond. How the light of others bounced back. And the light of a few burned out. How broken bits of light painted a kaleidoscopic picture of the human condition.

Phil and I learned to value the whole spectrum. We learned to spot inconsistencies in others by adjusting our own light source. We learned to keep glowing no matter how dark it gets.

Not long after we moved to Camp Dodge we had dinner with a couple in our neighborhood, a well-educated pair, gifted and giving who were engaged in important volunteer work. How I had bristled when they politely broached the topic of religion and the husband questioned why we had left ours behind.

"I believe we were called out of the ministry," was Phil's firm but courteous reply.

chapter 19: Orb

"Dear Phil, I hope you don't mind me writing," began an email sent the morning of May 2, 2006 by a woman from South Wales. "I just wanted to tell you about something strange that's just happened. I've been reading a book by Robert A Johnson - Balancing Heaven and Earth and last night I had a dream where I'd won a competition because I'd chosen the number five and your name was on the entry form. I've never heard of you before so it was a real surprise when I found your name on the internet.

Lately I've been reading Eckhart Tolle and lots of books on synchronicity. Don't quite know what this means but just thought I'd write and let you know about it.

Best wishes
[name omitted]
Pontypridd
South Wales
Great Britain"

Phil was stunned by the email. This was no ordinary business exchange from someone who had discovered his website. And, upon further inspection, it didn't appear to be a scam. It was intimate dialogue from a woman he'd never met about a dream she'd had about him.

Phil pondered the information she had shared. He had never heard of Robert Johnson, or his book, or for that matter, his co-author Jerry Ruhl. Though he did discover that Ruhl had once served as trustee of the C.G. Jung Society of Colorado, and Phil wondered, for a brief moment, if her email was a clue that he should contact Ruhl.

"Synchronicity is a very powerful force that shapes our lives in unexpected and surprising ways," Phil told the woman from Wales in a reply email. *"In the instance of your dream I do not know the significance of my name appearing on the entry form, but if you gain more clarity on the significance I would enjoy hearing about it ..."*

"Thanks to getting back to me," she responded. *"I knew you would somehow. If I learn anymore I'll let you know, definitely. It's strange but often I experience synchronistic events, I can just never seem to work their meaning ..."*

Phil sympathized with the woman's frustration; and so did I. We too had experienced synchronistic events and had found it a challenge to 'work their meaning.'

It seemed almost necessary to rewire our brains to comprehend them. Or, at least upgrade our perceptions, like computer software, to better access the information.

That, or blow off those mysteries entirely — as if they were nonsense, which was certainly simpler.

That same year, I picked up a copy of Carl Sagan's book *The Demon-Haunted World; Science as the Candle in the Dark.* I had yet to become richer, thinner or prettier pursuing spheres and I was tired of the wait. Our vision of the world was skewed, I decided, and it was time to clear that up.

"From the first page to the last, this book is a manifesto for clear thought," read a quote from the Los Angeles Times on the cover of the book.

And written on the back of the book was this thought-provoking challenge to readers who dared peer inside: *"How can we make intelligent decisions about our increasingly technology-driven lives if we don't understand the difference between myths of pseudoscience, New Age thinking and fundamentalist zealotry and the testable hypotheses of science?"*

For those of you who aren't familiar with Carl Sagan *(I didn't know anything about him before reading his book)* ... Sagan was an American Astronomer *(among many other talents)* who advocated skeptical inquiry and the scientific method. He popularized astronomy and astrophysics; was the face of the television series Cosmos; published more than 600 scientific papers and articles and wrote, co-wrote or edited more than 20 books. And he won more than two dozen prestigious awards and honors for his work including a Pulitzer, a Peabody and two Emmy's, along with NASA's distinguished public service medal.

The least I could do was read his last book, now ten years old, published around the time of his death in 1996. It seemed quit responsible of me. Or, at least get Phil to read it to me and translate it for me.

Sagan's childhood was a complete contrast to ours I discovered one afternoon as I settled into an overstuffed chair in Phil's office and listened to him begin reading from the introduction of Sagan's book.

From Sagan's earliest school days, he knew he wanted to be a scientist; from the moment when he first learned "that the stars are mighty suns."

"I'm not sure I even knew the meaning of the word "science" then, but I wanted somehow to immerse myself in all that grandeur," Phil read, quoting Sagan. *"I was gripped by the splendor of the Universe, transfixed by the prospect of understanding how things really work, of helping to uncover deep mysteries, of exploring new worlds—maybe even literally."*

As Sagan grew older, his romance with science never waned. It was to him an 'imaginative and disciplined' way to illuminate our world.

"Not explaining science seems to me perverse. When you're in love, you want to tell the world," Sagan explained in his book. *"But there's another reason: Science is more than a body of knowledge; it is a way of thinking ..."*

Phil paused, and, as is customary of his reading style, began scanning pages forward until he discovered, on page 14, Sagan's distaste for what he called "pseudoscience:"

"Pseudoscience speaks to powerful emotional needs that science often leaves unfulfilled. It caters to fantasies about personal powers we lack and long for (like those attributed to comic book superheroes today, and earlier, to the gods.) In some of its manifestations, it offers satisfaction of spiritual hungers, cures for disease, promises that death is not the end ..."

I smiled as I listened. Not with a sense of smugness — as if I knew this man to be wrong — but rather, a feeling of relief: that I had the aptitude and open-mindedness to consider his arguments.

That wasn't the case for nearly four decades of my life. I grew up in a demon-haunted world, with this cautionary passage from the New Testament tattooed on my forehead: *"Keep your senses, be watchful. Your adversary, the Devil, walks about like a roaring lion, seeking to devour [someone]."*

It wasn't easy to let go of that mindset. It comprised a chain of words linked to my character. Words like: loyalty; self-sacrifice and eternal salvation.

I would have never touched a book like Sagan's back then.

Appealing to my logic meant fine-tuning the pre-existing beliefs bequeathed to me. And I became proficient at it. I learned to play the Bible like a piano — my swift fingers directing the pages like a keyboard to produce what sounded like harmonious melodies.

Until the day the music died.

When a restricted repertoire no longer engaged me, I had to step away from the ivories completely, because the compositions I had learned were grooved into my brain.

I had focused my entire life on preserving my beliefs. It was time to "un-focus" my attention in order to see my world anew.

It was then, that I identified the boundaries imposed on me by my ancestors — the limits intended to keep me from ever straying far from my roots. An assortment of intricate rules that worked like a deadbolt, in my head, to ensure my behavior was predictable and manageable.

They were summed up in a few often-recited scriptures: *"Train up a boy according to the way for him; even when he grows old he will not turn aside from it,"* which prompted anxious and inexperienced parents to douse us children in cautionary tales about being stoned to death in public for disobedience; or, getting thrown to the lions as a sacrificial lamb for our unwavering devotion.

That was topped off with those ecclesiastical proclamations read to us from powerful and wealthy archetypes like wise King Solomon *(once my favorite muse)*, that made educational pursuits in the field of science rather irrelevant. For, King Solomon said: *"There is nothing new under the sun."*

When I read that scripture nowadays, in context with its surrounding verses, it sounds like the king was in a melancholy frame of mind *(—it takes one to know one—)* with his hypothesis of life that seemed more than a little gloomy: '*That which has come to be, that is what will come to be; and that which has been done, that is what will be done ... there is no remembrance of people of former times, nor will there be of those also who will come to be later. There will prove to be no remembrance even of them among those who will come to be still later on.*'

That's rather odd rhetoric from a man whose name lives on in infamy if you ask me. And astronauts weren't walking on the moon in his day ...

"Science arouses a soaring sense of wonder," Phil continued reading; having returned to an earlier section of the book that he had skipped. *"If it were widely understood that claims to knowledge require adequate evidence before they can be accepted, there would be no room for pseudoscience. But a kind of Gresham's Law prevails in popular culture by which bad science drives out good.*

"All over the world there are enormous numbers of smart, even gifted, people who harbor a passion for science. But that passion is unrequited,"

Phil read on. "Surveys suggest that some 95 percent of Americans are "scientifically illiterate." That's just the same fraction as those African Americans, almost all of them slaves, who were illiterate just before the Civil War — when severe penalties were in force for anyone who taught a slave to read. Of course there's a degree of arbitrariness about any determination of illiteracy, whether it applies to language or to science. But anything like 95 percent illiteracy is extremely, serious ..."

"And I thought artists had it tough in school," I blurted out, feeling suddenly sorry for the nerdy kids.

Then Phil reached a point in Sagan's material that clearly separated our time from the past.

"I don't know to what extent ignorance of science and mathematics contributed to the decline of ancient Athens," Phil spoke for Sagan. *"But I know that the consequences of scientific illiteracy are far more dangerous in our time than in any that has come before ..."*

Sagan then proceeded to list but a few dangers that make it *"perilous and foolhardy for the average citizen to remain ignorant"* about such things as air pollution, toxic and radioactive wastes, acid rain, topsoil erosion, tropical deforestation, exponential population growth, ozone depletion and global warming. Not to mention the "social ramifications" of fission and fusion power, supercomputers, radon, food additives, morning-after pills, alleged 'hereditary antisocial predispositions' and government eavesdropping on the lives of its citizens to name but a few.

"How can we affect national policy — or even make intelligent decisions in our own lives — if we don't grasp the underlying issues?" Sagan asked his readers. Then his tone turned serious. *"As I write, (in 1995) Congress is dissolving its own Office of Technology Assessment — the only organization specifically tasked to provide advice to the House and Senate on science and technology. Its competence and integrity over the years have been exemplary. Of the 535 members of the U.S. Congress, rarely in the twentieth century have as many as one percent had any significant background in science. The last scientifically literate President may have been ..."*

"Thomas Jefferson!" I blurted out, having no idea where that answer came from.

"Thomas Jefferson," Phil read on, his head bobbing; his face registering surprise on my behalf.

The very thought of it was quite scary. *"Jefferson lived a long time ago,"* I muttered, at which point Phil replied, *"No kidding."*

And it bothered Sagan too, Phil discovered, scanning the book's index about Thomas Jefferson. Further into his material Sagan highlighted Jefferson's foundational contribution to America with the Declaration of Independence and Sagan lamented the *lack* of similarly-minded people today.

"At the time, there were only about two and a half million citizens of the United States," Sagan wrote. *"Today there are about a hundred times more. So if there were ten people of the caliber of Thomas Jefferson then, there ought to be 10 x 100 = 1,000 Thomas Jefferson's today. Where are they?"*

Ironically, I remembered our frustration in our 20s in Oxford when Phil and I were often starved for the company of intellectually curious folks that could carry on expansive conversations without freezing up if the topic stretched past their convictions. Even during our visits to Headquarters, in New York, we found no such comrades. Those that would engage at all, had their lifestyles to protect and preferred to preach 'official policy' if the conversation reached uncomfortable proportions. We had no idea, back then, that our frustrations echoed society as a whole.

Or, to some degree, echoed Sagan's. He had a way of assessing society's progress over time, over centuries, and it was shocking for us to learn how 'beliefs' stifled advancement, or reversed it, with disturbing consequences for our ancestors.

"[Hippocrates] is still remembered 2,500 years later for the Hippocratic Oath," Phil continued reading, about to divulge the complexities of bucking the status quo. *"But he is chiefly celebrated because of his efforts to bring medicine out of the pall of superstition and into the light of science. In a typical passage Hippocrates wrote: "Men think epilepsy divine, merely because they do not understand it. But if they called everything divine which they do not understand, why, there would be no end of divine things."*

Hippocrates urged careful and meticulous observation in diagnosing disease, Sagan explained, quoting Hippocrates: *"Leave nothing to chance. Overlook nothing. Combine contradictory observations. Allow yourself enough time ..."*

But what was most interesting about Hippocrates, according to Sagan, was his honesty; his willingness to admit the *"limitations of the physician's knowledge,"* based on the limited options available in his day.

If only religious leaders were so humble, I thought. But they get to play the trump card — the 'God' card — when their religious mysteries are challenged.

Back in his day, Hippocrates was already performing surgeries and cauterization. But in a shocking turn of events, progress in medicine in his homeland came to a halt not long after he died — 2,500 years ago!

"While medicine in the Islamic world flourished, what followed in Europe was truly a dark age. Much knowledge of anatomy and surgery was lost," Phil kept reading from Sagan's book. *"Reliance on prayer and miraculous healing abounded. Secular physicians became extinct. Chants, potions, horoscopes, and amulets were widely used. Dissections of cadavers were restricted or outlawed, so those who practiced medicine were prevented from acquiring firsthand knowledge of the human body. Medical research came to a standstill."*

As Phil recited some quote about a historian named Edward Gibbon saying something about, *'in the revolution of 10 centuries, not a single discovery was made to exalt the dignity or promote the happiness of mankind ...'* my brain froze up. I couldn't believe what I was hearing. Could it really be so, that very few people ever born have a desire to change and grow?

"What does that mean?" I asked, stunned by the implications. *"I don't understand ..."*

"For 10 centuries there was no progress," Phil answered in a matter-of-fact tone. *"And that's basically what he's [Sagan and other scientists] are trying to say about now. People are enraptured by the myth of a lost Atlantis, but know nothing about the 'molecular building blocks of life sitting out there in the cold, tenuous gas between the stars.'"*

Phil then dived back into the text to prove his point, quoting something about Queen Anne who, in the last 17 years of the seventeenth century, was pregnant 18 times. Only five of them were live births and only one of those children survived infancy. And that child died before reaching adulthood. And she had the best medicine money could buy in her day.

That story allowed Sagan to expound upon the advances in science in recent years that have made it easier to keep children alive — everything from public health and sanitation measures to molecular biology. Smallpox has been wiped out, he said, and places that still have malaria-carrying mosquitoes are vanishing. But Sagan reminded readers that pseudoscience has hardly vanished.

"We can pray over the cholera victim, or we can give her 500 milligrams of tetracycline every 12 hours," Sagan barks.

Had Phil and I still been affiliated with our childhood faith we would have been considered heretics for reading Sagan's book, I remembered with a shiver. But it had been more than a decade since our departure and our 'free will' had come of age. In the process, we didn't lose our morals *(so there.)*

"It's time to look above and beyond — to hover, to orb!" I offered aloud, remembering dreams during my sleep where I'd had a feeling I was hovering near a ceiling looking down on a room.

Sagan saw his cosmic connection as something different than Phil's and mine. It was based on the findings of modern nuclear astrophysics but it was to him no less astonishing: *"Except for hydrogen, all the atoms that make each of us up — the iron in our blood, the calcium in our bones, the carbon in our brains — were manufactured in red giant stars thousands of light-years away in space and billions of years ago in time. We are, as I like to say, starstuff."*

Sagan's perspective in a weird way, it occurred to me, made life seem even more precious — our lives more original; our accomplishments more rare. What if we didn't answer to a mute invisible master? That we believe gives us permission to judge our fellow humans? Or, do deplorable things to them based on problematic interpretations of ancient texts?

When I thought about it from that angle a strange thing happened. It put responsibility for my thoughts and actions squarely on my own shoulders. And that caused me pause ...

As Phil took a break from his reading, he began to recall a past dinner conversation he had with a friend. This well-spoken and informed man had served on a world energy assessment team for the U.S. Geological Survey and was often invited to give presentations to a variety of organizations about the team's findings. One of those lectures was before a group of religious fundamentalists who upon hearing that society would soon reach peak oil capacity began to cheer. Members of the audience coyly suggested that humanity should use as much oil as we can, as fast as we can, to bring on Armageddon — as if they were helping their God fulfill his master plan.

Armageddon: that word had cast a shadow over my life for as long as I could remember. And what an undertaking it had been for me to wean myself from *welcoming* the end of the world. Not that we humans have things under control, by a long shot. On its current course, our civilization is headed for a heap of trouble. But it doesn't take a dead prophet to confirm that.

I wonder though, if some of our ancestors would have been so insensitive to the planet, and the creatures living on it, if they hadn't presumed a Supreme Being was going to save the day.

It was these realizations, over time, that began to ground me to my surroundings; that yanked me out of the past and repurposed me for the here and now.

Not that I dismissed my upbringing. Favorite lessons learned in childhood from legendary characters in the Old and New Testaments were embedded in my psyche. But so were a few puzzling stories that seemed oddly adolescent for the creator of the universe — for the almighty king in the sky, introduced to me in picture books. And if I were a critic, those revelations would be unsettling if simplified to these few sound bytes ...

You see, shortly after Sky King created man *(and especially wo-man)* he regretted the whole dang thing. And to cleanse earth of his mess, he drowned nearly every living being ... then promised he'd never do that again if man behaved.

He destroyed the next bunch of waywards by fire and sulfur. After He had scrambled the native tongue of his people, and scattered them to the four corners of the earth for their arrogant efforts to build a tower that stretched towards heaven. Soon enough, his people demanded a king made of flesh. And He granted them their wish, but later regretted that, too. All of which occurred in the first book of Genesis ... as if Sky King, was learning on the fly, how to manage things *'in the beginning.'* Followed by His jealous and vengeful phase — when insubordinates were threatened with *seven times* the usual punishment; or, He subjected their heirs to *four generations* of shame. Finally, His star-studded son appeared on earth, and sacrificed himself for the ingrates. And his son's advocates vowed to mimic his heroic, peace-loving behavior ... but many of them instead led holy wars in his name for a painfully prolonged period thereafter.

We haven't really heard from Sky King since. (But for the revelation, a fellow named John received about 2,000 years ago, that said most of us should expect to be destroyed any day now.)

— — —

One could argue that if a parent displayed that kind of mercurial behavior toward his or her offspring, they'd likely produce some fanatical descendents. *(Tell me I did NOT just say that ...)*

All I'm thinking *is* ... it appears to me *that* ... the originator, or origins, of this spectacular universe; our magnificent planet; our astonishing and varied species — deserves better storytelling now. An upgrade from 1.0 to 2.0, in software-speak.

Especially in lieu of my time spent as creative director of The Agency in Denver, when my intellect grew in proportion to my paycheck. It was there that I indulged my left brain in a little comparative analysis. When I recalled a scripture I had once frequently recited, a text that in part said this: *"All Scripture is inspired of God and beneficial for teaching, for reproving, for setting things straight ..."*

One day, I pondered that passage more than usual — in particular, the phrase "inspired of God." In my role as creative director it was my job to inspire my cohorts — to offer ideas and direct the completion of assignments. And there's where things got interesting. I utilized the services of several different graphic designers, a few paid employees at The Agency, plus a talented freelancer that we used when deadlines and workloads required extra hands. I recalled the diversity in their styles, work habits, and creations. On occasion, I'd give two of them the same assignment. But the results were always different, based on the creative interpretations of each designer.

That's when I rethought the concept of "inspired of." Sovereign downloads — it seemed to me, were at the mercy of human interpretation; at the mercy of an individual's perceptions and qualifications to convey an "inspiration."

That awakening continued when I became a writer. I realized that my stories that went to print in our newspapers were the end result of my ability — or lack thereof — to properly interpret a person's life; or unfolding events. I also understood the complexities of passing that information along to an editor who might, on any given day, change or rearrange a word or sentence, in attempts to better convey the information for me. I knew those changes at times altered my entire message, and not always for the better. Early on in my career I often lost sleep over it.

My role as a professional communicator proved to be the most humbling and exasperating experience of my life. And I pondered that in relation to the Bible. The many different writers who claimed to have recorded historic dialogue long after much of it had occurred. Not to mention the many alternative translations of that book that have sprung up over the centuries — authors, of which, charged their counterparts with tainting certain words or verses. What meanings had gotten lost? I wondered. What meanings had been changed, entirely? And must I worry myself, either way?

I recalled a comment attributed to Jesus, spoken to his apostle's back in the day, which goes like this: *"Most truly I say to you, He that exercises faith in me, that one also will do the works that I do; and* ***he will do works greater than these*** *..."* — this from a man who was credited with raising the dead.

— — —

Just like that, the Good Book I had grown up with was no longer *absolute*. The insights I'd gleaned from its stories remained precious to me, but the 'package' was not foolproof.

Under those circumstances, it seemed only appropriate that I not beat my fellowman over the head with it, to justify my upbringing or mask my insecurities. With the exception of one scripture, maybe — the principles of which were *amazing*, it seemed to me, and should be embraced *this very instant!* A passage attributed to Moses about the "Jubilee Year." Based on interpretations I have read, it was a liberating event that occurred every 50 years when masters freed their slaves and farmers rested their land and mortgaged properties reverted back to rightful owners and creditors waved people's indebtedness! Presumably to prevent the wealthy few from forming a monopoly ... wow, what a concept ...

"I have a foreboding of an America in my children's or grandchildren's time — when the United States is a service and information economy," Phil resumed reading from Sagan's book. *"When nearly all the key manufacturing industries have slipped away to other countries; when awesome technological powers are in the hands of a very few, and no one representing the public interest can even grasp the issues; when the people have lost the ability to set their own agendas or knowledgeably question those in authority; when, clutching our crystals and nervously consulting our horoscopes, our critical faculties in decline, unable to distinguish between what feels good and what's true, we slide, almost without noticing, back into superstition and darkness."*

Phil stopped and shook his head. At which point I blurted out this astonishing realization: *"Why do we assume that those who came before us have the answers?! Why can't it possibly be that we are all circling the elephant? Our ancestors and us! Spiritualists and Scientists! That if we connect all our data, it allows for a quantum leap in understanding? All at once — a gargantuan leap forward!"*

My outburst hung in the air as Phil rose and headed for the bathroom. And I began to contemplate other instances, aside from reading Sagan's book, when I had stepped outside the comfort zone of my upbringing and read books about the mystical world of the Q'ero of Peru, and the healing traditions of the Kabbalah.

How Phil and I had once slipped into a sweltering sweet lodge, packed with strangers, presided over by a Native American medicine man, after we had first tied tobacco into tiny pouches and offered up silent prayers during an oenikika purification ceremony.

How we had sat crossed legged in meditation in the Great Stupa of Dharmakaya that housed the ashes of a respected Buddhist teacher; and we once received individual blessings, in person, from Sri (Amma) Karunamayi, a Hindu holy leader who is believed to be the incarnation of the Divine Mother, Saraswati, Goddess of Knowledge and Creativity.

Those experiences did not occur in one brief experimental period, as if we were sampling exotic foods at a buffet, but rather over several years. When our perceptions were shifting, and we embraced unusual encounters with awe — instead of resisting them — as if there might be a lesson to be learned from each of them at that very moment in our lives.

What a stretch, I realized, for someone birthed and burped into a way of thinking that spanned Adam to Armageddon. A package complete with guaranteed heroics — *"you will be persecuted on account of my name"* — that came with built in rewards for the faithful — *"you will be with me in paradise"* — and threats of damnation for those who were not — *"down to Hades you will come"* — that was meant to be inescapable.

But I had escaped somehow.

I had traded absolute for immeasurable. And though my legs wobbled at first, I found my way — experiencing the same marvelous "attitude" adjustments, along my path that had always been there — a message in a book that I was drawn to read at the right moment; certain animal encounters that were unusually memorable; even the occasional chance meeting with a stranger — aware that the exchange between us might have been just for me; or was two-fold in nature, or intended just for him or her.

But I no longer felt the need to label those experiences. Nor, did I dismiss them as nothingness. I knew otherwise: I was linked to something vast and grand.

"This is exactly what Sagan's introduction was about." Phil said, returning to his spot on the couch and resuming our previous conversation. *"When he went to school there was no sense of "wonder" — it was, 'follow the rules.' That's why science appealed to him. I think he's a brilliant, brilliant man ... But he thinks science will save the day. Science is the way and 'I can show you how!' But, some scientists in their sterile white lab coats are demanding reverence like priests, demanding obedience to the rational reductionist way — attempting to create the mathematics of a marriage, or a broken heart, which is why its not surprising that some people who sense something missing to that story respond to it by*

retreating to the comfort of their superstitions and post-Enlightenment views ..."

"And what's your solution?" I replied, now irritated by his doubt. *"Spiritualists and Scientists meet in the middle? At the center of Sphere-tuality?"*

"We can't get into that argument — religion and superstition versus science. Humanity doesn't have enough time," Phil answered me. *"Its simple math: more people less breathable air, more people less drinkable water, more people less cultivatable land.*

"What we face today generations past did not face. Take the Taliban: A small group of guys 6,000 miles away get pissed and rock the world — never possible before this moment.

"This is where that sense of "wonder" Sagan spoke of becomes absolutely necessary to our survival," Phil continued. *"It's what I call 'spherical not knowing.'"*

"Here we go with the sphere, again..." I sighed; baffled that Phil managed to slip it into every conversation. *"Why not use the word "marvel" instead,"* I interrupted, but Phil talked right through it ...

"With all our knowledge, all our knowing — our PhDs; our fame, our money, our politics — humanity has arrived at this **place** *... and it's NOT GOOD. A sense of wonder, of "not knowing" is the wisest attitude we can have right now. And, as we connect the dots, and the sphere of our consciousness expands, so will its integrity. And from that will emerge new behaviors."*

Arguably, *spherical marvel* had a ring to it, I decided, daydreaming (as Phil chatted on) that if I were clutching a giant ball while falling from the sky I might bounce when I hit ground.

"Everyone believes they know the answers," Phil concluded. *"When, in fact, we don't know the questions."*

— — —

Over the course of the next few days we revisited Sagan's book and read more intriguing things, like matter and antimatter are being created from nothing throughout the Universe all the time. And once in every great while your car will spontaneously ooze through the brick wall of your garage and be found the next morning in the street — the results of quantum mechanics, Sagan explains — something called vacuum fluctuations and barrier tunneling.

If that doesn't make sense to you, I urge you to read Sagan's book.

In the end, we were struck by this observation of Sagan's: *"At the time of writing there are three claims in the ESP field which, in my opinion, deserve serious study: (1) that by thought alone humans can (barely) affect random number generators in computers; (2) that people under mild sensory deprivation can receive thoughts or images "projected" at them; and (3) that young children sometimes report the details of a previous life, which upon checking turn out to be accurate and which they could have not known about in any other way than reincarnation. I pick these claims not because I think they're likely to be valid (I don't), but as examples of contentions that might be true. The last have at least some, although still dubious, experimental support. Of course, I could be wrong."*

— — —

Phil never heard from the woman from South Wales again.

But he did buy the book she had mentioned in her email — a candid memoir by Robert A. Johnson about his life as a noted Jungian analyst titled, *Between Heaven and Earth.* It included a story about his brief encounter in the late 1940s, at the age of 26, with Carl Jung himself — the famed founder of analytical psychotherapy who was by then in his 70s.

Between Heaven and Earth became one of Phil's favorite books. Phil's "introverted" personality was similar to Johnson's and he felt a kinship to Johnson regarding some of his life experiences and perspectives. And Phil was especially moved by Carl Jung's perception of Johnson, after he had deciphered the meaning of one of Johnson's very elaborate dreams.

"Even if you never produce anything of social value, your relationship with the collective unconscious will justify your reason for being on the face of this earth," Jung had told Johnson, adding: *"Do not join anything. This will just be poison for you."*

The young Johnson was taken aback by Jung's advice, but also moved by it. *"Please remember, it is what you* ***are*** *that heals, not what you know,"* Jung had further said.

Later in life, as Johnson pondered that rare meeting with Jung, he wrote about it in his book. And Phil related strongly to Johnson's summary:

"This is the essence of what I learned from Dr. Jung: listen to your interior intelligence, take it seriously, stay true to it, and — most important — approach it with a religious attitude. His psychological term for this is individuation — discovering the uniqueness of yourself, finding out what you are not and finding out what you are. Individuation relates

to wholeness, but it is not some indiscriminate wholeness but rather your particular relationship to everything else. You get to the whole only by working with the particularity of your life, not by trying to evade or rise above the specificity of your life. This is the blending of heaven and earth."

chapter 20: Resuscitate

"I've had this craving lately ... to slip off my reporter cap — a job consumed with recording the pursuits and opinions of others — and sing wildly about a few of my own."

Those were the first words of a four-part newspaper series that I began the winter of 2004. It all started when I blurted out a plan earlier that fall, during a staff meeting at my weekly newspaper agency, to upstage the dailies who would soon print their annual holiday fitness stories. The one's where folks lose weight and readers follow along.

"If you're going to embarrass yourself in front of total strangers, why not lose weight AND become a Pop Star all at the same time?" I told my editor and fellow reporters.

It was obvious to them that the crash test dummy in this little experiment I was proposing would be me.

"I could lose about 30 pounds and buff up enough to fit into some stylish outfit," I kept talking. *"While I'm at, I could learn to sing well enough to perform one song in a popular nightclub, like say, the historic Little Bear. Heck, life is short! Right?!"*

Everybody laughed. And that's when my heart began pounding wildly. The idea had been so spontaneous that morning despite the absurdity of it that I could barely process what had happened. I had just sabotaged myself. But in all actuality, I was saving my life.

Five years had passed since we left the city and moved to a mountain cabin. Five years since I had become a community reporter — a position that held the attention of young journalists fresh out of college for a year on average, before they skipped town to upgrade their resumes and salaries.

Five years that we had scratched out a meager existence, with no end to our struggle in sight and I was turning 50 in a few months.

I recalled the many nights I had tossed and turned in my bed; the sheets damp from my premenopausal condition; and my brow damp from agony over back taxes we owed to the government. Those nights — and there were countless numbers of them; I swore the world would be a better place without me.

Eventually, that despair metamorphosed into something different: the resolve of an 80-year-old. The passion I'd once had as a young adult, that I would help make a difference in the world, had passed. I'd given it my best shot, with lackluster results. I would live the remainder of my days in a thankful but passive state, I decided. I'd remain curious in my job as a reporter for the sole sake of others, careful to record their stories as they pursued their passions.

Despite that resolve, however, a confounding spunk stirred within me on occasion.

It began to surface in the form of poetry; bits and pieces of songs I was compelled to scribble on the backs of bills and margins of newspapers. Nothing to rival Joni Mitchell, mind you, mostly half-baked insights:

"Must have done something many lives ago, I wasn't sorry for.
Got a guilt and pain I can't explain, braced for even score...
I've put my angst to canvas; I've walked through a labyrinth.
Been a Sunday crossword puzzle, but the anguish just won't lift..."

It was as if some part of me was crying out. I'd been somber long enough and it was time to sing!

But when I stretched my vocal chords one afternoon singing backup for Sinéad O'Connor in the privacy of my living room, I wound down like a radio with a dead battery. I was deflated by the fact that I had no musical training and my appearance had conspicuously deviated from a favorite black and white photo on my bed stand, taken when I was 29 years old. My long, chestnut hair was thick, my skin, smooth and tight. I was wearing a white dress with ruffles and leaning against a wooden fence post in a romantic pose at William Faulkner's home in Oxford.

"What are you doing? You're almost 50. You'll never be a singer now."

Soon after, at a local Safeway, I snatched up a copy of *Country Weekly* even though I had never read the magazine before. A subheading on the front page had jumped out at me: "George Strait: How He Became an Overnight Success." I was motivated to buy it, even though I had been allergic to country music for about three decades, thanks to my parent's addiction to it when I was a teen.

The story was about Strait's impulse one afternoon in 1986 to buy a game board at Toys "R" Us that featured a stack of cards with 2,500 advertising slogans. Near broke, he sprang for the $39 game because *he had to,* he recalled in the interview. One phrase, "overnight mail" jumped out at him. Then with the help of three fellow songwriters, he converted the slogan to a song titled "Overnight Male" and he finally had his first hit.

I guess I can thank George Strait for my impetuous outburst to my workmates the fall of 2004 — when I vowed to lose weight and learn to sing by my 50th birthday the spring of 2005. And chronicle those experiences despite my already heavy workload.

"Well ... maybe ... it could be kind of fun ... sort of a satire on those other 'lose-weight, new-me' stories," my editor, unexpectedly replied. *"Maybe you can dye your hair pink ... wear a dog collar ... and sing punk rock."*

"Or go country-western with 'big hair' ..." someone else suggested. They all laughed again.

Not exactly what I had in mind. But at least the idea hadn't been rejected.

"I know a voice coach!" I said in haste, remembering a woman I had once interviewed who might be interested in participating in the project.

At which point the editor said he knew a local fitness guru who might be willing to help. And the deal was sealed a few minutes later.

That's when I realized I was about to expose myself — and Phil — when he found out — to a level of vulnerability I had never before experienced. My success or failure would be on display for thousands of residents in the string of Front Range communities where I lived, worked and bought groceries. *(OMG!)*

Thus began my resuscitation.

Under any other circumstances it may have never occurred. But it happened under the watch of an eccentric and daring editor who had just been hired by our newspaper three months earlier. His past experiences with large news agencies and periodicals were notable. He was also a New York Times best-selling true-crime author and had been mentored in his younger years by a Pulitzer-prize winning journalist.

Under his tutelage I would learn the art of narrative writing. But it took me awhile to get the hang of it ...

Many weeks rolled by before I finished the first segment of my four-part series — after a first draft had fallen short of expectation followed by multiple changes. And my editor by then was pissed!

"I WANT this story for the week of December 28," he told me in a staff meeting. *"It's sort of got that New Year's resolution tone to it."*

Of course that date came and went.

"HAVE IT TO ME by Thursday night," he said, ranting about another publication deadline that sped by without my cooperation.

"This story HAS to go in this week!" he ordered me in an email on yet another occasion. *"In fact, it should have been READY — already; the layout worked on today!"*

But I didn't reply. Maybe he'd forget, I wagered.

Finally, I found my direction. And a theme and message began to appear on my computer screen. I had known for some time that to capture reader's attention my story would need to be about more than weight loss and voice lessons. I would need to share tidbits of my life — explain my desires and disappointments along with my current challenges.

So I searched my memories for a time in my past that would set the stage for this unfolding saga. It was a carefree moment after the death of my mother when my father and I escaped our world through music.

"A Bible, a red and white two-door Plymouth Fury, and a wooden stereo cabinet, resembling a fine piece of furniture, comprised our few prized possessions," I wrote in that first segment, remembering our priorities in those days.

"Tucked inside the stereo case were record albums of blues and country titles, and — as if to challenge our piety — Elvis-The-Pelvis in a shiny suit of gold lame.

"... In those days, my head was filled with poems and rhythms."

— — —

By the time I'd written my first segment in the series, I'd discovered my voice coach was a perfectionist and would "show me the door" if I didn't practice — rigorously — which tied my stomach into knots. And my professional fitness trainer, it seemed to me, was being forced to deploy techniques that were well beneath his expertise: *"She's a rank beginner and we're working on huge changes,"* he wrote in a sidebar piece to my story offering circuit training tips for interested readers. *"My approach with her is the most basic I've used in 15 years as a strength coach. But knowing where to start is often the hardest part, and we're on our way ..."*

I had also discovered this: *"It's not hard to understand why many people don't even bother to rekindle those parts of them that are dying, prematurely,"* I wrote in the article. *"Overcoming the necessary obstacles to achieve a dream or two can be, well, brutal."*

The editor titled my series: "Finding Her Voice." And his choice of words would have deeper meaning to my life than either of us could then imagine.

— — —

I suppose you're wondering the outcome of my undertaking?

The short answer would be "yes" I reached my goal.

I lost 32 pounds. And I sang 10 songs before 80-plus diners at a local venue without fainting. But ... it took four months longer than planned to accomplish it.

Under those circumstances, I missed the target date to sing on my 50th birthday. But a friend hosted a surprise birthday party for me anyway, which was covered by my newspaper. It was newsworthy because it was my first ever birthday bash, since birthday celebrations had been a "no-no" during my childhood.

Eventually, after the help of *two different voice coaches,* I hit the stage with a talented piano player and belted out a full set of songs, which included George Gershwin's "Summertime," and Sting's, "Fields of Gold;" a tune by Norah Jones; one by Bonnie Raitt, then John Lennon; Garth Brooks and a few others, the titles of which now escape me.

I was fit as a fiddle thanks to the local fitness guru. I looked smart in a black ensemble created by a local fashion designer. And my 12-year-old glasses had been replaced with contact lenses, thanks to the generosity of a local ophthalmologist.

My progress became a community affair as participants donated their services or reduced them on my behalf; or sacrificed their time to see me through, including a community member who donated the use of her sound equipment.

It was a groovy collaboration. I had served the community as a reporter for five years and they were there for me during my resuscitation.

Heck, Phil was even energized by my experience. He met with an attorney and filed our back taxes. He had secured a noteworthy business project which made it possible to begin monthly payments.

(For those of who you who clicked your tongues at us back in Chapter 18 when I first wrote about the IRS fiasco, you should know as I edit this chapter we've taken care of that business, though we could have bought a nice new car for what we paid in dues and penalties!)

I would later win two awards for the four-part series. My publisher would discuss the project during a presentation at an annual corporate convention. And community members in my readership area would speak of it for years to come.

"I feel 15 years younger," I told the audience the night of my musical performance. And I felt like I looked it, too, which gave me the courage to

say a lot of crazy things to friends back then, like: *"I want to perform with Eminem!"*

It made perfect sense at the time. Despite our age difference and experiences, he and I had something in common. We had both escaped our limits. His life story made into the movie "8 Mile" had reminded me of that pursuit. And the lyrics of his theme song, *"Lose Yourself,"* had been an inspiration to me:

"You better lose yourself in the music, the moment You own it, you better never let it go. You only get one shot, do not miss your chance to blow. This opportunity comes once in a lifetime, yo"

Those lyrics proved true in my case. Soon after my singing debut in 2005 my unconventional editor and my newspaper agency parted ways. Had I not seized the moment, under his watch, it would have never happened.

The experience had expanded me — just like living in the Hollywood Hills once did. For a while after that I sang at church events in Denver and even once got paid for a performance. But the distractions of my personal life began to surface again — a disturbing family tragedy ... the worsening economy ...

One day, after a dreadful performance at a friend's funeral, I realized my novice venture into the music world would require significantly more training and that would have to wait.

The experience had rejuvenated me, but not for the purpose of launching a music career. *(Not yet, anyway ;-)* It had renewed my spirit for the final leg of our personal journey. The one Phil and I began long ago: The Journey To The Sphere.

Had Phil's book soared to the top of the New York Times bestseller list right after it was finished in 2004, it's doubtful you'd be reading this memoir. We'd have been basking in the glory of his and our accomplishments by now. But he and RLL were too frazzled after its completion to hammer away at the process of selling their message — a philosophical treatise from two "unknown" talents — to the big name publishing houses in New York. Instead, they paid to have in printed on their own and then dispersed it the best they knew how in small circles. And when that didn't gain them instant notoriety ... they sighed heavily and scratched their heads.

*"You need to tell **YOUR** story,"* had been the admonition of one business friend of Phil's who read an early draft of his book back in the late 1990s. But the thought of writing yet another book on the heels of *Being*

Spherical was unimaginable to both Phil and I. We greatly desired an extended tropical vacation.

"I'm SPENT, do you hear me!" I scolded Phil at the thought of it, remembering the worn-out old woman in Thomasville with the burnt circle on her butt.

"Without me, there would have been no story to tell!" Phil snapped at me, a bit testy himself. That was some audacity, I thought. But he did have a point. The other fellows I knew as a teenager hardly seemed the type to initiate this kind of adventure. And for that matter, none of the girls Phil knew *would have tolerated it!*

But after my grandiose resuscitation I could finally revisit the idea. And in preparation I did one last thing as part of my make-over experience. I stopped coloring my hair. Underneath that pretty auburn dye was a mane of white. It was time to own it. I had after all earned it ... so much for feeling "15 years younger."

I would soon enough reach into the depths of my bowels to retrieve our story and that would require the steeled resolve that comes with white hair.

Meanwhile, I had more to learn as a writer. And that would happen under the watch of my fourth and final editor; a man who had once been copy chief at two major dailies and had earned a staff Pulitzer. What a talent he was to know, before I quit my job as a journalist the fall of 2008 after nine years in the business.

chapter 21: Parts

One year after Phil and RLL completed *Being Spherical* we got a call from a woman dear to our hearts who had suffered a nasty blow to the head. Her experience would cause us to contemplate the topic of "parts" versus "whole" — like we once did in our younger years in Mississippi.

A closing garage door slammed into the top of the woman's head as she exited the building too slowly, damaging the vertebrae in her neck. But the jarring incident did more than damage her spine, requiring months of bed rest. It ignited memories of childhood abuses that had lay dormant for decades.

A short time before the conk on her noggin she had begun to remember the horrific details of a violent sexual attack she endured as a little girl, an outdoor assault that had knocked her unconscious when her head hit a rock. Worse still, it involved a minister who had once stayed with her family. Now interned, more memories came flooding back to her involving other perpetrators, one of which she believed to be her father. Her extreme experiences, at such a tender age, prevented the developing aspects of her tiny being from fully integrating, leaving those aspects or parts of herself, broken and disconnected.

The controversial diagnosis she received, we would come to know as we followed her progress, was called "Dissociative Identity Disorder." And it is controversial. And we won't begin to infer that we can speak to such complexities here. So we won't.

But we did know this about this bright and lively woman: Her negative experiences had affected every aspect of her life. Her health problems were extensive and included many surgeries. She had developed addictions to painkillers. She was often suicidal. And she reacted different ways on different days to life's dramas — unable to connect the dots of her own behaviors.

What she did do well was rush through life and burn through money. Until a garage door grounded her.

Finally, she was ready to slowly connect the pieces of her life. And on good days, there was a calmness about her that had once been absent.

The steps in the development of her particular disorder (that happens most often in childhood) are theorized to involve harm by a trusted caregiver that splits off the awareness and memory of the traumatic event in order for the child to survive in the relationship. "Dissociation becomes a coping mechanism" for the individual when faced with further stressful situations, according to a bestselling psychiatric nursing publication about the topic.

As we learned more about this woman's condition we couldn't help but reflect on the 'coping mechanisms' that our society at large has developed over time – which, in an odd way, seemed similar to those who have been physically or emotionally abused.

Why are there so many folks suffering from serious depression, we wondered? (More than 8 million Americans seriously consider suicide each year, according to information recently released in a new government study.)

Why so many taking prescription medications? Why so many taking illegal drugs and over-indulging in alcohol? Committing suicide and worse – shooting total strangers in schools and universities, in shopping malls and restaurants and churches?

Why are so many people seeking to 'dissociate' from reality?

– – –

Since we're on the topic of "parts," it seems only practical of me to reference a brief section of Phil and RLL's book.

It has to do with the Ford Pinto. And surprise of all surprises, we once owned one.

As conveyed in their book, the story of the Ford Pinto is a dramatic example of the compartmentalization that has affected our world.

In the 1970s, when oil prices soared U.S. automakers faced serious competition from small fuel-efficient cars manufactured in Asia. In response, the automakers rushed smaller cars to market. Ford Motor Company's popular and successful entry was the Pinto. But, during production, tests revealed that rear-end collisions could cause the gas tanks to rupture and the doors to jam. Those two conditions, plus a small spark, could turn the Pinto into an incinerator.

That prompted Ford to generate its now-famous internal memo — a cost/benefit analysis of fuel tank redesign for the Pinto. According to its estimates, the unsafe tanks would cause approximately 180 burn deaths, 180 serious burn injuries and 2,100 burn vehicles.

Ford calculated that it would have to pay $200,000 per wrongful death lawsuit, $67,000 per injury and $700 per vehicle, for a total cost to the company of $49.5 million. Design alterations, on the other hand, would cost $11 per car, or $137 million.

The auto companies took their case before the federal regulators and argued that it would be financially prudent to let the design stay as it is. And they were able to delay fuel tank regulations for eight years.

Ford eventually changed the Pinto design because lawyers discovered Ford's knowledge of the problem and outraged jurors awarded huge sums of money to victims.

But it's safe to say, the people who determined it was more cost effective to cremate living human beings looked and acted just like the rest of us. They had homes and families. They did favors for friends. They were good to their parents, even went to church. They did not consider themselves to be evil monsters, but it's a sure bet their own families didn't drive Pintos.

And here's the kicker to that story folks ... Ford's estimated cost of fixing the flaws turned out to be incorrect. The actual cost per car was $1, not $11.

Of course, the Pinto was not an isolated case. Before and after the Pinto, in areas such as children's apparel, cigarettes, coal mining, shipping and the environment, there have been hundreds of publicized and thousands of unpublicized cases of good people making decisions that seem to violate the most basic human values.

What happened was simply this: the people who made those choices were focused solely on the responsibilities of their boxes. They did not see or feel responsibility for the larger consequences of their actions. They were just doing their jobs.

The bottom line is, when we compartmentalize our lives, values are applied inconsistently and expediently.

That is the *"absolute and terrible cost"* wrote Phil and RLL, for having an outdated mindset that allows us to *"pray in church and write death warrants at work."*

All right, I'm done referencing their book.

Now flash forward nearly 40 years to the subprime mortgage scandals and you'll see the similarities. Or, think of our dysfunctional healthcare in this country. When we read statistical data in the news that says 80 percent of Americans have healthcare and we think that's a pretty good average overall, we are operating mechanistically. We are forgetting that 20 percent — *or 50 million people* — do not. Now, let me translate that in human terms: if these folks get scared or angry because their children, spouses or aging parents are dying without proper medical care *they won't behave like machines,* I assure you!

— — —

No wonder our anxieties are off the charts. We've been reduced to bits and pieces for so long now. We sense things but can't connect the dots. We haven't been allowed to.

Perhaps that's how people who should know better say the darnedest things. And believe them, to boot.

At the end of the Bush administration, a prominent politician made the following comment to the Associated Press about the unfolding economic crisis: *"I don't think anybody saw it coming."*

And he wasn't alone in that view.

At which point I fidget in my chair and write the following:

"Seriously? You didn't ***feel*** *it coming? Didn't* ***smell*** *it, maybe?"* Oh, I forgot. Machines can't feel. They can't smell.

Truth be told, many of us grew accustomed to being parts in a machine. Found comfort in the clang and buzz. And we dismissed those of us who blew a head gasket or lost a few screws. But you can't dismiss us anymore ...

It's time to connect our puzzle pieces, people.

chapter 22: Whole

It's Saturday, October 31, 2009. Barack Obama has been in office 10 months and his blockbuster ratings have declined over his approach to the exhaustive list of challenges he faced upon his arrival in office.

Among the commentaries about him is a piece by New York Times Op-Ed Columnist Thomas Friedman. And Phil can't wait to read it to me ... perhaps you'll figure out why when I share a few of his thoughts below:

"More and more lately, I find people asking me: What do you think President Obama really believes about this or that issue?" Phil read Friedman's piece aloud. "I find that odd. How is it that a president who has taken on so many big issues, with very specific policies — and has even been awarded a Nobel Prize for all the hopes he has kindled — still has so many people asking what he really believes?

"I don't think that President Obama has a communications problem, per se," Phil continued reading from Friedman's column. "He has given many speeches and interviews broadly explaining his policies and justifying their necessity. Rather, he has a "narrative" problem.

"He has not tied all his programs into a single narrative that shows the links between his health care, banking, economic, climate, energy, education and foreign policies. Such a narrative would enable each issue and each constituency to reinforce the other and evoke the kind of popular excitement that got him elected ..."

Just then, Phil jerked his head up from his computer screen and said to me, in an excited tone of voice: "If the president used The Sphere for his "narrative," that would change everything!"

— — —

In the fall of 2006, Phil did a little research project the results of which, I believe, will fascinate you. He explored how many people in one month had searched for the word "whole" on one particular Internet search engine. And he was stunned by what he found.

There were only 215,000 searches on the word. Roughly 110,000 were for whole foods; 43,000 were for whole life insurance; followed by 6,300 searches for song lyrics about a "Whole New World." Miscellaneous searches on the word represented the rest.

But nobody searched for the word as it relates to, for example, the whole of our lives; the whole of our companies; the whole of our relationships or our connection to our whole planet.

By comparison, there were an incalculable number of hits on words like war, money, sex and dating.

That proved to be a scary little research project for us. Do you know why?

If you asked yourself how you arrive at the most important decisions of your life regarding your education, career, the growth of your business, your marriage, your relationship with your children; your community — even politics — you might easily say: "*I look at the whole picture!*"

Well, honey, that's a load of crap. You've barely scratched the *whole* surface.

When you do, phrases such as "think whole" and "see whole" will be a natural part of your vocabulary. They will populate internet search engines. You will find pages and pages and pages of deeply valuable references on the topic instead of a few links to: "whole grain."

Speaking of whole grain, it's hard to believe it was 31 years ago that Dick Doc introduced Phil and me to whole grain and whole vitamins, which started us on this whole journey.

A journey that has taught us that *thinking whole* and *seeing whole* and *being whole* involves so much more than whole foods or whole life insurance.

It must involve every aspect of our lives to ensure best possible outcomes under any conditions — but especially under the worst of conditions. And that should be shouted from the highest rooftops. Or rather, it should flood the Internet.

Oddly enough, over the last six years since Phil completed his book, we've attempted to convey that very message, on a shoe-string budget, without the backing of a sophisticated marketing team. We created several functional *(translation: not necessarily glamorous)* web sites touting the value of seeing whole.

We paid for ad words on two different search engines to test people's interest and even attracted visitors!

We bought hosting sites imagining they'd one day be useful. Get this: "MyWholeMate," or how about "LeapSphere," "SphereofIntimacy," "SphereofFailure" "SphereofSuccess," "BeWholed" and "Spheretuality."

(You laugh, but at least we tried ...)

But we couldn't afford to keep advertising the concept long-term. Discouraged, we eventually quit that approach, thinking we had failed to craft the perfect 10 second blurb. As if we had to champion the cause like some kind of politician.

And Oh, My Gosh, I almost forgot ... Phil even filed 44 pages of a second patent with the U.S. Patent Office for the purpose of creating an official template or map for a holistic frame of mind.

"Though not always stated, the true goal in life for humans — whether individually, in our families and relationships, our communities and countries, our activities, organizations, companies and governments — is to be healthy, to be complete, to be whole. [But] Our mechanistic training works against this objective ..." Phil wrote in the patent.

He titled it, "System Reflectment Processes and Activities" and straight away he began to describe a process for *"identifying and evaluating the elements that come together to constitute or shape the whole of any system."*

"The most advanced work in defining systems at this time is in ecology," Phil also wrote in his patent document. *"While great progress is being made these attempts still are largely based on mechanistic views and approaches. More importantly even the most advanced work in this field has no universality or standardization allowing the approach to be applied to companies, marriages, communities, finances, education projects or other systems. This invention is a process called "reflectments." This reflective process is a standardized, universally applicable, repeatable and trainable process that is used to identify the elements that constitute any system ..."*

Had Phil and I not encountered the children in Oxford, had he not designed a Healthcare Career Readiness Sphere as one of his first significant client applications of The Sphere technology, back in 2005, he may not have readily recognized the need for a systematized approach to defining whole. But he had. And in the process, he had learned to seek out and identify critical elements of a person's life or business — what he called "nodes" on the sphere of their existence that impacted all other aspects of their sphere. He had learned too that these nodes, as they related to other nodes, created entirely different outcomes depending upon the person or situation.

(If you're having difficulty picturing what nodes on a sphere looks like you can google "Hoberman sphere toys." They resemble geodesic domes. Note the nodes or nodules that link that sphere toy together. Now, imagine each of those nodules standing for something, say, some aspect of your health, your career, your relationship, your business, etc.)

Back to the patent for a minute ... To make it as simple as possible for people to assimilate, Phil began to label various nodes with descriptive titles like "Butterfly Nodes," "Disposition Nodes" and "Accelerator Nodes;" "Kernel Code Nodes" and "Trump Nodes" to name but five of the 15 listed in his patent.

"The position of a butterfly node, as seen in context on a sphere, can alter our understanding — though not definitely — of the rest of a person's sphere, of a company's sphere," Phil said to me trying to explain his patent one day. *"The reality that a single node can fundamentally alter our understanding of a person's sphere is part of systems science. A small change in a node can have an exponential impact on the overall shape or condition of that sphere. And simultaneously, my sphere technology helps users become aware that a small change can, in fact, create discontinuous change. Which means it can create a much, much larger impact on a person's life or a company than would be expected in simple cause-and-affect mechanistic approaches. And the last thing I would say, that you should be aware of, is this growing awareness on my part, that nodes themselves are unique; that there are different types of nodes, not only different "kinds" of nodes, but also different "types," each of which gives us an enhanced understanding of our spheres."*

The Sphere and its many kinds and types of nodes along with the interplay between them, Phil believed, would provide outcomes that would aid people to accept the principles of systems science in everyday life. It could release them from the linear-only, step-by-step, mechanistic ways in which people have addressed life's complexities for far too long. The details of which would, of course, be transparent to users of The Sphere and only relevant to those called upon to authenticate its value, those who could expand upon its many uses for the masses.

Additionally, Phil also introduced "filters," "tangibles," "intangibles," "internal" and "external" factors along with much more in the patent ... did I mention it was 44 pages?

Now I've stressed myself out. That's because the topic is a sensitive one to me. Being whole seems so "natural" an idea, when you think about it, that we humans seem to believe we already function that way. We fail to realize that *centuries* of mechanistic programming have "trumped" our inborn sensibilities, have trained us to compartmentalize everything we do; have permeated society in ways we have yet to comprehend.

But, to be fair, what the heck does whole actually mean? Who really knows?

For years, a few of the more "advanced" thinkers in our society have attempted to answer that question by describing four compartments: the physical, mental, emotional and spiritual parts of our lives. But what exactly makes up the physical aspects of our lives? What comprises the emotional, spiritual and mental aspects?

Truth is, we have no agreed upon definition of these; much less how they interact to shape or form the condition of being human.

Even worse, we attempt to analyze these four aspects with a mechanistic mindset. As four *separate* compartments. And this interferes with our ability to see how these parts of our lives inter-relate.

When we have a so-called spiritual problem we go to a reverend or priest. If we have mental or emotional problems we might go to a psychologist or psychiatrist to address those; health problems — a medical doctor who often specializes in the "part" of our body that is ailing.

But in actuality, our physical well-being is directly linked to our emotional, mental and spiritual wellbeing and vice versa. They are all interconnected. But our professional advisors, presiding over these four separate compartments of our lives, are not connected. They don't talk to one another. And laws often prohibit sharing information, which can impede progress. In fact, we often spend *years* connecting the dots of our own personal experiences.

I'm thinking we could accomplish so much more in life if "pulling ourselves together" didn't take so dang long. How about you?

That's why when the opportunity presents itself, Phil invites audience members during his business seminars to take one minute and jot down on a piece of paper what they believe comprises a "whole person."

And surprisingly, when audience members compare their lists, the answers are rarely if ever the same. Why?

"We've never had this discussion!" Phil tells them.

Even more important, if we were able to identify a suitable collection of elements that encompass a whole person, how might we visualize those inter-relations?

"Whole ... comprises all the essential elements that come together to form or shape the condition of your life," Phil often tells people during those business seminars. *"And that means there are more than four — there are many."*

I can't help but remember the lazy afternoon back in 1998 when Phil, after reading a book about an indigenous medicine wheel, sat down at his computer and began to create two spheres — one designed to offer insights into a person's health; the second, designed to identify what he called "business equilibrium." He then began to craft a series of questions intended to be impartial; intended to capture a person's views without an underlying agenda, the answers of which were displayed on sectors of his newly formed sphere charts.

Phil was on cloud nine that September day. And he kept at it after that improving on the concept and approach, even multiplying the number of data points by more than 500 percent, which eventually years later captured the attention of more than a dozen Ph.D.s. Including the leader of a futuristic think tank; a former IBM executive who, according to his list of credentials, was one of that company's most decorated 'idea laureates.'

"For many of us, mechanical thinking has been hardwired into our DNA," he wrote in a email to Phil. *"For people in government, the tools at their disposal were all created generations ago and tweaked around the edges to give the appearance of being modernized. As we have moved to global business operations, we have not grown the regulatory systems to match ..."*

The futurist wrapped up his email with this statement: *"I like the way you use the sphere to help expand people's thinking. Most are so immersed in their little world that they continually miss the big picture of what's happening around them. You may indeed have the perfect tool for reinventing our systems."*

(Hoot, Hoot!)

That's why The Sphere comes in handy as a metaphor *and* as a visual aid. It provides a way — perhaps for the very first time — to glimpse a more whole-is-tic image of our lives. An introduction to systems science, you might say. A simple way to eliminate old phrases like, "I'm a well-oiled machine." Or, "my marriage needs a tune-up."

Or try this on for size: the internal combustion engine was to the Industrial Age, what The Sphere is to systems, what The Sphere is to complex systems — to our century of complexity.

Adding to the concept of a sphere, when we picture the various components (or aspects) of our life as "nodes" on a sphere, we can immediately begin to see how each of those relates to all others. Seeing our lives in context that way, offers us speed and dexterity as we engage in changing our path and patterns.

Now, here's where it gets fun. The very act of seeing our life in context changes us. It alters our views. Simply put: it's easier to adjust our perceptions once we've seen our reflection. How? When we see the shape of our life we become more aware. We see how to change it. Voila! Not so scary!

Emerging from that experience can be qualities that serve us well. For example, we may become more flexible with less hesitation; we may become more responsive, more adaptable and more responsible.

Phil identifies these and other outcomes as "emergents."

"These emergents come from the act of seeing our life in context," Phil says. *"I literally see this in rooms of people as they start to see the whole of their life; their relationship or their company. They start to verbalize what they see, give meaning to their individual sphere. They start to tell their whole story and in so doing begin to talk about what they can do — right now, today — to change things."*

Each person's story, the sphere of their lives, has its own unique characteristics. That's because individual circumstances vary considerably. And that's why several-step programs to success don't work for everybody. We're all at different starting points and there are too many variables.

Which means ... (now brace yourselves) "standards" and "norms" are incomplete indicators, at best, for painting a picture of society. We are not robots. We are dynamic. We are systems. Our relationships are systems. So are our companies. In fact, we are systems within systems with the capacity to flex and adapt beyond our wildest imagination.

Here's another reason why The Sphere as metaphor is very useful at this moment in time: it mirrors the World Wide Web.

The Web is a manifestation of our interconnectedness — of our interdependence. Traditional hierarchies and concentrated power sources are becoming obsolete. And it is possible today for society to experience a leaping together of people, ideas and events.

But most people are still stuck somewhere in the middle of our changing worldview. Much of our vocabulary is still punctuated with machine terminologies; our lifestyles linked to rational self-interest.

As an example of that confusion note a New York Times headline the fall of 2008: "Reaching for the right *levers* in an anxious situation." And the subtitle: "Without the bailout plan they lobbied for, the Treasury and Federal Reserve will have to dig deep into their *toolkits*." Note the mechanistic terms "levers" and "toolkits." But further along in the same story the reporter wrote that the "crisis of confidence in American financial markets had *metastasized* to money markets everywhere." Note the switch to a biological comparison — metastasized.

Fact is a lot of young people who grew up on the Web function as systems already.

It's you in-between'ers that are having difficulty finding your "see" legs. And there are millions and millions of you out there — those of you *(and me)* — old enough to have been influenced by or trained in mechanistic business models. You; who still function by those standards, you who can't break free of them and keep imposing them on others.

To illustrate the value of changing the way we see our world, here's a fitting finale to this chapter ...

In history, the Greeks were highly advanced in their abilities in math. Some of those mathematicians are still remembered centuries later for contributing new elements of thinking to their society. But when the Romans became the dominate world power after the Greeks, skilled mathematicians were surprisingly absent in that culture. That's because they were being held hostage by the Roman numbering system. *(Ever heard of Roman numerals?)* Turns out, the way the Romans visualized their numbers made it impossible to do advanced math. But the Romans were so immersed in it — so invested in that method of calculation — they had no idea it was restricting them from moving forward in areas of science, astronomy and medicine.

Having said that, ponder what I say next — it's key to your passage from an outdated mindset to a new one: How you *visualize* has a dramatic impact on what you *realize.*

chapter 23: Reflect

It was our infatuation with a house that caused us to stop and reflect more than usual on the popular self-help techniques available today. You know the ones that teach us how to achieve our greatest desires and be our best selves. The advocates of those systems maintain that our life experiences are the direct result of the "choices" we make, of the things we "attract." They tell us that living in the moment — in the "now" — can heal the past and the future.

Their advice seemed simple enough and the projected outcomes sounded amazing. But try as we may, Phil and I hadn't perfected those techniques in our lives. And from what we could tell, a lot of other folks hadn't either.

It was this frustrating reality that prompted us to embark on a mind-walk to grasp what we were missing. Our mind-walks are often rowdy rows that push buttons and press boundaries. And this particular mind-walk would span several weeks until we attained what appeared to be a staggering level of clarity.

It all started deep in the heart of winter as 2007 surrendered to 2008 when Phil and I slipped into our car one afternoon and drove up a popular road that featured a panoramic view of one of Colorado's 14,000-foot peaks. Along the route, we traveled past luxury homes built next to a partially frozen river. Toward the end of the road I noticed a "for sale" sign beside a long dirt driveway.

I hadn't indulged my fantasies in a long time. What was the use? I thought. Nothing had come of them, so far.

Even so, I asked Phil to stop the car and I snatched up a spec sheet about the property. The price was substantial but it was after all just a daydream. By the time we arrived home I had convinced Phil to play along further as we logged onto the Internet and viewed a virtual tour of the house and its manicured land.

It was gorgeous by traditional standards. But it did not inspire us. Had we the money to buy it, we wouldn't have, for we were drawn to uncanny beauty that stirred and disturbed us.

We recalled an unconventional home that had once inspired us nine years earlier on the Front Range above Denver. It resembled a Frank Lloyd Wright design. It was situated on 25 acres; was surrounded by verdant mountaintops and backed up to a giant rock face. We were captivated by its unusual presentation: a long narrow dwelling framed by floor-to-ceiling windows that offered sunrise and sunset views, plus an expansive rock wall that began outside the structure and cut straight through the middle of it, inset with twin fireplaces.

It was January of 1999 when we discovered the home that was at the time for sale. The very weekend John Elway led the Denver Bronco's to their second straight NFL Championship and the city had burst into joy with the sounds of car horns and whoops and hollers from balcony windows.

The next weekend a gracious realtor showed us around the place and we determined right then and there that if there were such things as "dream homes" this was ours.

"I am so in love with it that I can hardly think of anything else," Phil wrote in his journal in an oddly sentimental entry about visiting the property. *"My soul and my spirit were at peace and felt at home."*

It didn't matter that it was 17-years-old and paled in size to the mansions in other upscale sections of the community. We loved it because we understood it. It was organic architecture that blended shelter with nature. It was one-of-a-kind; handsomely eccentric, which repelled the more practical homebuyers.

We returned soon after with friends visiting from California who also admired its distinctive characteristics, noting that it cost about the same as their small home in a populated neighborhood of Pasadena.

We even scouted a few fine furniture stores imagining how we might better decorate the place then the last owners who had failed to do justice to the dwelling with their selections.

Little more than four years had passed since our painful departure from Hollywood. And it was conceivable that we could reestablish a lifestyle that matched our ambition.

Phil's new venture, a web-based digital asset management company, was taking off and he and his partner were in discussions with investors.

On our last trip to the property I picked up an attractive stone near the driveway for a keepsake and we spoke to the trees — as if they were kindred spirits — informing them of our desire to be there — to share their space, to walk among them.

Back in the city, we placed the stone atop the fireplace in our penthouse apartment and got on with life, which by fall had veered away from our grandiose dream. We landed instead in a cabin in the woods and began our journey to full-sight *(or, more candidly, we began our journey through purgatory.)*

One day, a year or so into our stay at the cabin, we took the keepsake stone back to our dream home and placed it on the ground. We were dumfounded by the turn of events that had steered us away from this precious place. And returning the stone was our way of letting it go.

Now, nine years later, our thoughts returned to the dream home. And unbelievably when we researched the property online we discovered it was once again for sale! "Mountain Sanctuary on 25 acres" the new listing read.

It seemed impossible odds and triggered hope within us that our assent from purgatory was imminent. It appeared to be a sign that we would soon have the money to buy it, which meant — in self-help terms — that we had finally manifested what we desired.

We recalled recent events that proved a financial breakthrough could happen any day regarding Phil's work and invention. As evidence, there was his well-received keynote address delivered to several hundred financial advisors in Florida. One naval officer was so excited by Phil's presentation that he couldn't sleep that night in his hotel room and instead paced the floor.

"I suspect Spherical Counseling is the "next big thing" in counseling in general and for Personal Financial Management in particular," the naval officer later wrote Phil in an email.

And there was the productive three-hour meeting Phil had had with a U.S. Department of Defense official regarding the possible use of his sphere technology within that agency.

Armed with anticipation, we once again traipsed through a few fashionable furniture stores and indulged ourselves in the imaginary process of decorating the place.

I was awestruck by the realization that a single incident — in this case, finding our dream home for sale, again — could so swiftly resurrect my enthusiasm for life that had been pummeled to death by an unmerciful string of disappointments.

Over the next few weeks we began to experience other strange occurrences, too. An article in the February edition of *The Oprah Magazine* caught my eye while standing in the checkout line of a grocery store and I snatched it up. It was one of maybe two times that I had ever purchased that publication and it reminded me of the time I picked up *Country Weekly* from a newsstand back in 2004, read an article about George Strait, and a few months later had learned to sing.

Here was the teaser in the *"O"* magazine:

"Was it coincidence or magic? Alice Gorman wrote 100 things she wanted in a man, burying the list in a closet. And then, oddly enough, a man who matched the list almost exactly strolled into her life. Seriously, people, how did that happen? After you read the story Martha Beck, O's life coach, explains why it worked ..."

When I got home, I devoured Gorman's narrative. Then I read Beck's summation, which went like this:

"I don't mean to rain on anyone's parade, but there's considerable evidence that — brace yourself — not all our thoughts come true," Beck wrote a few paragraphs into her story. *"If thinking were absolute power, every plane carrying an aviophobe would crash, and every lottery ticket would win. Humans are often afflicted by things they aren't thinking about (I, for one, don't believe AIDS babies lie around brooding about immune disorder). And although we've all read about celebrities who wrote themselves prescient checks for millions of dollars when they were just starting out, plenty of people write such checks without ever accumulating enough to finance their own funerals."*

Why magic lists worked for some, and not others, Beck believed, had to do with their level of awareness, at which point she eloquently elaborated on that message in her own words.

Her story, it seemed to me, added a level of thoughtfulness to the notion of positive thinking and the law of attraction.

Soon after, I shared the article with Phil. Then, in an uncharacteristic move, he turned on the television one afternoon during a break in his schedule and found himself glued to an Oprah segment. To his surprise, one of the guests was Martha Beck and the show's topic involved the same information she had shared in her magazine article. Now that was *spooky* we thought to ourselves.

But something was still bothering us about the overall concept — had been since we watched a movie called "The Secret" two years earlier that introduced the "law of attraction," which was at the time all the rage. After seeing the film, a heated debate followed between Phil and me when I became mesmerized by the movie's message. I had personally experienced the value of positive thinking after a bout of negative thinking had temporarily imprisoned me. So, the underlying theme of the motion picture seemed plausible. But Phil was put off by it. It oversimplified the topic, he believed, and could harm people if they did not achieve the projected results, rather quickly.

So we dug in deep, to the tips of our toes, and stumbled on a concept that seemed to connect a few dots between the Woo-Woo world and the rational world.

The concept involved momentum — as it relates to our past and our future, though it took some time for us to make sense of it.

"While we experience life in the 'moment,'" Phil said on a February day of that year, *"it is imperative that we recognize that this moment is not isolated from the rest of our life. It is the convergence of our past and our future."*

It was an odd take on things, I thought. But it was perhaps more holistic; more spherical.

He struggled to find an example of what he meant then settled on an imaginary one.

"If I'm in med school, the classes I have taken in the past will determine what classes I take in the future. The 'now' is a reflection of the past and the future ..." he said, gesturing with his left and right hands. *"There are even degrees to the past. There's an immediate past, inter-mediate past, and far past, that is shaping what I am doing now. Last week shaped this week ..."*

And that's important because? I replied, cranking my hand at the wrist in a circular motion, as if to say, 'give me something more.' (Sarcasm, I had discovered, can be useful during long-winded conversations.)

"Our life is less about 'choices' ... and more about the momentum of our life ..." he said, stringing thoughts together in a sentence to see if they connected. *"We can literally get to a point where we have no say in our lives."*

"That's why we sometimes hear stories about people, who get cancer, or their house burns down, or they go blind and they turn around and say it was a great blessing," he went on. *"They've been through an unimaginable thing and they're saying it was the best thing that ever happened to them. They say that because their momentum was carrying them forward in life and they didn't know how to stop it, or couldn't stop it. Then they lose their eyesight and it gives them a completely different perspective on life."*

Phil took a deep breath and sat back in his chair. *"The tragedy made them stop. Made them reflect. And shift ... their views,"* he said.

After that, the topic of momentum began to consume our lives to such an extent that I literally took a week off work to clear my schedule and make way for more spontaneous brainstorming sessions. Such as the following discussion:

"We have been shaped in this moment by our past experiences — our ideals, lifestyles, beliefs and battle scars — whether they are good or bad or boring — that's our mass," Phil said, more or less speaking about our own personal lives; about America in general and the world-at-large.

Combining the idea of "mass" with "momentum" when applied to our personal lives seemed a new thought entirely.

"That's heavy, man," I said, mocking his dialogue, once again. Then, thinking myself clever I came up with a T-shirt slogan right there on the spot.

"Hey man, I'm going to kick your mass!"

But Phil ignored my shenanigans as if I were a five-year-old and kept on talking until he'd talked himself out that day.

A short time later, while glancing through *Time Magazine* Phil scanned an article about a physics professor who drove 150 miles per hour in a NASCAR race. And something about the article sent Phil spinning.

By then, he had begun using a different phrase for 'living in the now.' He called it the "spherical moment" — as if imagining the elements of our lives on a sphere, in context, was a more holistic way to comprehend our "now."

"I have not recognized the impact that momentum plays in the spherical moment!" he told me in an excited tone after reading the race car story. *"It's a much greater influencer than I had previously realized."*

Then, his eye-brows arched and he voice boomed," *The past is driving us! That's it!"*

Finally, it had clicked: Momentum is mass times velocity.

"I will have to spend some time on this to really get it all figured out," Phil said, sounding like a scientist in a laboratory. *"But it appears that the momentum from our past, which is a result of our mass and velocity, not only shapes the spherical moment but is actually shaping our expectations of, and in many cases the reality of, our future."*

Phil was on a roll and his dialogue continued to the point of exhaustion on his part.

"It was the car at 150 miles per hour that really made me start to realize this," he said.

"If that race car was approaching an intersection the driver could not easily slow to a stop like a car doing 30 miles per hour could. Its momentum would carry it through the intersection unless the driver slammed on the brake, or ..." Phil changed thoughts in mid-sentence, *"... and let's not forget there is an unstated assumption, belief or expectation on the driver's part that the road will continue on front of him. We don't expect the road to suddenly end or make a sharp turn because we can't negotiate a stop or a turn going 150 miles per hour ..."*

We both stared out the window as he sped on with that line of reasoning.

"Humankind, or at least the western world in general, but America specifically, has significant momentum from our past that has created the expectation that the road will continue on, straight ahead, in front of us."

Phil sputtered to a stop, then resumed.

"My point is, without a new vision of our future we have no chance to alter it," he said, cupping his hands in front of him to form a sphere; pressing all the fingertips of both hands together. *"Our momentum will carry us through this moment; we humans will give it little if any real thought, because of our underlying assumptions."*

It seemed a mind-twister, but when I pinched my brows in contemplation I managed to decipher what he was trying to say.

We, of course, had to ramble on a bit about the momentum of a tractor trailer rig versus a small car, or for that matter a ship in the ocean. But the concept was beginning to sink in.

It was during this period that I happened to photograph Phil scribbling notes on a napkin in a restaurant. And I couldn't help but marvel at the value I added to this relationship.

But there's more to it than that: Besides giving Phil someone to stare at during these lengthy mind-walks *(—he hates talking to himself—)* I actually give him heck, frequently.

I thought you were all about spheres! I challenged him during one of his momentum marathons. What the hell are we talking cars for? And the past, intersecting with the future! That sounds **mechanistic**. That's linear ...

At which point he explained himself.

"We experience time linear," he said. *"You must deal with the physical manifestation of linear time otherwise you get into astrophysics. A car is one of the most common shared experiences we currently understand. It's simple: If we're traveling along at 150 miles an hour — or 60 miles an hour — and the light turns red, WE CAN'T STOP."*

"Momentum becomes the wild card," Phil continued. *"And the spherical moment is experienced differently for each one of us — depending on our momentum.*

"Here is where it really gets fun," he concluded. *"The greater our momentum, the briefer our moment; the more certain our course based on our beliefs. All we can do at that point is hope the road is straight, that there are no sudden stops or sharp turns ..."*

Then Phil turned philosophical.

"For fifteen years I've seen us approaching a moment — an awakening. We humans are on a course that is unsustainable on every front. If I had gone to the world with that message in 1993 no one would have heard a word I said. We didn't have the Web; we didn't have an idea of connections. In 15 years the world has so profoundly changed ...

"When this moment comes — this moment coming — we're already in a huge consilience — but apparently the crescendo of that; we are approaching the moment when humanity will potentially be open to what was inconceivable the day before ..." Phil said, pausing to take a breath.

"There is a critical moment coming — it's not yet here but it may be here next week, when humanity for the first time in human existence will have the option of making the decision to see the world anew ... but they won't do it without someone connecting the dots for them. Somebody has to show them what's going on ..."

At that point we had a side discussion of folks in the past that "connected dots" for their fellowman, such as Gandhi, for instance, and Martin Luther King Jr. ... then we remembered Hitler ...

Phil paused, and balanced his pen on his leg aware that "momentous" times make way for all sorts of characters when folks don't connect the dots.

"Hitler hit 'a moment,'" Phil said, his tone cautious. *"Five years earlier, not a chance; five years later, not a chance in hell — he hit that* ***moment*** *..."*

I began to squirm in my chair, overloaded by mass and velocity and *whatever* ... when Phil threw my past in my face. He reminded me of our own momentum involving our childhood religion and the beliefs that once drove us. It took us *years* to slow that momentum; to jettison our mass and change our course. But our fellow countrymen don't have that kind of time.

"Choice" had just lost its fizz. In and of itself, it wasn't nearly as powerful as self-help advocates liked to preach. We must understand choice in context with the elements that comprise our existence; the beliefs and experiences that have shaped our current condition — our now — to realize the limits of our choices.

On that note, I slipped to the floor and curled up with my dogs.

"Stop, reflect, envision, shift, then engage," Phil spoke up, stringing several words together in a simple directive. *"That's what we must do — as individuals and as a nation — if we want to slow our momentum and jettison our mass. We must stop and reflect on what got us here. We must envision a new path. We must shift our view entirely to engage in effective change. Otherwise there's no choice but to face ..."* I heard Phil say before his voice trailed off and a shadow spread across the room.

— — —

There it was, several weeks-worth of inspiration ignited by a single incident — finding our dream home for sale. Our Mountain Sanctuary on 25-acres. But, I worried: *"What if that was the sole purpose of finding it — to inspire us to think deeper thoughts?"* The money to buy it after all was not yet "in the bank," as they say, reminding me that our capacity to "attract," by self-help standards, remained undeveloped.

chapter 24: Dog-eared

"You're one of those glass half full people," a co-worker told me over lunch the spring of 2008. He said it as if my optimism was rooted in genetics or social advantage or most likely, naiveté. Because, he added: *"You trust people too much."*

His depiction of me was unexpected. But I smiled offering no rebuttal. My hard-earned navigational skills could not easily be explained. Especially, when they were cloaked by odd behaviors, on my part, and a blemished vocabulary riddled with curse words that resembled Tourette Syndrome. *(No disrespect intended.)*

The dichotomy of my personal life and my day job — as deadline-driven small-town journalist, often forced to report the same community events year in and year out; and interview the same community leaders and volunteers regarding different local issues —triggered bizarre brain activity.

Take the day a visiting journalism professor showed up for a staff meeting to critique the cover photos we ran in our four newspapers. He was a firecracker; had captured images of five U.S. presidents; many U.S. Opens and four Super Bowls. One of his Super Bowl photos, in fact, hung in the NFL Hall of Fame.

I watched quietly from the sidelines as he reviewed the work of fellow journalists featured onscreen in a slide show. Then, he began to analyze a sampling of mine with what appeared to be an unnecessary level of politeness. *'Um,* ***do you mind*** *... if I tell you what I think?'* He tested; his tone too perky.

"Go ahead, SCREW ME!!" I cried out, as the whole room gasped. At which point the good-natured professor who was seated near me leaned over and whispered his phone number in my ear.

I was dog-eared, for sure. Both Phil and I were. But we were real. We had wriggled ourselves free of our gears and levers. We could feel.

Before my grandiose resuscitation, when I lost weight and learned to sing, "glass empty" would have described me. Back then my life was gridlocked. It was unsuccessful, as defined by so-called experts. Even though I had glimpsed, during that stationary period in the cabin, insights that made my spirits soar.

On good days, I felt like a kid in velvet pants standing beside a brand new bike licking an ice cream cone.

On others, when I got stuck like a scratched CD overanalyzing my uncertainties, I would freak and weep.

One day I teared up for no obvious reason during a casual conversation with my newspaper publisher, a friendly and sensitive fellow.

Here's a number to call he said that summer slipping me a torn piece of paper that directed me to the Corporate HR Department. He then explained a "confidential" program the company offered that paid for mental health services. Employees were entitled to five free appointments with a trained psychotherapist without it showing up on their health record.

I had never been to a bona fide shrink before. But that day in June I picked up the phone and dialed the number of a highly-recommended counselor in my area. I would finally find out if I was mentally ill. *(That would explain everything...)*

The woman's office was in a high rise; the kind with a bank on the bottom and hallways filled with other professional services on the floors above. She was dressed in business attire and had black shoulder length hair, but for a streak of it that was white and curled into an "s" on her forehead, which gave her an air of sophistication.

I filled out the necessary paperwork got past the initial introductory consultation and then unwrapped myself. During one session I produced photos and mementos of the disruptions and milestones of my life as if they were clues on a game board.

In no time we had breezed through the allotted sessions and I braced myself for her analysis.

*"You've experienced **so much loss**,"* she said in a soft, sympathetic tone. But there was no grim diagnosis to follow. No prescriptions or referrals, other than a few books I might like to read, one of which I already had.

*"You just needed a **witness**,"* she said, defining what her role had become during our sessions together.

When I rose to leave she thrust her right hand towards mine smiled and said: *"It's an honor to know you."*

For all I knew, she used that line on all her patients. But on that particular day, it felt good when she said it to me.

— — —

If our life journey had been reduced to mere statistics for common analysis it might have appeared doomed from the start.

I went to nine different schools in Colorado before graduating at 17. Phil went to 11 different schools in four states before graduating at 16. We married too young at 18. We had no savings account. We had no trust fund. We had no college degree. We ventured into parts unknown with simplistic plans. We burned through 28 cars together (— including a few company cars —) from Ramblers, Plymouths, Chevy's, Oldsmobile's and a Ford Pinto; to Volvos, Audis, a Saab, Land rover, Jeep and Prius. *(Not to mention the few we owned as teens before we got hitched — such as Phil's Volkswagen Beetle named Herbie.)*

We've lived in seven states together — one of them three times. Before marriage, during our childhood, I moved 13 times (that I can remember) and Phil, 15. After marriage, Phil and I moved 16 more times — and we're not in the military. *(As an aside, Phil and I made a stab at stability by living in only three different homes during a 20-year period. Meaning, the number of moves during the rest of those years was frequent.)*

We've been bankrupt and homeless — once requiring the mercy of a relative to take us in. But we've also enjoyed the indulgence of a three-story A-Frame on 10-acres, as part of a company perk.

For 14 years of our 36-year marriage, we lived in modular dwellings *(that's polite for trailers)*. But we've also lived in a brick loft in an artists' colony; and a log cabin, in a historic writers' colony. We've lived in tiny towns and big cities; in a penthouse apartment with a killer view and a luxury home with tear-shaped pool. We married in the city of lost souls and once lived in the city of angels.

(I just figured out why I've never been attracted to those orchestrated reality shows. Real life, unscripted and un-choreographed, is far more frightening ... er ... **fascinating** to me.)

We've started eight different businesses and were employed by five-plus corporations. We've worked, if you count religion, in about 14 different fields — from modest enterprises to highly professional endeavors. Phil has traveled to 13 countries; me, five. Phil co-authored a sophisticated book and was issued a U.S. Patent. And I, in the role of reporter, once scored a private hour-long interview with a prominent senator when he was considering his third run for president of the United States. *('You and 200 other reporters wish,' his spokesperson had snidely replied when I pursued the interview; until I pestered him to death.)* Not to mention the 23 journalism awards I've earned *(O.K. four of them were staff awards, but still ...)*

We've lost family in death and in life; we've lost friends who could not come to terms with our changes; lifestyles that we prized; our dignity on many occasions; and beliefs that were encoded in our genes.

But we've never been to rehab and we still have all our body parts! *(Wait, Phil did lose his appendix.)*

— — —

Gosh, that was a painful recall session just now. It stirred memories of polite but critical folks we've encountered along the way who assumed we were brilliant fuck-ups. *(OMG could it be?)* While others have inferred that our pitching-sea experiences are part of a celestial plan. But maybe it was nothing more than this: We tapped the Universe within us to sculpt something useful from madness.

Whatever the reason, there are nights when I'm lying in bed — a cool mountain breeze kissing my cheeks from an open window; my favorite man and dogs curled up beside me —that the most magnificent peace envelopes me. It is a bliss that gurus speak of.

chapter 25: Release

It was Phil's mother, that feisty redhead that taught me a most important lesson about letting go; about seeing life anew.

She was 68 when she divorced her husband of 52 years in 2005 and began to live alone for the first time in her life.

She moved into an apartment village with a park-like setting and it was here that she contemplated her future while walking along the commons. She had no assets to her name. And her job security at an outsourcing company was tenuous at best. Yet, despite those odds, hope stirred within her.

Two years earlier, at a banquet hall in Texas, she had celebrated 50 years of marriage to the Good Son in front of 50 guests. In a renewal ceremony officiated by a tribal chief of the Cherokee Nation (from Mexico) the pair exchanged meat and cornbread; drank from the same vessel and huddled under a handmade blanket to reflect their continued life-journey together.

The renewal ceremony had been a dream of the Good Son's. For years he'd been exploring his Cherokee ancestry. And this was a chance for him to acknowledge his native roots.

But it was more than that, really. The goal had become his lifeline. Six years earlier he was diagnosed with prostate cancer and a doctor had given him a grim prognosis: *"Two to five years to live."* Setting his sights on his 50th wedding anniversary kept him going, along with the remedial steps he took to beat the disease.

And the Feisty Redhead had gone along, for it was the decent thing to do. But in the end she faced a dilemma she could not have imagined. What to do if he lived?

Their relationship had long ago turned to drudgery; his character too "difficult and obnoxious" for her to bear. But she had stuck by him, imagining she was sparing her children the demanding role of caring for him as he grew older.

She had after all done so for decades — burying her feelings like pockets of poison throughout her body, which only weakened her. Over time, she endured a dozen surgeries and nearly died more than once from frightening ailments. But she willed herself on for the sake of her offspring. She was the primary breadwinner when their father was seized by depression. (*"You've got to do what you've got to do,"* she'd say to her children, living it by example.) And she was their rock, the dozens of times he had uprooted his family and moved them.

When he was gone she could die in peace, she had decided. She could *"get this life over with."*

But he didn't die. In fact, his physical condition improved. And after years of secluded convalescence he took a job in his old hometown, at the Feisty Redhead's suggestion, which pleased him. Yet, there was no real change in his disposition, for he had not come to terms with the black hole in his soul that was sucking his family in.

In his younger years, swept up in the inconsistent existence of a traveling salesman, fueled by an illusion of instant wealth, seeking to escape the assembly line of life, he had become a "self-deluded," "self-defeating," "all-American dreamer and loser" as some critics have described his kind — the kind Arthur Miller depicted in his Pulitzer-winning play *Death of a Salesman.*

As the years rolled on, his had become a life filled with mishaps and dubious associates; of migraine headaches and visits to hospital emergency rooms — of secrets ... until the Good Son wasn't anymore.

One night, 52 years into his marriage to the Feisty Redhead, he began to "rant and rave" as usual when the Feisty Redhead arrived home from work.

That very evening as they dined together at a local cafeteria she found the strength to let go of the toxic relationship.

"I can't do this anymore," she told him simply and clearly. "I'm done."

— — —

Five months after her divorce the Feisty Redhead kissed another man. She was standing on a bridge above a serene lake in the park surrounding her apartment village. Her spine tingled and she felt like a teenager.

She had met the man 18 months earlier, when she and Phil's father, at the urging of a relative, had attended a weekend retreat together featuring transformational self-help techniques. The first night of the event she was unhappy to be there and unwilling to cooperate with the tall, silver-haired instructor when he engaged the small audience in exercises.

"Prove it to me!" she'd said, frustrated with his message. Followed by, *"I'll get to it later!"* when he suggested she experience his methods.

But the second day of the program took them both by surprise when, in the middle of an exercise, the Silver-haired Instructor looked directly at her and blurted out: *"We are going to do something important together!"*

Upon uttering the words he bolted from the room embarrassed by his outburst. His work and reputation was of utmost importance to him and he was stunned by his behavior.

The Feisty Redhead shrugged off his comment, unable to decipher its meaning. But others in the room found it curious.

"I've never seen anybody put you on the run before!" said a client seated at the table when the Silver-haired Instructor returned to his post.

Over time, during teleconferencing calls, he could not ignore the powerful connection he felt to the Feisty Redhead; and she to him.

"*What in the world is this?"* he pondered.

"What in the heck is going on?" she wondered, too.

One spring evening on a visit with family to Florida the Feisty Redhead was especially moved by the beauty of the setting sun slipping effortlessly into the ocean. Afterwards with pen and paper in hand she began to write the following poem titling it, *Let Me Just Be Me:*

"There is no right and there is no wrong; Just feelings and emotions that may run quite strong. Various decisions are before us that we may make. Many directions and paths we each can take ..."

For the first time in her life the Feisty Redhead realized she had options that had never before crossed her mind. She could make different decisions than she was accustomed to and produce different outcomes.

Initially, she was suspended by her own shame: *"I've screwed up as much as anybody in this life,"* she chastised herself, remembering the mistakes she had made. *"What gives me the right?"*

But she knew ... somehow she knew, despite her hesitations, that it was time to experience her world anew.

It was the fall of that same year that she bid farewell to Phil's father.

As she contemplated her future, walking along the commons of her apartment village, the Silver-haired Instructor joined her on those walks.

Six years had passed since his wife of 42 years had died of cancer, but he'd had no desire to pursue another mate. He was content with single life, busy with his work — his mission — that took root decades earlier, before his hair had turned gray.

It was 1977, while attending a health food convention in Las Vegas that he had a most unusual encounter with a numerologist.

'Things are going to get very difficult in the world. And people are going to have a lot of difficulty handling it ...' the numerologist, in so many words, had told him that day. Then, he added: *'You are going to be instrumental in helping people get through these rough times.'*

The news came as a shock: *"I can't solve my own problems,"* he thought back then. *"How can I be of use to others?"*

Some years passed and he and his wife got on with raising their sons. Then one summer he found himself in Sedona, Arizona, immersed in the classes of a self-help teacher who claimed to have, on his deathbed at the age of 42, discovered a way to recover his health and achieve inner peace by "releasing" negative emotions — and for that matter positive ones; acknowledging them and then letting them go without feeling a need to hold on to them. That teacher's techniques were so effective that his supporters continued his work after he died, at the ripe old age of 84.

But the Silver-haired Instructor forged his own path combining that teacher's techniques with his own insights that came to him in a state of meditation one afternoon in the early 1990s.

His approach proved to be inspiring to others, too. And soon enough he launched his own modest coaching business instructing people in his simple methods. His message was less about achieving wealth or finding the perfect relationship and more about achieving spiritual equilibrium to thrive in a difficult world. And his clients over time grew to include doctors, actors and business professionals who sought his assistance.

The Silver-haired Instructor declared his unconditional love for the Feisty Redhead the spring of 2007 on the same bridge where they had first kissed. She was about to turn 70 and he was 72. During a private wedding ceremony the pair vowed to live their lives together by "spirit direction."

"... Not only for our benefit and pleasure, but also for the benefit of all other people we can support through this expression of our spirituality," they recited to one another, before slipping on matching wedding bands engraved with a statement in Egyptian hieroglyphics that described their special bond.

They spent their honeymoon in Ireland and upon their return began a productive life together. By then, the poem the Feisty Redhead had penned two years earlier in Florida had turned up in a poetry book; and the story of her romantic union on the bridge had been printed in a newsletter, published by staff at her apartment village. Simultaneously, many of her long-standing health issues began to diminish and her eyes sparkled with mischief. She experienced a promotion on the job and received lavish year-end bonuses.

The pair behaved like youngsters in shopping markets and restaurants prompting total strangers, energized by their presence, to say the nicest things to them. One winter soon after their marriage a photo of the handsome couple — their bodies splayed like snow angels in deep white powder — made the front page of a community newspaper.

Before the Silver-haired Instructor lost his first wife to cancer, she had gifted him with a message: *"You're going to find someone you are going to be very happy with,"* she told him.

As I write this chapter the end of 2009 the Silver-haired Instructor and Feisty Redhead are playing in Vienna.

— — —

To be honest, Phil and I were skeptical of the Silver-haired Instructor's approach. We often challenged his methods and sparred with him during telephone conversations. We balked at his choice of words and phrases — self-help terms that too often fail people by our observations.

One day, when the cheery couple called from Texas to chat, Phil was in no mood for conversation. A business deal had fallen through and he had reached a moment of great disappointment. The journey to The Sphere was taking far too long and he was overcome by exasperation.

"You've hit a wall! Speak to him about it?" I told Phil. *"What have you got to lose?"*

With great reluctance he agreed, only because the Silver-haired Instructor was now "family."

Their conversation went on for some time as the Silver-haired Instructor began coaxing Phil's long-buried feelings to the fore and ever-so-gently helped him release them.

Surprisingly, when the call ended Phil's dark mood had lifted providing him strength to face another day.

Over time, we began to grasp from the Silver-haired Instructor how to tune in to subtle sensations in our bodies as we released our emotions — twitches, tingles and pains that we had trained ourselves to ignore.

We learned the value of not resisting those feelings, be they negative or positive ones, when we experienced them. We learned to acknowledge each and every one of them before letting them go — a wakefulness that took some time to develop.

Learning to tune into our bodies and emotions in this way reminded me, in principle, of how we had tuned in to nature after moving to the cabin in the woods by acknowledging the energy in stones; the healing power of plants and the behavior of wildlife. In that way we were "waking up" to our surroundings. This time, we were waking up the best part of ourselves.

But I would argue here (— and we did with the Silver-haired Instructor, plenty —) that we had already tuned in to our inner selves long ago.

In fact, I could fire off example after example of our "spiritual" pursuits; our "meditative practices" and the "awareness's" we had achieved along the way.

But eventually, during our discussions with him, we realized our vocabulary was colored with "struggle" words — primarily because our life-journey had personified struggle. Our upbringing had sent us packing along the back roads of society as adults. It had branded us outsiders, doomed to run alongside the fast track to prosperity without a boarding pass. We had endured the ordeal. But that which had once defined us, was now dragging us down.

Our vocabulary did not match our best of thoughts, the results of which seemed to move us forward in fits and starts. It's a powerful experience when what we say and what we think are in sync; it was beginning to dawn on us.

"I'm so sorry you've had such a difficult life," the Feisty Redhead told her firstborn son during that time, as she began to cry.

Her firstborn, conceived when she was only 17 — an "XY" chromosome born of Promise and Prestige, with blond hair and blue eyes that concealed his native past, but for his short wide feet gifted by the White Cherokee. The boy with the Hollywood smile — a smile that reflected his uncharacteristic exuberance for life; an exuberance that had been severely strained by the sheer weight of his purpose. An aging full grown man now, with graying temples, who — without formal higher education — was attempting dethrone a mechanistic metaphor that we humans have relied on for nearly 400 years.

(Tall order, he knows ...)

And there was me — who had stood by Phil's side in "the fight," for as long as I can remember.

Like Soldiers of War, Phil and I had learned extreme survival skills that were now hard to part with and on some level seemed valuable to maintain.

But that which once made us strong, had now weakened us. It was camouflaging our gifts and disrupting our outcomes.

(Damn! Life's so hard to figure out, ain't it?! Oops, more struggle words...)

As we altered our vocabulary, and released stored emotions that no longer served us, we did indeed begin to feel better. However, Phil's business had not recovered from its slump, despite predictions by the Silver-haired Instructor that it was possible to "attract" the necessary resources.

One day after Phil had released his anxieties over money the phone rang. On the other end of the receiver was his mother, the Feisty Redhead. She discovered he was in a financial pickle and sent him a check right away.

Her generosity at that moment was a life-saver but oddly enough it angered us.

"Why didn't the money come by way of a new business project?" Phil grilled the Silver-haired Instructor over the phone after his mother's call. *"Why did it have to come from my aging mother?"*

It was a blow to our self-esteem. We had not yet learned to "let go" of expectation regarding our circumstances as they unfolded. We wanted to control them. When outcomes didn't match our expectations we formed judgments.

"We are here for you no matter how long it takes," I heard the Silver-haired Instructor say a few weeks later, as tears sprang from my eyes.

By then he and I were becoming close — his sense of humor, easy-going nature and slapdash driving habits, strangely familiar to my own dead father's. And his love for us seemed to know no bounds, reminding me of the love Phil and I once felt for the people in Thomasville and Oxford.

Then it dawned on me: Had Phil scored that business project and attracted the necessary money the moment he wanted it, we would have never connected so personally with the Feisty Redhead and Silver-haired Instructor. We would have gone about our lives, meeting only on special occasions, and would have missed the joy of their companionship, which included this refresher course for life: *If you're constipated with negativity, it's time for a foul movement.*

Never underestimate the unexpected encounters in life that provide us with a precious shift in thought. That's a lesson from the Feisty Redhead and the Silver-haired Instructor that Phil and I cherish.

I'm thankful too for the encounter I had the fall of 2008 with an eccentric woman in her 60s that indirectly inspired me to quit my job as a newspaper reporter. I discovered her from a story tip; about a weekend retreat being held in my coverage area. She was bohemian in appearance — her face framed by a wild grey mane — and possessed of wit and awareness.

She was once headstrong and driven, "on top of her game," as she liked to tell it; traveling the country as a corporate saleswoman, until it all came to a screeching halt.

It happened the year she moved from suburbia to a home in the Rockies to be "closer to nature." She was proud of her accomplishments by then, having raised her son alone after her husband died years earlier in a work-related accident.

Life was good.

Then for no obvious reasons she lost control of it. She felt displaced and inauthentic; depressed and confused.

"It seemed to come out of nowhere," she told me during my interview with her. *"It was internal. It was tumultuous, and the main thing that I remember was the rising of a deep, deep desire — a yearning that gnawed at me — to turn inward. I had this career, (but) I couldn't do it anymore. I was exhausted emotionally and physically; I felt every single cell in my body was sick."*

When she sought medical help she was given antidepressants. Her company gave her time off "to work things out," and friends recommended she visit a spiritual adviser — in particular, a former physician who had researched alternative healing that focused on the use of energy techniques.

It was this doctor that gave her an insight about the human condition. He explained a center of consciousness inside each of us that we can "go to" to enliven ourselves — a place outside "the mind" that can sustain a person no matter what they are going through.

"He called it 'the heart,' " she explained. *"You can call it 'self,' (or) God consciousness ... It is the center of your being tied to consciousness."*

Soon after, she resigned from her corporate position and began a two-year journey of "internal inquiry." As part of that journey the saleswoman-turned-bohemian hiked the Colorado Trail relying on her savings to sustain her.

During her "awakening" process she became aware that the dramas and dreams that fuel a person's motivation are most often solidified during childhood. Whether those experiences are traumatic or incidental they can set in motion behaviors and outcomes that continue through adulthood.

By the time I interviewed The Bohemian about her upcoming retreat 10 years had passed since her trek along the Colorado Trail. And she had developed a few techniques that she believed could be useful to others who sensed a major transition was eminent in their lives.

"My art is that I know how to unweave the weaving," she told me during the interview. *"All of us are living in a network tapestry of who we are ... I can show people how to unweave that — to see their essence; their soul. If they didn't have those parents, who would they be? If they didn't have that tapestry, who would they be? But, not by making up another story. Who would they be, uncontrived?"*

Admittedly, my editor was skeptical of the woman's approach.

"Is this some kind of a cult?" he asked me suspiciously, when he heard details of the story I was compiling.

"I don't know. I don't think so," had been my reply. Then he reminded me as usual to get quotes from sources that could authenticate her claims.

The story ran the week before her scheduled retreat. And there was a respectable turnout for an introductory session she hosted the night before it began. I know this because I attended it.

"This work is about what you are able to see of yourself," The Bohemian explained to those gathered. *"It vitalizes every area of your life but is not intended to make you 'feel better.' It is intended to point you toward whom and what you are."*

Afterwards, I anted up the funds for the weekend adventure that drew a small but inspiring gang of working professionals, including an executive with a petroleum company.

And I'm not sorry for that experience to this day.

As we sat huddled in a semi-circle The Bohemian shared a childhood memory that had shaped her life. Then she encouraged us to do the same: asking us to reflect upon the sights and sounds or images that spontaneously came to us during the session.

Surprisingly, I recalled a rather mundane scene from my early life.

My father was at work. And my crippled mother was in bed. I was in the kitchen of our tiny Denver apartment having hatched a plan to be helpful. I would wash the dirty dishes ...with laundry powder, which at the time made sense.

When my father came home to the mess, I saw on his face a great weariness and a sense of burden washed over me.

That sense of burden washed over me from time to time throughout my life, I began to remember. When I couldn't please my stepmother, or God; when I failed myself, my husband or a church elder; a friend or workmate and "I'm sorry" became a repetitive part of my everyday language.

But the kitchen scene wasn't the only childhood memory I shared during the retreat in my circle of peers.

I saw a small dog hit by a milk truck one afternoon in front of our apartment house, I told The Bohemian. I watched the dog drag its broken body to the curb to die near the house where my own mother lay dying, slowly.

It doesn't take much to sketch a picture of your life at an impressionable age, The Bohemian explained.

Just a few experiences here or there, trivial or traumatic — or both, intersecting — that transform a feeling, a remark or an image into a perception. A perception that influences a decision, that becomes a pattern, that becomes a journey.

That very evening, as I was driving home from the retreat, I was puzzled by the traffic jam on the mountain road where I lived. As I drew nearer to the object that cars were swerving to miss I saw a beautiful red fox that had been hit by a car. I nearly fainted as I pulled to a stop in front of it. As I exited my vehicle it dragged its broken body right past me to the side of the road and crawled into a culvert. I fought back tears as a neighbor woman approached the ditch with a dog cage and some food hoping to lure it out.

As I climbed back into my car, I was stunned by the coincidence of the scene. I was jarred by familiar feelings of dread and helplessness that had surfaced.

The next day, toward the end of the two-day program, as our intimate group exchanged stories again in a semi-circle, I told them about the injured red fox.

"For years ... I've had this feeling ... that I was running from something," I told The Bohemian, between sobs. *"I thought maybe ... I was afraid of death." I said, before pausing to catch my breath. "But the truth is ... I've been afraid to* ***live****."*

— — —

What does all that have to do with me quitting my job?

It was time to. But I needed a little reminder of who I am to find the courage to let go.

On the final day of our gathering, The Bohemian urged us to choose a word that modeled the life we intended — an "archetype" name that befit us most. And I chose Freedom.

I gave my two-week's notice about two weeks after attending the retreat.

As I reflected back on my unexpected encounter with The Bohemian, I was strengthened by a comment she made to me about my writing technique. In particular, the article I had written about her. She thanked me for transforming her personal story and her complex esoteric expressions into something simple and digestible for the average reader.

"You have a real gift," The Bohemian told me, her eyes misting over. *"You are strong and powerful and I'm so inspired by you."*

chapter 26: Costs

It was a sunny summer day in 2009 when Phil swapped his standard attire of blue jeans and vest for a pair of modern black slacks — the kind you'd find in a Banana Republic store — topped off by a Gold Trumpeter cashmere jacket, before heading to a meeting with a vice president of a global outsourcing company that employed tens of thousands of people in many countries.

The encounter had been arranged by two hotshot entrepreneurs — industrious 29-year-olds that had discovered Phil through a technology meet-up group. Within days the young men had established their own company and web site to sell Phil's spherical approach as a business solution and they were cold-calling high-profile executives to introduce it.

Their spontaneity was a stark contrast to the businessman in his 60s — a successful entrepreneur and respected Ph.D., with whom Phil had formed a working relationship over the last two years. The man took nine months to complete his new web site, featuring a new product that incorporated Phil's methods.

His slow methodical approach, as it compared to the young men, who were engaged at the speed of change, exposed the great disconnect that people from varying age groups experience today.

Our world has changed almost overnight. And few of us grasp the cost of those changes — of all that must be lost, rather quickly, to navigate our way.

(Note to stable-cravers: Imagine navigating a starship through an asteroid field ...

C-3PO: Sir, the possibility of successfully navigating an asteroid field is approximately 3,720 to 1.

Han Solo: Never tell me the odds.

I digress ...)

Heading out the door on that sunny morning Phil's demeanor was hopeful; as it had been for the most part over the last 10 years — hopeful that one day his message would be timely.

And suddenly there it was, the words he had been waiting to hear, a universal awareness that something was truly amiss. Not temporarily but in totality. That a great shift in thought and itinerary was upon us.

'We are experiencing a growing rebellion on the part of both customers and employees against the very foundational structure of how our industry has always worked,' the vice president of the global outsourcing company conveyed, without remorse, during the meeting. *'Our business model and approach has reached the end of its lifecycle.'*

And it was only the beginning of other productive meetings to follow in the days afterwards when Phil met with a noted medical doctor and a psychologist both of whom were championing the necessity of *"bringing together systems which have historically been separate."*

Phil and his young colleagues also met with a roomful of professionals representing a national initiative that was seeking to urgently improve outcomes in education.

The initiative called STEM, backed by the federal government, national foundations and corporation's targeted science, technology, engineering and math students.

"It is not saying that our traditional way of teaching is not very effective — it is ***anti-effective,"*** a Nobel Laureate who was affiliated with the Colorado STEM initiative had reported.

It caused Phil pause when he remembered a recent meeting he'd had with a group of MBA graduate students at a noted business college. He was disturbed by the fact that they had no awareness of complex adaptive systems. They had received no instruction in those sciences — in how complexity impacts the business world. These students had been trained as mechanics to manage the "old ways. "

They had paid a substantial price for that education but were now being deprived of the opportunity to rest on their laurels and savor it. They would have to release that which was no longer applicable and move on to what was now relevant — *and quickly.*

Phil had great empathy for those students. He knew the drill. He had interned in many schools-of-thought and many vocations only to lose them during his costly journey to The Sphere.

He had learned to educate himself in the moment — gathering critical knowledge as he needed it, in context with the sphere of his circumstances. And so had I.

Unconventional as that approach had appeared to be, it had its virtues. Armed with the goal of seeking whole, we spotted in our 20s issues brewing in our former faith a dozen years before such matters came to light as part of a national controversy. It was as if that practice, of seeking whole, cued us in to an emerging awareness — a combination of conditions that made it impossible to ignore any longer.

And not only that: Phil had managed on several occasions, to design technology products that were years ahead of the curve in the business world. Furthermore, we had experienced enough natural disasters combined with economic downturns — had lived through the emotional and financial after effects of them — that we could actually *feel* the Great Recession coming on before few people dared speak of it. We knew life wouldn't be getting 'back to normal' afterwards.

And while President Bush, some have said, squandered one of the greatest opportunities for nation-building after 9/11, we did watch in awe as he and other political leaders in 2008, behaved uncharacteristically towards capitalism — almost heretical.

"What they did to address the economic crash went against the beliefs of a capitalistic free market — probably went against their own personal beliefs regarding a capitalistic free market," Phil sometimes ranted back then — *"one created to allow companies to grow or fail based on their own capabilities; based on the market that drives their outcomes. These leaders instead have begun bailing out companies and financial institutions deemed "too big to fail" with billions upon billions [now trillions] of dollars as if to prop up the economy, (which fortunately it did, on behalf of America and the world) but, unfortunately, as such offered a way to pretend the Great Recession was an aberration, when in actuality its message to us reveals something systemic."*

None of those realizations were miraculous on our part. And seeking whole hadn't eliminated our need for tutorial-style instructions for certain parts of our information-gathering, but it had streamlined our activities. We were awake to the confluence of elements encompassing us, and our world, and we were learning to react accordingly.

And now our past experiences had come full circle, it seemed. Our baptism by mayhem — of living life on the edge — of running companies on the brink of change — had made it possible for Phil to comprehend in small measure the predicament folks now face in all industries.

We had learned that life isn't about "fitting in," like parts in a machine. Life is dynamic and synergistic.

And that state of mind even has its own scent. The explanation of which was cited to me by an alternative veterinarian I once interviewed, a man who often delivered this quotable quote: *"Change your thoughts, change your chemistry."*

Phil and I had changed our thoughts, which in turn had changed our chemistry. And while I'm sure the doctor meant that phrase in terms of one's biology, I couldn't help but think it was the reason some folks wrinkled their noses at Phil and I. We had the smell of the future all over us.

In fact, Phil and I had become the poster pair of this insight, offered up to Phil by his maternal grandfather when he was young: *If you remove the training wheels from your bike too soon, then lose the bolts to replace them, you'd better: a) Learn to live with it, and b) Learn to ride without training wheels.*

We now face a future, as a nation, that requires a fresh form of fearlessness to navigate today's unknowns — fearlessness stripped of *expectation and agenda*. It is the bold way, in these extraordinary times, to uncover new resources.

And we do have resources, people. More than you know.

If we imagine our life as a sphere with many nodes, we'll realize that money is only one node on the sphere of our assets. It's not the "center" of our world.

That means old phrases like "return on investment" can have a broader significance than monetary recovery, alone. Our investment in ourselves — our growth and originality; sensitivity and skillfulness often delivers dividends. Our fortune becomes our vigilance and versatility. So we can thrive, or at least hopefully survive, uncertain times.

But our fortune, America's fortune, will come by trial and error — by losing our way and finding it. By arriving and departing. By crashing and then soaring. By recognizing we are soiled, and recoiling from the thought of it. By submerging ourselves and then orbiting above it all. By stopping; reflecting, releasing and envisioning; by shifting our worldview — by connecting our parts and experiencing whole.

Trial and error is a *"powerful process for solving problems in a complex world,"* according to economist Tim Harford, author of, Adapt: Why Success Always Starts with Failure. *"In the face of seemingly intractable problems ... We will have to make an uncomfortable number of mistakes, and learn from them, rather than cover them up or deny they happened, even to ourselves. This is not the way we are used to getting things done. "*

— — —

Where's the danger in that?

Even though we sense we are at a moment of great change, our environments are booby-trapped with mechanical explosive devices. Mechanistic thinking still permeates our vocabulary. It impacts our strategies; dictates our financial disbursements, shackles us with legalities and restricts our humanity.

Having said that, did you know that right now The United States has the greatest number of laws of any country at any time in history? And not surprisingly the U.S. leads the world in incarcerations?

And that phenomenon appears to be getting worse, according to a Wall Street Journal piece that ran in 2009 about Boston civil-liberties lawyer, Harvey Silverglate.

Mr. Silverglate authored the book, "Three Felonies a Day" and he estimates that the average American now unwittingly commits three felonies a day because of vague laws. And new technology adds its own complexity, making innocent activities potentially criminal. New technologies like the Web *"scare legislators because they don't understand them and want to control them,"* Mr. Silverglate says.

Speaking of problems with laws, I am reminded of the murder case of little Pamela Powers back in 1968 that took a whopping 15 years to settle. Even though, shortly after the murder, the man who killed her (and left her half-naked body on the side of the road in a snowstorm) turned himself in!

Turns out an investigator, while transporting the assailant, managed to get him to divulge the whereabouts of the child for the sake of the family who was grieving during the Christmas holiday. But that exchange violated a technicality in the law involving the *man's* rights. And it triggered years of costly legal battles, which forced the child's family to face multiple court proceedings. Books have been written about it.

What have we done to ourselves, people?! WHAT HAVE WE DONE!!

It's time, as a society, to take a good hard look at our reflection.

— — —

"I can't believe we've allowed ourselves to be labeled consumers!" Phil said one warm afternoon as he slipped two Portobello mushrooms on the grill. *"It's a one-dimensional view — that our sole purpose for existence is to devour — is to buy; buy; buy! That's the reason there is an America — because King George viewed the colonies as an economic engine to feed Britain. And that led to the Boston Tea Party and ultimately the*

Revolution. And this country formed a different kind of government," Phil paused, and reached from his soap box to the refrigerator where he pulled out a jar of pickled red peppers. *"But we've stepped backwards in time. Our government officials and corporate leaders call us — not citizens, not patriots, not human beings, but consumers! They analyze us like they do crops!"*

"Whateverrr ..." I said, modestly impressed by his ranting. Then thinking myself clever, I replied: *"Then, we must once again become modern-day pilgrims!"*

Perhaps he was right about the "crop" illustration. It's hard to imagine how else the chief legal officer of Countrywide Financial in 2007 could in good conscious tell a colleague: *"We are going to keep making these [subprime] loans until the last second they are legal,"* saying those words after a gathering of virtual Who's Who in banking had voiced their concerns during a private meeting in a U.S. senate building over the looming foreclosure fiasco. *(Phil discovered that little detail in a 2009 BusinessWeek article titled: How Banks are Worsening Foreclosure Crisis.)*

Do you remember, earlier in this book, when I ran down the list of respected corporations who had gone out of business in recent years after executives at those firms went to prison for draining company funds for their own personal gain?

And not long after that, respected brokerage firms paid hundreds of millions (each) in penalties for knowingly recommending those fraudulent stocks to investors?

And then some of those same brokerage firms went out of business for their participation in the subprime mortgage scandal that followed? When lenders were rewarded with greater sales commissions for the more risky mortgages they secured, and drew unqualified buyers to the table, lured by the patriotic promise of the American Dream, who couldn't possibly afford to pay for it?

Scandals, the enormity of which, cost millions of middleclass American jobs, destroyed retirement funds, and toppled the financial infrastructures of other countries?

Too bad it didn't end there.

In July of 2009, the *New York Times* reminded us that **cancerous** ideals are hard to eradicate, if left unchecked.

The *Times* story, *Subprime Brokers Resurface as Dubious Loan Fixers*, featured a California firm whose owner had amassed a "fortune" during the housing boom, before it tanked, by specializing in exotic mortgages that were most prone to foreclosure. Then, after that business played out, he and his team began working for a loan modification company that targeted as clients those people he had already *screwed! (Word and italics mine.)*

For fees reaching several thousand dollars, with most of the money collected upfront, the California firm promised to negotiate with lenders to lower payments on the now-delinquent mortgages of suffering Americans. The *Times* article quoted the owner of the company as saying: *"We just changed the script and changed the product we were selling."*

What was the new script? *'You got a raw deal.'*

Soon enough people found the scam appalling. But not before more damage to Americans had been done.

According to the *Times,* more than 650 complaints were filed with the Better Business Bureau and the Federal Trade Commission in a lawsuit filed against the company that alleges it "frequently exaggerated its rates of success; advised clients to stop making their mortgage payments; did little or nothing to modify loans and failed to promptly refund fees."

"I had people calling me crying, and we were telling them, 'You can pay me or you can lose your house,' " said one young salesman who later 'felt really bad' about his participation in the scheme and agreed to a Times interview. *"People were giving me every dime they had, opening credit cards. But I never saw one client come out of it with a successful loan modification."*

And his was no small operation. The company he worked for had 700-plus employees. It was among dozens of similar companies that were accused the spring of 2009 by state and federal authorities of fraudulent business practices, according to the *Times.* On the same day that the Federal Trade Commission sued that California firm it brought action against four similar companies and sent letters of warning to 71 others. By summer, when more lawsuits surfaced, an enforcement campaign to address the mess had spread to 23 states.

Some of the clients called from motels, their belongings piled in boxes, weeping as they recounted losing their homes the salesman told the *Times.*

"The agents let most calls go to voicemail, playing the most dramatic messages over speakerphones for communal amusement," he said. *"Guys would sit there and laugh ... 'This lady's going crazy,' that sort of thing."*

— — —

How heartless. How unbelievable.

Let's pause for a moment of silence for those who endured such pain and humiliation ... and while you're at it, allow this realization to sink into your head: their suffering did not occur at the hands of foreigners and terrorists.

— — —

And it wasn't an isolated case of abuses on home soil. You see, since I began writing this book, an American named Bernie Madoff was sentenced to 150 years in prison for defrauding thousands of investors of billions of dollars.

This man, who once served as a non-executive chairman of the NASDAQ stock exchange, was convicted of a Ponzi scheme that has been called the largest investor fraud ever committed by a single person. Allow me a quick recap:

His victims, it has been reported, included prominent society figures and politicians; those in sports and entertainment. They also included average hardworking smart folks.

For example, Madoff's scheme wiped out the savings of three generations of one family — the grandparents' retirement; the children's investments and grand-children's college funds. Another victim was a 90-year-old man — 30 years retired — who had to return to the workforce after losing $700,000.

And Madoff cost Nobel laureate and Nazi death camp survivor Elie Wiesel, big time. Wiesel, a Boston University humanities professor, lost his personal wealth to Madoff's scam, and $15.2 million belonging to his charitable organization, *The Elie Wiesel Foundation for Humanity,* formed after he won the Nobel Peace Prize in 1986, nearly wiping out the non-profit.

This on top of everything else this man had endured. The ripple effects of which are huge.

Wiesel was introduced to Madoff through a friend who had known him for decades, Wiesel has said in media discussions. Madoff presented himself as a "philanthropist." And the two had discussions about "ethics" over dinner.

"It was a personal tragedy for me and my wife," Wiesel said of their loss. *"Everything was gone."*

(Sound of soft whistling here ...)

Those stories are a reminder that — despite our strengths and accomplishments —when we lose our decency we arrive at moments of *great frailty* and *great immorality,* which affect us *collectively.*

How is this possible? We live in an inter-connected, inter-dependent world. *(Ponder that last sentence very carefully ...)*

As I write this chapter the unemployment rate is at a 26-year high and news headlines are featuring "Big Brands" going bankrupt in America. And the Federal Reserve is predicting that it could take half a dozen years for the economy and job market to 'get on a path' to recovery. But that's *IF* consumers return to spending. And people aren't spending like they used to.

Millions instead find themselves attracted to web sites that encourage new levels of resourcefulness. And feature articles, like, "Stop Paying for Things You Don't Need," as part of a humble awakening.

"A big coordinated garage sale in my neighborhood recently gave me a surprising wakeup call," wrote the author of an online newsletter that attracts roughly eight million monthly hits. *"All I could think of as I walked from one yard to the next was all the dumb decisions that led to this colossal display of stuff — purchased with dollars, now offered for pennies."*

— — —

Now, without being too repetitive at this point in this book, I'll remind you one last time: The grand finale of two philosophical thoughts is upon us. We've had permission for a few hundred years to be self-indulgent without responsibility because we were just parts in the big machine. (Key words: Renee Descartes and Adam Smith.) But those beliefs, as they were experienced concurrently in history, proved deadly.

(Of course, there's a little more to it than that. But what good is it to overload you at this point? Oh, I already have, you say? Oops!)

The fabric of our colorful country is stressed; the edges frayed. What we do next (— or, um, *immediately* —) is crucial.

Now, let me get back to that "cancerous ideals" analogy that I mentioned at the beginning of this section. I'm going to share a brief bit of data about cancer of the body with you — something new about the disease, recently released, that has created some controversy. It's the idea that cancer can vanish without conventional treatments — but how?

I quote here from a *New York Times* article on the subject, written by a science reporter:

"The old view is that cancer is a linear process," said Dr. Barnett Kramer, associate director for disease prevention at the National Institutes

of Health. *"A cell acquired a mutation, and little by little it acquired more and more mutations. Mutations are not supposed to revert spontaneously."*

The science reporter then followed that quote with this observation:

So, Dr. Kramer said, the image was *"an arrow that moved in one direction."* But now, he added, it is becoming increasingly clear that cancers require more than mutations to progress. **They need the cooperation of surrounding cells and even, he said, "the whole organism, the person,"** whose immune system or hormone levels, for example, can squelch or fuel a tumor. Cancer, Dr. Kramer said, is a dynamic process.

Now here's where it gets really interesting.

At first (according to the *Times* reporter) that view was hard for some cancer doctors and researchers to accept. But some of the skeptics have changed their minds and decided that — contrary as it seems to everything they had thought — cancers can disappear on their own.

Note one final quote from the *Times* article:

"At the end of the day, I'm not sure how certain I am about this, but I do believe it," said Dr. Robert M. Kaplan, the chairman of the department of health services at the School of Public Health at the University of California, Los Angeles, adding, *"The weight of the evidence suggests that there is reason to believe."*

— — —

Having written all that, I venture to say this: It sounds like cancer depends on the whole organism to survive. If that's the case, then I suspect the same is true for cancerous ideals. They need the cooperation of 'We the People.' If *we* don't *cooperate,* than the cancer might very well vanish.

— — —

It's time to see the whole picture at all costs.

And I'll warn you, as you uncover *your whole potential* — as your vision of the world expands — your family, friends and workmates may be puzzled by the shift in your conversations and behaviors. But be patient with them. Let's trust they'll come 'round soon enough.

Until then, our definition of heroes should expand to include folks who have abandoned their mechanistic training cold-turkey and stepped through the looking glass; who are paying the hefty price to *feel* what's going on in the world.

(And when you do feel what's going on — truly connect the dots ... its O.K. to poop your pants. There's some scary sh**! going down right now.)

— — —

Now you know why I had to do it. Why I had to capture a snapshot of America during these extraordinarily difficult times, when the world-at-large is also seized with alarm. Why I had to study that snapshot with a magnifying glass. And search for my reflection in it.

I had to remember, so I would not forget.

Its how I knew, absolutely knew, that I and you, dear readers, are the ones who have been blessed with the whole burden. Us — all of us: from the baby boomers to Generation X'ers; the "Y's" and "Millennials."

We like Abraham Lincoln cannot escape our destiny, bequeathed to us by previous generations.

But ours is not a 19th Century War to be fought with smoothbore muskets. Or a 20th Century War to waylay by means of atomic radiation. It cannot be stopped by merciless machines — lest we obliterate our civilization. *(The weaponry is already available.)*

Ours is a campaign of transformation — a conversion from clunkers and beaters to complex adaptive creatures; from passive to responsive; from consumers to caretakers.

I'm going to wrap this chapter up with a war story, which may seem rather peculiar. But most of you folks out there seem to like war stories and this one has a point that transcends war for wars sake. It's about taking chances when all odds are against you. I trust you will figure out the reason why I'm including it here when you read it.

Phil found the story online shortly after I began writing this book and I felt compelled to save it. It was an obituary posted by the Associated Press written about a Vietnam War hero named John Ripley. The story referenced a videotaped interview with Ripley, who was a retired Marine Colonel, by the U.S. Naval Institute for its Americans at War program. Ripley was credited with stopping a column of North Vietnamese tanks by blowing up a pair of bridges during the 1972 Easter Offensive of the Vietnam War.

That day in 1972, according to Ripley, he and about 600 South Vietnamese had been ordered to "hold and die" against 20,000 North Vietnamese soldiers with about 200 tanks. The only way to slow the enormous force with the tiny force was to blow up the bridge.

"I'll never forget that order, 'hold and die'," Ripley was quoted as saying in the article. But that did not stop him from crawling under the bridge under heavy gunfire and rigging 500 pounds of explosives that brought down the twin spans.

"The idea that I would be able to even finish the job before the enemy got me was ludicrous," Ripley remembers, adding: *"When you know you're not going to make it, a wonderful thing happens: You stop being cluttered by the feeling that you're going to save your butt."*

chapter 27: Assets

I read somewhere recently ... in a medical book, in fact, that losing a parent young can be detrimental to a child's very existence. Studies have revealed these predictors: that these children often suffer early death, suicide, mental illness, high blood pressure, heart disease and tumors.

I was stunned. Here I was alive at 55 — no small feat, apparently.

I've read that marrying young, more often than not, ends in early divorce — but not in our case.

We've heard that fundamentalist religions may incorporate cultish tactics to attract and maintain followers. But we were raised in that environment and grew from the experience in spite of it.

I know what its like to grow up with beliefs you'd stake your life on, only to realize that some beliefs have expiration dates.

I've read that losing one's faith can be a mind-blowing affair. And Phil and I would concur, but we didn't lose our integrity when we lost our religion.

We know it's feasible to scrape the foundation of your life and rebuild it — improved.

We won't argue that a privileged upbringing and costly degrees from prestigious universities offers advantage. But we also know that a couple of kids living on the wrong side of the tracks; who played in the earth near train yards where smelting plants had once spewed toxic waste, can still experience, as adults, quantum leaps in lifestyle and awareness. In search of our wholeness, we collected shards of light that flickered far and wide from others.

We know what it feels like when you don't fit the mold for venture capital or business loans. What it means to go it alone and still get up and go.

We know that life is not fair. That short people get no respect. That losing your job, home, car, credit and friends can be shameful and devastating. That it's possible to lose yourself during those experiences. But we also know it's possible to save yourself; to carve yourself into a finely cut diamond and offer it, no matter its size, as a gift to the world.

We've seen people waste themselves and their potential as much as humanity has wasted the environment. And here we are, as a people, as a nation, as a world, because of it. We must now trust there are enough gemstones "out there" to bounce light and sparkle in this dark period.

It's time to excavate our human potential like never before. It's time to collaborate in ways we have yet to imagine.

And if society must sacrifice something substantial at this time, let it be selfish agendas instead of selfless soldiers.

Having pondered all that, I can't help but cherish the hidden assets Phil and I uncovered along our way that have sustained us — the ones we've mined from within or discovered outside ourselves from unexpected connections ... like the flap of a butterfly's wings ... that have produced life-altering experiences that no expert or study could predict.

— — —

It was a mere seven months after Phil and I had moved to the old folk's mobile home park in Yucaipa, California, in our mid-30s, that British computer scientist Tim Berners-Lee presented a simple document to his employer proposing a lofty idea.

"Suppose all the information stored on computers everywhere, were linked," the Computer Scientist had imagined, before writing that paper. *"Suppose I could program my computer to create a space in which anything could be linked to anything."*

When he proposed the idea to his superiors, at the European Organization for Nuclear Research (CERN) in Geneva, in March of 1989, he wrote about it in this way: *"Imagine making a large three-dimensional model, with people represented by little spheres, and strings between people who have something in common at work."*

At first nothing happened. And in 1990 he tried to revive his plan. But that proposal got shelved, too. Even when he came up with a name for it, dubbing it the "World Wide Web," friends thought it would never work because it was too long a phrase.

Each time the Computer Scientist explained his vision of the World Wide Web, it was difficult for people to imagine it without him having a way to demonstrate it. It was "too complicated," people told him, which shocked him because he knew it was actually quite simple.

"People had to be able to grasp the web in full which meant imagining a whole world populated with web sites and browsers," he would later say in his book, Weaving the Web, about those early days. *"They had to sense the abstract information space that the web could bring into being. It was a lot to ask."*

He came to the conclusion he would have to create it on his own. He began the programming in October of 1990. By mid-November he had developed a point and click browser. By December, it was up and running.

Why am I writing about the man who invented the World Wide Web? In a chapter called "Assets?"

The short answer is this: there's something about his invention that has deep relevance for you and I today.

So let's get back to it.

Before the Computer Scientist started programming the Web he made a simple decision — what Phil likes to call a "pure thought." He decided to create a system with common rules that would be acceptable to everyone.

And that turned out to be very few rules at all.

"This notion seemed impossible until I realized (that) the diversity of different computer systems and networks could be a rich resource," the Computer Scientist further explained, *"something to be represented, not a problem to be eradicated."*

He settled for three foundational protocols that would allow *"one computer to talk to another, in such a way, that when all computers everywhere did it, the system would thrive, not break down."*

These involved three types of technology, terms of which even I, a non-techie, have heard of. Acronyms like: HTML (which stands for Hypertext markup language); and "http" which means Hypertext Transfer Protocol; and universal resource identifiers called URI's, which nowadays are known as URL's.

And the fundamental property to his design was simply this: the Web had to be completely decentralized. That would be the only way, according to the Computer Scientist, that *"a new person somewhere could start to use it without asking for access from anyone else. Most ... systems still depended on some central node to which everything had to be connected and whose capacity eventually limited the growth of the system as a whole. I wanted the act of adding a new link to be trivial; if it was, then a web of links could be spread evenly across the globe. So long as I didn't introduce some central link database everything would scale nicely. There would be no special nodes, no special links. Any node would be able to link to any other node. This would give the system the flexibility that was needed and be the key to a universal system."*

Now here's where his design got a little confusing for folks, to hear him tell it. There was nothing beyond it, there was no central computer "controlling" the Web; no single network on which these protocols worked — not even an organization anywhere that "ran" the Web.

In other words there was no one in control, no one in charge.

The Web was not a physical "thing" that existed in a certain "place." It was "space" in which information could exist.

By being able to reference anything with equal ease, the Web could also represent associations between things that might seem unrelated but for some reason did actually share a relationship, he also explained.

Everything about the Web, and the Computer Scientist who envisioned it, excited Phil as we were going over the material for this chapter — Phil seated on the floor below my desk caressing the Web guy's book.

"He built the Web and gave it away!!" Phil said, somewhat oversimplifying the details — as he later filled them in — that this computer scientist had indeed conceptualized and designed the Web, programming the first generation of it himself, laying the groundwork for it and then, with permission from his employer CERN, gave it away. All of which underscored Phil's point that: *"It's the ultimate example of a system — of how a self-organizing system works!*

"Think about it! The summer of 1991 there were between 10 and 100 daily hits on the Web! The fall of 1994 there were only 200 servers on the Web ... "

Phil was quite inspired to speak on about it and all I could do was type as fast as he could talk.

"By following those protocols everything on the web emerged!" Phil continued. *"That's all there is to the story. From that vision and protocols it created a "space" from which emerged Amazon. That allowed Yahoo and Google to emerge and You Tube. That's all that happened! It's profound. It's huge. It's historic. This is how transformation happens. This is how leaps are made. A man creates something with three protocols, gives it away, and in just 15 years we have Ebay and online banking and Facebook. That's what we are talking about!"*

Whose the "we"? I ribbed him.

"Systems scientists!" he deadpanned, as if he were one of them. At which point he steered the conversation towards how unanticipated emergents are the key to our survival as a nation and a world.

"How can we address the, 'more people less breathable air' scenario? The 'more people less drinkable water' 'more people less food, less land' scenarios?" Phil said. *"Or, the amount of water it takes to make a pair of blue jeans or a 2-liter bottle of soda? We can't solve those problems doing it the way we've always done it. We have to do something completely new. The Web proves it can be done. A guy gives it away and it fundamentally alters our life and our world,"* Phil kept repeating himself, which he often does.

Then he began to rant about the underwhelming attention the computer scientist was getting in 2011 during the 20th year anniversary of his invention.

*"The average person has no clue that one person created the Web (— which is something different than, but a part of, the Internet—) sitting in a little office in Switzerland, not the United States. On every front his creation invalidates selfish business practices. It discredits hierarchies. It scares business people and entrepreneurs. He changed the world on a scale AND IN A SHORTER PERIOD OF TIME than probably any other single individual. But we don't talk about it because we don't understand it. We talk about millionaires and billionaires, some of whom have paid fines — sometimes more than a billion dollars — for harming others to build their empires ... But Tim Berner's Lee, at the end of the day, didn't make billions of dollars. He didn't get much credit; he didn't get control of it, he doesn't get to drive it. It just happens and it scares us because we think you are supposed to build an organization; someone is supposed to run it; you are supposed to have all these rules and someone is supposed to be in charge and all this "Sh**!" which is not necessarily true. He just created three protocols that work with or without him, or anyone else. This goes against what WE HAVE BEEN TOLD about how things are supposed to work."*

"Don't forget Wikipedia," I chimed in. The success of Wikipedia involved what economists have come to describe as "peer production" — a previously unimagined phenomenon for sharing work among peers.

"A bunch of chaotic hackers doing as good a job as Encyclopedia Britannica," was the way author Joshua Cooper Ramo described it in his book Age of the Unthinkable.

Who could have imagined such collaborations even a decade ago?

"That's what emergents are!" Phil said, putting a spin on the word "emergence" by spelling it differently, which he believed made it a noun.

"But, we have to be prepared for them, open to them," Phil cautioned me, like I didn't already know that. *"The concept of emergents is neutral —*

but the specifics of what emerges from our spheres can result in negative or positive outcomes."

I thought this chapter was about *assets,* I cut in.

"At the end of the day, our assets are our emergents. Emergents are the final product — the payoff," he replied. *"Each and everything we do strengthens or weakens the integrity of our spheres — the sphere of our family, our communities, our companies and our country.*

"That's why it's critical we think in terms of a sphere, in terms of a whole. And theoretically that should be easy to do, but it goes against everything we've been trained for the last several hundred years.

"We've been immersed and indoctrinated in a belief system that is built upon the idea that all we have to do is consider the 'figures and motions of our parts' to remedy our ills," Phil said, quoting French philosopher Rene Descartes. *"Our society has been built upon the idea of rational self-interest,"* he added, referencing Scottish Philosopher Adam Smith. *"As those ideals coalesced we were reduced to parts in the big machine and felt no responsibility for our indulgences."*

"If only people had a few simple protocols to live by — just like the World Wide Web — that would unleash their unimagined potential," I thought aloud.

"They do." Phil replied in all seriousness. *"There are three simple protocols that will work right now — at this very moment: 1.) Seek to see the whole of every situation. 2.) Learn to define, evaluate and connect all elements that comprise the whole of any situation. 3.) Act to enhance the spherical integrity of any and all spheres you are connected to.*

"What's critical about this is — and it has to be emphasized — this concept is simple, it's natural and intuitive. When we momentarily and fearlessly release ourselves from political, religious or scientific expectations and agendas," Phil concluded. *"It reinforces what we already know inside but had no way to validate. There are no beliefs required. The act of seeing the whole transforms everything."*

And just then something awesome occurred to me. The Sphere introduced to the world as a Wikipedia-type application. Where people from all around could collaborate online together on a host of subjects by contributing their own individual awareness's to the sphere question sets. Their thoughts filling out the nodes of one whole topic, for instance. A real participatory way for us to soar past the limits and barriers of our working memory and address our complexities in exciting new ways.

"We could call it the Spheres of Our Lives," Phil blurted out, being uncharacteristically poetic, rhyming his phrase with a longstanding

television series, before reminding me of this little detail: to build that kind of a platform requires resources that, up to this point, he has yet to obtain.

— — —

Having pondered all that, I can't help but cherish the hidden assets Phil and I uncovered along our way that have sustained us. Flexibility, adaptability and responsiveness — to name but a few characteristics — that have emerged from our expanding sphere of awareness. We've observed how fields and particles have materialized from our chaos. How patterns of disruption have given way to energy flow and quantum leaps. We understand how our connections have self-organized in response to internal and external stimuli. How the nodes of our spheres have transmitted and received information, which happens in every system.

We found a way to connect the dots of our world, which produced unimaginable outcomes. Not that our lives were comparable to, say, Oprah Winfrey or Steve Jobs. But we have traveled farther than we could have ever imagined, under the circumstances.

chapter 28: Facets

"Today, most people admire diamonds for two exceptional attributes: their hardness and their brilliance ..." began a Nova article Phil discovered while I was completing this book. Immediately after, I had him forward the link to me so I could re read it. There was something about the piece that seemed so appropriate to what he and I had discovered on our Journey to The Sphere. What all Americans must now comprehend about each other: We're not a clog in a wheel; we're not a part in a machine. We're multifaceted, like diamonds.

"Scholars knew of diamonds' unrivaled hardness since antiquity, but its unique optical properties went unrecognized until comparatively recently ..." I scanned the material again, captivated by it. *"Deeply colored rubies, emeralds, and sapphires were far more prized as adornments."* Hmmm, I didn't know that, I thought to myself. And I didn't know this, either: *"Owners accumulated the seemingly indestructible diamond pebbles, as found in their unpolished natural state, as talismans against defeat and symbols of their own "manly" virtues, without ever seeing diamonds as objects of beauty."* Then I stopped to ponder, quite deliberately, the paragraphed that followed:

"Brazilian gold miners of the 18th century cast aside a fortune in unrecognized diamonds while panning for the precious metal. Diamond's familiar ornamental role represents a relatively recent development — a consequence in part of scientists' growing understanding of the nature of light ..."

And that's when it hit me. When we polish our facets we discover hidden assets. We shine.

— — —

So here we are. Our deep cuts carved into facets, over time — over a long time.

No wonder I champion old people. I keep imagining that someday, no matter our age, our value will shine through.

That Phil and I had to reach this very moment before you could see us, before you could hear us — when your perceptions of life are beginning to fail you and now you will find meaning in our journey.

We have a contribution to make. And I'll bet there are others like us who do too ...

An economist by the name of David Galenson happened to explore the life cycles of artistic creativity in his book *Old Masters and Young Geniuses*. Look at what he said during a presentation in 2007 sponsored by the Center for Social Innovation — part of the Stanford graduate school of business:

"In today's hyperkinetic world of instant internet links and television sound bites we've become conditioned — I would say brainwashed — into believing that the innovative people who make important contributions to our culture and our economy are all whiz kids —prodigies — fresh from the most prestigious art schools and institutes of technology who leap to sudden dramatic discoveries and quickly become rich and famous. In fact, however, these young geniuses may be matched in both number and importance by much less conspicuous late bloomers who spend much of their lives working patiently and tirelessly in obscurity only gradually arriving at the achievements that ultimately gain them recognition."

(Holy Molly ... what did that last sentence just say?)

As Phil and I offer up the pages of this book to you — thought clear through — as we plug our story into the shared collective — into the world that is ours and yours — at this very instant — as the information seeps into your mind; as you digest it, as it connects with your consciousness — I trust this read worthwhile.

— — —

"If you look closely at a faceted diamond, you can see that it soaks up white light and breaks it apart like a prism," the Nova article concluded. *"Diamonds sparkle and dance with colored light; each of its dozens of facets produces its own dazzling display. Other natural gemstones disperse white light to some degree, but none comes close to diamond's ability to reveal the rainbow."*

chapter 29: "X"

Phil got the call the morning of March 13, 2010.

His father had died. And for a brief moment sadness settled over him like nightfall.

Gone was the man who once believed he'd retire rich in his 20s. The man who loved boxing and football in high school and sent postcards to his firstborn son from the road as a traveling salesman — one of which pictured Phil's favorite horse, Roy Roger's Trigger.

Dead was the man who led his son into unsafe abandoned mines.

Who catapulted his family down a rocky mountain, hasty to leave the main road in his tiny Fiat, and find a different path, until the Feisty Redhead demanded he stop the car — right now! — and let her and her children out!

Deceased was the man who set a field ablaze, attempting to burn some trash, and later cut off a toe when cutting the grass.

Who endangered child no. 3 — a toddler straddled on his knee — while driving a tractor with a side mower atop a steep hill. How Phil had come running when his father yelled for help, the man thrusting the baby girl at his 13-year-old boy, moments before he leapt from the machinery which then tumbled into wreckage.

Done, was the man who warned his son, "Don't tell your mother!" regarding so many things — even those movies in his car he was "storing for a friend." Pornographic: wasn't that what he had called them?

Vanished, was the man who had bequeathed discord. Who confounded his children — all four of them, when the last child arrived — with partial truths and incomplete data that sent them in four different directions. Phil, when he was younger, challenging his father's logic and motivations on far too many occasions.

Phil's sadness was eclipsed minutes later by an unforgettable emptiness. Emptiness over what his father had become. And what he had not become.

March 13. The very date Phil was scheduled to attend the first National Coffeehouse Day. An event spearheaded by a new grassroots movement known as Coffee Party USA.

And he did. Go. And listen. And watch. And share a few thoughts ... in between phone calls with family members who were making burial arrangements for his deceased dad.

He and I had traveled to a nearby community to attend one of 370 coffeehouse discussions that day. To observe citizens attempt to find common ground over the state of America and the volatile political climate. We watched people line up and add their signature to a civility pledge and seat themselves around tables in an ice-cream parlor that served coffee.

Phil's surprising involvement with Coffee Party USA was due to an unexpected introduction two weeks earlier to the movement's founders, who lived in Washington D.C.

The introduction came through one of the hotshot young businessmen who believed in Phil's technology and concept.

"*WOW, Guys, I joined the Coffee Party on FB,*" read an email to Phil from one of the hotshots. "*This movement has generated over 6k fans in 3 weeks. Washington Post is doing a story on them. MTV is airing [their] documentary at the link below. I contacted the founder. Going to see if [name omitted] can build the website for them ...*"

Soon after, he called Phil on his cell phone.

"*How do we tell them they should do a sphere, they don't have any money?*" The Hotshot asked Phil.

One of the founders was a 38-year-old award-winning filmmaker and activist — the other, a 41-year-old documentary filmmaker and activist who had studied political theory at Oxford. She was a former *New York Times* strategy analyst who had immigrated to America at the age of nine with her family from South Korea.

It was late January of 2010 when the Oxford-trained Activist posted her concerns on Facebook about a group of citizens calling themselves the Tea Party who were intent on reshaping the political landscape by means of protests and extreme political tactics. She strongly disagreed with that approach and a flurry of instant Facebook responses, of people agreeing with her, prompted the formation of Coffee Party USA. Two weeks later on February 14, she posted a video on You Tube, filmed by her companion, the Award-winning Filmmaker, explaining Coffee Party's purpose: to hold people accountable for obstructing progress in government and to engage citizens in the political process through civil dialog.

The Oxford-trained Activist was eloquent in expressing her views and Phil found it refreshing. But he was cautious about getting involved.

Theology had trumped politics for the better part of our lives. You could hardly call us politically savvy citizens. I had only registered to vote in 2000 at the age of 45, and Phil in 2004, when he was almost 50 — both of us choosing to be "independent" voters over championing a particular side. That's because we had taken sides in our past. We had blindly advocated the supremacy of our conservative religious beliefs over all others. Taking sides, it now seemed to us, had blatant limitations.

"*My initial thought would be that the role of The Sphere in this type of situation would be to understand the perceptions of the Coffee Party, Tea Party, and other citizen organizations as they relate to one another, and to help them visually see where they agree,*" Phil told the young hotshots. "*If this is a road that we were to consider going down it would be important that we be seen as a neutral third party or The Sphere will be assumed to be biased.*"

As far as the group's lack of money, Phil could identify. But America was in trouble. So Phil decided to step up, the only way he knew how — with The Sphere. And there would be no charge for it. Perhaps the collaboration would be beneficial in ways neither he nor they could predict.

And so it was that the hotshots touted The Sphere to the Coffee Party founders — some grandiose speech about "*introducing a new technology created by a long haired philosophy guy that is going to change the world. 'This is it!' I think you will see this will change the political climate; could short cut to the heart and meat of these issues!*" one of them said.

And the Coffee Party founders were excited about what they heard — especially after Phil expounded upon his approach during a teleconference call with them.

"*It's really amazing ... it fits almost exactly with things that I have read that have shaped my world view,*" the Oxford-trained Activist told Phil during their first conversation together. "*Things like chaos theory, uncertainty principle, Gaia theory — all these things that have shaped my understanding; it all came together in your presentation and is kind of mind-blowing to me.*"

Why not use The Sphere as a dialog map for Coffeehouse discussions, Phil suggested to her? Talking is a linear process, but The Sphere is a presentation of multiple conversations — it's a reference point for interaction.

That was on a Sunday. Two days later, Phil had already built a working prototype of the Coffee Sphere. And by that Thursday, March 4, after exhausting round-the-clock efforts on his part; after a team of people had approved the questions; after debugging and beta testing, a Coffee Sphere link was posted on the new Coffee Party website — complete with short videos of how to read a sphere and a way for citizens to share and compare their answers with other citizens.

Phil dubbed that first Coffee Party Sphere the "first cup" intending to create more spheres over time that would enable people to drill down to the root of their chosen topics more thoroughly.

Thirty-eight days after Phil had launched The Coffee Sphere, when the group's fan base had grown to roughly 250,000 people, he was invited to share the results of 10,000 Coffee Sphere participants at a public forum in Washington D.C., which produced some encouraging feedback.

There was, of course, the fellow that called Phil a "huckster," and another who blogged that he 'needed coffee to stay awake through Phil's speech.' But others seemed to grasp The Sphere's usefulness and they wrote about it in this way:

"A very powerful tool for political self-awareness and action," wrote a blogger from Las Vegas. *"This Sphere model surpasses other matrixes that I have used in demonstrating the calculus of the inter-connectedness of issues ... Perhaps we could send it to the three branches of our government, state houses, county and city counsels, the U.N.?"*

And another blogger wrote:

"If we could get a large percentage of the American electorate to enter into the Sphere process, we would start to see ourselves as one nation, one people — and our strength would begin to gather."

Early on, Phil had discovered patterns in the data emerging from responses of citizens who had used the Coffee Sphere. But there was no sexy way to convey the information to the media.

This is what Phil found: participants did not believe the government was very effective in providing essential services. This was true regardless of age, gender, race, location or political affiliation of the Sphere users. In addition, Sphere users did not believe that politicians had the "fortitude" to make the changes required. Sphere users believed that the interests of the American people were not being put first by the federal government. And they believed the political system would require major changes to initiate proper solutions.

That was heavy-duty stuff. It meant, in a nutshell, that focusing on — or fighting over — "specific" political issues wouldn't do much good in the long run. It indicated an overhaul was in order.

The core team of Coffee Party was energized by Phil's findings. But time slipped by while they determined what to do with it.

Instead, crusaders in the group began scrambling for three top political issues to champion. And who could blame them? Phil was projecting the message of 'seeing whole' on the political process, but what were the immediate rewards of that approach? What were the risks of it?

"*Finding common ground involves seeing issues in context and seeking solutions in line with that awareness,*" Phil had told the core team. "*All the issues on The Coffee Sphere are important — almost equally so. There is no clear No. 1, 2 or 3. We could use a forced ranking technology to create an artificial hierarchy for these issues, but what would be the point?*" Phil continued explaining his observations.

"*If we say the top priority is jobs, for example, and our congressman says, 'o.k. I'll get you jobs,' but his execution of that plan impacts healthcare solutions, or environmental solutions ... then, maybe jobs shouldn't have been No. 1 on the list in that sense ...*

"*The wild card to me that became evident on The Coffee Sphere was "us" — you and I and our fellow Americans,*" Phil pressed on. "*We agree that the issues America faces are numerous — all, serious. And, we admit that we have not been very involved in addressing them.*"

Phil had strategically placed three different questions on the Coffee Sphere about citizen involvement. And a special thing happened in the process. As participants completed their answers, their attitude about helping out their country in the future had improved. The act of reading the questions and rating their understanding of them had increased their awareness. And Phil couldn't wait to share that little detail with the core team.

"*By the time (citizens) had spent 15 minutes with The Sphere — when they finally reached the very last question that basically repeated the fourth question, their answers had changed!*" Phil told them in an excited tone. "*There was a 16 percent increase in their willingness to be more involved in helping to shape the future of America. That's a transformation in view!*"

Of course follow-through by citizens was another matter, and Phil knew that. But he was still encouraged by what he had found.

"*If you want three things to tell congressmen here they are: 1.) We won't champion one important issue to the detriment of another. 2.) We have lost confidence in the political environment and its ability to successfully address the issues. 3.) We recognize our failure as citizens to be involved. We plan to be more engaged in shaping the future of America,"* Phil said, adding: *"Perhaps the second cup of Coffee should be designed to determine our willingness to follow through?"*

For several weeks Phil served on the core team of the movement. Often directing the flood of phone calls emails and chats between them at all hours of the day and night. And I pitched in, in small ways, where I could be useful.

In fact, one of the hotshots canceled his own plans to travel with his family on a special vacation to Europe to assist the cause in its infancy. There was an infectious hope among the volunteers that reminded Phil and I, in small measure, of what we once felt in Thomasville and Oxford. But this time we were connecting with individuals that would have otherwise been impossible to meet under our old belief systems.

We knew what that meant. Headquarters would want our heads on a platter, if we were still members of that religion. And our former associates from those bygone days would be dismayed if they knew. We were supposed to be "no part of the world" yet here we were: responsible, engaged, citizens.

We imagined Dick Doc would be proud of us, though, if he were alive today.

We had come so far ... We had traded a life that buried our minds in the past, in the stories of our forefathers, for a life that was tuned into *right now*. As if being thoroughly "present" — as if becoming our best selves *right now* — as if flexing and adapting in *real time* to our surroundings — could alter everything about our future.

I'll admit I was jazzed to be involved in a bona fide political cause as it unfolded.

Some days, I had a sense that something quite remarkable could result from it. But on other days, I observed how the training and perceptions of the team of volunteers got in the way — ours, included — and the momentum of our collective views prevented us from fully following our hearts in a bold new direction.

Reality began to surface for Phil and me on the first National Coffeehouse Day, March 13. When the coordinator in charge of facilitating the meeting, unable to flex and adapt to the crowd, stuck strictly to his 'to-do' list. A list, that among its prompters, encouraged people to spend time drawing political slogans on poster boards with magic markers.

I was startled by the sight of it. It looked like fun, to be clear — a distraction from the difficult political climate. And it made for good photo opportunities. But it felt like grade school to me.

I couldn't help but count the heads of those in attendance at the hour-long event, most of whom were working professionals. There were more than 40. Some of whom had traveled more than an hour to be there. Which meant many hours had been spent on what, exactly? Multiply that by 370 meetings across the country ...

What's more, people came with Coffee Sphere's in hand to use them, but the local coordinator did not discuss them. And that seemed like a wasted opportunity to me.

I was embarrassed to be counting heads. What did I know about the political process, honestly? I admired the crowd's easygoingness that day. But Phil and I had become so mindful of our energy — which was our primary asset — that we could no longer relate. We thought folks were in a big hurry to get to the bottom of issues? We thought Americans were stressed and their resources limited?

So it was, a few weeks into our involvement with the movement that we began to observe it from a distance.

From our vantage point, having no political training, the movement appeared to be practicing politics as usual, with a "civility" clause added on. Under those circumstances, how could it inspire genuine transformation in the political arena, we wondered?

Turns out the Coffee Party and Tea Party were both "systems" in action. They had emerged as a result of America's anxieties. One, shouting angry demands, the other demanding civility.

The Coffee Party had risen up virtually overnight because of social media; because its founder posted a grievance on Facebook that eventually led to hundreds of thousands of fans clicking the "like" button.

And the beginnings of the Tea Party, in 2009, had been similar.

In fact, one writer for the *National Journal* magazine identified the Tea Party's strength to affect change by explaining it in systems science terms, which was very astute of him.

It was due in part, he surmised, to the 'radical decentralization' of the headless Tea Party organization; made possible by modern technology. The Tea Party appeared to come out of nowhere, starting as a network of people 'disillusioned with President Bush's Republicans and disheartened by President Obama's election,' the writer wrote. They began to *"talk about doing something. What they didn't realize was that they were already doing something. In the very act of networking, they were printing the circuitry for a national jolt of electricity."*

The needed spark, the writer continued, came in February of 2009 when a CNBC journalist aired a diatribe against the bank bailout and that, according to one prominent Tea Party coordinator, became the group's 'source code.' That made it possible for them to stage rallies in 50 cities organized virtually overnight by amateurs. And that led to a second round of rallies, shortly after, drawing an estimated 600,000 people to more than 600 events — blowing the mind of experienced political operatives, the writer further explained.

"The movement probably could not have arisen before the advent of free conference calling," the *National Journal* writer noted.

Complex adaptive systems comprise our world now — systems from which emerge our collective concerns; systems that reflect our current views — be they productive or non-productive.

What I'm trying to say is this: the fact that the aforementioned movements emerged was inevitable. They hit a nerve, *ahite?* If they hadn't, others most likely would have. That's important to comprehend. If we don't understand what these emergents signify; if we don't understand how to interact in the midst of one — how to exploit all the sparkles of light that have been captured — we may drain our precious resources. We may grow weary of emergents, at a time when they comprise our key assets.

We must ask ourselves: do we know how to allow our lives, our work, our politics, to self-organize? Not *know* everything? Not *control* everything? To be open to bursts of illumination that come from unanticipated places, from unexpected faces? Or, do we automatically snuff them out?

Ten months after the Coffee Party formed, the Tea Party backed the political candidates of its choice in winning back enough congressional seats in the November 2010 election to begin dismantling policies the 'other' party had just established. Based on those results, it could appear that the Tea Party had utilized its assets best, by enforcing its choices. But it was caught up in the loop of compromise — of taking back what had been lost.

"Compromise is winning a battle but is not the winning of the war," a professor who has studied conflicts in marriage told Phil around that time.

This professor, an astute articulate man who had come to value The Sphere in his work as an educator further explained compromise in this way: *"Compromise at its heart does not consider the other. Its purpose is to maneuver the obstacle of the other's difference. After compromise neither party is motivated by what they feel they were coerced to give up. There is no sense of working together."*

What that means in terms of our political parties is kind of scary, huh?

We've gone from debaters to haters; from two-halves-of-a-whole to gladiators. Under the circumstances unless our political parties stop, reflect and shift their beliefs — unless they realize that which defined them is now dragging them down — it's likely they'll engage in a dogfight to the death.

I suppose that would be fine if politics was just a game. And maybe that's all it is, you think? A competition, the amusements of which go like this: More people less breathable air, more people less drinkable water, more people less cultivatable land ... everybody take your places, get ready, set and go.

Arguably, we've gotten a little addicted to competition over the past 40 years — what with all the sports arenas that have sprouted up in our cities since the early 1970s. And all the sophisticated video games we've developed. Its understandable why folks might favor rowdy rows over, say, achieving something better *together*.

But listen up as I swap the words "competition and rivalry" for "partner and friend." Did you feel that? Did you feel the "grrrr and aurgh" dissolve into an "ahhhh"?

Phil and I were grateful for the "wakeup call" the Coffee Party inspired within us. Phil was glad for the connections he'd made with so many talented and dedicated people. But it seemed quite important that we follow our own path to its completion without getting sidetracked any further — that we apply our energy and resources to the completion of this book.

"It is my assertion that humanity is prepared for a leap," Phil said as we redirected our efforts. *"We've come to that spot where our beliefs are being stretched past their limits, like a rubber band; the tension so great that we can't extend ourselves any further. We are stuck. Some of us are demanding we go backwards. But when our founding fathers met, they didn't know what would come from that, they were acting in the moment. And, they brought their agendas. And, we paid a price for them where compromises were made — just one instance, slavery, which led to a bloody civil war. But America is at a different place, and we can't afford that outcome,"* Phil hesitated, remembering in our own lives how, at certain times, when burdened with one too many things, one additional obstacle, one more catastrophe, how we had collapsed. How great the price we had paid to recover.

"I am saying release the rubber band. Break free and make the leap. To what? We don't know the specifics, but we do know that science has prepared us for it for 100 years. We are not being asked as a society for a leap of faith, science has set the stage. We were taught that our world is a mechanism and a mechanism cannot exceed its specifications. But humans and all human activities are complex adaptive systems. As we make that leap — as we let go of the belief that our experiences right now must be controllable and predictable, as we conjure up the courage to trust that we have what it takes to get to the other side of this ..." Phil sighed, knowing that was a tall order, *"...When we start to see our experiences in terms of systems, it literally and fundamentally alters how we think. I personally don't know how to fix the economy. And no one individual does. But I know we cannot battle this to the death like gladiators. We must collaborate. We must allow for self-organization, which happens at the edge of chaos, in turbulence. We have to allow this process. If we try to clamp everything down — attempt to control our chaos, our turbulence, try and stop it, we interfere with what comes next."*

[What Phil was stating was grounded in a book he'd read when he was submerged at Walhalla. Introducing Chaos was its title, and it contained this short commentary by Llya Prigogine a Belgium chemist and respected contributor to chaos theory: *"Far-from-equilibrium studies led me to the conviction that irreversibility has a constructive role. It makes form. It makes human beings."* The authors of that book further explained Prigogine's observation in this way: *"Irreversible time is not an anomaly, but relates to reversible time. This is not an either/or situation. Reversibility applies in closed systems only. Irreversibility applies to the rest of the universe."* And the authors also made this insightful statement in their book: *"The flow of energy in these systems allows them spontaneously to self-organize — creating and maintaining a structure in far from equilibrium conditions. Such systems also create novel structures and new modes of behavior. Self-organized systems are thus said to be creative."*]

"I know I'm not trained in systems science, and I know many of those researchers aren't street fighters," Phil further spoke. *"They sit in their ivory towers and contemplate their findings, much of their work still trapped by the vocabulary and concepts of reductionism — saying systems can't be predicted and controlled, but being obligated to find ways to predict and control them — not creating practical applications for use in our chaotic daily lives, but devising elaborate papers written in*

high-minded language that are valuable, true, but largely impractical in any form for the current complex dramas playing out in the lives of us out here. In our jobs, our marriages, our healthcare. I'm just saying 'guys,' there's a way to use systems science to improve our situation. From our activities will emerge — this is systems science — that which we seek will emerge ... "

And there you go. That's why Phil and I are in persistent pursuit of the whole picture.

We know our quest falls in line behind a whole list of others with more prestigious resumes than ours — scientists, inventors, futurists and business leaders. Phil and I are commoners by comparison with a down-to-earth spin on the topic. But we have been driven to similar conclusions as they have, tapping into the same cosmic awareness. The awareness that compartmentalized thinking is killing us now. It is restricting every good thing we do.

Robert Johnson said the most amazing thing in his memoir, Between Heaven and Earth. That's the book Phil has grown quite fond of since first being introduced to it in an email from a stranger back in 2006, from the woman who lived in Wales. (Remember her?)

This is what Johnson said:

"If holiness (deriving from the root word whole) means to bring one's personality to a state of wholeness, it involves finding the missing parts or the faculties that are lacking in our nature and restoring them to a dignified place in our personality."

— — —

What an experience this has been for Phil and I — reflecting on our own life experiences in this book as they relate to the rest of humanity. As they relate to the past and the future. As they relate to our scary present time — right here, right now. Even as I write these words I am reminded of the information map in a shopping mall — the diagram with the "x" on it that says *"you are here."*

We are here.

During the writing of this book a young man in Italy riding his horse along a pristine beach was overtaken by poisonous fumes from rotting algae; fumes of which immediately killed his horse and knocked him unconscious. More than 70 beaches are now plagued with the lethal algae and environmentalists believe that pollutants from intensive farming are responsible.

Meanwhile, tons of trash floating in the ocean washed up on the shore of a beautiful Hawaiian Island last year.

During the writing of this book, a fire department in Tennessee refused to respond to a house fire because the person living there hadn't paid the $75 fee for rural coverage. The house burned to the ground and four animals died in the fire. And, in San Francisco, a suicidal man drowned in the bay as police, fire crews and others watched idly from the shore. Why? Officials blamed a department policy, stemming from budget cuts that prevented them from jumping in to save him. A representative of the fire department explained that, due to 2009 budget cuts, his crews lacked the training and gear to enter the water. And a Coast Guard boat couldn't access the area because the water was too shallow.

During the writing of this book the United Kingdom experienced the worst civil unrest and riots in generations. The Prime Minister was quoted in a media report as saying: *"This has been a wake-up call for our country. Social problems that have been festering for decades have exploded in our face ..."* It was also reported that both the Prime Minister and a Labour Party Leader agreed that, 'following recklessness by bankers, the lawmakers' expense check scandal, and media phone hacking saga, all sectors of society had a share of the blame.'

But it's complex, costly and politically unpopular to deal with those issues. Reportedly, that same Prime Minister has refused to budge on budget cuts that will slash programs designed to address social concerns, believing that *"jittery financial markets"* would *"take fright at any sign of backtracking ..."*

During the writing of this book a Kansas-based church released a hostile memo announcing that 'God hates Elizabeth Edwards,' after her death, along with plans to protest her funeral because of her tolerance for gays. (The announcement triggered a surprising outpouring of support for Mrs. Edwards from hundreds of others who were appalled by the church's behavior — a church that had also scorned the deaths of U.S. soldiers.)

Meanwhile, a gay celebrity blogger who built his reputation on bullying famous people, the act of which drew millions to his website, publicly apologized for his antics and re-branded his website to reflect an upbeat change in attitude from "hater" to "sassy."

During the writing of this book, the National Institute of Mental Health released its annual report stating the United States is now the most anxious nation in the world. Stress-related ailments cost the nation $300 billion every year in medical bills and lost productivity, while our usage of sedative drugs keeps skyrocketing. Also reported, was this finding: the average high school student today *"has the same level of anxiety as the average psychiatric patient in the early 1950s."*

In a separate news item, Pope Benedict somberly addressed Vatican cardinals and bishops about the revelations of abuse in 2010 that had reached *"an unimaginable dimension."* The Pope declared: *"We must ask ourselves what was wrong in our proclamation, in our whole way of living the Christian life, to allow such a thing to happen."*

During the writing of this book Phil and I discovered this unsettling bit of research about the way we humans choose to process information: We actually have a "delete" function in our brains. It's the section of our brains called the dorsolateral prefrontal cortex. It's behind the forehead and is one of the last areas of the brain to develop in young adults. It plays a crucial role in suppressing so-called "unwanted representations." It gets rid of "those thoughts that don't square with our preconceptions." Phil discovered the information in a December 2009 issue of *Wired Magazine,* part of a series about the value of exploring our failures, titled: *The Neuroscience of Screwing Up*. The article featured a researcher who studied how scientists study things — how they fail and succeed. He spent a year studying four biochemistry labs at Stanford University and another four years analyzing the data.

"The reason we're so resistant to anomalous information — the real reason researchers automatically assume that every unexpected result is a stupid mistake — is rooted in the way the human brain works," the article explained: *"Over the past few decades, psychologists have dismantled the myth of objectivity. The fact is, we carefully edit our reality, searching for evidence that confirms what we already believe. Although we pretend we're empiricists — our views dictated by nothing but the facts — we're actually blinkered, especially when it comes to information that contradicts our theories."*

On top of that, during the writing of this book, Phil and I learned how entire societies can collapse and die, which made us shudder even more:

1.) According to a *New York Times* piece written by a senior fellow at the Annenberg Norman Lear Center at the University of Southern California, we are living in an increasingly post-idea world — a world in which big, thought-provoking ideas that can't instantly be monetized are of so little intrinsic value that fewer people are generating them and fewer outlets are disseminating them, the Internet notwithstanding. Bold ideas are almost passé, the article explained.

2.) But according to a *New Scientist* piece, cited in a different *New York Times* article, to keep growing, *"societies must keep solving problems as they arise. Yet success generates a larger population, more specialists, more resources to manage, more information to juggle – and ultimately, less bang for your buck."*

"Eventually," says one author quoted in the article, who is an anthropologist with Utah State University, *"all the energy and resources available to a society are required just to maintain its existing level of complexity. Then when the climate changes or barbarians invade, overstretched institutions break down and civil order collapses."*

"We get seduced by the complicated in Western society," another professor from the Schulich School of Business in Ontario is quoted as saying in the article. *"We're in awe of it and we pull away from the duty to ask simple questions, which we do whenever we deal with matters that are complex."*

Meanwhile, America's triple A credit rating was downgraded by Standard & Poor's under what some believe to be controversial circumstances, the ramifications of which remain unknown. Yet, some economists and politicians are not worried about the financial troubles of America and other countries believing that "technology will save us."

However, according to an August 2011 *Forbes* article, a once tranquil neighborhood above the Hollywood Hills sign in Los Angeles, a secluded area of *"winding roads dotted with hideaway homes and panoramic vistas that has always drawn a smattering of sightseers ... seeking to climb"* up to the popular landmark is now experiencing perilous gridlocks because of technology, GPS technology to be precise, that two years ago began providing exact directions to the sign, allowing *"tourists to easily navigate a maze of narrow streets, dead-man's curves and tiny cul-de-sacs."* Now, *"scores of tourists pour into the neighborhood daily in rental cars and tour vans, causing safety hazards and headaches ranging from sheared off fire hydrants to fender-benders to blocked driveways, not to mention noise, trash and car exhaust at four main picture-taking vistas."*

"It can take me 40 minutes to get out of my driveway. What if I had an emergency with my child?" a production designer, who bought his home there 12 years ago, was quoted as saying in one report. *"It's like being in Times Square."*

By the way, did I mention that during the writing of this book, the Chinese government warned that its own rising demand for rare earth minerals may soon force it to stop exporting the precious elements? (Did you know that many of today's high-tech devices, from computer hard drives to hybrid cars rely on rare earth minerals to function properly?)

During the writing of this book we learned this about the qualities of the best type of leaders during periods of crisis, as explained by Dr. Nassir Ghaemi, who is the director of the Mood Disorders Program at Tufts Medical Center. He said in his new book, A First-Rate Madness: *"We will see that our greatest crisis leaders toil in sadness when society is happy, seeking help from friends and family and doctors. Sometimes they're up, sometimes they're down, but they're never quite well. Yet when calamity occurs, if they are in a position to act, they can lift up the rest of us; they can give us the courage we may have temporarily lost, the fortitude that steadies us. Their weakness is, in short, the secret of their strength."*

Hmmmm ... we have a delete button in our brains for those times we don't like what we hear. We humans aren't able to process bold new ideas right now because they can't be instantly "monetized." We've stopped asking simple questions because we're overloaded by complexity. And complexity can collapse entire civilizations. Some people think technology will save us, but in fact, technology is also making our world more complex. But, let's see, so-called "madmen" may be the best leaders to get us through times of crisis ... GOOD GOLLY! (Breathe in through the nostrils and out through the mouth; breathe in through the nostrils and out through the mouth ...)

Astonishingly, during the writing of this book, more than 200 new species were discovered in the Pacific Islands of Papua New Guinea, including *"fanged frogs, grunting fish, and tiny bear-like creatures."* They were found in a proverbial 'lost world' accessible only by a combination of small plane, dinghy, helicopter and by foot. They ranged in variety from mammals and amphibians to insects and plants. The discoveries are being seen as *"fresh evidence of the richness of the world's rainforests,"* according to one report. *"And the explorers hope their finds will add weight to calls for international action to prevent the demise of similar ecosystems."*

Even more astounding was the news of an archaeological excavation underway in Turkey: *"a vast and beautiful temple complex, a structure so ancient that it may be the very first thing human beings ever built."* It predates the Great Pyramid by 7,000 years, and Stonehenge, by 6,000 years. It is believed to have been crafted and arranged by prehistoric people who had not yet developed metal tools or even pottery. But the site contains 16 foot high towers, weighing seven to ten tons, and is decorated with elaborately carved foxes, lions, scorpions and vultures *"twisting and crawling on the pillar's broad sides."*

Surprisingly, excavations on the site began more than a decade ago, though I'd never heard of it until recently. The discovery is so unique, it could rewrite history.

"*Many people think that it changes everything,*" said a Stanford archaeology director. "*It overturns the whole apple cart. All our theories were wrong.*"

"*To carve, erect and bury rings of seven-ton stone pillars would have required hundreds of workers, all needing to be fed and housed ...*" said the archaeologist who discovered the site, adding: "*We're 6,000 years before the invention of writing here.*"

Ponder what he just said for a moment ...

I'll tell you what. I'm willing to let go of all of it — all my hard-earned perspectives and even my attachment to our personal discoveries during this journey of ours, just to peer through the looking glass. There is so much yet to consider. I'm not frightened by it. The thought of it invigorates me! What have we got to lose? We're enveloped in drama and angst. We've played that tune well. It's stuck in our heads like a scratched CD, repeating itself. Come on now, what else have we got?

Recently, I've had the unexpected pleasure of experiencing sensations in my body from past moments of joy; when I was giddy, silly and light-hearted. Sensations I'd forgotten. That I had lost. Dang that *felt good.*

I want to experience those emotions more. I want to reflect them, transmit them and attract them. I want to shout, "*I trust in the good of us — I must!*"

— — —

"*Guess what I've decided?!*" I jabbed Phil, when I'd just about finished this chapter. "*I don't think people should read this book!*

"*They should buy it, of course, and then burn it. Collect the ashes and grind them into a fine powder. Funnel the soot into a balloon. Fill the balloon with helium. Suck hard and laugh. We could pitch our frightening and tumultuous, wildly boisterous somewhat insightful journey, as the anecdote for mankind's queasiness — for their uneasiness about what lies ahead.*"

Phil stared at me blankly and then corrected my vocabulary: "*I think you meant antidote.*"

"*My God man, get a sense of humor!*" I nearly wept.

At which point Phil pulled out his journal (true story) in an attempt to please me and read something about the ... "*five key assets we must have to set aside our beliefs and expectations of how life should be.*" How we must look at the big picture — all of the elements; how we must connect the dots of our life to identify our strengths and build upon them; how we must take positive action to enhance and increase the integrity of our spheres — the spheres of our family, our community and our country. And when we do, we will experience "the gift" of systems as everything self-organizes. And from that will emerge the qualities we require and desire to address the challenges we face.

"It's the gift of The Sphere! Like, 'The Gift of the Deer!' " Phil blurted out, recalling the title of an old paperback in another one of his oddly poetic moments before reminding me that introverts don't laugh at stupid ideas like burning this book.

Phil, ever the toughy — a little too tough and crotchety these days when folks fail to turn loose of the "old ways." Him, often dubbing them clueless old farts with ignorant agendas; which makes him an ass, albeit a wise ass. And me a brat for calling him an ass, prompting the occasional verbal resolution from me like we once did in our 20s: *"I, Pamela Lawson, do hereby vow to become the kind of extraordinary woman Phil Lawson would be inspired to respect,"* yada yada yada, prompting Phil to cough up, *"I promise to acknowledge it if I'm ever mistaken,"* etcetera and so on.

All kidding aside ...

It's happening, people. Can you feel it? A consilience is upon us. If you don't bond with that word, then Renaissance will do. Everything about our existence and our understanding of life is metamorphosing — right now, when we are bankrupt and bled of our strength. And yet we rise. And we rise. And we rise ... until we are there.

epilogue: Home

Move. That directive was hard for me to hear in the middle of writing this book. But Phil and I were forced to pack up our belongings on short notice the summer of 2009 and leave the quant mountain community that had been our home for 10 years.

It was so abrupt an ending to our pilgrimage to The Sphere that I never saw it coming. Neither of us did.

We couldn't have predicted that the owner's of Camp Dodge would join the growing ranks of unfortunate Americans who were financially tapped out due to mounting healthcare costs, along with the ongoing recession, and were forced to sell their own house quickly — then downsize and move into ours.

We moved to the only place we could find with questionable credit on short notice: an empty house owned by a friend that was headed for foreclosure.

We were scared. We were confounded.

Conjuring up what little optimism we had left, we dubbed our new dwelling the "halfway house" — suspended as we were, between nowhere and somewhere.

When we escaped to a cabin in the woods in 1999 we hoped it would take a year or two for Phil to complete his book and contribute what he believed was an important message to society. But it took *far* longer. And we made the best of it — trapped as we were between completing the journey and paying the price for it.

Eventually, we felt like the ancient bristlecone pines looked, clinging to the mountainside near the summit of Mount Evans, bent and gnarled by extreme weather.

And that mystified our friends and business acquaintances. Most of them had been conditioned along with the rest of America to believe that financial abundance was the guaranteed outcome of hard work.

And there had been an astonishing level of hard work on Phil's part. And mine.

But along the way we had discovered sobering research about the length of time it takes before "innovative achievements coalesce" — before a person masters a clear thought. It takes at least 10 years Harvard professor, Howard Gardner, says. Others have touted the 10,000 hour ratio necessary before one becomes an "expert" in a given field.

Either way, Phil had spent the time. In fact, after crunching some numbers of my own I had discovered that Phil had invested roughly 24,000 hours developing a solid foundation for his spherical message, technology and various applications. And I had his back the whole way.

Yet, how could we ever justify our un-credentialed life — rich of experience but short on financial rewards? It made no sense by the current standards of society. *(Even though spirited people, in this country, of all places, should **not** have to defend the pioneer spirit.)*

We'd spent more than a decade in volunteer mission work — shrouded in poverty. Fifteen years navigating our way in the corporate world — without the competitive advantage of a college degree. Only to bookend those experiences by 10 years of rustic cabin life where we observed the movements of nature and we studied the habits of society ... in order to see through them and beyond them. A simplistic existence, for a certainty, that forced us to sit with ourselves — quietly and completely — and view the glory and grime of our own reflection. Until, we mastered a way to see our world anew.

It's tough to exist on the fringes of American life when you're driven to do something unexpected, and uncharted. Such pursuits appear frivolous and invaluable; irrational and careless. There is no support system built to sustain it. It's a fragile existence void of frills, safety nets and sympathy from outsiders.

Heck, we didn't even own our own home.

And wouldn't qualify for a home loan until hell freezes over, I discovered, after calling a mortgage broker. And that's even if I rounded up a 70 percent down payment.

It was staggering to realize that a credit score could so thoroughly strip a person of their character; could reduce a person's accomplishments — despite great sacrifice — to a pitiless mathematical equation.

Home, will have to be a state of mind for me I resolve *(reluctantly)* that encompasses more than a sticks-and-stone dwelling. I'm alive on this precious earth in Halfway House. And I will release my anxiousness each time realtors parade through it with potential buyers hungry for a short sale. For now, this arrangement must suffice.

On this property, perched high on a hill, songbirds ride the breeze and clouds shape shift with the weather. And I plunge my fingers into damp earth to save delicate perennials from the chokehold of noxious weeds.

I am struck by the beauty of change and I reach for my camera as I once did on my deathbed in Mississippi eager to wake up to life again.

I photograph my dog peering at a deer through a picture window; and Phil peeking past his computer at a dense garden. I photograph Mountain Blue Bells swaying with the wind and a snake skin that a slithery creature deposited at the base of a bush.

My motivation to finish this tome departed when we first arrived at Halfway House. *"Who really cares?"* I thought, too wounded to write the remaining half of it. Until, my inspiration eventually surfaced again, like a marshmallow in hot chocolate.

As if it's become my calling to tell this story as the limits of our society are giving way. It's become our duty — Phil's and mine to report back to you from the front lines of bewilderment. To testify what we've been taught: *"It's going to be O.K. ... but not like we thought."*

— — —

P. S. It's the spring of 2010. And we've been told it's time to move, again. But my book is not yet done and my sense of humor is now *all gone.* When, what to my steeled nerves does appear, but a tiny crack in our reflective mirror. And over the course of a startling few weeks a series of phone calls and plans are complete ... and we find ourselves unpacking our plates in the brilliant sunlight of a precious place: our beloved Mountain Sanctuary on 25 acres.

"FINALLY, our outsides match our insides!" I cried out soon after our arrival here, humbled by our abrupt change in circumstance; feeling right at home in this dignified dwelling that is anchored to a solid rock wall with sunrise and sunset views.

I couldn't help but remember then ... the stories I had learned as a kid, the one's that transcend religious creed — the legends that are in fact embedded within. If only we learn how to live into them. They go something like this: You're never too old for miracles. But, you may have to wander 38 years to reach your promise land. So, if your perfectly planned life is stolen from you and you feel like a slave ... *invent a way to free yourself.*

[The End]

To share your thoughts and join the discussion about this book, visit:

www.TheOKbook.com

To learn more about Phil's work with The Sphere, visit:

www.Spherit.com

To order a copy of Phil's book, **Being Spherical: Reshaping Our Lives and Our World for the 21st Century**, visit: Amazon.com

ABOUT THE AUTHORS

Pamela Powers Lawson

Pamela was a journalist for nine years before writing this book. She has written roughly 2,900 stories, conducted more than 9,000 interviews and has received numerous first-place journalism awards.

Before becoming a journalist Pamela served as creative director for an image bank and multi-media company. In addition, she was once a photo-illustrator working in the publishing, periodical and entertainment industries. While living in the Hollywood Hills, her assignments included Harlequin Romance book covers. Other projects included work for Turner Broadcasting (Nicole Kidman movie poster) St. Martin's Press (book covers) and Palm Springs Life Magazine (cover and spreads).

Phil Lawson

Phil is an inventor, author, technology designer and the Founder/CEO of Spherit Inc. Details of Phil's patented technology and approach are explained in the book, Being Spherical —Reshaping Our Lives and Our World for the 21st Century. Spherit Inc aids companies, individuals and communities to connect the dots in complex situations, quickly. His proprietary online visualization system has been used in many applications including management consulting; the US Army for marriage counseling; non-profits in working with high risk youth; adults for education and job readiness; colleges and state departments of labor, education and human resources.

Prior to their business endeavors, Phil and Pam spent 10 years in the Southern United States in volunteer mission work in social change and integration activities.

Currently, Phil is working to establish the World Center for Complexity Solutions to apply his methodology and technology in developing practical applications for individuals, organizations and communities to successfully navigate 21st Century complexity.

Made in the USA
Charleston, SC
04 October 2011